Technology and Scholarly Communication

Technology and Scholarly Communication

EDITED BY

Richard Ekman and Richard E. Quandt

UNIVERSITY OF CALIFORNIA PRESS

Berkeley   Los Angeles   London

Published in association with The Andrew W. Mellon Foundation

University of California Press
Berkeley and Los Angeles, California

University of California Press, Ltd.
London, England

© 1999 by
The Regents of the University of California

Library of Congress Cataloging-in-Publication Data
Technology and scholarly communication / edited by Richard Ekman and
  Richard E. Quandt.
      p.   cm.
    Papers presented at a conference held April 1997 at Emory
  University, Atlanta, Ga.
    Includes bibliographical references and index.
    ISBN 0-520-21762-4 (alk. paper). — ISBN 0-520-21763-2 (alk.
  paper)
      1. Scholarly electronic publishing—United States—Congresses.
  2. Libraries—United States—Special collections—Electronic
  information resources—Congresses. 3. Research libraries—United
  States—Congresses.   I. Ekman, Richard.   II. Quandt, Richard E.
  Z479.T43   1999
  686.2'2544—dc21   98-30679
                                                              CIP

Printed in the United States of America
9 8 7 6 5 4 3 2 1

The paper used in this publication meets the minimum requirements of American National
Standard for Information Sciences—Permanence of Paper for Printed Library Materials,
ANSI Z39.48-1984.

CONTENTS

PREFACE

The Andrew W. Mellon Foundation has a long-standing interest in the vitality of both research libraries and scholarly publishing. In the 1970s and early 1980s, the Foundation made large grants for the cataloging of collections and for the general support of the leading independent research libraries and university libraries. The Foundation also offered assistance to university presses. In the late 1980s, escalating operating costs at research libraries, especially for acquisitions, prompted a detailed empirical study of trends in both materials acquired and expenditures. The resulting work, *University Libraries and Scholarly Communication*,[1] demonstrated that research libraries were spending more of their funds on acquisitions, but were buying a smaller share of what was available or what might be regarded as desirable to purchase by any reasonable standard. The situation seemed inherently unstable, and changes were inevitable.

At the time our report appeared, there was also reason to hope that solutions to at least some of these problems might be found through thoughtful utilization of the then-new information technologies. There was, however, only very limited experience with the application of these technologies to the scholarly communication process—from the electronic publication of works of scholarship, to ways of organizing and cataloging materials, to the provision of electronic access to the source materials for doing scholarship. We therefore decided that the Foundation might be able to make a significant contribution by supporting a variety of natural experiments in different fields of study using diverse formats—including the electronic equivalents of books, journals, manuscripts, sound recordings, photographs, and working papers. This initiative was launched in 1994, and to date the Foundation has made 30 grants totaling $12.8 million in support of projects that attempt to evaluate the effects on actual patterns of scholarly use and measurable costs when electronic approaches to scholarly communication are introduced.

Selection of these projects has been guided by Richard Ekman, secretary of the Foundation and a senior program officer, and Richard E. Quandt, Hughes-Rogers Professor of Economics Emeritus at Princeton University and senior advisor to the Foundation.[2] Ekman and Quandt have worked closely with the directors of these projects since their inception and, late in 1996, concluded that the time had come for the first exchange of reports on results achieved through projects funded by the earliest grants. Accordingly, they organized a conference, graciously hosted by Emory University in Atlanta in April 1997, at which some two dozen papers were presented (most of which were authored by the directors of these early projects). Some 60 other individuals participated in the conference, including librarians, publishers, and leaders in the field of information technology. Sessions were organized under the following headings: "Economics of Electronic Publishing—Cost Issues"; "The Evolution of Journals"; "Journal Pricing and User Acceptance"; "Patterns of Usage"; "Technical Choices and Standards"; "Licenses, Copyright, and Fair Use"; "Multi-Institutional Cooperation"; and "Sustaining Change."

The papers in this volume constitute most of those that were presented at the Atlanta conference. None of the conclusions put forth in these papers is definitive—it is too early for that. But they do demonstrate that a substantial amount of learning has already taken place about how to operate more effectively in light of changed economic and technological circumstances; how to set prices for scholarly products in order to make them sustainable in the long run; and how to make these new electronic resources as attractive and useful to students and scholars as traditional books and journals have been. In addition to reporting on "where we have been," these papers offer insights into the potential of information technology and well-informed statements about the future of the publishing and library worlds. The Foundation intends to follow these projects for some years to come and also to learn from the results of additional projects that have been approved more recently and could not be included in the April 1997 conference.

The papers in this volume are best regarded, then, as contributions to the opening of areas of inquiry rather than as fixed judgments about fields that are continuing to change very rapidly. It is a pleasure to applaud the work of the authors of these papers and also to congratulate Richard Ekman and Richard Quandt on the excellent work they have done in organizing and stimulating new thinking in the broad field of scholarly communication. The most daunting challenge, in my view, is how to improve scholarship, learning, and teaching while simultaneously reducing the costs of libraries and other institutions that will continue to work under intense budgetary pressures. The papers in this extremely useful volume will serve their purpose if they provoke as well as inform.

William G. Bowen

NOTES

1. Anthony M. Cummings, Marcia L. Witte, William G. Bowen, Laura O. Lazarus, and Richard H. Ekman (Association of Research Libraries, 1992).

2. Ekman has overall Foundation responsibility for its work with libraries, university presses, scholarly communication, historical societies, and centers for advanced study in addition to duties in other program areas (including the Foundation's work with Latin American libraries and archives) and for other aspects of the management of the Foundation. Quandt has been responsible for the development of the Foundation's program in Eastern Europe, which has, among other accomplishments, led to the automation and modernization of dozens of university and national libraries; he has also been working closely with another Foundation staff member, Thomas I. Nygren, on the development of similar library projects in South Africa.

Introduction: Electronic Publishing, Digital Libraries, and the Scholarly Environment

Richard E. Quandt and Richard Ekman

INTRODUCTION

By now it is commonplace to observe that the economic position of research libraries has been deteriorating for at least 20 or more years and that derivative pressures have been experienced by publishers of scholarly monographs. The basic facts have been discussed in Cummings et al. (1992), and the facts and their interpretations have been analyzed in countless articles[1]—ground that we do not need to cover from the beginning. Contemporaneously with these unfavorable changes, an explosive growth has occurred in information technology: processing speeds of computers have doubled perhaps every 18 months, hard-disk storage capacities have changed from 10 Mbytes for the first IBM-XTs to 6 to 8 Gbytes, and networks have grown in speed, capacity, and pervasiveness in equal measure. In chapter 21 of this volume, Michael Lesk shows that the number of Internet hosts has grown 10-fold in a four-year period. Parallel with the hardware changes has come the extraordinary development of software. The Web is now a nearly seamless environment about which the principal complaint may be that we are being inundated with too much information, scholarly and otherwise.

Some five years ago, more or less isolated and enthusiastic scholars started to make scholarly information available on the growing electronic networks, and it appeared that they were doing so at very low cost (per item of information). A few electronic journals started to appear; the hope was voiced in some quarters that modern information technology would supplant the traditional print-based forms of scholarly communication and do so at a substantially lower cost. The Association of Research Libraries, compiler of the *Directory of Electronic Scholarly Journals, Newsletters, and Academic Discussion Lists* since 1991, reports that there are currently approximately 4,000 refereed electronic journals.

The Andrew W. Mellon Foundation, which has had a long-standing commitment to support research libraries in their mission, announced a new initiative in 1994 with the dual objective of (1) supporting electronic and digital publishing and library projects that would make significant contributions to assisting scholarly communication, and (2) supporting them in a manner that would, at the same time, permit detailed and searching studies of the economics of these projects. The objective of the projects was not so much the creation of new hardware or software, but the thoughtful application of existing hardware and software to problems of scholarly communication—in Joseph Schumpeter's terms, the emphasis was to be more on "innovation" than on "invention." The Foundation also planned to diversify its portfolio of projects along functional lines—that is, to work with publishers as well as libraries; to deal with journals as well as monographs, reference works, and multimedia approaches; and to support liberal arts colleges as well as research universities. All grantees were required to include in their proposals a section that outlined the methodology to be used in the project to track the evolution of developmental and capital costs as well as continuing costs (the supply side of the equation) and to measure the usage of any new product created, preferably under varying pricing scenarios (the demand side of the equation). Out of these efforts, it was hoped, the outlines of a "business plan" would emerge from which one could ultimately judge the long-term viability of the product created by the project and examine whether it did, indeed, save libraries money in comparison with the conventional print-based delivery mechanism for an analogous product (Ekman and Quandt 1994).

The papers in the present volume represent, for the most part, the findings and analyses that have emerged from the first phase of the Foundation's grant making in this area. They were all presented and discussed at a conference held under the auspices of the Foundation at the Emory University Conference Center in Atlanta, Georgia, on April 24–25, 1997.[2] They fall roughly into five categories: (1) papers that deal with important technical or methodological issues, such as techniques of digitizing, markup languages, or copyright; (2) papers that attempt to analyze what has, in fact, happened in particular experiments to use electronic publishing of various materials; (3) papers that deal specifically with the patterns of use and questions of productivity and long-term viability of electronic journals or books; (4) papers that consider models of how electronic publishing could be organized in the future; and (5) papers that deal with broader or more speculative approaches.

The purpose of this introductory essay is not to summarize each paper. Although we will refer to individual papers in the course of discussion, we would like to raise questions or comment on issues emerging from the papers in the hope of stimulating others to seek answers in the coming months and years.

INFORMATION TECHNOLOGY AND THE PRODUCTIVITY PUZZLE

The argument in favor of the wholesale adoption of the new information technology (IT) in universities, publishing houses, libraries, and scholarly communication rests on the hope—indeed the dogma—that IT will substantially raise productivity. It behooves us to take a step back to discuss briefly the general relationship between IT, on the one hand, and economic growth and productivity increases on the other.[3]

There seems to be solid agreement among experts that the trend growth rate of real GDP in the United States has been between 2.0 and 2.5% per annum during the past 20 years, with 2.2% being perhaps the best point estimate. About 1.1% of this increase is accounted for by the growth in the labor force, leaving 1.1% for annual productivity growth. This figure is very unremarkable in light of the miracles that are supposed to have occurred in the past 20 years in IT. Technology communications and information gathering have grown tremendously: for example, some steel factories now have hardly any workers in them, and banking is done by computers. Yet the productivity figures do not seem to reflect these savings. Admittedly, there are measurement problems: to the extent that we overestimate the rate of inflation (and there is some evidence that that we do), we also underestimate the rate of growth of GDP and productivity. It may also be true that our measurement of inflation and hence productivity does not correctly measure the quality improvements caused by IT: perhaps an argument in support of that view is that the worst productivity performance is seen to be in industries in which measurement of output is chronically very difficult (such as in financial intermediaries). But it is difficult to escape the conclusion that IT has not delivered what the hype surrounding it has claimed.

What can we say about the effects of IT in universities, libraries, and publishing houses, or in teaching, research, and administration? Productivity increases are clearly a sine qua non for improvement in the economic situation of universities and libraries, but labor productivity increases are not enough. If every worker in a university produces a greater output than before and the university chooses to produce the greater output without diminishing the number of workers employed (who now need more and more expensive equipment to do their work), its economic situation will not improve. As a minimum, we must secure increases in "total factor productivity"; that is, real output per real composite input ought to rise. But will this improvement be forthcoming? And how do we measure labor or total factor productivity in an institution with highly varied products and inputs, most of which cannot be measured routinely by the piece or by weight or volume? What is the "output contribution" of students being able to write papers with left and right margins aligned and without—thanks to spell checkers—too many spelling errors? What is the output contribution (that is, the contribution to producing "truth" in particle physics) of Ginsparg's preprint server in Los Alamos?

Scott Bennett's important contribution to this volume (chapter 4) gives a specific example of how one might tackle the question of the effect of IT on productivity in teaching and shows that the answer depends very much on the time horizon one has in mind. This conclusion is important (and extremely reasonable). The investments that are necessary to introduce IT in teaching need to be amortized, and that takes time. One need look only as far as the eighteenth and nineteenth centuries to recognize that the inventions that fueled the Industrial Revolution did not achieve their full effects overnight; on the contrary, it took many decades for the steam engine, railroads, and later, electricity to diffuse throughout the economy. Hence, even the most productive IT breakthroughs in an isolated course will not show up in overall university productivity figures: the total investment in IT technology is too small a fraction of aggregate capital to make much difference.[4]

In the papers by Malcom Getz (chapter 6) and Robert Shirrell (chapter 10), we have examples of the potential impact on research productivity. Getz illustrates why libraries will prefer to buy large packages of electronic journals, and Shirrell stresses that productivity is likely to be higher (and costs lower) over longer horizons. By coincidence, both authors happened to choose as their specific illustration the *American Economic Review*.

Bennett's, Getz's, and Shirrell's papers, among others, suggest that much could be learned by studying academic productivity more systematically and in more detail. We need to study particular examples of innovation in teaching and to analyze the productivity changes that occur over *suitably long horizons* and with full awareness that a complete understanding of productivity in teaching must cope with the problem of how to measure whether students have learned faster or better or more. We also need to pay more explicit attention to research productivity, mindful of the possibility that research productivity may mean different things in different disciplines.

But these considerations raise particularly murky questions. When journals are electronic and access to information is much faster and requires less effort, do scholars in the sciences and social sciences write more papers and do humanists write more books? Or do they write the same number of articles and books, but these writings are better than they would have been without the IT aids? What measures do we have for scholarly productivity? Obviously, every self-respecting tenure-and-promotion committee will shudder at the thought that productivity is appropriately measured by the quantity of publications; but how do we measure quality? And what is the relationship between the quality of access to information and the quality of ideas? While we agree with Hal Varian's view (chapter 25) that journals tend to have an agreed-upon pecking order and we find his suggestions for a new model of electronic publishing fascinating and promising, we still believe that in the short run, much could be learned by studying the impact of particular IT advances on scholarly productivity in specific fields.

It is possible that in the short run our views about productivity enhancements from IT in universities, libraries, and publishing houses must be expressions of faith. But unlike previous eras, when inventions and innovations did not always lead to self-conscious and subsequently documented examinations of the productivity effects, we have remarkable opportunities to measure the productivity effects in the discrete applications of IT by universities, libraries, and scholarly presses, and thus provide earlier feedback on the innovation process than would otherwise occur.

MEASURING DEMAND AND SUPPLY: THE FOUNDATIONS
FOR PRICING STRATEGIES AND SURVIVAL

It may be too facile a generalization to say that the early, "heroic" period of electronic library products was characterized by enormous enthusiasm on the part of their creators and not much concern about costs, usage, and business plans. But the early history of electronic publishing is filled with examples of devoted academics giving freely of their time and pursuing their dreams in "borrowed" physical space and with purloined machine cycles on computers that were originally obtained for other purposes. An instructive (and amusing) example of this phenomenon can be found in the papers by Richard Hamilton (chapter 12) and James J. O'Donnell (chapter 24), which describe the early days of the *Bryn Mawr Reviews* and how the editors improvised to provide space, hardware, and labor for this effort. Creating electronic library products seemed to be incredibly easy, and it was.

But as we gradually learned what was *technically* possible,[5] started to learn *what users might like or demand,* and realized the scope of the efforts that might be involved in, say, digitizing large bodies of materials, it was unavoidable that sooner or later even not-for-profit efforts would be informed by the realities of the marketplace. For example, if we create an electronic counterpart to an existing print-based journal, should the electronic counterpart look identical to the original? What search capabilities should there be? Should the corpus of the electronic material be added to in the future? What are the staffing requirements of creating and maintaining an electronic publication? (See, for example, Willis G. Regier [chapter 9].) Marketplace realities were further compounded by the recognition that commercial publishers were looking to enter the field of electronic publication. In their case the question of pricing had to be explicitly considered, as is amply illustrated in the paper by Karen Hunter (chapter 8).

Of course, pricing cannot be considered in the abstract, and the "proper" pricing strategy will generally depend on (1) the objectives to be accomplished by a pricing policy, (2) costs, and (3) demand for the product. While it is much too early in the development of electronic information products to propose anything beyond casual answers, it is not too early to consider the dimensions of these problems. We shall briefly discuss each of three key elements on which pricing has to depend.

Objectives to Be Accomplished

The important fact is that there are numerous agents in the chain from the original creator of intellectual property to the ultimate user. And the creator—the author—may himself have divided interests. On the one hand, he may want to have the largest conceivable circulation of the work in question in order to spread his academic reputation. On the other hand—and this point is characteristically relevant only for books—he may want to maximize royalty income. Or, indeed, the author may have a compromise solution in mind in which both royalty income and circulation get some weight.

Next in line comes the publisher who is well aware that he is selling a differentiated product that confers upon him some monopoly power: the demand curve for such products is downward sloping and raising the price will diminish the quantity demanded.[6] The market motivations of commercial and not-for-profit publishers may not be very different, but in practice, commercial publishers appear to charge higher prices. Since print-based materials are difficult to resell (or copy in their entirety), publishers are able to practice price discrimination—that is, sell the identical product at different prices to different customers, as in the case of journal subscriptions, which are frequently priced at a higher level for libraries than for individuals.[7] The naive view might be that a commercial publisher would charge a price to maximize short-term profit. But the example of Elsevier, particularly in its TULIP Project, suggests that the picture is much more complicated than that. While Elsevier's design of TULIP may not be compatible with long-run profit maximization, the correct interpretation of that project is still open to question.

Scholars and students want access to scholarly materials that is broad and inexpensive to them, although they do not much care whether their universities bear a large cost in acquiring these materials. On the other hand, academic administrators want to contain costs,[8] perhaps even at the risk of reducing the flow of scholarly information, but also have a stake in preserving certain aspects of the journal and book production process (such as refereeing) as a way of maintaining their ability to judge academic excellence, even if this approach adds to the cost of library materials. The libraries, on the other hand, would like to provide as large a flow of information to their clients as possible and might seek the best combination of different library materials to accomplish this objective.

While none of us can clearly foresee how the actual prices for various types of electronic library products will evolve, there are two general ways in which electronic library products can be defined and two general ways in which they can be priced. Either the product itself can be an individual product (for example, a given journal, such as *The Chicago Journal of Theoretical Computer Science*, or a particular monograph, or even an individual paper or chapter), or it can be a bundle of journals or monographs with the understanding that the purchaser in this latter case buys the entire bundle or nothing. If the product is a bundle, a further question is whether the items bundled are essentially similar (that is, good substitutes for one another), as would be the case if one bundled into a single product 20 economics journals; whether the items bundled are sufficiently dissimilar so that they would not be good substitutes for one another, such as Project MUSE; or whether the bundle is a "cluster of clusters" in the sense that it contains several subsets that have the characteristic of high substitutability within but low substitutability across subsets, as is the case in JSTOR.[9]

With regard to pricing, the vendor may offer site licenses for the product (however defined in light of the discussion above), which provide the purchaser with very substantial rights of downloading, printing, and so on, or charge the user each time the user accesses the product (known as "charging by the drink"). The principal difference here is not in who ultimately bears the cost, since even in the latter case universities may cover the tabs run up by their members. Two contrasting approaches, JSTOR and Project MUSE, are described in the papers by Kevin M. Guthrie (chapter 7) and Regier, respectively. In the case of JSTOR, both initial fees and annual maintenance charges vary by the size of the subscribing institution. Project MUSE, in addition, offers—not unproblematic—discounts for groups of institutions joined in consortia.

Costs

Several papers in this volume discuss the issue of costs. The complexity of the cost issues is staggering. Everybody agrees that journals as well as monographs have first-copy costs, which much resemble what the economist calls fixed costs, and variable costs. Printing, binding, and mailing are fairly sizable portions of total costs (23% for the *American Economic Review* if we ignore the fixed component and more like 36% if we include it), and it is tempting to hope that electronic publications will completely avoid these costs. (It is particularly bothersome that the marginal cost of producing an additional unit of an electronic product is [nearly] zero; hence a competitive pricing strategy would prescribe an optimal price of zero, at which, however, the vendor cannot make ends meet.) While it is true that publishers may avoid these particular costs, they clearly incur others, such as hardware, which periodically needs to be replaced, and digitizing or markup costs. Thus, estimates by Project MUSE, for example, are that to provide both the print-based and the electronic copies of journals costs 130% of the print-based publication by itself, whereas for *Immunology Today*, the combined price is set at 125% of the print version (see chapter 8). But these figures just underscore how much in the process is truly variable or adjustable: one could, presumably, save on editorial costs by requiring authors to submit papers ready to be placed on the Web (to be sure, with some risk of deteriorating visual quality).[10]

Most important, the cost implications of electronic publication are not only those costs from actually producing the product. Suddenly, the costs incurred by other entities are also affected. First is the library. Traditionally the library has borne costs as a result of providing access to scholarly information: the book or journal has to be ordered, it has to be cataloged, sometimes bound (and even rebound), shelved and reshelved, circulated, and so on. But electronic products, while they may offer some savings, also bring new costs. Libraries, for example, now have to provide workstations at which users can access the relevant materials; they must devote resources to archiving electronic materials or to providing help desks for the uninitiated. The university's computer center may also get involved in the process. But equally important, the costs to a user may also depend on the specific type of electronic product. Meanwhile, to the extent that a professor no longer has to walk to the library to consult a book, a benefit is conferred that has the effect of a de facto cost reduction. But let us agree that university administrators may not care much about costs that do not get translated into actual dollars and cents and that have to be actually disbursed (as Bennett points out). Nevertheless, there may well be actual costs that can be reduced. For example, a digital library of rare materials may obviate the need for a professor to undertake expensive research trips to distant libraries (which we may therefore call avoided costs). This factor may represent a saving to the university if it normally finances such trips or may be a saving to the National Science Foundation or the National Endowment for the Humanities if they were to end up paying the tab. The main point is that certain costs that used to be deemed *external* to the library now become internal to a broader system, and the costs of the provision of information resources must be regarded, as a minimum, on a university-wide basis. Hence these costs belong not only in the librarian's office (who would not normally care about the costs of professors' research trips) but in the provost's office as well.

Finally, we should note that many types of electronic products have up-front development costs that, given the current state of the market for such products, may not be recouped in the short run. (See, for example, Janet H. Fisher [chapter 5].) But to the extent that electronic library products will be more competitive at some future time, investing in current development efforts without the expectation of a payback may be analogous to the infant industry argument for tariff protection and may well have a lot of justification for it.

Usage and Demand

One area that we know even less about than costs is usage and demand. The traditional view has been that scientists will adapt rapidly to electronic publications, whatever they may be, and the humanists will adapt rather slowly, if at all. The picture is probably more complicated than that.

Some kinds of usage—for example, hits on the Web—may be easy to measure but tell us correspondingly little. Because hits may include aimless browsing or be only a few seconds in duration, the mere occurrence of a hit may not tell us a great deal. Nor are we able to generate in the short run the type of information from which the econometrician can easily estimate a demand function, because we do not have alternative prices at which alternative quantities demanded can be observed. But we can learn much from detailed surveys of users in which they describe what they like and what they do not like in the product and how the product makes their lives as researchers or students easier or harder (see the surveying described by Mary Summerfield and Carol A. Mandel in chapter 17). Thus, for example, it appears that critical mass is an important characteristic of certain types of electronic products, and the TULIP project may have been less than fully successful because it failed to reach the critical mass.

Electronic library products make access to information easier in some respects and certainly faster; but these benefits do not mean that the electronic information is always more convenient (reading the screen can be a nuisance in contrast to reading the printed page), nor is it clear that the more convenient access makes students learn better or faster. In fact, the acceptance of electronic products has been slower than anticipated in a number of instances. (See the papers about the *Chicago Journal of Theoretical Computer Science* [chapter 5], Project MUSE [chapters 9 and 15], JSTOR [chapters 7 and 11], and the Columbia On-line Books project [chapter 17].) But all the temporary setbacks and the numerous dimensions that the usage questions entail make it imperative that we track our experiences when we create an electronic or digital product; only in the light of such information will we be able to design products that are readily acceptable and marketable at prices that ensure the vendor's long-term survival.

A special aspect of usage is highlighted by the possibility that institutions may join forces for the common consortial exploitation of library resources, as in the case of the Associated Colleges of the South (Richard W. Meyer [chapter 14]) and Case Western Reserve/Akron Universities (Raymond K. Neff [chapter 16]). These approaches offer potentially large economies but may face new problems in technology, relations with vendors, and consortial governance (Andrew Lass [chapter 13]). When the consortium is concerned not only with shared usage, but also with publishing or compilation of research resources (as in the cases of Project MUSE and the Case Western/Akron project), the issues of consortial governance are even more complex.

A LOOK INTO THE FUTURE: QUESTIONS BUT NO ANSWERS (YET)

A key question is not whether electronic publishing will grow in the future at the expense of print-based publishing nor whether electronic access to scholarly materials in universities will account for an increasing share of all access to such materials. The answers to both these broad questions are clearly "yes." But some of the more important and interrelated questions are the following:[11] (1) How will the costs of electronic and conventional publishing evolve over time? (2) How will products be priced? (3) What kind of use will be made of electronic information products in teaching and in research? (4) How will the use affect the productivity of all types of academic activities? (5) What will be the bottom line for academic institutions as a result of the changes that are and will be occurring?

At present, the cost comparison between electronic and conventional publications may be ambiguous, and the ambiguity is due, in part, to our inability to reduce first-copy costs substantially: electronic publications save on fulfillment costs but require high initial investments and continued substantial editorial involvement. Andrew Odlyzko, in chapter 23, argues that electronic journals *can* be published at a much lower per-page cost than conventional journals, but this reduction does not appear to be happening yet. Even if we were able to reduce costs substantially by turning to electronic journals wholesale, the question for the future of library and university budgets is how the costs of electronic journals will increase over time relative to other university costs.

Curiously, most studies of the determinants of journal prices have focused on what makes one journal more expensive than another and not on what makes journal prices increase faster than, say, the prices of classroom seats.[12] If electronic journals were half the price of comparable print-based journals, universities could realize a one-time saving by substituting electronic journals for print-based ones; but if these journals increased in price over time as rapidly as paper journals, eventually universities would observe the same budget squeeze that has occurred in the last decade.

In speculating about the future evolution of costs, we can paint both optimistic and pessimistic scenarios. Hardware capabilities have increased enormously. PC processors have gone from 8-bit processors running at just over 4 Mhertz to 32-bit processors running at 450 Mhertz. Any given piece of software will run blindingly fast on a PC of the latter type in comparison with one of the former. But there is a continuing escalation of software: as soon as faster PCs appear on the market, more demanding software is created that will not perform adequately on an older PC. Will software developments continually make our hardware obsolete? If so, we may be able to carry out more elaborate functions, but some may not serve directly the objective of efficient access to scholarly information and all will be at the cost of an unending stream of equipment upgrades or replacements. On the other hand, some software improvements may reduce first-copy costs directly. It is not difficult to imagine a "learned-paper-writing software" that has the feel of a Windows 95 application, with a drop-down menu that allows the user to select the journal in whose style the paper is to be written, similarly to select mathematical notation, and so on.[13] Perhaps under such circumstances editing and copyediting might consist of little more than finding errors of logic or substance. Furthermore, as the complexity of hardware and software grows, will the need for technical support staff continue to grow and perhaps represent an increasing share of the budget?[14] It would take a crystal ball to answer all these questions. The questions provide, perhaps, some justification for O'Donnell's skeptical paper in this volume about the possibilities of measurement at this early stage in the history of electronic libraries.

Other questions asked at the beginning of this section cannot be answered in isolation from one another. The usage made of electronic products—which, one imagines, will be paid for mostly by universities and other academic institutions—will depend on the price, and the price will clearly depend on the usage: as in the standard economic model, quantity and price are jointly determined, neither being the independent cause of the other. But it is certain that usage will lag behind the hype about usage. Miller (1997) cites a state legislator who believes that the entire holdings of the Harvard University library system have (already) been digitized and are available to the public free of charge, and at least one East European librarian has stated that conventional library acquisitions are no longer relevant, since all important material will be available electronically.

In returning to the productivity puzzle, it is important to be clear about what productivity means. One may be awed by the fact that some 30 years ago the number of shares traded daily on the New York Stock Exchange was measured in the millions or perhaps tens of millions, whereas today a day with 700 million shares traded is commonplace. However, the productivity of the brokerage industry is *not* measured by the number of shares traded, but by the value added per worker in that industry, a figure that exhibits substantially lower rates of growth. Likewise, in instruction or research, productivity is not measured by the number of accesses to information but by the learning imparted (in instruction) or by the number of ideas or even papers generated (in research). If information gathering is a relatively small portion of total instructional activity (that is, if explanation of the underlying logic of an argument or the weaving of an intellectual web represent a much larger fraction), the productivity impact in teaching may end up being small. If information gathering is a small portion of research (that is, if performing laboratory experiments or working out solutions to mathematical models are much larger fractions), then the productivity impact in research may end up being low. And in these fundamental instructional and research activities there may be no breakthroughs resulting from the information technology revolution, just as you still need exactly four people to perform a string quartet and cannot increase productivity by playing it, say, twice as fast (see Baumol and Bowen 1966).

Teaching and research methods will change, but less rapidly than some may expect. The change will be more rapid if searching for the relevant information can be accomplished effectively. Effective search techniques are less relevant for instructional units (courses) in which the professor has canned the access procedures to information (such as the art course materials described in Bennett's paper in this volume). But individualized electronic products are not likely to sweep the broad ranges of academia: the specific art course at Yale, discussed by Bennett, is likely to be taught only at Yale despite the fact that it is similar to courses taught at hundreds of universities. For scholars who are truly searching for new information, Web searches that report 38,732 hits are not useful and suggest that neither students nor faculty members are well trained in effective search techniques.[15] It is fortunate that important new research into better search algorithms is being carried out. Librarians will play a vital role in this process by helping to guide scholars toward the best electronic sources, just as they have helped generations of scholars to find their way among print-based sources. This new role may, of course, require that librarians themselves redefine their functions to some extent and acquire new expertise; but these changes are happening anyway.

And what about the bottom line? This question is the most difficult one of all, and only the wildest guesses can be hazarded at this time. Taking a short-run or intermediate-run perspective (that is, a period of time up to, say, seven years from now), we do not expect that the revolution in information technology is going to reduce university costs; in fact it may increase them. Beyond the intermediate horizon, things may well change. Hardware costs may decline even more precipitously than heretofore, software (including search engines) may become ever more effective, and the cost savings due to information technology that are *not* centered on library activities may become properly attributed to the electronic revolution. In the long run, the budgetary implications are probably much more favorable than the short- or intermediate-term implications. But what we need to emphasize is that the proper way of assessing the longer term evolution of costs is not by way of one part of an institution—say, the library—or even by way of an individual institution viewed as a whole system, but ideally by way of an interdependent multi-institutional system. Just as electronic technology may provide a university with savings that do not fall within the traditional library budget, thus implying that savings are spread university-wide, so too will the savings be spread over the entire higher educational system. Even though some costs at individual institutions may rise, we are confident that system costs will eventually fall.

NOTES

1. See, for example, Astle and Hamaker (1988), Joyce and Mertz (1985), Joyce (1990), Kingma and Eppard (1992), Chressanthis and Chressanthis (1993a, 1993b, 1994a, 1994b), Noll and Steinmueller (1992), Petersen (1989, 1990), Quandt (1996), and Thatcher (1992).

2. A small number of additional papers, by authors not involved in Foundation projects, was commissioned on topics deemed particularly relevant for electronic and digital libraries.

3. For more detailed discussion of these issues, see Blinder (1997) and Blinder and Quandt (1997).

4. As a parallel, note that investment in computers and related equipment accounted for less than 10% of gross investment in the U.S. economy in 1996. For a comprehensive account of the economics of the "computer revolution," see Sichel (1997).

5. For example, digitizing in a myriad different ways: see Anne R. Kenney's remarkable benchmarks in chapter 2.

6. Technically speaking, the sellers of such products are monopolistic competitors.

7. But price discrimination emerging from the difficulty of reselling cannot be the whole story, because it seems largely confined to journals and not to monographs.

8. Louisiana State University, among others, has replaced journal subscriptions with a liberal document delivery service, saving hundreds of thousands of dollars annually.

9. Bakos and Brynjolfsson (1997) argue that under certain simplifying assumptions, the latter strategy permits the vendor to realize substantial profit while at the same time inflicting only modest deadweight loss on the purchaser.

10. The question of the quality of presentation versus the cost is one of the important trade-offs that the academic profession may have to face in the future. See Andrew Odlyzko (chapter 23).

11. By "interrelated" we mean that some of these questions cannot be answered in isolation: the answer to one may well depend on the answer to another one.

12. See, for example, Chressanthis and Chressanthis (1993a, 1993b, 1994a, 1994b) and Petersen (1989, 1990). For a notable exception that does deal with the issue of which journal prices are increasing, see Noll and Steinmueller (1992).

13. Analogies are the Netscape HTML Editor or the Microsoft FrontPage Editor that permit one to write HTML code practically without knowing anything about HTML.

14. It is a common perception that the amount of time spent on software installation and on the maintenance of computer and software integrity is substantially larger today than it was in the "good old days" of DOS, a mere five years ago.

15. The vastly different outcomes that may occur when different search algorithms are applied to the same database is well illustrated in Besser and Yamashita (1997).

PART ONE

Technological Fundamentals

CHAPTER 1

Making Technology Work for Scholarship
Investing in the Data

Susan Hockey

The introduction of any kind of new technology is often a painful and time-consuming process, at least for those who must incorporate it into their everyday lives. This is particularly true of computing technology, where the learning curve can be steep, what is learned changes rapidly, and ever more new and exciting things seem to be perpetually on the horizon. How can the providers and consumers of electronic information make the best use of this new medium and ensure that the information they create and use will outlast the current system on which it is used? In this chapter we examine some of these issues, concentrating on the humanities, where the nature of the information studied by scholars can be almost anything and where the information can be studied for almost any purpose.

Today's computer programs are not sophisticated enough to process raw data sensibly. This situation will remain true until artificial intelligence and natural language processing research has made very much more progress. Early on in my days as a humanities computing specialist, I saw a library catalog that had been typed into the computer without anything to separate the fields in the information. There was no way of knowing what was the author, title, publisher, or call number of any of the items. The catalog could be printed out, but the titles could not be searched at all, nor could the items in the catalog be sorted by author name. Although a human can tell which is the author or title from reading the catalog, a computer program cannot. Something must be inserted in the data to give the program more information. This situation is a very simple example of markup, or encoding, which is needed to make computers work better for us. Since we are so far from having the kind of intelligence we really need in computer programs, we must put that intelligence in the data so that computer programs can be informed by it. The more intelligence there is in our data, the better our programs will perform. But what should that intelligence look like? How can we ensure that we make the right decisions in creating it so that computers can really do what we want? Some scholarly communication and digital library projects are beginning to provide answers to these questions.

NEW TECHNOLOGY OR OLD?

Many current technology and digital library projects use the new technology as an access mechanism to deliver the old technology. These projects rest on the assumption that the typical scholarly product is an article or monograph and that it will be read in a sequential fashion as indeed we have done for hundreds of years, ever since these products began to be produced on paper and be bound into physical artifacts such as books. The difference is that instead of going only to the library or bookstore to obtain the object, we access it over the network—and then almost certainly have to print a copy of it in order to read it. Of course there is a tremendous savings of time for those who have instant access to the network, can find the material they are looking for easily, and have high-speed printers. I want to argue here that delivering the old technology via the new is only a transitory phase and that it must not be viewed as an end in itself. Before we embark on the large-scale compilation of electronic information, we must consider how future scholars might use this information and what are the best ways of ensuring that the information will last beyond the current technology.

The old (print) technology developed into a sophisticated model over a long period of time.[1] Books consist of pages bound up in sequential fashion, delivering the text in a single linear sequence. Page numbers and running heads are used for identification purposes. Books also often include other organizational aids, such as tables of contents and back-of-the-book indexes, which are conventionally placed at the beginning and end of the book respectively. Footnotes, bibliographies, illustrations, and so forth, provide additional methods of cross-referencing. A title page provides a convention for identifying the book and its author and publication details. The length of a book is often determined by publishers' costs or requirements rather than by what the author really wants to say about the subject. Journal articles exhibit similar characteristics, also being designed for reproduction on pieces of paper. Furthermore, the ease of reading printed books and journals is determined by their typography, which is designed to help the reader by reinforcing what the author wants to say. Conventions of typography (headings, italic, bold, etc.) make things stand out on the page.

When we put information into electronic form, we find that we can do many more things with it than we can with a printed book. We can still read it, though not as well as we can read a printed book. The real advantage of the electronic medium is that we can search and manipulate the information in many different ways. We are no longer dependent on the back-of-the-book index to find things within the text, but can search for any word or phrase using retrieval software. We no longer need the whole book to look up one paragraph but can just access the piece of information we need. We can also access several different pieces of information at the same time and make links between them. We can find a biblio-graphic reference and go immediately to the place to which it points. We can merge different representations of the same material into a coherent whole and we can count instances of features within the information. We can thus begin to think of the material we want as "information objects."[2]

To reinforce the arguments I am making here, I call electronic images of printed pages "dead text" and use the term "live text" for searchable representa-tions of text.[3] For dead text we can use only those retrieval tools that were de-signed for finding printed items, and even then this information must be added as searchable live text, usually in the form of bibliographic references or tables of contents. Of course most of the dead text produced over the past fifteen or so years began its life as live text in the form of word-processed documents. The ob-vious question is, how can the utility of that live text be retained and not lost for-ever?

ELECTRONIC TEXT AND DATA FORMATS

Long before digital libraries became popular, live electronic text was being created for many different purposes, most often, as we have seen, with word-processing or typesetting programs. Unfortunately this kind of live electronic text is normally searchable only by the word-processing program that produced it and then only in a very simple way. We have all encountered the problems involved in moving from one word-processing program to another. Although some of these problems have been solved in more recent versions of the software, maintaining an electronic document as a word-processing file is not a sensible option for the long term un-less the creator of the document is absolutely sure that this document will be needed only in the short-term future and only for the purposes of word processing by the program that created it. Word-processed documents contain typographic markup, or codes, to specify the formatting. If there were no markup, the docu-ment would be much more difficult to read. However, typesetting markup is am-biguous and thus cannot be used sensibly by any retrieval program. For example, italics can be used for titles of books, or for emphasized words, or for foreign words. With typographic markup, we cannot distinguish titles of books from for-eign words, which we may, at some stage, want to search for separately.

Other electronic texts were created for the purposes of retrieval and analysis. Many such examples exist, ranging from the large text databases of legal statutes to humanities collections such as the *Thesaurus Linguae Graecae* (TLG) and the *Tré-sor de la langue française*. The scholars working on these projects all realized that they needed to put some intelligence into the data in order to search it effectively. Most project staff devised markup schemes that focus on ways of identifying the refer-ence citations for items that have been retrieved; for example, in the TLG, those items would be the name of the author, work, book, and chapter number. Such markup schemes do not easily provide for representing items of interest within a text, for example, foreign words or quotations. Most of these markup schemes are specific to one or two computer programs, and texts prepared in them are not easily interchangeable. A meeting in 1987 examined the many markup schemes for humanities electronic texts and concluded that the present situation was "chaos."[4] No existing markup scheme satisfied the needs of all users, and much time was being wasted converting from one deficient scheme to another.

Another commonly used method of storing and retrieving information is a relational database such as, for example, Microsoft Access or dBASE or the mainframe program Oracle. In a relational database, data is assumed to take the form of one or more tables consisting of rows and columns, that is, the form of rectangular structures.[5] A simple table of biographical information may have rows representing people and columns holding information about those people, for example, name, date of birth, occupation, and so on. When a person has more than one occupation, the data becomes clumsy and the information is best represented in two tables, in which the second has a row for each occupation of each person. The tables are linked, or related, by the person. A third table may hold information about the occupations. It is not difficult for a human to conceptualize the data structures of a relational database or for a computer to process them. Relational databases work well for some kinds of information, for example, an address list, but in reality not much data in the real world fits well into rectangular structures. Such a structure means that the information is distorted when it is entered into the computer, and processing and analyses are carried out on the distorted forms, whose distortion tends to be forgotten. Relational databases also force the allocation of information to fixed data categories, whereas, in the humanities at any rate, much of the information is subject to scholarly debate and dispute, requiring multiple views of the material to be represented. Furthermore, getting information out of a relational database for use by other programs usually requires some programming knowledge.

The progress of too many retrieval and database projects can be characterized as follows. A project group decides that it wants to "make a CD-ROM." It finds that it has to investigate possible software programs for delivery of the results and chooses the one that has the most seductive user interface or most persuasive salesperson. If the data include some nonstandard characters, the highest priority is often given to displaying those characters on the screen; little attention is paid to the functions needed to manipulate those characters. Data are then entered directly into this software over a period of time during which the software interface begins to look outmoded as technology changes. By the time the data have been entered for the project, the software company has gone out of business, leaving the project staff with a lot of valuable information in a proprietary software format that is no longer supported. More often than not, the data are lost and much time and money has been wasted. The investment is clearly in the data, and it makes sense to ensure that these data are not dependent on one particular program but can be used by other programs as well.

STANDARD GENERALIZED MARKUP LANGUAGE (SGML)

Given the time and effort involved in creating electronic information, it makes sense to step back and think about how to ensure that the information can outlast the computer system on which it is created and can also be used for many different purposes. These are the two main principles of the Standard Generalized Markup Language (SGML), which became an international standard (ISO 8879) in 1986.[6] SGML was designed as a general purpose markup scheme that can be applied to many different types of documents and in fact to any electronic information. It consists of plain ASCII files, which can easily be moved from one computer system to another. SGML is a descriptive language. Most encoding schemes prior to SGML use prescriptive markup. One example of prescriptive markup is word-processing or typesetting codes embedded in a text that give instructions to the computer such as "center the next line" or "print these words in italic." Another example is fielded data that is specific to a retrieval program, for example, reference citations or author's names, which must be in a specific format for the retrieval program to recognize them as such. By contrast, a descriptive markup language merely identifies what the components of a document are. It does not give specific instructions to any program. In it, for example, a title is encoded as a title, or a paragraph as a paragraph. This very simple approach ultimately allows much more flexibility. A printing program can print all the titles in italic, a retrieval program can search on the titles, and a hypertext program can link to and from the titles, all without making any changes to the data.

Strictly speaking, SGML itself is not a markup scheme, but a kind of computer language for defining markup, or encoding, schemes. SGML markup schemes assume that each document consists of a collection of objects that nest within each other or are related to each other in some other way. These objects or features can be almost anything. Typically they are structural components such as title, chapter, paragraph, heading, act, scene, speech, but they can also be interpretive information such as parts of speech, names of people and places, quotations (direct and indirect), and even literary or historical interpretation. The first stage of any SGML-based project is document analysis, which identifies all the textual features that are of interest and identifies the relationships between them. This step can take some time, but it is worth investing the time since a thorough document analysis can ensure that data entry proceeds smoothly and that the documents are easily processable by computer programs.

In SGML terms, the objects within a document are called elements. They are identified by a start and end tag as follows: <title>Pride and Prejudice</title>.

The SGML syntax allows the document designer to specify all the possible elements as a Document Type Definition (DTD), which is a kind of formal model of the document structure. The DTD indicates which elements are contained within other elements, which are optional, which can be repeated, and so forth. For example, in simple terms a journal article consists of a title, one or more author names, an optional abstract, and an optional list of keywords, followed by the body of the article. The body may contain sections, each with a heading followed by one or more paragraphs of text. The article may finish with a bibliography. The paragraphs of text may contain other features of interest, including quotations, lists, and names, as well as links to notes. A play has a rather different structure: title; author; cast list; one or more acts, each containing one or more scenes, which in turn contain one or more speeches and stage directions; and so on.

SGML elements may also have attributes that further specify or modify the element. One use of attributes may be to normalize the spelling of names for indexing purposes. For example, the name Jack Smyth could be encoded as <name norm="SmithJ"> Jack Smyth</name>, but indexed under S as if it were Smith. Attributes can also be used to normalize date forms for sorting, for example, <date norm=19970315>the Ides of March 1997</date>. Another important function of attributes is to assign a unique identifier to each instance of each SGML element within a document. These identifiers can be used as a cross-reference by any kind of hypertext program. The list of possible attributes for an element may be defined as a closed set, allowing the encoder to pick from a list, or it may be entirely open.

SGML has another very useful feature. Any piece of information can be given a name and be referred to by that name in an SGML document. These names are called entities and are enclosed in an ampersand and a semicolon. One use is for nonstandard characters, where, for example, é can be encoded as é thus ensuring that it can be transmitted easily across networks and from one machine to another. A standard list of these characters exists, but the document encoder can also create more. Entity references can also be used for any boilerplate text. This use avoids repetitive typing of words and phrases that are repeated, thus also reducing the chance of errors. An entity reference can be resolved to any amount of text from a single letter up to the equivalent of an entire chapter.

The formal structure of SGML means that the encoding of a document can be validated automatically, a process known as parsing. The parser makes use of the SGML DTD to determine the structure of the document and can thus help to eliminate whole classes of encoding errors before the document is processed by an application program. For example, an error can be detected if the DTD specifies that a journal article must have one or more authors, but the author's name has been omitted accidentally. Mistyped element names can be detected as errors, as can elements that are wrongly nested—for example, an act within a scene when the DTD specifies that acts contain scenes. Attributes can also be validated when there is a closed set of possible values. The validation process can also detect unresolved cross-references that use SGML's built-in identifiers. The SGML document structure and validation process means that any application program can operate more efficiently because it derives information from the DTD about what to expect in the document. It follows that the stricter the DTD, the easier it is to process the document. However, very strict DTDs may force the document encoder to make decisions that simplify what is being encoded. Free DTDs might better reflect the nature of the information but usually require more processing. Another advantage of SGML is very apparent here. Once a project is under way, if a document encoder finds a new feature of interest, that feature can simply be added to the DTD without the need to restructure work that has already been done. Many documents can be encoded and processed with the same DTD.

TEXT ENCODING INITIATIVE

The humanities computing community was among the early adopters of SGML, for two very simple reasons. Humanities primary source texts can be very complex, and they need to be shared and used by different scholars. They can be in different languages and writing systems and can contain textual variants, nonstandard characters, annotations and emendations, multiple parallel texts, and hypertext links, as well as complex canonical reference systems. In electronic form, these texts can be used for many different purposes, including the preparation of new editions, word and phrase searches, stylistic analyses and research on syntax, and other linguistic features. By 1987 it was clear that many encoding schemes existed for humanities electronic texts, but none was sufficiently powerful to allow for all the different features that might be of interest. Following a planning meeting attended by representatives of leading humanities computing projects, a major international project called the Text Encoding Initiative (TEI) was launched.[7] Sponsored by the Association for Computers and the Humanities, the Association for Computational Linguistics, and the Association for Literary and Linguistic Computing, the TEI enlisted the help of volunteers all over the world to define what features might be of interest to humanities scholars working with electronic text. It built on the expertise of groups such as the Perseus Project (then at Harvard, now at Tufts University), the Brown University Women Writers Project, the Alfa Informatica Group in Groningen, Netherlands, and others who were already working with SGML, to create SGML tags that could be used for many different types of text.

The TEI published its *Guidelines for the Encoding and Interchange of Electronic Texts* in May 1994 after more than six years' work. The guidelines identify some four hundred tags, but of course no list of tags can be truly comprehensive, and so the TEI builds its DTDs in a way that makes it easy for users to modify them. The TEI SGML application is built on the assumption that all texts share some common core of features to which can be added tags for specific application areas. Very few tags are mandatory, and most of these are concerned with documenting the text and will be further discussed below. The TEI Guidelines are simply guidelines. They serve to help the encoder identify features of interest, and they provide the DTDs with which the encoder will work. The core consists of the header, which documents the text, plus basic structural tags and common features, such as lists, abbreviations, bibliographic citations, quotations, simple names and dates, and so on. The user selects a base tag set: prose, verse, drama, dictionaries, spoken texts, or terminological data. To this are added one or more additional tag sets. The options here include simple analytic mechanisms, linking and hypertext, transcription of primary sources, critical apparatus, names and dates, and some methods of handling graphics. The TEI has also defined a method of handling nonstandard alphabets by using a Writing System Declaration, which the user specifies. This method can also be used for nonalphabetic writing systems, for example, Japanese. Building a TEI DTD has been likened to the preparation of a pizza, where the base tag set is the crust, the core tags are the tomato and cheese, and the additional tag sets are the toppings.

One of the issues addressed at the TEI planning meeting was the need for documentation of an electronic text. Many electronic texts now exist about which little is known, that is, what source text they were taken from, what decisions were made in encoding the text, or what changes have been made to the text. All this information is extremely important to a scholar wanting to work on the text, since it will determine the academic credibility of his or her work. Unknown sources are unreliable at best and lead to inferior work. Experience has shown that electronic texts are more likely to contain errors or have bits missing, but these are more difficult to detect than with printed material. It seems that one of the main reasons for this lack of documentation for electronic texts was simply that there was no common methodology for providing it.

The TEI examined various models for documenting electronic texts and concluded that some SGML elements placed as a header at the beginning of an electronic text file would be the most appropriate way of providing this information. Since the header is part of the electronic text file, it is more likely to remain with that file throughout its life. It can also be processed by the same software as the rest of the text. The TEI header contains four major sections.[8] One section is a bibliographic description of the electronic text file using SGML elements that map closely on to some MARC fields. The electronic text is an intellectual object different from the source from which it was created, and the source is thus also identified in the header. The encoding description section provides information about the principles used in encoding the text, for example, whether the spelling has been normalized, treatment of end-of-line hyphens, and so forth. For spoken texts, the header provides a way of identifying the participants in a conversation and of attaching a simple identifier to each participant that can then be used as an attribute on each utterance. The header also provides a revision history of the text, indicating who made what changes to it and when.

As far as can be ascertained, the TEI header is the first systematic attempt to provide documentation for an electronic text that is a part of the text file itself. A good many projects are now using it, but experience has shown that it would perhaps benefit from some revision. Scholars find it hard to create good headers. Some elements in the header are very obvious, but the relative importance of the remaining elements is not so clear. At some institutions, librarians are creating TEI headers, but they need training in the use and importance of the nonbibliographic sections and in how the header is used by computer software other than the bibliographic tools that they are familiar with.

ENCODED ARCHIVAL DESCRIPTION (EAD)

Another SGML application that has attracted a lot of attention in the scholarly community and archival world is the Encoded Archival Description (EAD). First developed by Daniel Pitti at the University of California at Berkeley and now taken over by the Library of Congress, the EAD is an SGML application for archival finding aids.[9] Finding aids are very suitable for SGML because they are basically hierarchic in structure. In simple terms, a collection is divided into series, which consist of boxes, which contain folders, and so on. Prior to the EAD, there was no effective standard way of preparing finding aids. Typical projects created a collection level record in one of the bibliographic utilities, such as RLIN, and used their own procedures, often a word-processing program, for creating the finding aid. Possibilities now exist for using SGML to link electronic finding aids with electronic representations of the archival material itself. One such experiment, conducted at the Center for Electronic Texts in the Humanities (CETH), has created an EAD-encoded finding aid for part of the Griffis Collection at Rutgers University and has encoded a small number of the items in the collection (nineteenth-century essays) in the TEI scheme.[10] The user can work with the finding aid to locate the item of interest and then move directly to the encoded text and an image of the text to study the item in more detail. The SGML browser program Panorama allows the two DTDs to exist side by side and in fact uses an extended pointer mechanism devised by the TEI to move from one to the other.

OTHER APPLICATIONS OF SGML

SGML is now being widely adopted in the commercial world as companies see the advantage of investment in data that will move easily from one computer system to another. It is worth noting that the few books on SGML that appeared early in its life were intended for an academic audience. More recent books are intended for a commercial audience and emphasize the cost savings involved in SGML as well as the technical requirements. This is not to say that these books are not of any value to academic users. The SGML Web pages list many projects in the areas of health, legal documents, electronic journals, rail and air transport, semiconductors, the U.S. Internal Revenue Service, and more. SGML is extremely useful for technical documentation, as can be evidenced by the list of customers on the Web page of one of the major SGML software companies, INSO/EBT. This list includes United Airlines, Novell, British Telecom, AT&T, Shell, Boeing, Nissan, and Volvo.

SGML need not be used only with textual data. It can be used to describe almost anything. SGML should not therefore be seen as an alternative to Acrobat, PostScript, or other document formats but as a way of describing and linking together documents in these and other formats, forming the "underground tunnels" that make the documents work for users.[11] SGML can be used to encode the searchable textual information that must accompany images or other formats in order to make them useful. With SGML, the searchable elements can be defined to fit the data exactly and can be used by different systems. This encoding is in contrast with storing image data in some proprietary database system, which is common practice. We can imagine a future situation in which a scholar wants to examine the digital image of a manuscript and also have available a searchable text. He or she may well find something of interest on the image and want to go to occurrences of the same feature elsewhere within the text. In order to do this, the encoded version of the text must know what that feature of interest is and where it occurs on the digital image. Knowing which page it is on is not enough. The exact position on the page must be encoded. This information can be represented in SGML, which thus provides the sophisticated kind of linking needed for scholarly applications. SGML structures can also point to places within a recording of speech or other sound and can be used to link the sound to a transcription of the conversation, again enabling the sound and text to be studied together. Other programs exist that can perform these functions, but the problem with all of them is that they use a proprietary data format that cannot be used for any other purpose.

SGML, HTML, AND XML

The relationship between SGML and the Hypertext Markup Language (HTML) needs to be clearly understood. Although not originally designed as such, HTML is now an SGML application, even though many HTML documents exist that cannot be validated according to the rules of SGML. HTML consists of a set of elements that are interpreted by Web browsers for display purposes. The HTML tags were designed for display and not for other kinds of analysis, which is why only crude searches are possible on Web documents. HTML is a rather curious mixture of elements. Larger ones, such as <body>; <h1>, <h2>, and so on for head levels; <p> for paragraph; and <ul> for unordered list, are structural, but the smaller elements, such as <b> for bold and <i> for italic, are typographic, which, as we have seen above, are ambiguous and thus cannot be searched effectively. HTML version 3 attempts to rectify this ambiguity somewhat by introducing a few semantic level elements, but these are very few in comparison with those identified in the TEI core set. HTML can be a good introduction to structured markup. Since it is so easy to create, many project managers begin by using HTML and graduate to SGML once they become used to working with structured text and begin to see the weakness of HTML for anything other than the display of text. SGML can easily be converted automatically to HTML for delivery on the Web, and Web clients have been written for the major SGML retrieval programs.

The move from HTML to SGML can be substantial, and in 1996 work began on XML (Extensible Markup Language), which is a simplified version of SGML for delivery on the Web. It is "an extremely simple dialect of SGML," the goal of which "is to enable generic SGML to be served, received, and processed on the Web in the way that is now possible with HTML" (see *http://www.w3.org/TR/REC-xml*). XML is being developed under the auspices of the World Wide Web Consortium, and the first draft of the specification for it was available by the SGML conference in December 1996. Essentially XML is SGML with some of the more complex and esoteric features removed. It has been designed for interoperability with both SGML and HTML—that is, to fill the gap between HTML, which is too simple, and full-blown SGML, which can be complicated. As yet there is no specific XML software, but the work of this group has considerable backing and the design of XML has proceeded quickly.[12]

SGML AND NEW MODELS OF SCHOLARSHIP

SGML's objectlike structures make it possible for scholarly communication to be seen as "chunks" of information that can be put together in different ways. Using SGML, we no longer have to squeeze the product of our research into a single linear sequence of text whose size is often determined by the physical medium in which it will appear; instead we can organize it in many different ways, privileging some for one audience and others for a different audience. Some projects are already exploiting this potential, and I am collaborating in two that are indicative of the way I think humanities scholarship will develop in the twenty-first century. Both projects make use of SGML to create information objects that can be delivered in many different ways.

The Model Editions Partnership (MEP) is defining a set of models for electronic documentary editions.[13] Directed by David Chesnutt of the University of South Carolina, with the TEI Editor, C. Michael Sperberg-McQueen, and myself as co-coordinators, the MEP also includes seven documentary editing projects. Two of these projects are creating image editions, and the other five are preparing letterpress publications. These documentary editions provide the basic source material for the study of American history by adding the historical context that makes the material meaningful to readers. Much of this source material consists of letters, which often refer to people and places by words that only the author and recipient understand. A good deal of the source material is in handwriting that can be read only by scholars specializing in the field. Documentary editors prepare the material for publication by transcribing the documents, organizing the sources into a coherent sequence that tells the story (the history) behind them, and annotating them with information to help the reader understand them. However, the printed page is not a very good vehicle for conveying the information that documentary editors need to say. It forces one organizing principle on the material (the single linear sequence of the book) when the material could well be organized in several different ways (chronologically, for example, or by recipient of letters). Notes must appear at the end of an item to which they refer or at the end of the book. When the same note—for example, a short biographical sketch of somebody mentioned in the sources—is needed in several places, it can appear only once, and after that it is cross-referenced by page numbers, often to earlier volumes. Something that has been crossed out and rewritten in a source document can only be represented clumsily in print even though it may reflect a change of mind that altered the course of history.

At the beginning of the MEP project, the three coordinators visited all seven partner projects, showed the project participants some very simple demonstrations, and then invited them to "dream" about what they would like to do in this new medium. The ideas collected during these visits were incorporated into a prospectus for electronic documentary editions. The MEP sees SGML as the key to providing all the functionality outlined in the prospectus. The MEP has developed an SGML DTD for documentary editions that is based on the TEI and has begun to experiment with delivery of samples from the partner projects. The material for the image editions is wrapped up in an "SGML envelope" that provides the tools to access the images. This envelope can be generated automatically from the relational databases in which the image access information is now stored. For the letterpress editions, many more possibilities are apparent. If desired, it will be possible to merge material from different projects that are working on the same period of history. It will be possible to select subsets of the material easily by any of the tagged features. This means that editions for high school students or the general public could be created almost automatically from the archive of scholarly material. With a click of a mouse, the user can go from a diplomatic edition to a clear reading text and thus trace the author's thoughts as the document was being written. The documentary editions also include very detailed conceptual indexes compiled by the editors. It will be possible to use these indexes as an entry point to the text and also to merge indexes from different projects. The MEP sees the need for making dead text image representations of existing published editions available quickly and believes that these can be made much more useful by wrapping them in SGML and using the conceptual indexes as an entry point to them.

The second project is even more ambitious than the MEP, since it is dealing with entirely new material and has been funded for five years. The Orlando Project at the Universities of Alberta and Guelph is a major collaborative research initiative funded by the Canadian Social Sciences and Humanities Research Council.[14] Directed by Patricia Clements, the project is to create an Integrated History of Women's Writing in the British Isles, which will appear in print and electronic formats. A team of graduate research assistants is carrying out basic research for the project in libraries and elsewhere. The research material they are assembling is being encoded in SGML so that it can be retrieved in many different ways. SGML DTDs have been designed to reflect the biographical details for each woman writer as well as her writing history, other historical events that influenced her writing, a thesaurus of keyword terms, and so forth. The DTDs are based on the TEI but they incorporate much descriptive and interpretive information, reflecting the nature of the research and the views of the literary scholars in the team. Tag sets have been devised for topics such as the issues of authorship and attribution, genre issues, and issues of reception of an author's work.

The Orlando Project is thus building up an SGML-encoded database of many different kinds of information about women's writing in the British Isles. The SGML encoding, for example, greatly assists in the preparation of a chronology by allowing the project to pull out all chronology items from the different documents and sort them by their dates. It facilitates an overview of where the women writers lived, their social background, and what external factors influenced their writing. It helps with the creation and consistency of new entries, since the researchers can see immediately if similar information has already been encountered. The authors of the print volumes will draw on this SGML archive as they write, but the archive can also be used to create many different hypertext products for research and teaching.

Both Orlando and the MEP are, essentially, working with pieces of information, which can be linked in many different ways. The linking, or rather the interpretation that gives rise to the linking, is what humanities scholarship is about. When the information is stored as encoded pieces of information, it can be put together in many different ways and used for many different purposes, of which creating a print publication is only one. We can expect other projects to begin to work in this way as they see the advantages of encoding the features of interest in their material and of manipulating them in different ways.

It is useful to look briefly at some other possibilities. Dictionary publishers were among the first to use SGML. (Although not strictly SGML since it does not have a DTD, the *Oxford English Dictionary* was the first academic project to use structured markup.) When well designed, the markup enables the dictionary publishers to create spin-off products for different audiences by selecting a subset of the tagged components of an entry. A similar process can be used for other kinds of reference works. Tables of contents, bibliographies, and indexes can all be compiled automatically from SGML markup and can also be cumulative across volumes or collections of material.

The MEP is just one project that uses SGML for scholarly editions. A notable example is the CD-ROM of Chaucer's Wife of Bath's Prologue, prepared by Peter Robinson and published by Cambridge University Press in 1996. This CD-ROM contains all fifty-eight pre-1500 manuscripts of the text, with encoding for all the variant readings as well as digitized images of every page of all the manuscripts. Software programs provided with the CD-ROM can manipulate the material in many different ways, enabling a scholar to collate manuscripts, move immediately from one manuscript to another, and compare transcriptions, spellings, and readings. All the material is encoded in SGML, and the CD-ROM includes more than one million hypertext links generated by a computer program, which means that the investment in the project's data is carried forward from one delivery system to another, indefinitely, into the future.

MAKING SGML WORK EFFECTIVELY

Getting started with SGML can seem to be a big hurdle to overcome, but in fact the actual mechanics of working with SGML are nowhere near as difficult as is often assumed. SGML tags are rarely typed in, but are normally inserted by software programs such as Author/Editor. These programs can incorporate a template that is filled in with data. Like other SGML software, these programs make use of the DTD. They know which tags are valid at any position in the document and can offer only those tags to the user, who can pick from a menu. They can also provide a pick list of attributes and their values if the values are a closed set. These programs ensure that what is produced is a valid SGML document. They can also toggle the display of tags on and off very easily—Author/Editor encloses them in boxes that are very easy to see. The programs also incorporate style sheets that define the display format for every element.

Nevertheless, inserting tags in this way can be rather cumbersome, and various software tools exist to help in the translation of "legacy" data to SGML. Of course, these tools cannot add intelligence to data if it was not there in the legacy format, but they can do a reasonable and low-cost job of converting material for large-scale projects in which only broad structural information is needed. For UNIX users, the shareware program *sgmls* and its successor, *sp*, are excellent tools for validating SGML documents and can be incorporated in processing programs. There are also ways in which the markup can be minimized. End tags can be omitted in some circumstances, for example, in a list where the start of a new list item implies that the previous one has ended.

There is no doubt that SGML is considered expensive by some project managers, but further down the line the payoff can be seen many times over. The quick and dirty solution to a computing problem does not last very long, and history has shown how much time can be wasted converting from one system to another or how much data can be lost because they are in a proprietary system. It is rather surprising that the simple notion of encoding what the parts of a document are, rather than what the computer is supposed to do with them, took so long to catch on. Much of the investment in any computer project is in the data, and SGML is the best way we know so far of ensuring that the data will last for a long time and that they can be used and reused for many different purposes. It also ensures that the project is not dependent on one software vendor.

The amount of encoding is obviously a key factor in the cost, and so any discussion about the cost-effectiveness of an SGML project should always be made with reference to the specific DTD in use and the level of markup to be inserted. Statements that SGML costs x dollars per page are not meaningful without further qualification. Unfortunately at present such further qualification seems rarely to be the case, and misconceptions often occur. It is quite possible, although clearly not sensible, to have a valid SGML document that consists of one start tag at the beginning and one corresponding end tag at the end with no other markup in between. At the other extreme, each word (or even letter) in the document could have several layers of markup attached to it. What is clear is that the more markup there is, the more useful the document is and the more expensive it is to create. As far as I am aware, little research has been done on the optimum level of markup, but at least with SGML it is possible to add markup to a document later without prejudicing what is already encoded.

In my view, it is virtually impossible to make some general cost statements for SGML-based work. Each project needs to be assessed differently depending on its current situation and its objectives.[15] However, I will attempt to discuss some of the issues and the items that make up the overall cost. Many of the costs of an SGML-based project are no different from those of other computer-based projects in that both have start-up costs and ongoing costs.

Start-up costs can depend on how much computing experience and expertise there already is in the organization. Projects that are being started now have the advantage of not being encumbered by large amounts of legacy data and proprietary systems, but they also will need to be started from scratch with the three things that make any computer project work: hardware, software, and skilled people. Hardware costs are insignificant these days, and SGML software will work on almost any current PC or UNIX-based hardware. It does not need an expensive proprietary system. An individual scholar can acquire PC software for creating and viewing SGML-encoded text for under $500. Public domain UNIX tools cost nothing to acquire. That leaves what is, in my view, the most essential component of any computing project, namely, people with good technical skills. Unfortunately, these people are expensive. The market is such that they can expect higher salaries than librarians and publishers receive at the equivalent stages in their careers. However, I think that it is unwise for any organization to embark on a computer-based project without having staff with the proper skills to do the work. Like people in all other disciplines, computer people specialize in one or two areas, and so it is important to hire staff with the right computing skills and thus important for the person doing the hiring to understand what those skills should be. There are still not many SGML specialists around, but someone with a good basic background in computing could be trained in SGML at a commercial or academic course in a week or so, with some follow-up time for experimentation. This person can then use mailing lists and the SGML Web site to keep in touch with new developments. Having the right kind of technical person around early on in any computing project also means that there is somebody who can advise on the development of the system and ensure that expensive mistakes are not made by decision makers who have had little previous involvement with computing systems. The technical person will also be able to see immediately where costs can be saved by implementing shortcuts.

The one specific start-up cost with SGML is the choice or development of the DTD. Many digital library projects are utilizing existing DTDs—for example, the cut-down version of the TEI called TEILite—either with no changes at all or with only light modifications. However, I think that it is important for project managers to look hard at an existing DTD to see whether it really satisfies their requirements rather than just decide to use it because everyone else they know is using it. A project in a very specialized area may need to have its own DTD developed. This could mean the hiring of SGML consultants for a few days plus time spent by the project's own staff in specifying the objectives of the project in great detail and in defining and refining the features of interest within the project's documents.

Computer-based projects seldom proceed smoothly, and in the start-up phase, time must be allowed for false starts and revisions. SGML is no different here, but by its nature it does force project managers to consider very many aspects at the beginning and thus help prevent the project from going a long way down a wrong road. SGML elements can also be used to assist with essential aspects of project administration, for example, tags for document control and management.

Ongoing costs are largely concerned with document creation and encoding, but they also include general maintenance, upgrades, and revisions. If the material is not already in electronic form, it may be possible to convert it by optical character recognition (OCR). The accuracy of the result will depend on the quality of the type fonts and paper of the original, but the document will almost certainly need to be proofread and edited to reach the level of quality acceptable to the scholarly community. OCR also yields a typographic representation of a document, which is ambiguous for other kinds of computer processing. Whether it comes from word processors or OCR, typographic encoding needs to be converted to SGML. It is possible to write programs or purchase software tools to do this, but only those features that can be unambiguously defined can be converted in this way. Any markup that requires interpretive judgment must be inserted manually at the cost of human time. Most electronic text projects in the humanities have had the material entered directly by keyboarding, not only to attain higher levels of accuracy than with OCR, but also to insert markup at the same time. More often than not, project managers employ graduate students for this work, supervised by a textbase manager who keeps records of decisions made in the encoding and often assisted by a programmer who can identify shortcuts and write programs where necessary to handle these shortcuts.

There are also, of course, costs associated with delivering SGML-encoded material once it has been created. These costs fall into much the same categories as the costs for creating the material. Start-up costs include the choice and installation of delivery software. In practice, most digital library projects use the Opentext search engine, which is affordable for a library or a publisher. The search engine also needs a Web client, which need not be a big task for a programmer. Naturally it takes longer to write a better Web client, but a better client may save end users much time as they sort through the results of a query. Opentext is essentially a retrieval program, and it does not provide much in the way of hypertext linking. INSO/EBT's suite of programs, including DynaText and DynaWeb, provides a model of a document that is much more like an electronic book with hypertext links. INSO's Higher Education Grant Program has enabled projects like MEP and Orlando to deliver samples of their material without the need to purchase SGML delivery software. INSO offers some technical support as part of the grant package, but skilled staff are once again the key component for getting a delivery system up and running. When any delivery system is functioning well, the addition of new SGML-encoded material to the document database can be fully automated with little need for human intervention unless something goes wrong.

Experience has shown that computer-based projects are rarely, if ever, finished. They will always need maintenance and upgrades and will incur ongoing costs more or less forever if the material is not to be lost. SGML seems to me to be the best way of investing for the future, since there are no technical problems in migrating it to new systems. However, I find it difficult to envisage a time when there will be no work and no expense involved with maintaining and updating electronic information. It is as well to understand this and to budget for these ongoing costs at the beginning of a project rather than have them come out gradually as the project proceeds.

SGML does have one significant weakness. It assumes that each document is a single hierarchic structure, but in the real world (at least of the humanities) very few documents are as simple as this.[16] For example, a printed edition of a play has one structure of acts, scenes, and speeches and another of pages and line numbers. A new act or scene does not normally start on a new page, and so there is no relationship between the pages and the act and scene structure. It is simply an accident of the typography. The problem arises even with paragraphs in prose texts, since a new page does not start with a new paragraph or a new paragraph with a new page. For well-known editions the page numbers are important, but they cannot easily be encoded in SGML other than as "empty" tags that simply indicate a point in the text, not the beginning and end of a piece of information. The disadvantage here is that the processing of information marked by empty tags cannot make full use of SGML's capabilities. Another example of the same problem is quotations spanning over paragraphs. They have to be closed and then opened again with attributes to indicate that they are really all the same quotation.

For many scholars, SGML is exciting to work with because it opens up so many more possibilities for working with source material. We now have a much better way than ever before of representing in electronic form the kinds of interpretation and discussion that are the basis of scholarship in the humanities. But as we begin to understand these new possibilities, some new challenges appear.[17] What happens when documents from different sources (and thus different DTDs) are merged into the same database? In theory, computers make it very easy to do this, but how do we merge material that has been encoded according to different theoretical perspectives and retain the identification and individuality of each perspective? It is possible to build some kind of "mega-DTD," but the mega-DTD may become so free in structure that it is difficult to do any useful processing of the material.

Attention must now turn to making SGML work more effectively. Finding better ways of adding markup to documents is a high priority. The tagging could be speeded up by a program that can make intelligent tagging guesses based on information it has derived from similar material that has already been tagged, in much the same way that some word class tagging programs "learn" from text that has already been tagged manually. We also need to find ways of linking encoded text to digital images of the same material without the need for hand coding. Easier ways must be found for handling multiple parallel structures. All research leading to better use of SGML could benefit from a detailed analysis of documents that have already been encoded in SGML. The very fact that they are in SGML makes this analysis easy to do.

NOTES

1. Ian Graham's *HTML Sourcebook: A Complete Guide to HTML 3.0*, 2d ed. (Wiley, 1996), especially the beginning of chapter 3, gives an excellent overview of the characteristics of a book in the context of a discussion of the design of electronic resources. The third edition of this book was published early in 1997.

2. Jay David Bolter's *Writing Spaces: The Computer, Hypertext, and the History of Writing* (Erlbaum, 1991) expands on some of these ideas. See also George Landow, *Hypertext: The Convergence of Contemporary Critical Theory and Technology* (Johns Hopkins, 1992) and my own *Knowledge Representation*, a paper commissioned as part of the Getty Art History Information Program (now the Getty Information Institute) Research Agenda for Humanities Computing, published in *Research Agenda for Networked Cultural Heritage* (Getty Information Institute, 1996), 31–34, and also available at *http://www.ahip.getty.edu/agenda/represen.html*.

3. These terms, among others, have been used by the Model Editions Partnership *(http://mep.cla.sc.edu)*.

4. This was the planning meeting for the Text Encoding Initiative project. It was held in November 1987.

5. C. J. Date, *An Introduction to Database Systems,* 4th ed. (Addison Wesley, 1986), is a good introduction to relational database technology.

6. By far the most useful starting point for information about SGML is the very comprehensive Web site at *http://www.oasis-open.org/cover/*. This site is maintained and updated regularly by Robin Cover of the Summer Institute for Linguistics.

7. The TEI's Web site is at *http://www.uic.edu/orgs/tei*. It contains links to electronic versions of the TEI Guidelines and DTDs as well as to projects that are using the DTD.

8. See Richard Giordano, "The Documentation of Electronic Texts Using Text Encoding Initiative Headers: An Introduction," *Library Resources and Technical Services* 38 (1994): 389ff, for a detailed discussion of the header from the perspective of someone who is both a librarian and a computer scientist.

9. More information about the EAD can be found at *http://lcweb.loc.gov/ead*. This site has examples of the Library of Congress EAD projects. Others can be found via links from the SGML Web site.

10. This example can be seen at *http://www.ceth.rutgers.edu/projects/griffis/project.htm*. The site also provides instructions for downloading the Panorama SGML viewer.

11. See Yuri Rubinsky, "Electronic Texts the Day After Tomorrow," in *Visions and Opportunities in Electronic Publishing: Proceedings of the Second Symposium, December 5–8, 1992,* ed. Ann Okerson (Association for Research Libraries, 1993), 5–13, also available at *http://arl.cni.org:80/scomm/symp2/rubinsky.html*. Rubinsky was the founder of SoftQuad and a leading figure in the SGML community until his tragic early death in January 1996.

12. There is a useful set of Frequently Asked Questions (FAQ) on XML at *http://www.ucc.ie/xml/*. See also the XML section of the SGML Web site at *http://www.oasis-open.org/cover/related.html*.

13. See note 3.

14. The Orlando Project's Web site is at *http://www.ualberta.ca/ORLANDO*.

15. For a more detailed and very useful discussion of these issues, see Liora Alschuler, *ABCD . . . SGML: A User's Guide to Structured Information* (International Thompson Computer Press, 1995), especially chapters 5 through 9. Alschuler shares my view that it is very difficult to make general statements about the value of SGML-based projects since SGML can mean so many different things. Chapter 4 of her book consists of a series of case studies. It begins with a caveat: "anyone looking for a picture of a typical SGML implementation, look elsewhere," and then goes on: "These case studies represent the richness and diversity of real-world implementations, not the mythical norm." Elsewhere Alschuler notes that "ultimately the most profound impact of converting to structured information may be on the products you produce rather than on the methods you use to produce them" (186).

16. In order to deal with the problem of overlap, the Wittgenstein Archives at the University of Bergen *(http://www.hit.uib.no/wab)* have devised their own encoding scheme, MECS (Multi-Element Code System). MECS contains some of the properties of SGML, but has simpler mechanisms for structures that are cumbersome in SGML. However, the use of their own encoding scheme has meant that they have had to develop their own software to process the material.

17. For a longer discussion of new questions posed by the use of SGML and especially its perceived lack of semantics, see C. M. Sperberg-McQueen's closing address to the SGML92 conference at *http://www.oasis-open.org/cover/sgml92sp.html*. He notes: "In identifying some areas as promising new results, and inviting more work, there is always the danger

of shifting from 'inviting more work' to 'needing more work' and giving the impression of dissatisfaction with the work that has been accomplished. I want to avoid giving that impression, because it is not true, so I want to make very clear: the questions I am posing are not criticisms of SGML. On the contrary, they are its children. . . . SGML has created the environment within which these problems can be posed for the first time, and I think part of its accomplishment is that by solving one set of problems, it has exposed a whole new set of problems."

CHAPTER 2

Digital Image Quality

From Conversion to Presentation and Beyond

Anne R. Kenney

There are a number of significant digital library projects under way that are designed to test the economic value of building digital versus physical libraries. Business cases are being developed that demonstrate the economies of digital applications to assist cultural and research institutions in their response to the challenges of the information explosion, spiraling storage and subscription costs, and increasing user demands. These projects also reveal that the costs of selecting, converting, and making digital information available can be staggering and that the costs of archiving and migrating that information over time are not insignificant.

Economic models comparing the digital to the traditional library show that digital will become more cost-effective *provided* the following four assumptions prove true:

1. that institutions can share digital collections,
2. that digital collections can alleviate the need to support full traditional libraries at the local level,
3. that use will increase with electronic access, and
4. that the long-term value of digital collections will exceed the costs associated with their creation, maintenance, and delivery.[1]

These four assumptions—resource sharing, lower costs, satisfaction of user demands with timely and enhanced access, and continuing value of information—presume that electronic files will have relevant content and will meet baseline measures of functionality over time. Although a number of conferences and publications have addressed the need to develop selection criteria for digital conversion and to evaluate the effective use of digitized material, more rhetoric than substantive information has emerged regarding the impact on scholarly research of creating digital collections and making them accessible over networks.

I believe that digital conversion efforts will prove economically viable only if they focus on creating electronic resources for long-term use. Retrospective

sources should be carefully selected based on their intellectual content; digital sur-
rogates should effectively capture that intellectual content; and access should be
more timely, usable, or cost-effective than is possible with original source documents. In sum, I argue that long-term utility should be defined by the informational value and functionality of digital images, not limited by technical decisions
made at the point of conversion or anywhere else along the digitization chain. I
advocate a strategy of "full informational capture" to ensure that digital objects
rich enough to be useful over time are created in the most cost-effective manner.[2]

There is much to be said for capturing the best possible digital image. From a
preservation perspective, the advantages are obvious. An "archival" digital master
can be created to replace rapidly deteriorating originals or to reduce storage costs
and access times to office back files, provided the digital surrogate is a trusted representation of the hard copy source. It also makes economic sense, as Michael
Lesk has noted, to "turn the pages once" and produce a sufficiently high-level
image so as to avoid the expense of reconverting at a later date when technological advances require or can effectively utilize a richer digital file.[3] This economic
justification is particularly compelling as the labor costs associated with identifying, preparing, inspecting, and indexing digital information far exceed the costs of
the scan itself. In recent years, the costs of scanning and storage have declined
rapidly, narrowing the gap between high-quality and low-quality digital image
capture. Once created, the archival master can then be used to generate derivatives to meet a variety of current and future user needs: high resolution may be
required for printed facsimiles, for on-screen detailed study,[4] and in the future for
intensive image processing; moderate to high resolution may be required for character recognition systems and image summarization techniques;[5] and lower resolution images, encoded text, or PDFs derived from the digital masters may be required for on-screen display and browsing.[6] The quality, utility, and expense of all
these derivatives will be directly affected by the quality of the initial scan.[7]

If there are compelling reasons for creating the best possible image, there is
also much to be said for not capturing more than you need. At some point, adding
more resolution will not result in greater quality, just a larger file size and higher
costs. The key is to match the conversion process to the informational content of
the original. At Cornell, we've been investigating digital imaging in a preservation
context for eight years. For the first three years, we concentrated on what was technologically possible—on determining the best image capture we could secure. For
the last five years, we've been striving to define the minimal requirements for satisfying informational capture needs. No more, no less.

DIGITAL BENCHMARKING

To help us determine what is minimally acceptable, we have been developing a
methodology called benchmarking. Digital benchmarking is a systematic proce-

dure used to forecast a likely outcome. It begins with an assessment of the source documents and user needs; factors in relevant objective and subjective variables associated with stated quality, cost, and/or performance objectives; involves the use of formulas that represent the interrelationship of those variables to desired outcomes; and concludes with confirmation through carefully structured testing and evaluation. If the benchmarking formula does not consistently predict the outcome, it may not contain the relevant variables or reflect their proper relationship—in which case it should be revised.

Benchmarking does not provide easy answers but a means to evaluate possible answers for how best to balance quality, costs, timeliness, user requirements, and technological capabilities in the conversion, delivery, and maintenance of digital resources. It is also intended as a means to formulate a range of possible solutions on the macro level rather than on an individual, case-by-case basis. For many aspects of digital imaging, benchmarking is still uncharted territory. Much work remains in defining conversion requirements for certain document types (photographs and complex book illustrations, for example); in conveying color information; in evaluating the effects of new compression algorithms; and in providing access on a mass scale to a digital database of material representing a wide range of document types and document characteristics.

We began benchmarking with the conversion of printed text. We anticipate that within several years, quality benchmarks for image capture and presentation of the broad range of paper- and film-based research materials—including manuscripts, graphic art, halftones, and photographs—will be well defined through a number of projects currently under way.[8] In general, these projects are designed to be system independent and are based increasingly on assessing the attributes and functionality characteristic of the source documents themselves coupled with an understanding of user perceptions and requirements.

Why Do Benchmarking?

Because there are no standards for image quality and because different document types require different scanning processes, there is no "silver bullet" for conversion. This frustrates many librarians and archivists who are seeking a simple solution to a complex issue. I suppose if there really were the need for a silver bullet, I'd recommend that most source documents be scanned at a minimum of 600 dpi with 24-bit color, but that would result in tremendously large file sizes and a hefty conversion cost. You would also be left with the problems of transmitting and displaying those images.

We began benchmarking with conversion, but we are now applying this approach to the presentation of information on-screen. The number of variables that govern display are many, and it will come as no surprise that they preclude the establishment of a single best method for presenting digital images. But here, too, the urge is strong to seek a single solution. If display requirements paralleled conversion requirements—that is, if a 600 dpi, 24-bit image had to be presented on-screen, then *at best,* with the highest resolution monitors commercially available, only documents whose physical dimensions did not exceed 2.7" × 2.13" could be displayed—and they could not be displayed at their native size. Now most of us are interested in converting and displaying items that are larger than postage stamps, so these "simple solutions" are for most purposes impractical, and compromises will have to be made.

The object of benchmarking is to make informed decisions about a range of choices and to understand in advance the consequences of such decisions. The benchmarking approach can be applied across the full continuum of the digitization chain, from conversion to storage to access to presentation. Our belief at Cornell is that benchmarking must be approached holistically, that it is essential to understand at the point of selection what the consequences will be for conversion and presentation. This is especially important as institutions consider inaugurating large-scale conversion projects. Toward this end, the advantages of benchmarking are several in number.

1. Benchmarking is first and foremost a management tool, designed to lead to informed decision making. It offers a starting point and a means for narrowing the range of choices to a manageable number. Although clearly benchmarking decisions must be judged through actual implementations, the time spent in experimentation can be reduced, the temptation to overstate or understate requirements may be avoided, and the initial assessment requires no specialized equipment or expenditure of funds. Benchmarking allows you to scale knowledgeably and to make decisions on a macro level rather than to determine those requirements through item-by-item review or by setting requirements for groups of materials that may be adequate for only a portion of them.

2. Benchmarking provides a means for interpreting vendor claims. If you have spent any time reading product literature, you may have become convinced, as I have, that the sole aim of any company is to sell its product. Technical information will be presented in the most favorable light, which is often incomplete and intended to discourage product comparisons. One film scanner, for instance, may be advertised as having a resolution of 7500 dpi; another may claim 400 dpi. In reality, these two scanners could provide the very same capabilities, but it may be difficult to determine that without additional information. You may end up spending considerable time on the phone, first getting past the marketing representatives and then closely questioning those with a technical understanding of the product's capabilities. If you have benchmarked your requirements, you will be able to focus the discussion on your particular needs.

3. Benchmarking can assist you in negotiating with vendors for services and products. I've spent many years advocating the use of 600 dpi bitonal scanning for printed text, and invariably when I begin a discussion with a representative of an imaging service bureau, he will try to talk me out of such a high resolution, claiming that I do not need it or that it will be exorbitantly expensive. I suspect the representative is motivated to make those claims in part because he believes them and in part because the company may not provide that service and the salesperson wants my business. If I had not benchmarked my resolution requirements, I might be persuaded by what this salesperson has to say.

4. Benchmarking can lead to careful management of resources. If you know up front what your requirements are likely to be and the consequences of those requirements, you can develop a budget that reflects the actual costs, identify prerequisites for meeting those needs, and, perhaps most important, avoid costly mistakes. Nothing will doom an imaging project more quickly than buying the wrong equipment or having to manage image files that are not supported by your institution's technical infrastructure.

5. Benchmarking can also allow you to predict what you can deliver under specific conditions. It is important to understand that an imaging project may break at the weakest link in the digitization chain. For instance, if your institution is considering scanning its map collection, you should be realistic about what ultimately can be delivered to the user's desktop. Benchmarking lets you predict how much of the image and what level of detail can be presented on-screen for various monitors. Even with the most expensive monitor available, presenting oversize material completely, with small detail intact, is impractical.

Having spent some time extolling the virtues of digital benchmarking, I'd like to turn next to describing this methodology as it applies to conversion and then to move to a discussion of on-screen presentation.

CONVERSION BENCHMARKING

Determining what constitutes informational content becomes the first step in the conversion benchmarking process. This can be done objectively or subjectively. Let's consider an objective approach first.

Objective Evaluation

One way to perform an objective evaluation would be to determine conversion requirements based on the process used to create the original document. Take resolution, for instance. Film resolution can be measured by the size of the silver crystalline clusters suspended in an emulsion, whose distinct characteristics are appreciated only under microscopic examination. Should we aim for capturing the properties of the chemical process used to create the original? Or should we peg resolution requirements at the recording capability of the camera or printer used?

There are objective scientific tests that can measure the overall information carrying capacity of an imaging system, such as the Modulation Transfer Function, but such tests require expensive equipment and are still beyond the capability of most institutions except industrial or research labs.[9] In practical applications, the resolving power of a microfilm camera is measured by means of a technical test chart in which the distinct number of black and white lines discerned is multiplied by the reduction ratio used to determine the number of line pairs per millimeter. A system resolution of 120 line pairs per millimeter (lppm) is considered good; above 120 is considered excellent. To digitally capture all the information present on a 35 mm frame of film with a resolution of 120 lppm would take a bitonal film scanner with a pixel array of 12,240.[10] There is no such beast on the market today.

How far down this path should we go? It may be appropriate to require that the digital image accurately depict the gouges of a woodcut or the scoops of a stipple engraving, but what about the exact dot pattern and screen ruling of a halftone? the strokes and acid bite of an etching? the black lace of an aquatint that becomes visible only at a magnification above $25\times$? Offset publications are printed at 1200 dpi—should we choose that resolution as our starting point for scanning text?

Significant information may well be present at that level in some cases, as may be argued for medical X rays, but in other cases, attempting to capture all possible information will far exceed the inherent properties of the image as distinct from the medium and process used to create it. Consider for instance a $4'' \times 5''$ negative of a badly blurred photograph. The negative is incredibly information dense, but the information it conveys is not significant.

Obviously, any practical application of digital conversion would be overwhelmed by the recording, computing, and storage requirements that would be needed to support capture at the structure or process level. Although offset printing may be produced at 1200 dpi, most individuals would not be able to discern the difference between a 600 dpi and a 1000 dpi digital image of that page, even under magnification. The higher resolution adds more bits and increases the file size but with little to no appreciable gain. The difference between 300 dpi and 600 dpi, however, can be easily observed and, in my opinion, is worth the extra time and expense to obtain. The relationship between resolution and image quality is not linear: at some point as resolution increases, the gain in image quality will level off. Benchmarking will help you to determine where the leveling begins.

Subjective Evaluation

I would argue, then, that determining what constitutes informational content is best done subjectively. It should be based on an assessment of the attributes of the document rather than the process used to create that document. Reformatting via digital—or analog—techniques presumes that the essential meaning of an original can somehow be captured and presented in another format. There is always some loss of information when an object is copied. The key is to determine whether that informational loss is significant. Obviously for some items, particularly those of intrinsic value, a copy can serve only as a surrogate, not as a replacement. This determination should be made by those with curatorial responsibility and a good understanding of the nature and significance of the material. Those with a trained eye should consider the attributes of the document itself as well as the immediate and potential uses that researchers will make of its informational content.

Determining Scanning Resolution Requirements for Replacement Purposes

To illustrate benchmarking for conversion, let's consider the brittle book. For brittle books published during the last century and a half, detail has come to represent the size of the smallest significant character in the text, usually the lowercase *e*. To capture this information—which consists of black ink on a light background—resolution is the key determinant of image quality.

Benchmarking resolution requirements in a digital world have their roots in micrographics, where standards for predicting image quality are based on the Quality Index (QI). QI provides a means for relating system resolution and text legibility. It is based on multiplying the height of the smallest significant character, h, by the smallest line pair pattern resolved by a camera on a technical test target, p: QI $= h \times p$. The resulting number is called the Quality Index, and it is used to forecast levels of image quality—marginal (3.6), medium (5.0), or high (8.0)—that will be achieved on the film. This approach can be used in the digital world, but the differences in the ways microfilm cameras and scanners capture detail must be accounted for.[11] Specifically, it is necessary to make the following adjustments:

1. Establish levels of image quality for digitally rendered characters that are analogous to those established for microfilming. In photographically reproduced images, quality degradation results in a fuzzy or blurred image. Usually degradation with digital conversion is revealed in the ragged or stairstepping appearance of diagonal lines or curves, known as *aliasing*, or "jaggies."

2. Rationalize system measurements. Digital resolution is measured in dots per inch; classic resolution is measured in line pairs per millimeter. To calculate QI based on scanning resolution, you must convert from one to the other. One millimeter equals 0.039 inches, so to determine the number of dots per millimeter, multiply the dpi by 0.039.

3. Equate dots to line pairs. Again, classic resolution refers to line *pairs* per millimeter (one black line and one white line), and since a dot occupies the same space as a line, two dots must be used to represent one line pair. This means the dpi must be divided by two to be made equivalent to p.

With these adjustments, we can modify the QI formula to create a digital equivalent. From QI = $p \times h$, we now have QI = 0.039 dpi $\times$ $h/2$, which can be simplified to 0.0195 dpi $\times$ h.

For bitonal scanning, we would also want to adjust for possible misregistration due to sampling errors brought about in the thresholding process in which all pixels are reduced to either black or white. To be on the conservative side, the authors of AIIM TR26–1993 advise increasing the input scanning resolution by at least 50% to compensate for possible image detector misalignment. The formula would then be QI = 0.039 dpi $\times$ $h/3$, which can be simplified to 0.013 dpi $\times$ h.

So How Does Conversion Benchmarking Work?

Consider a printed page that contains characters measuring 2 mm high or greater. If the page were scanned at 300 dpi, what level of quality would you expect to obtain? By plugging in the dpi and the character height and solving for QI, you would discover that you can expect a QI of 8, or excellent rendering.

You can also solve the equation for the other variables. Consider, for example, a scanner with a maximum of 400 dpi. You can benchmark the size of the smallest character that you could capture with medium quality (a QI of 5), which would be .96 mm high. Or you can calculate the input scanning resolution required to achieve excellent rendering of a character that is 3 mm high (200 dpi).

With this formula and an understanding of the nature of your source documents, you can benchmark the scanning resolution needs for printed material. We took this knowledge and applied it to the types of documents we were scanning— brittle books published from 1850 to 1950. We reviewed printers' type sizes commonly used by publishers during this period and discovered that virtually none utilized type fonts smaller than 1 mm in height, which, according to our benchmarking formula, could be captured with excellent quality using 600 dpi bitonal scanning. We then tested these benchmarks by conducting an extensive on-screen and in-print examination of digital facsimiles for the smallest font-sized Roman and non-Roman type scripts used during this period. This verification process confirmed that an input scanning resolution of 600 dpi was indeed sufficient to capture the monochrome text-based information contained in virtually all books published during the period of paper's greatest brittleness. Although many of those books do not contain text that is as small as 1 mm in height, a sufficient number of them do. To avoid the labor and expense of performing item-by-item review, we currently scan all books at 600 dpi resolution.[12]

Conversion Benchmarking beyond Text

Although we've conducted most of our experiments on printed text, we are beginning to benchmark resolution requirements for nontextual documents as well. For non-text-based material, we have begun to develop a benchmarking formula that would be based on the width of the smallest stroke or mark on the page rather than a complete detail. This approach was used by the Nordic Digital Research Institute to determine resolution requirements for the conversion of historic Icelandic maps and is being followed in the current New York State Kodak Photo CD project being conducted at Cornell on behalf of the Eleven Comprehensive Research Libraries of New York State.[13] The measurement of such fine detail will require the use of a 25 to 50× loupe with a metric hairline that differentiates below 0.1 mm.

Benchmarking for conversion can be extended beyond resolution to tonal reproduction (both grayscale and color); to the capture of depth, overlay, and translucency; to assessing the effects of compression techniques and levels of compression used on image quality; to evaluating the capabilities of a particular scanning methodology, such as the Kodak Photo CD format. Benchmarking can also be used for evaluating quality requirements for a particular category of material—halftones, for example—or to examine the relationship between the size of the document and the size of its significant details, a very challenging relationship that affects both the conversion and the presentation of maps, newspapers, architectural drawings, and other oversized, highly detailed source documents.

In sum, conversion benchmarking involves both subjective and objective components. There must be the means to establish levels of quality (through technical targets or samples of acceptable materials), the means to identify and measure significant information present in the document, the means to relate one to another via a formula, and the means to judge results on-screen and in-print for a sample group of documents. Armed with this information, benchmarking enables informed decision making—which often leads to a balancing act involving trade-offs between quality and cost, between quality and completeness, between completeness and size, or between quality and speed.

DISPLAY BENCHMARKING

Quality assessments can be extended beyond capture requirements to the presentation and timeliness of delivery options. We began our benchmarking for conversion with the attributes of the *source documents*. We begin our benchmarking for display with the attributes of the *digital images*.

I believe that all researchers in their heart of hearts expect three things from displayed digital images: (1) they want the full-size image to be presented on-screen; (2) they expect legibility and adequate color rendering; and (3) they want images to be displayed quickly. Of course they want lots of other things, too, such as the means to manipulate, annotate, and compare images, and for text-based material, they want to be able to conduct key word searches across the images. But for the moment, let's just consider those three requirements: full image, full detail and tonal reproduction, and quick display.

Unfortunately, for many categories of documents, satisfying all three criteria at once will be a problem, given the limitations of screen design, computing capabilities, and network speeds. Benchmarking screen display must take all these variables into consideration *and* the attributes of the digital images themselves as user expectations are weighed one against the other. We are just beginning to investigate this interrelationship at Cornell, and although our findings are still tentative and not broadly confirmed through experimentation, I'm convinced that display benchmarking will offer the same advantages as conversion benchmarking to research institutions that are beginning to make their materials available electronically.[14]

Now for the good news: it is easy to display the complete image and it is possible to display it quickly. It is easy to ensure screen legibility—in fact, intensive scrutiny of highly detailed information is facilitated on-screen. Color fidelity is a little more difficult to deliver, but progress is occurring on that front.[15]

Now for the not-so-good news: given common desktop computer configurations, it may not be possible to deliver full 24-bit color to the screen—the monitor may have the native capability but not enough video memory, or its refresh rate cannot sustain a nonflickering image. The complete image that is quickly displayed may not be legible. A highly detailed image may take a long time to deliver, and only a small percent of it will be seen at any given time. You may call up a photograph of Yul Brynner only to discover you have landed somewhere on his bald pate.

Benchmarking will allow you to predict in advance the pros and cons of digital image display. Conflicts between legibility and completeness, between timeliness and detail, can be identified and compromises developed. Benchmarking allows you to predetermine a set process for delivering images of uniform size and content and to assess how well that process will accommodate other document types. Scaling to 72 dpi and adding 3 bits of gray may be a good choice for technical reports produced at 10-point type and above but will be totally inadequate for delivering digital renderings of full-size newspapers.

To illustrate benchmarking as it applies to display, consider the first two user expectations: complete display and legibility. We expect printed facsimiles produced from digital images to look very similar to the original. They should be the same size, preserve the layout, and convey detail and tonal information that is faithful to the original. Many readers assume that the digital image on-screen can also be the same, that if the page were correctly converted, it could be brought up at approximately the same size and with the same level of detail as the original. It is certainly possible to scale the image to be the same size as the original document, but most likely the information contained therein will not be legible.

If the scanned image's dpi does not equal the screen dpi, then the image on-screen will appear either larger or smaller than the original document's size. Because scanning dpi most often exceeds the screen dpi, the image will appear larger on the screen—and chances are that not all of it will be represented at once. This is because monitors have a limited number of pixels that can be displayed both horizontally and vertically. If the number of pixels in the image exceeds those of the screen and if the scanning dpi is higher, the image will be enlarged on the screen and will not be completely presented.

The problems of presenting completeness, detail, and native size are more pronounced in on-screen display than in printing. In the latter, very high printing resolutions are possible, and the total number of dots that can be laid down for a given image is great, enabling the creation of facsimiles that are the same size—and often with the same detail—as the original.

The limited pixel dimensions and dpi of monitors can be both a strength and a weakness. On the plus side, detail can be presented more legibly and without the aid of a microscope, which, for those conducting extensive textual analysis, may represent a major improvement over reviewing the source documents themselves. For instance, papyrologists can rely on monitors to provide the enlarged view of fragment details required in their study. When the original documents themselves are examined, they are typically viewed under a microscope at 4 to 10× magnification.[16] Art historians can zoom in on high-resolution images to enlarge details or to examine brush strokes that convey different surfaces and materials.[17] On the downside, because the screen dpi is often exceeded by the scanning dpi and because screens have very limited pixel dimensions, many documents cannot be fully displayed *if* legibility must be conveyed. This conflict between overall size and level of detail is most apparent when dealing with oversized material, but it also affects a surprisingly large percentage of normal-sized documents as well.

Consider the physical limitations of computer monitors: typical monitors offer resolutions from 640 × 480 at the low end to 1600 × 1200 at the high end. The lowest level SVGA monitor offers the possibility of displaying material at 1024 × 768. These numbers, known as the pixel matrix, refer to the number of horizontal by vertical pixels painted on the screen when an image appears.

In product literature, monitor resolutions are often given in dpi, which can range from 60 to 120 depending on the screen width and horizontal pixel dimension. The screen dpi can be a misleading representation of a monitor's quality and performance. For example, when SVGA resolution is used on a 14″, 17″, and 21″ monitor, the screen dpi decreases as screen size increases. We might intuitively expect image resolution to increase, not decrease, with the size of the monitor. In reality, the same amount of an image—and level of detail—would be displayed on all three monitors set to the same pixel dimensions. The only difference would be that the image displayed on the 21″ monitor would appear enlarged compared to the same image displayed on the 17″ and 14″ monitors.

The pixel matrix of a monitor limits the number of pixels of a digital image that can be displayed at any one time. And if there is insufficient video memory, you will also be limited to how much gray or color information can be supported at any pixel dimension. For instance, while the three-year-old 14″ SVGA monitor on my desk supports a 1024 × 768 display resolution, it came bundled with half a megabyte of video memory. It cannot display an 8-bit grayscale image at that resolution and it cannot display a 24-bit color image at all, even if it is set at the lowest resolution of 640 × 480. If I increased its VRAM, I would be bothered by an annoying flicker, because the monitor's refresh rate is not great enough to support a stable image on-screen at higher resolutions. It is not coincidental that while the most basic SVGA monitors can support a pixel matrix of 1024 × 768, most of them come packaged with the monitor set at a resolution of 800 × 600. As others have noted, network speeds and the limitations of graphical user interfaces will also profoundly affect user satisfaction with on-screen presentation of digital images.

So How Does Display Benchmarking Work?

Consider the brittle book and how best to display it. Recall that it may contain font sizes at 1 mm and above, so we have scanned each page at 600 dpi, bitonal mode. Let's assume that the typical page averages 4″ × 6″ in size. The pixel matrix of this image will be 4 × 600 by 6 × 600, or 2400 × 3600—far above any monitor pixel matrix currently available. Now if I want to display that image at its full scanning resolution on my monitor, set to the default resolution of 800 × 600, it should be obvious to many of you that I will be showing only a small portion of that image—approximately 5% of it will appear on the screen. Let's suppose I went out and purchased a $2,500 monitor that offered a resolution of 1600 × 1200. I'd still only be able to display less than a fourth of that image at any one time.

Obviously for most access purposes, this display would be unacceptable. It requires too much scrolling or zooming out to study the image. If it is an absolute requirement that the full image be displayed with all details fully rendered, I'd suggest converting only items whose smallest significant detail represents nothing smaller than one third of 1% of the total document surface. This means that if you had a document with a one-millimeter-high character that was scanned at 600 dpi and you wanted to display the full document at its scanning resolution on a 1024 × 768 monitor, the document's physical dimensions could not exceed 1.7″ (horizontal) × 1.3″ (vertical). This document size may work well for items such as papyri, which are relatively small, at least as they have survived to the present. It also works well for items that are physically large *and* contain large-sized features, such as posters that are meant to be viewed from a distance. If the smallest detail on the poster measured 1″, the poster could be as large as 42″ × 32″ and still be fully displayed with all detail intact.[18]

Most images will have to be scaled down from their scanning resolutions for on-screen access, and this can occur a number of ways. Let's first consider full display on the monitor, and then consider legibility. In order to display the full image on a given monitor, the image pixel matrix must be reduced to fit within the monitor's pixel dimensions. The image is scaled by setting one of its pixel matrixes to the corresponding pixel dimension of the monitor.[19]

To fit the complete page image from our brittle book on a monitor set at 800 × 600, we would scale the vertical dimension of our image to 600; the horizontal dimension would be 400 to preserve the aspect ratio of the original. By reducing the 2400 × 3600 pixel image to 400 × 600, we will have discarded 97% of the information in the original. The advantages to doing this are several: it facilitates browsing by displaying the full image, and it decreases file size, which in turn decreases the transmission time. The downside should also be obvious. There will be a major decrease in image quality as a significant number of pixels are discarded. In other words, the image can be fully displayed, but the information contained in that image may not be legible. To determine whether that information will be useful, we can turn to the use of benchmarking formulas for legible display.

Here are the benchmarking resolution formulas for scaling bitonal and grayscale images for on-screen display:[20]

$$\text{dpi} = \text{QI}/(.03h)$$
$$\text{QI} = \text{dpi} \times .03h$$
$$h = \text{QI}/(.03\text{dpi})$$

Note: Recall that in the benchmarking resolution formulas for conversion, dpi refers to the scanning resolution. In the scaling formulas, dpi refers to the image dpi (not to be confused with the monitor's dpi).

Let's return to the example of our 4″ × 6″ brittle page. If we assume that we need to be able to read the 1-mm-high character but that it doesn't have to be fully rendered, then we set our QI requirement at 3.6, which should ensure legibility of characters in context. We can use the benchmarking formula to predict the scaled image dpi:

$$\text{dpi} = \text{QI}/.03h, \text{ or}$$
$$\text{dpi} = 3.6/(.03 \times 1), \text{ or}$$
$$\text{dpi} = 120$$

The image could be fully displayed with minimal legibility on a 120 dpi monitor. The pixel dimensions for the scaled image would be 120 × 4 by 120 × 6, or 480 × 720. This full image could be viewed on SVGA monitors set at 1024 × 768 or above; slightly more than 80% of it could be viewed on my monitor set at 800 × 600.

We can also use this formula to determine a preset scaling dpi for a group of documents to be conveyed to a particular clientele. Consider a scenario in which your primary users have access to monitors that can effectively support an 800 × 600 resolution. We could decide whether the user population would be satisfied with receiving only 80% of the document if it meant that they could read the smallest type, which may occur only in footnotes. If your users are more interested in quick browsing, you might want to benchmark against the body of the text rather than the smallest typed character. For instance, if the main text were in 12-point type and the smallest lowercase *e* measured 1.6 mm in height, then our sample page could be sent to the screen with a QI of 3.6 at a pixel dimension of 300 × 450, or an image dpi of 75—well within the capabilities of the 800 × 600 monitor.

You can also benchmark the time it will take to deliver this image to the screen. If your clientele are connected via ethernet, this image (with 3 bits of gray added to smooth out rough edges of characters and improve legibility) could be sent to the desktop in less than a second—providing readers with full display of the document, legibility of the main text, and a timely delivery. If your readers are connected to the ethernet via a 9600-baud modem, however, the image will take 42 seconds to be delivered. If the footnotes must be readable, the full text cannot be displayed on-screen and the time it will take to retrieve the image will increase. Benchmarking allows you to identify these variables and consider the trade-offs or compromises associated with optimizing any one of them.

CONCLUSION

Benchmarking is an approach, not a prescription. It offers a means to evaluate choices for how best to balance quality, costs, timeliness, user requirements, and technological capabilities in the conversion, delivery, and presentation of digital resources. The value of this approach will best be determined by extensive field testing. We at Cornell are committed to further refinement of the benchmarking methodology, and we urge others to consider its utility *before* they commit considerable resources to bringing about the brave new world of digitized information.

NOTES

1. Stephen Chapman and Anne R. Kenney, "Digital Conversion of Library Research Materials: A Case for Full Informational Capture," *D-Lib Magazine* (October 1996).

2. Currently, scanning is the most cost-effective means to create digital files, and digital imaging is the only electronic format that can accurately render the information, page layout, and presentation of source documents, including text, graphics, and evidence of age and use. By producing digital images, you can create an authentic representation of the original at minimal cost and then derive the most useful version and format (e.g., marked-up text) for transmission and use.

3. Michael Lesk, *Image Formats for Preservation and Access: A Report of the Technology Assessment Advisory Committee to the Commission on Preservation and Access,* Commission on Preservation and Access, Washington, DC, July 1990.

4. See Charles S. Rhyne, *Computer Images for Research, Teaching, and Publication in Art History and Related Disciplines,* Commission on Preservation and Access, Washington, DC, January 1996, p. 4, in which he argues that "with each jump in [on-screen image] quality, new uses become possible."

5. Interesting work is being conducted at Xerox PARC on image summarization. See Francine R. Chen and Dan S. Bloomberg, "Extraction of Thematically Relevant Text from Images," paper presented at the fifth annual Symposium on Document Analysis and Information Retrieval, Las Vegas, April 15–17, 1996.

6. An interesting conclusion from a project on the use of art and architectural images at Cornell focused on image size guidelines to support a range of user activities. For browsing, the project staff found that images must be large enough for the user to identify the image, but small enough to allow numerous images to be viewed simultaneously—the physical size on the screen preferred by users was 1.25″ to 2.25″ square. For viewing images in their entirety, images were sized to fit within a 5.5″ square; for studying, detailed views covering the entire screen were necessary; and for "authoring" presentations or other multimedia projects, users preferred images that fit in a half-inch square. See Noni Korf Vidal, Thomas Hickerson, and Geri Gay, "Developing Multimedia Collection and Access Tools, Appendix V. Guidelines for the Display of Images" (report delivered to the Council on Library Resources, April 1996), 14–17.

7. A number of leading experts advocate this approach, including Michael Ester of Luna Imaging, Inc. See, for example, Michael Ester, "Digital Images in the Context of Visual Collectons and Scholarship," *Visual Resources* 10 (1990): 11–24; and "Specifics of Imaging Practice," *Archives and Museum Informatics: Hands-on Hypermedia and Interactivity in Museums,* Selected Papers from the Third International Conference, San Diego, CA, October 9–13, 1995.

8. Roger S. Bagnall, *Digital Imaging of Papyri: A Report to the Commission on Preservation and Access,* Commission on Preservation and Access, Washington, DC, September 1995; Janet Gertz, *Oversize Color Images Project, 1994–1995 Final Report of Phase I,* Commission on Preservation and Access, Washington, DC, August 1995; Picture Elements, Inc., *Guidelines for Electronic Preservation of Visual Materials, Part I,* Report to the Library of Congress, March 2, 1995. Michael Ester argues that an "archival image" of a photograph cannot be benchmarked through calculations but should be pegged to the "functional range of an institution's reproduction sources." See page 11 in Ester, *Digital Image Collections: Issues and Practice,* Commission on Preservation and Access, Washington, DC, December 1996. For a critique of this approach, see Chapman and Kenney, "Digital Conversion."

9. Don Williams, "What Is an MTF and Why Should We Care?" *RLG Diginews* 2(1) (February 15, 1998), *http://www.rlg.org/preserv/diginews.*

10. Anne R. Kenney and Stephen Chapman, "Film Scanning," Chapter 7 in *Digital Imaging for Libraries and Archives,* Cornell University Library, Ithaca, NY, 1996, p. 169.

11. ANSI/AIIM MS23–1991, *Practice for Operational Procedures/Inspection and Quality Control of First-Generaton, Silver Microfilm and Documents,* Association for Information and Image Management; ANSI/AIIM TR26–1993, *Resolution as It Relates to Photographic and Electronic Imaging,* Association for Information and Image Management; and Kenney and Chapman, *Tutorial: Digital Resolution Requirements for Replacing Text-Based Material: Methods for Benchmarking Image Quality,* Commission on Preservation and Access, Washington, DC, April 1995.

12. For a description of this verification process, see Anne R. Kenney, "Digital-to-Microfilm Conversion: An Interim Preservation Solution," *Library Resources and Technical Services* (October 1993): 380–401; (January 1994): 87–95.

13. Anne R. Kenney and Oya Y. Rieger, *Using Kodak Photo CD Technology for Preservation and Access,* Cornell University Library, Ithaca, NY, 1998.

14. A fuller explanation of the display benchmarking process is included in Anne R. Kenney and Stephen Chapman, Chapter 2 in *Digital Imaging for Libraries and Archives,* Cornell University Library, Ithaca, NY, 1996, pp. 76–86.

15. Improvements in managing color digitally may be forthcoming from an international consortium of industry leaders working to develop an electronic prepress industry standard. Their "International Color Consortium Profile Format" is intended to represent color consistently across devices and platforms.

16. See Peter van Minnen, "Imaging the Duke Papyri," (December 1995) *http:// odyssey.lib.duke.edu/papyrus/texts/imaging.html,* and Roger S. Bagnall, *Digital Imaging of Papyri: A Report to the Commission on Preservation and Access,* Commission on Preservation and Access, Washington, DC, September 1995.

17. Rhyne, *Computer Images,* 5.

18. The formula for calculating the maximum percentage of a digital image that can be displayed on-screen is as follows:

    a. If both image dimensions < the corresponding pixel dimensions *(pd)* of the screen, 100% of the image will be displayed.

    b. If both image dimensions > the corresponding pixel dimensions of the screen, % displayed = *horiz. screen pd* × *vertical screen pd* × 100 image's horiz. pd × image's vertical pd.

    c. If one of the image's dimensions < the corresponding pixel dimension of the screen, % displayed = *image's opposite pixel dimension* × 100.

19. The scaling formula for complete display of image on screen is as follows:

    a. When digital image aspect ratio < screen aspect ratio, set image's horizontal pixel dimension to the screen's horizontal pixel dimension.

    b. When digital image aspect ratio > screen aspect ratio, set image's vertical pixel dimension to the screen's vertical pixel dimension.

20. This formula presumes that bitonal images are presented with a minimum level of gray (3 bits or greater) and that filters and optimized scaling routines are used to improve image presentation.

CHAPTER 3

The Transition
to Electronic Content Licensing
The Institutional Context in 1997

Ann S. Okerson

INTRODUCTION

The public discourse about electronic publishing, as heard at scholarly and library gatherings on the topic of scholarly communications, has changed little over the past several years. Librarians and academics fret about the serials crisis, argue about the influence of commercial offshore publishers, wonder when the academic reward system will begin to take electronic publications into account, and debate what steps to take to rationalize copyright policy in our institutions. There is progress in that a wider community now comes together to ponder these familiar themes, but to those of us who have been party to the dialogue for some years, the tedium of ritual sometimes sets in.

At Yale, subject-specialist librarians talk to real publishers every day about the terms on which the library will acquire their electronic products: reference works, abstracts, data, journals, and other full-text offerings. Every week, or several times a week, we are swept up in negotiating the terms of licenses with producers whose works are needed by our students and faculty. Electronic publications are now a vital part of libraries' business and services. For example, at a NorthEast Research Libraries Consortium (NERL) meeting in February 1997, each of the 13 research library representatives at the table stated that his or her library is expending about 6–7% of its acquisitions budget on electronic resources.

This essay will offer some observations on the overall progress of library licensing negotiations. But the main point of this essay will be to make this case: in the real world of libraries, we have begun to move past the predictable, ritual discourse. The market has brought librarians and publishers together; the parties are discovering where their interests mesh; and they are beginning to build a new set of arrangements that meet needs both for access (on the part of the institution) and remuneration (on the part of the producer). Even though the prices for electronic resources are becoming a major concern, libraries are able to secure crucial and significant use terms via site licenses, use terms that often allow the customer's students, faculty, and scholars significant copying latitude for their work (including articles for reserves and course packs), at times more latitude than what is permitted via the fair use and library provisions in the Copyright Act of the United States. In short, institutions and publishers perhaps do not realize how advanced they are in making a digital market, more advanced at that, in fact, than they are at resolving a number of critical technological issues.[1]

WHY DO CONTRACTS OR LICENSES (RATHER THAN COPYRIGHT) GOVERN ELECTRONIC CONTENT?

Society now faces what seems to be a powerful competitor for copyright's influence over the marketplace of cultural products, one that carries its own assumptions about what intellectual property is, how it is to be used, how it can be controlled, and what economic order can emerge as a result.

For convenience's sake, the codification of intellectual property is assigned to the early eighteenth century. That time period is when the evolving notion of copyright was enacted into law, shaping a marketplace for cultural products unlike any seen before. In that eighteenth-century form, copyright legislation depended in three ways on the technologies of the time:

1. The power of copyright was already being affirmed through the development of high-speed printing presses that increased the printer's at-risk capital investment and greatly multiplied the number of copies of a given original that could be produced (and thus lowered the selling price).
2. An author could begin to realize financial rewards through signing over copyright to a publisher. Owning the copyright meant that the publisher, who had assumed the expense and risk of publication, stood to gain a substantial portion of the publication revenue.
3. Punishment for breaking the law (i.e., printing illegal copies) was feasible, for the ability to escape detection was relatively slight. The visibility and the capital costs of establishing and operating a printing press meant that those who used such presses to violate copyright were liable to confiscatory punishment at least commensurate with the injury done by the crime itself.

In the 1970s, technology advances produced the photocopier, an invention that empowered the user to produce multiple copies cheaply and comparatively unnoticed. In the 1980s, the fax machine took the world by storm, multiplying copies and speeding up their distribution. Computer networking technology of the 1990s marries the convenience, affordability, and ease of distribution, eclipsing the power of all previous technologies. We can attribute the exponential increase in electronic content, at least indirectly, to the current inhabitants of the White House. The Clinton-Gore campaign of 1992 introduced the Internet to the general public, and this administration has been passionately committed to rapid development of the National Information Infrastructure (NII) and determined to advance the electronic marketplace. Part of that commitment arises from national leaders' unwavering faith that electronic networks create an environment and a set of instruments vital to the overall economic growth of the United States.

While copyright (that is, the notion that creative works can be owned) is still and probably always will be recognized as a fundamental principle by most players in the information chain, many believe that its currently articulated "rules" do not effectively address either the technical capabilities or reader needs of a high-speed information distribution age. It could be argued (and many educators do) that the nineteenth- and twentieth-century drafters of copyright law intended to lay down societally beneficial and, by extension, technologically neutral principles about intellectual property ownership and copying,[2] but in fact Thomas Jefferson knew nothing of photocopiers, and the legislators who crafted the 1976 Copyright Act of the United States knew nothing of computer networks. Had they even begun to imagine such things, the law might have been written differently—and in fact the case can be made that it should now be written differently.[3] So to many people, the gulf between copyright laws or treaties and the universe that those laws ought to address today feels vast and deep. Therefore, instead of relying on national copyright law, surrounding case law, international treaties, and prevailing practice to govern information transactions for electronic information, copyright holders have turned to contracts (or licenses, as they are more commonly called in the library world) as the mechanism for defining the owner, user, and uses of any given piece of information.

That is, the license-contract is invoked because the prospective deal is for both parties a substantial transaction (in cash or in consequence). The new atmosphere creates a new kind of marketplace or a market for a new kind of product, and neither the selling nor the buying parties are sure of the other or of their position vis-à-vis the law and the courts. Publishers come to the table with real anxieties that their products may be abused by promiscuous reproduction of a sort that ultimately saps their product's marketability, while libraries are fearful that restrictions on permitted uses will mean less usable or more expensive products.

In short, what licensing agreements have in common with the copyright regime is that both accept the fundamental idea of the nature of intellectual property—that even when intangible, it can be owned. Where they differ is in the vehicle by which they seek to balance creators', producers', and users' rights and to regulate the economy that springs up around those rights. Copyright represents a set of general regulations negotiated through statutory enactment. Licenses, on the other hand, represent a market-driven approach to this regulation through deals struck between buyers and sellers.

WHEN DID THIS MODE OF DOING BUSINESS BEGIN FOR LIBRARIES?

The concept of a license is old and fundamentally transparent. A license is essentially a means of providing use of a piece of property without giving up the ownership. For example, if you own a piece of property and allow another to use it without transferring title, you may, by law of contract, stipulate your conditions; if the other party agrees to them, then a mutually agreeable deal has come into being. A similar transaction takes place in the case of performance rights for films and recordings. This example moves from the tangible property mode of real estate, in which exclusive licenses (granting of rights to only one user) are common, to the intangible property mode of intellectual property such as copyright, in which nonexclusive licenses are the norm. The owner of a movie theater rarely owns the cans of film delivered weekly to the cinema, holding them instead under strict conditions of use: so many showings, so much payment for each ticket sold, and so on. With the right price such an arrangement, like the economic relationship between author and publisher that is sanctioned by copyright, can be extraordinarily fruitful. In the license mode of doing business (precisely defined by the legal contract that describes the license), the relationships are driven entirely by contract law: the owner of a piece of property is free to ask whatever price and set whatever conditions on use the market will bear. The ensuing deal is pure "marketplace": a meeting of minds between a willing buyer and a willing seller. A crucial point here is that the license becomes a particularly powerful tool for that property owner who has a copyright-protected monopoly.

Most academics began to be parties to license agreements when personal computer software (WordStar, WordPerfect) appeared in the 1980s in shrink-wrap packages for the first time. Some purchasers of such software may have read the fine print on the wrapper that detailed the terms and conditions of use, but most either did not or have ceased to do so. The thrust of such documents is simple: by opening the package the purchaser has agreed to certain terms, terms that include limited rights of ownership and use of the item paid for. In many ways, this mode of licensing raises problematic questions,[4] but in other ways, such as sheer efficiency, shrink-wrap licensing suggests the kind of transaction that the scholarly information marketplace needs to achieve. It is noteworthy that the shrink-wrap license has moved easily into the World Wide Web environment, where it shows itself in clickable "I agree" form. The user's click supposedly affirms that he or she has said yes to the user terms and is ready to abide by them. The downsides and benefits are similar to those of shrink-wrapped software.

The phenomenon of institutional licensing for electronic content has evolved in a short time. Over the past 20 years or so, the licensing of software has become a way of life for institutions of higher education. These kinds of licenses are generally for systems that run institutional computers or on-line catalogs or software packages (e.g., for instruction or for office support). The licenses, often substantial in scale and price, are arranged by institutional counsel (an increasingly over-worked segment of an educational institution's professional staff) along with information technology managers.

Libraries' entrée into this arena has been comparatively recent and initially on a small scale. In fact, the initial library business encounter with electronic content may not have happened via license at all, but rather via deposit account. Some 20 years ago, academic and research libraries began accessing electronic information through mediated searching of indexing and abstracting services provided by consolidators such as Dialog. Different database owners levied different per hour charges (each database also required its own searching vocabularies and strategies), and Dialog (in this example) aggregated them for the educational customer. For the most part, libraries established accounts to which these searches (usually mediated by librarians or information specialists) were charged.

By the late 1980s, libraries also began to purchase shrink-wrapped (prelicensed) content, though shrink-wrapped purchases did not form—and still do not—any very visible part of library transactions. Concurrently, a number of indexing and abstracting services offered electronic versions directly to libraries via CD-ROM or through dial-up access (for example, an important early player in this arena was ISI, the Institute for Scientific Information). It was at this point, within the last ten years, that library licenses gradually became recognized as a means to a new and different sort of information acquisition or access. Such licenses were often arranged by library subject specialists for important resources in well-defined areas of use. The license terms offered to libraries were accepted or not, the library customer regarding them mostly as nonnegotiable. Nonacceptance was most often a matter of affordability, and there seemed to be little room for the library customer to affect the terms. Complaints about terms of licenses began to be (and persist in being) legion, for important reasons such as the following:

- *Potential loss of knowledge.* By definition, licenses are arranged for specific periods of time. At the end of that time, librarians rapidly discovered, if the license is not renewed, prior investment can become worthless as the access ceases (for example, where a CD-ROM must be returned or perhaps stops being able to read the information; or where connections to a remote server are severed).

- *License restrictions on use and users.* In order to reduce or curtail the leakage of electronic information, institutions are often asked to ensure that only members of the institution can use that information.,

- *Limitations on users' rights.* Initial license language not infrequently asks that institutional users severely limit what and how much they may copy from the information resource and may prescribe the means by which such copying can be done.

- *Cost.* In general, electronic licenses for indexing and abstracting services cost significantly more than print equivalents.[5]

WHAT HAS HAPPENED TO INCREASE LIBRARIES' AWARENESS OF LICENSES?

1. Sheer numbers have increased. Thousands of information providers have jumped into the scholarly marketplace with electronic products of one sort or another: CDs, on-line databases, full text resources, multimedia. Many scientific publishers, learned societies, university presses, full-text publishers, and vendor/aggregators, as well as new entrants to the publishing arena, now offer beta or well-tested versions of either print-originating or completely electronic information. The numbers have ballooned in a short two to three years, with no signs of abating. For example, *NewJour,* the on-line forum for announcing new e-journals, magazines, and newsletters, reports 3,634 titles in its archive as of April 5, 1997, and this figure does not include the 1,100 science journal titles that Elsevier is now making available in electronic form.[6] The Yale University Library licenses more than 400 electronic resources of varying sizes, types, media, and price, and it reviews about two new electronic content licenses a week.

2. The attempt by various players in the information chain to create guidelines about electronic fair use has not so far proved fruitful. In connection with the Clinton Administration's National Information Infrastructure initiative, the Working Group on Intellectual Property Rights in the Electronic Environment called upon copyright stakeholders to negotiate guidelines for the fair use of electronic materials in a variety of nonprofit educational contexts. Anyone who wished to participate was invited to do so, and a large group calling itself CONFU, the Conference on Fair Use, began to negotiate such guidelines for a variety of activities (such as library reserves, multimedia in the classroom, interlibrary loans, etc.) in September 1994.[7] The interests of all participants in the information chain were represented, and the group quickly began to come unstuck in reaching agreements on most of the dozen or more areas defined as needing guidelines. Such stalemates should come as no surprise; in fact, they are healthy and proper. Any changes to national guidelines, let alone national law or international treaty, should happen only when the public debate has been extensive and consensus has been reached. What many have come to realize during the current licensing activities is that the license arrangements that libraries currently are making are in fact achieving legislation's business more quickly and by other means. Instead of waiting on Congress or CONFU and allowing terms to be dictated to both parties by law, publishers and institutions are starting to make their peace together, thoughtfully and responsibly, one step at a time. Crafting these agreements and relationships is altogether the most important achievement of the licensing environment.

3. Numerous formal partnerships and informal dialogues have been spawned by the capabilities of new publications technologies. A number of libraries collaborate with the publishing and vendor communities as product developers or testers. Such relationships are fruitful in multiple ways. They encourage friction, pushback, and conversation that lead to positive and productive outcomes. Libraries have been offered—and have greatly appreciated—the opportunity to discuss at length the library licenses of various producers, for example, JSTOR, and libraries feel they have had the opportunity to shape and influence these licenses with mutually satisfactory results.

4. Library consortia have aggressively entered the content negotiating arena. While library consortia have existed for decades and one of their primary aims has been effective information sharing, it is only in the 1990s (and mostly in the last two to three years) that a combination of additional state funding (for statewide consortia), library demands, and producers' willingness to negotiate with multiple institutions has come together to make the consortial license an efficient and perhaps cost-effective way to manage access to large bodies of electronic content. An example of a particularly fruitful marketplace encounter (with beautiful as well as charged moments) occurred from February 3 to 5, 1997, as a group of consortial leaders, directors, and coordinators who had communicated informally for a year or two through mailing list messages arranged a meeting at the University of Missouri–St. Louis. The Consortium of Consortia (COC, as we sweepingly named ourselves) invited a dozen major electronic content vendors to describe their products briefly and their consortial working arrangements in detail.[8] By every account, this encounter achieved an exceptional level of information swapping, interaction, and understandings, both of specific resources and of the needs of producers and customers. That said, the future of consortial licensing is no more certain than it is for individual library licenses, though for different reasons.[9]

5. Academia's best legal talent offers invaluable support to libraries. Libraries are indebted to the intelligent and outspoken lawyerly voices in institutions of higher learning in this country. The copyright specialists in universities' general counsel offices have, in a number of cases, led in negotiating content licenses for the institution and have shared their strategies and knowledge generously. Law school experts have published important articles, taught courses, contributed to Internet postings, and participated in national task forces where such matters are discussed.[10]

6. The library community has organized itself to understand the licensing environment for its constituents. The Association of Research Libraries (ARL) has produced an introductory licensing brochure,[11] the Council on Library Resources/Commission on Preservation and Access has supported Yale Library's creation of an important Web site about library content licensing,[12] and the Yale Library offers the library, publisher, vendor, and lawyer world

a high-quality, moderated, on-line list where the issues of libraries and producers are aired daily.[13]

7. Options are limited. Right now, licensing and contracts are the only way to obtain the increasing number of electronic information resources that library users need for their education and research.

SOME NOTABLE CHALLENGES
OF THE LIBRARY LICENSING ENVIRONMENT TODAY

I identify these challenges because they are important and need to be addressed.

1. *Terms of use.* This area needs to be mentioned at the outset, as it has caused some of the most anguished discussions between publishers and libraries. Initially, many publishers' contract language for electronic information was highly restrictive about both permitted users and permitted uses. Assumptions and requirements about how use ought to be contained have been at times ludicrous, for example, in phrases such as "no copies may be made by any means electronic or mechanical." Through dialogue between librarians and producers, who are usually eager to market their work to happy customers, much of this language has disappeared from the first draft contracts presented to library customers. Where libraries are energetic and aggressive on behalf of their users, the terms of use can indeed be changed to facilitate educational and research goals. The Yale Library, for example, is now party to a number of licenses that permit substantial amounts of copying and downloading for research, individual learning, in-the-classroom learning, library reserves, course packs, and related activities. Interlibrary loan and transmission of works to individual scholars in other organizations are matters that still need a great deal of work. However, the licenses of 1996 and 1997 represent significant all-around improvements and surely reinforce the feeling that rapid progress is being made.

2. *Scalability.* Institutional electronic content licenses are now generally regarded as negotiable, mostly because the library-customer side of the marketplace is treating them as such (which publishers seem to welcome). Successes of different sorts have ensued (success being defined as a mutually agreeable contract), making all parties feel that they can work together effectively in this new mode. However, negotiations are labor intensive. Negotiation requires time (to develop the expertise and to negotiate), and time is a major cost. The current method of one-on-one negotiations between libraries and their publishers seems at the moment necessary, for many reasons, and at the same time it places new demands on institutional staff. Scalability is the biggest challenge for the licensing environment.

   • Clearly, it is too early to shift the burden onto intermediaries such as subscription agencies or other vendors who have vested interests of their own. So far their intervention has been absent or not particularly success-ful. In fact, in some of the situations in which intermediaries purvey elec-tronic databases, library customers secure less advantageous use terms than those libraries could obtain by licensing directly from the publishers. This is because those vendors are securing commercial licenses from the producers whereas libraries are able to obtain educational licenses. Thus, it is no surprise that in unveiling their latest electronic products and ser-vices, important organizations such as Blackwell's *(Navigator)* and OCLC *(EJO—Electronic Journals On-line)* leave license negotiating for the journal content as a matter between the individual journal publishers and their li-brary customers.

- The contract that codifies the license terms is a pervasive document that covers every aspect of the library/producer relationship, from authorized uses and users to technology base, duration, security mechanisms, price, liability, responsibility, and so on. That is, the license describes the full di-mensions of the "deal" for any resource. The library and educational communities, in their attempts to draft general principles or models to ad-dress content licensing, characteristically forget this important fact, and the results inevitably fall short in the scaling-up efforts.

3. *Price.* Pricing models for electronic information are in their infancy; they tend to be creative, complicated, and often hard to understand.[14] Some of these models can range from wacky to bizarre. Consortial pricing can be particularly complex. Each new model solves some of the equity or revenue problems associated with earlier models but introduces confusion of its own. While pricing of electronic resources is not, strictly speaking, a problem with the license itself, price has been a major obstacle in making electronic agree-ments. The seemingly high price tags for certain electronic resources leave the "serials crisis" in the dust.[15] It is clear that academic libraries, particu-larly through their consortial negotiators, expect bulk pricing arrangements, sliding scales, early signing bonuses, and other financial inducements that publishers may not necessarily feel they are able to offer. Some of the most fraught moments at the St. Louis COC meeting involved clashes between consortial representatives who affirmed that products should be priced at whatever a willing buyer can or will pay, even if this means widely inconsis-tent pricing by the vendor, and producers who affirmed the need to stick with a set price that enables them to meet their business plan.

4. *The liability-trust conundrum.* One of the most vexing issues for producers and their licensees has been the producers' assumption that institutions can and ought to vouch for the behavior of individual users (in licenses, the sections that deal with this matter are usually called "Authorized or Permitted Users" and what users may do under the terms of a license is called an "Authorized or Permitted Use") and the fact that individual users' abuses of the terms of

a license can kill the deal for a library or a whole group of libraries. Working through this matter with provider after provider in a partnership/cooperative approach poses many challenges. In fact, this matter may be a microcosm of a larger issue: the development of the kind of trust that must underlie any electronic content license. Generally the marketplace for goods is not thought of in terms of trust; it regarded as a cold cash (or virtual cash) transaction environment. Yet the kinds of scaled-up scholarly information licenses that libraries are engaging with now depend on mutual understanding and trust in a way not needed for the standard trade—or even the print—market to work. In negotiating electronic content licenses, publishers must trust—and, given the opening up of user/use language, it seems they are coming to trust—their library customers to live up to the terms of the deal.

In part, we currently rely on licenses because publishers do not trust users to respect their property and because libraries are fretful that publishers will seek to use the new media to tilt the economic balance in their favor. Both fears are probably overplayed. If libraries continue to find, as they are beginning to do, that publishers are willing to give *the same or even more* copying rights via licenses as copyright offers, both parties may not be far from discovering that fears have abated, trust has grown, and the ability to revert to copyright as the primary assurance of trust can therefore increase. But many further technological winds must blow—for example, the cybercash facility to allow micropayment transactions—before the players may be ready to settle down to such a new equilibrium.

5. *The aggregator aggravation (and opportunity).* The costly technological investments that producers need to make to move their publications onto an electronic base; the publishing processes that are being massively reconceived and reorganized; and not least, the compelling vision of digital libraries that proffer information to the end user through a single or small number of interfaces, with a single or modest number of search engines, give rise to information aggregators of many sorts:[16] those who develop important searching, indexing, and/or display softwares (AltaVista, OpenText, etc.); those who provide an interface or gateway to products (Blackwell's, etc.); and those who do all that plus offer to deliver the information (DIALOG @CARL, OCLC, etc.). Few publishers convert or create just one journal or publication in an electronic format. From the viewpoint of academic research libraries, it appears that the electronic environment has the effect of shifting transaction emphasis from single titles to collections or aggregations of electronic materials as marketplace products.

In turn, licensing collections from aggregators makes libraries dependent on publishers and vendors for services in a brand new way. That is, libraries' original expectation for electronic publications, no more than five years ago, was that publishers would provide the data and the subscribing library or groups of libraries would mount and make content available. But mounting and integrating electronic information requires a great deal of capital, effort, and technological sophistication as well as multiple licenses for software and content. Thus, the prognosis for institutions meeting all or most of their users' electronic information needs locally is slim. The currently emerging mode, thus, takes us to a very different world in which publishers have positioned themselves to be the electronic information providers of the moment.[17]

The electronic collections offered to the academic library marketplace are frequently not in configurations that librarians would have chosen for their institutions had these resources been unbundled. This issue has surfaced in several of Yale Library's negotiations. For example, one publisher of a large number of high-quality journals made only the full collection available in e-form and only through consortial sale. By this means, the Yale Library recently "added" 50 electronic journal titles to its cohort, titles it had not chosen to purchase in print. The pricing model did not include a cost for those additional 50 titles; it was simply easier for the publisher to include all titles than to exclude the less desirable ones. While this forum is not the place to explore this particular kind of scaling up of commercial digital collections, it is a topic of potentially great impact on the academic library world.

6. *The challenge of consortial dealings.* Ideally, groups of libraries acting in consort to license electronic resources can negotiate powerfully for usage terms and prices with producers. In practice, both licensors and licensees have much to learn about how to approach this scaled-up environment. Here are some of the particularly vexing issues:

- Not all producers are willing to negotiate with all consortia; some are not able to negotiate with consortia at all.

- In the early days of making a consortial agreement, the libraries may not achieve any efficiencies because all of them (and their institutional counsel) may feel the need or desire to participate in the negotiating process. Thus, in fact, a license for 12 institutions may take nearly as long to negotiate as 12 separate licenses.

- Consortia overlap greatly, particularly with existing bodies such as cataloging and lending utilities that are offering consortial deals to their members. It seems that every library is in several consortia these days, and many of us are experiencing a competition for our business from several different consortia at once for a single product's license.

- No one is sure precisely what comprises a consortial "good deal." That is, it is hard to define and measure success. The bases for comparison between individual institutional and multiple institutional prices are thin, and the stated savings can often feel like a sales pitch.

- Small institutions are more likely to be unaffiliated with large or powerful institutions and left out of seemingly "good deals" secured by the larger, more prosperous libraries. Surprisingly enough, private schools can be at a disadvantage since they are generally not part of state-established and funded consortial groups.

- In fact, treating individual libraries differently from collectives may, in the long run, not be in the interests of publishers or those libraries.

7. *Institutional workflow restructuring.* How to absorb the additional licensing work (and create the necessary expertise) within educational institutions is a challenge. I can foresee a time when certain kinds of institutional licenses (electronic journals, for example) might offer standard, signable language, for surely producers are in the same scaling-up bind that libraries are. At the moment, licenses are negotiated in various departments and offices of universities and libraries. Many universities require that license negotiation, or at least a review and signature, happen through the office of general counsel and sometimes over the signature of the purchasing department. In such circumstances, the best result is delay; the worst is that the library may not secure the terms it deems most important. Other institutions delegate the negotiating and signing to library officers who have an appropriate level of responsibility and accountability for this type of legal contract. Most likely the initial contact between the library and the electronic provider involves the public service or collections librarians who are most interested in bringing the resource to campus.

One way of sharing the workload is to make sure that all selector staff receive formal or informal training in the basics and purposes of electronic licenses, so that they can see the negotiations through as far as possible and leave only the final review and approval to those with signing authority.[18] In some libraries, the licensing effort is coordinated from the acquisitions or serials departments, the rationale being that this is where purchase orders are cut and funds released for payment. However, such an arrangement can have the effect of removing the publisher interaction from the library staff best positioned to understand a given resource and the needs of the library readers who will be using it. Whatever the delegation of duties may be at any given institution, it is clear that the tasks must be carved out in a sensible fashion, for it will be a long time before the act of licensing electronic content becomes transparent. Clearly, this new means of working is not the "old" acquisitions model. How does everyone in an institution who should be involved in crafting licensing "deals" get a share of the action?

SUCCEEDING (NOT JUST COPING)

On the positive side, both individual libraries and consortia of libraries have reported negotiating electronic content licenses with a number of publishers who have been particularly understanding of research library needs. In general, academic publishers are proving to be willing to give and take on license language and terms, provided that the licensees know what terms are important to them. In many cases, librarians ask that the publisher reinstate the "public good" clauses of the Copyright Act into the electronic content license, allowing fair use copying or downloading, interlibrary loan, and archiving for the institutional licensee and its customers. Consortial negotiations are having a highly positive impact on the usefulness and quality of licenses.

While several downsides to the rapidly growing licensing environment have been mentioned, the greatest difficulty at this point is caused by the proliferation of licenses that land on the desks of librarians, university counsel, and purchasing officers. The answers to this workload conundrum might lie in several directions.

1. *National or association support.* National organizations such as ARL and the Council on Library and Information Resources (CLIR) are doing a great deal to educate as many people as possible about licensing. Practicing librarians treasure that support and ask that licensing continue to be part of strategic and funding plans. For example, the Yale Library has proposed next-step ideas for the World Wide Web Liblicense project. Under discussion are such possibilities as: further development of a prototype licensing software that will enable librarians to create licenses on the fly, via the World Wide Web, for presentation to producers and vendors as a negotiating position;[19] and assembling a working group meeting that involves publisher representatives in order to explore how many pieces of an academic electronic content are amenable to standardization. Clearly, academic libraries are working with the same producers to license the same core of products over and over again. It might be valuable for the ARL and other organizations to hire a negotiator to develop acceptable language for certain key producers—say the top 100—with the result that individual libraries would not need to work out this language numerous times. Pricing and technology issues, among others, might nonetheless need to remain as items for local negotiation.

2. *Aggregators.* As libraries, vendors, and producers become more skilled as aggregators, the scaling issues will abate somewhat. Three aggregating directions are emerging:

   • Information bundlers, such as Lexis-Nexis, OCLC, UMI, IAC, OVID, and a number of others offer large collections of materials to libraries under license. Some of these are sizeable take-it-or-leave-it groupings; others allow libraries to choose subsets or groups of titles.

   • Subscription agents are beginning to develop gateways to electronic resources and to offer to manage libraries' licensing needs.

   • Consortia of libraries can be considered as aggregators of library customers for publishers.

3. *Transactional licensing.* This paper treats only institutional licenses, be they site licenses, simultaneous user/port licenses, or single-user types. An increasing number of library transactions demand rights clearance for a piece at a time (situations that involve, say, course reserves or provision of articles that are not held in the library through a document supplier such as CARL). Mechanisms for easy or automatic rights clearance are of surpassing importance, and various entities are applying considerable energies to them. The academic library community has been skittish about embracing the services of rights management or licensing organizations, arguing that participation would abrogate fair use rights. It seems important, particularly in light of recent court decisions, that libraries pay close attention to their position vis-à-vis individual copies (when they are covered by fair use and when they are not, particularly in the electronic environment) and take the lead in crafting appropriate and fair arrangements to simplify the payment of fees in circumstances when such fees are necessary.[20]

BEYOND THE LICENSE?

As we have seen, the content license comes into play when the producer of an electronic resource seeks to define a "deal" and an income stream to support the creation and distribution of the content. Yet other kinds of arrangements are possible.

1. *Unrestricted and for free.* Some important resources are funded up front by, for example, governments or institutions, and the resources are available to all end users. Examples include the notable Los Alamos High Energy Physics Preprints; the various large genome databases; the recent announcement by the National Institutes of Health of MEDLINE's availability on-line; and numerous university-based electronic scholarly journals or databases. The number of such important resources is growing, though they may always be in the minority of scholarly resources. Characteristically, such information is widely accessible, the restrictions on use are minimal or nonexistent, and license negotiations are largely irrelevant or very straightforward.

2. *For a subscription fee and unrestricted to subscribers.* Some producers are, in fact, charging an on-line subscription fee but licenses need not be crafted or signed. The terms of use are clearly stated and generous. The most significant and prominent example of such not-licensed but paid-for resources is the rapidly growing collection of high-impact scientific and medical society journals published by Stanford University's HighWire Press.[21]

Both of these trends are important; they bear watching and deserve to be nurtured. In the first case, the up-front funding model seems to very well serve the needs of large scientific or academic communities without directly charging users or institutions; the databases are products of public- or university-funded research. In the second instance, although users are paying for access to the databases, the gap between the copyright and licensed way of doing business seems to have narrowed, and in fact the HighWire publications are treated as if copyright-governed. Over time, it would not be unreasonable to expect this kind of merger of the two constructs (copyright and contract) and to benefit from the subsequent simplification that the merger would bring.

In short, much is still to be learned in the content licensing environment, but much has been learned already. We are in a period of experimentation and exploration. All the players have real fears about the security of their livelihood and mission; all are vulnerable to the risks of information in new technologies; many are learning to work together pragmatically toward at least midterm modest solutions and are, in turn, using those modest solutions as stepping-stones into the future.

NOTES

1. Clifford Lynch in "Technology and Its Implications for Serials Acquisitions," *Against the Grain* 9, no. 1 (1997): 31. This article is based on a talk by Lynch at the November 1996 Charleston Conference. He identifies the key needs in building digital libraries as authentication, printing, individual item addressability, accessibility, and linkage. Lynch concludes with this insight: "The theme I want to underscore here is that we need to be very careful about whether we have technology that can deliver this electronic content *for which we are busy negotiating financial arrangements in acceptable ways on a broad systemic basis*" [emphasis is mine].

2. The position statement "Fair Use in the Electronic Age: Serving the Public Interest" is an outgrowth of discussions among a number of library associations regarding intellectual property and, in particular, the concern that the interests and rights of copyright owners and users remain balanced in the digital environment. This important position statement was developed by representatives of the following associations: American Association of Law Libraries, American Library Association, Association of Academic Health Sciences Library Directors, Association of Research Libraries, Medical Library Association, and Special Libraries Association. It espouses the philosophy that the U.S. copyright law was created to advance societal goals and well-being and embeds the notion of technological neutrality. It can be found at: *http://www.arl.org/info/frn/copy/fairuse.html*.

3. I have recently had the opportunity to read statements from the international publishing community in two major position papers originating with the International Publishers Copyright Council, the STM group of publishers, and the International Publishers Association. These documents affirm the following:

- Digital versions of works are not the same as print versions, because digital information can be manipulated and widely distributed. (The implication is that manipulation and distribution will happen and that it is happening with copyrighted works, often in an illegal manner.)
- Digital versions of works need even more protection than printed versions.
- Digital browsing is not the same as reading print: the very act of browsing involves reproducing copies (which immediately implicates and possibly violates copyright law).

- There should be no private or personal exemptions from copyright in the digital environment.
- There should be no exceptional copyright treatment for libraries in the digital environment—the exemptions for traditional materials, if carried over into the digital environment, will result in unfair competition with publishers.
- Digital lending (a digital analog to ILL) will destroy publishers.
- Publishers are now poised to offer and charge for electronic delivery of information and therefore they ought to be able to. Such services will replace most of the copying that libraries and individuals used to do in print.
- The role of libraries will be to provide access, select materials for users via what they choose to license, instruct users in the vast array of electronic sources and how to use them, and support users in searching and research and learning needs.

4. See the 30 June 1996 decision by the United States Court of Appeals, Seventh Circuit, in *ProCD v. Zeidenberg.* The question posed was: must buyers of computer software obey the terms of shrink-wrap licenses? The district court had said not. The court of appeals reversed this decision. ProCD (the plaintiffs) compiled information from more than 3,000 phone directories into one database with additional information such as zip code extensions and included their own searching software. They packaged the product, called Select-Phone, as a CD for personal sale in a shrink-wrap box. They also sold it to commercial companies in other formats, such as mailing lists. Mr. Zeidenberg bought SelectPhone at a shop in Madison, Wis., and formed a company to resell the information on the basis that factual information cannot be copyrighted. He made this information available over the Internet apparently quite cheaply. Zeidenberg argued that a person cannot be bound by the shrink-wrap license because the terms are not known at the time of purchase. They are inside the package and the purchaser cannot be bound by terms that are secret at the time of purchase. The judges' decision was that the shrink-wrap license is legal and that a buyer is bound by it.

5. See Martha Kellogg, "CD-ROM Products as Serials: Cost Considerations for Libraries," in *Serials Review* 17, no. 3 (1991): 49–60. The tables in this article, as a basis of comparison between print reference or indexing and abstracting works and their CD equivalents, show a difference of about 30% where resources are comparable. Recent e-mail from the University of Michigan Library suggests that differentials between print and electronic works are as high as 600%.

6. *NewJour* is a joint project of the Yale Library, the University of Pennsylvania, and the University of California, San Diego Library. Its fully searchable archive is located at *http://gort.ucsd.edu/newjour/*.

7. A good summary of the flavor, debates, and progress of CONFU can be found at *http://www.utsystem.edu/OGC/IntellectualProperty/confu.htm*. The CONFU interim report is available at *http://www.uspto.gov/web/offices/dcom/olia/confu/*.

8. For a list of the consortia that participated in the St. Louis meeting and descriptions of their activities, see the COC home page at Yale University Library: *http://www.library.yale.edu/consortia/*.

9. Ann Okerson, "Buy or Lease? Two Models for Scholarly Information at the End (or the Beginning) of an Era," *Daedalus* 125, no. 4 (1996): 55–76. This special issue on libraries is called "Books, Bricks, and Bytes." I suggest that one possible outcome of the new trend

to scaled-up consortial licensing activities is that the library marketplace will gain significant power and that publishers of scholarly information could find themselves in quite a different position than they are in the captive marketplace of today. It is possible to argue that such an outcome is very healthy; on the other hand, even librarians and scholars might find this outcome undesirable in that it would put today's specialized scholarly publications, with their attendant high prices, out of business. The *Daedalus* piece can also be found at *http://www.library.yale.edu/~okerson/daedalus.html.*

10. For example, an especially rich resource is the site of the University of Texas Office of General Counsel's Copyright Management Center. The center provides guidance and information to faculty, staff, and students concerning applicable law and the alternatives available to help accomplish educational objectives. A large number of materials, organized by topic, is accessible through this Web site. Some important documents are stored directly on the Web server. The principal author is Georgia Harper, copyright counsel for the University of Texas System. The URL is *http://www.utsystem.edu/ogc/intellectualprop erty/cprtindx.htm.*

The higher education community is indebted to, among others, Indiana University's Kenneth Crews, an important voice in CONFU (see, for example, the CETUS Fair Use document at *http://www.cetus.org/fairindex.html*); the University of North Carolina Law School's Lolly Gasaway, also a leader in CONFU and contributor of many important resources (see, for example, "When Works Pass Into the Public Domain" at *http://www .library.yale.edu/~okerson/pubdomain.html*); and Karen Hersey of the MIT Counsel's Office, a leader in crafting university-producer electronic license agreements and a frequent workshop presenter on this topic.

11. See "Licensing Electronic Resources: Strategic and Practical Considerations for Signing Electronic Information Delivery Agreements" at *http://www.arl.org/scomm/licens ing/licbooklet.html.*

12. See LIBLICENSE: Licensing Digital Information—A Resource for Librarians. This Web resource contains license vocabulary, licensing terms and descriptions, sample publishers' licenses, links to other licensing sites, and a bibliography about the subject. The URL is *http://www.library.yale.edu/~llicense/index.shtml.*

13. LIBLICENSE-L is a moderated list for the discussion of issues related to the licensing of digital information by academic and research libraries. To join the LIBLICENSE-L list, send a message to *listproc@lists.yale.edu.* Leave the subject line blank. In the body of the message, type: subscribe LIBLICENSE-L Firstname Lastname

14. A LIBLICENSE-L message of February 12, 1997, enumerated a dozen different pricing models for electronic resources, and correspondents added several more in subsequent discussion.

15. Several reasons are advanced for the higher cost of electronic resources versus comparable print resources: (1) the producers are making new R&D and technology investments whose significant prices are passed on to the customer; (2) producers of journals generally offer a package that includes print plus electronic versions, giving the customer two different forms of the same information rather than one only; (3) the functionality of electronic resources is arguably higher than that of the print version; (4) electronic resources are not marketed as single journals or books but as scaled-up collections, often of substantial heft (consider the corpora of humanities full texts marketed by Chadwyck-Healey, the large backfile collections of JSTOR, the full collection of Academic Press titles available under

its IDEAL program; it seems that there is little incentive for producers to create and sell one electronic item at a time); and (5) the publisher, in becoming the source or site or provider, is taking on many of the library's roles and costs.

16. A LIBLICENSE-L message of March 14, 1997, defined aggregators in the following way: " 'Aggregation' as used on this list means the bundling together or gathering together of electronic information into electronic collections that are marketed as a package. For example, DIALOG@CARL aggregates 300 databases; Academic Press's IDEAL aggregates 170+ journals; Johns Hopkins's Project MUSE is an electronic collection of 40+ journals, and so on. But the term 'aggregator' is more usually used in describing the supplier who assembles the offerings of more than one publisher, so one is more likely to hear Dialog, OCLC, Information Access, and UMI spoken of as aggregators, than The Johns Hopkins University Press."

17. License negotiations between libraries and producers now do take into account the matter of electronic archiving, or at least the parties pay lip service to perpetual access. For example, it is common for an electronic resource license to offer some form of access or data if the library cancels a license or if the provider goes out of business. However, while the license addresses this matter, the underlying solutions are far from satisfactory for either party. I leave the matter of archiving, a huge topic and concern, to other venues; clearly the whole underpinnings of libraries and culture are at stake, depending on the outcomes of the archiving dialogues that are in place now and will surely outlast our lifetimes.

18. At Yale, for example, after close discussions on this matter with the library to make sure that points of view were in synch, general counsel delegated library content licensing to senior library administration and it is now done by the associate university librarian for collections with considerable support and backstopping by Yale's public services and collections librarians in effective and productive teamwork.

19. In fact, the software development was funded by CLIR (formerly the Council on Library Resources) in June 1997, and its product is now available at *http://www.library.yale.edu/~llicense/software.shtml*).

20. The case, *Princeton University Press v. Michigan Document Services, Inc.*, asked the question: does a copy shop infringe on publishers' copyrights when it photocopies course pack materials? This material comprises book chapters and articles for students of nearby colleges and universities. The owner of Michigan Document Services argued that he was copying on behalf of the students and exercising their fair use rights. The recent appeal in the United States Court of Appeals for the Sixth Circuit found for the publishers. For extensive documentation on this matter, see Stanford's Fair Use site at *http://fairuse.stanford.edu/mds/*.

21. For the journals available through Stanford's HighWire, see *http://highwire.stanford.edu*.

PART TWO

Electronic Publishing:
Empirical Studies

CHAPTER 4

Information-Based Productivity

Scott Bennett

Convenience is a key word in the library lexicon. As service organizations, libraries give high priority to enhancing the convenience of their operations. Readers themselves regularly use the word to describe what they value.[1] By contrast, when NEXIS-LEXIS describes itself as a sponsor of public radio, it emphasizes not convenience but productivity for professionals. Does NEXIS-LEXIS know something that we are missing?

I think so. Talk about productivity is unambiguously grounded in the discourse of economics, whereas talk about convenience rarely is. Quite notably, The Andrew W. Mellon Foundation has self-consciously insisted that its programs in scholarly communication operate within the realm of economics. Foundation president William G. Bowen explains this focus, in speaking of the Foundation's JSTOR project, by observing that "when new technologies evolve, they offer benefits that can be enjoyed either in the form of more output (including opportunities for scholars to do new things or to do existing tasks better) or in the form of cost savings. . . . In universities electronic technologies have almost always led to greater output and rarely to reduced costs. . . . This proclivity for enjoying the fruits of technological change mainly in the form of 'more and better' cannot persist. Technological gains must generate at least some cost savings."[2] In its JSTOR project and the other scholarly communication projects it supports, the Foundation calls for attention "to economic realities and to the cost-effectiveness" of different ways of meeting reader needs. The Foundation wishes to promote change that will endure because the changes embody "more effective and less costly ways of doing [the] business" of both libraries and publishers.[3]

Productivity is the underlying measure of such effectiveness, so I want briefly to recall what economists mean by the word and to reflect on the problematic application of productivity measures to higher education. I will then describe a modest project recently undertaken to support one of the most famous of Yale's undergraduate courses. I will conclude with some observations about why the productivity of libraries and of higher education must command our attention.

PRODUCTIVITY

Productivity is one of the most basic measures of economic activity. Comparative productivity figures are used to judge the degree to which resources are efficiently used, standards of living are changed, and wealth is created.[4] Productivity is the ratio of what is produced to the resources required to produce it, or the ratio of economic outputs to economic inputs:

$$\text{Productivity} = \text{Outputs}/\text{Inputs}$$

Outputs can be any goods, services, or financial outcomes; inputs are the labor, services, materials, and capital costs incurred in creating the output. If outputs increase faster than inputs, productivity increases. Conversely, if inputs increase faster than outputs, productivity falls. Technological innovation has historically been one of the chief engines of productivity gain.[5]

Useful indicators of productivity require that both inputs and outputs be clearly defined and measured with little ambiguity. Moreover, the process for turning inputs into outputs must be clearly understood. And those processes must be susceptible to management if productivity increases are to be secured. Finally, meaningful quality changes in outputs need to be conceptually neutralized in measuring changes in productivity.

One need only list these conditions for measuring and managing productivity to understand how problematic they are as applied to higher education.[6] To be sure, some of the least meaningful outputs of higher education can be measured, such as the number of credit hours taught or degrees granted. But the outputs that actively prompt people to pursue education—enhanced knowledge, aesthetic cultivation, leadership ability, economic advantage, and the like—are decidedly difficult to measure. And while we know a great deal about effective teaching, the best of classroom inputs remains more an art in the hands of master teachers than a process readily duplicated from person to person. Not surprisingly, we commonly believe that few teaching practices can be consciously managed to increase productivity and are deeply suspicious of calls to do so.

Outside the classroom and seminar, ideas of productivity have greater acceptance. Productive research programs are a condition of promotion and tenure at research universities; and while scholars express uneasiness about counting research productivity, it certainly happens. The ability to generate research dollars and the number of articles and books written undeniably count, along with the in-

tellectual merit of the work. There is little dispute that many other higher education activities are appropriately judged by productivity standards. Some support
services, such as the financial management of endowment resources, are subject to
systematic and intense productivity analysis. Other academic support activities,
including the provision of library services, are expected to be efficient and productive, even where few actual measures of their productivity are taken.[7]

In many cases, discussion of productivity in higher education touches highly
sensitive nerves.[8] Faculty, for instance, commonly complain that administration is
bloated and unproductive. Concern for the productivity of higher education in-
forms a significant range of the community's journalistic writing and its scholarship.[9] This sensitivity reflects both the truly problematic application of productivity measures to much that happens in education and the tension between concerns
about productivity and quality. But it also reflects the fact that we are "unable and,
on many campuses, unwilling to answer the hard questions about student learning
and educational costs" that a mature teaching enterprise is inescapably responsible for answering.[10]

THE SCULLY PROJECT

A modest digital project undertaken in 1996 at Yale offers an opportunity to explore productivity matters. The project aimed at improving the quality of library
support and of student learning in one of the most heavily enrolled undergraduate courses at Yale. We wished to do the project as cost-effectively as possible, but
initially we gave no other thought to productivity matters. To echo Bowen's words,
we wanted to take the fruits of digital technology in the form of more output, as
"more and better." But the project provided an opportunity to explore possibilities
for cost savings, for reduced inputs. The project, in spite of its modest objectives
and scale (or perhaps exactly for those reasons!), became an instructive "natural
experiment" in scholarly communication very much like those supported by the
Mellon Foundation.

For decades, now Emeritus Professor Vincent Scully has been teaching his
renowned Introduction to the History of Art, from Prehistory to the Renaissance.
The course commonly enrolls 500 students, or about 10% of the entire undergraduate student body at Yale. Working with Professor Mary E. Miller, head of
the History of Art department, and with Elizabeth Owen and Brian Allen, head
Teaching Fellows with substantial experience in Professor Scully's course, Max
Marmor, the head of Yale's Arts Library, and his colleague Christine de Vallet un-
dertook to provide improved library support for this course. Their Scully Project
was part of a joint program between the University Library and Information
Technology Services at Yale designed to offer targeted support to faculty as they
employ digital technologies for teaching, research, and administration. The Scully
Project was also our first effort to demonstrate what it could mean to move from
film-based to digital-based systems to support teaching in art history.[11]

The digital material created for Professor Scully's students included:

- An extensive and detailed course syllabus, including general information about the course and requirements for completing it.

- A schedule of section meetings and a roster of the 25 Teaching Fellows who help conduct the course, complete with their e-mail addresses.

- A list of the four required texts and the six journal articles provided in a course pack.

- A comprehensive list of the works of art discussed in the course, along with detailed information about the artists, dates of creation, media and size, and references to texts that discuss the works.

Useful as this textual material is, it would not meet the course's key information need for images. The Scully Project therefore includes 1,250 images of sculptures, paintings, buildings, vases, and other objects. These images are presented in a Web image browser that is both handsome and easily used and contains a written guide advising students on study strategies to make the best use of the Web site.[12]

How did the Scully project change student learning? To answer that question, I must first describe how the library used to meet the course's need for study images. The library traditionally selected mounted photographs closely related to, but not necessarily identical to, the images used in Professor Scully's lectures. We hung the photographs in about 480 square feet of study gallery space in the History of Art department. Approximately 200 photographs were available to students for four weeks before the midterm exam and 400 photographs for four weeks before the final exam. In those exams, students are asked to identify images and to comment on them. With 500 students enrolled and with the photos available in a relatively small space for just over half of the semester, the result was extreme crowding of students primarily engaged in visual memorization. To deal with the obvious imperfections of this arrangement, some of Professor Scully's more entrepreneurial students made videotapes of the mounted photos and sold them for study in the residential colleges. Less resourceful students simply stole the photos from the walls.

The Scully Project employed information technology to do more and better.

- Students can study the slide images that Professor Scully actually uses in class rather than frequently different photographs, often in black-and-white and sometimes carrying outdated identifying labels.

- The 1,250 digital images on the Web site include not only those that Professor Scully uses in class, but also other views of the same object and still other images that the Teaching Fellows refer to in discussion sessions. Students now have easy access to three times the number of images they could see in the study gallery space. For instance, where before students viewed one picture of Stonehenge, they now can view eight, including a diagram of the site and drawings showing construction methods and details.

- Digital images are available for study throughout the semester, not just before term exams. They are also available at all hours of day and night, consistent with student study habits.

- The digital images are available as a Web site anywhere there is a networked computer at Yale. This includes the residential colleges, where probably three-fourths of undergraduates have their own computers, as well as computing clusters at various locations on campus.

- The images are usually of much better quality than the photographs mounted on the wall; they read to the screen quickly in three different magnifications; and they are particularly effective on 17″ and larger monitors.

- The digital images cannot be stolen or defaced. They are always available in exactly the form intended by Professor Scully and his Teaching Fellows.

Student comments on the Scully Project emphasized the convenience of the Web site. Comments like "convenient, comfortable, detailed all at the push of a button," and "fantastic for studying for exams" were common, as were grateful comments on the 24-hour-a-day availability of the images and the need not to fight for viewing space in the study gallery. One student told us, "it was *wonderful*. It made my life *so* much easier." Another student said, "it was very, very convenient to have the images available on-line. That way I could study in my own room in small chunks of time instead of having to go to the photo study. I mainly just used the Web site to memorize the pictures like a photo study in my room."[13]

Visual memory training is a key element in the study of art history, and the Scully Web site was used primarily for memorization. Reports from Teaching Fellows on whether the digital images enhanced student learning varied, and only two of the Fellows had taught the course before and could make comparisons between the photo study space and the Web site. The following statements represent the range of opinion:

- Students "did think it was 'cool' to have a web site but [I] can't say they *wrote* better or *learned* more due to it."

- "I don't think they learned more, but I do think it [the Web site] helped them learn more easily."

- The head Teaching Fellow for the course reported that student test performance on visual recognition was "greatly enhanced" over her previous experience in the course. Another Teaching Fellow reported that students grasped the course content much earlier in the semester because of the earlier availability of the Web site images.

- One Teaching Fellow expressed an unqualified view that students learned more, wrote better papers, participated in class more effectively, and enjoyed the course more because of the Scully Project.[14]

- Another Teaching Fellow commented, I "wish we had such a thing in my survey days!"

The Web site apparently contributed significantly to at least one key part of Professor Scully's course—that part concerned with visual memory training. We accomplished this improvement at reasonable cost. The initial creation of digital images cost about $2.25 an image, while the total cash outlay for creating the Web site was $10,500. We did not track computing costs or the time spent on the project by permanent university staff, but including these costs might well drive the total to about $17,200 and the per image cost to around $14. Using this higher cost figure, one might say we invested $34 for every student enrolled in the course, or $11 per student if one assumes that the database remains useful for six years and the course is offered every other year.

This glow of good feeling about reasonable costs, quality products, improved learning, and convenience for readers is often as much as one has to guide decisions on investing in information technology. Last year, however, Yale Professor of Cardiology Carl Jaffe took me up short by describing a criterion by which he judges his noteworthy work in instructional media.[15] For Professor Jaffe, improved products must help solve the cost problem of good education. One must therefore ask whether the Scully Project passes not only the test of educational utility and convenience set by Professor Scully's Teaching Fellows, but also the productivity test set by Professor Jaffe. Does the Scully Project help solve cost problems in higher education? Does it allow us to use university resources more productively?

ACHIEVING INFORMATION-BASED PRODUCTIVITY GAINS

For more than a generation, libraries have been notably successful in improving the productivity of their own operations with digital technology. It is inconceivable that existing staffing levels could handle today's circulation workload if we were using McBee punch cards or—worse yet—typewriter-written circulation cards kept in book pockets and marked with date stamps attached to the tops of pencils. While libraries have an admirable record of deploying information technology to increase the productivity of their own operations, and while there is more of this to be done, the most important productivity gains in the future will lie elsewhere. The emergence of massive amounts of textual, numeric, spatial, and image information in digital formats, and the delivery of that information through networks, is decisively shifting the question to one of teacher and reader productivity.

What does the Scully Project tell us about library, teacher, and reader productivity? To answer that question, I will comment first on a set of operational issues that includes the use of library staff and Teaching Fellows to select and prepare images for class use; the preservation of the images over time; and the use of space. I will assess the Scully Project both as it was actually deployed, with little impact on the conduct of classroom instruction, and as one might imagine it being deployed, as the primary source of images in the classroom. The operations I will describe are more or less under the university's administrative control, and savings achieved in any of them can at least theoretically be pushed to the bottom line or redirected elsewhere. I will also comment on student productivity. This is a much more problematic topic because we can barely imagine controlling or redirecting for productivity purposes any gains readers might achieve.

Productivity Gains Subject to Administrative Control

The comparative costs of selecting images and preparing them for instructional use in both the photographic and digital environments are set out in the four tables that follow. These tables are built from a cost model of more than three dozen facts, estimates, and assumptions about Professor Scully's course and the library support it requires.[16] The appendix presents the model, with some information obscured to protect confidentiality. I do not explain the details of the cost model here[17] but focus instead on what it tells us. One cautionary word is in order. The cost model generates the numbers given in the tables (rounded to the nearest dollar, producing minor summing errors), but these numbers are probably meaningful only to the nearest $500. In the discussion that follows, I round the numbers accordingly.

Table 4.1 compares the cost of library support for Professor Scully's course in its former dependence on photos exhibited in the study gallery and in its present dependence on digital images delivered in a Web site.[18]

Before the Scully Project, the university incurred about $7,000 in academic support costs for Professor Scully's course in the year it was taught. These costs over a six-year period, during which the course would be taught three times, are estimated at $22,000. As deployed in the fall of 1996, Web-site support for Professor Scully's course cost an estimated $21,000, or $34,000 over a six-year period. The result is a $12,500 balance arguing against digital provision of images in Professor Scully's course, or a 36% productivity loss in the use of university resources. However, a longer amortization period clearly works in favor of digital provision. The cost model suggests that the break-even point on the productive use of university resources comes in about 16 rather than 6 years.[19] This gradual improvement happens for the following reasons:

- The higher absolute cost of the digital images results from one-time staff and vendor cost of converting analog images to digital format. While there is some incremental growth in these costs over six years, staff costs for providing analog images grows linearly. The long-term structure of these costs favors digital provision.

- The cost of the "real" space of bricks and mortar needed to house the photo collection is substantial and grows every year. Similarly, the operation and maintenance of physical space carries the relative high increases of costs for staff and energy. By contrast, the "virtual" space of digital media is relatively inexpensive to begin with, and its unit cost is falling rapidly. Again, the long-term structure of costs favors digital provision.

TABLE 4.1. "As Done" Condition:
1,250 Images Used Primarily for Memory Training

1st Year and Cumulative 6-Year Expenses	400 Photos		1,250 Digital Images	
	1st Year	6-Year Total	1st Year	6-Year Total
Preparation of images				
Full-time library staff for photo collection	797	2,392	6,200	7,440
Library student staff	10	30		
Selection of digital images for digitizing			6,200	7,440
Digitization of images			2,800	3,360
Web site design			1,500	1,500
Selection of images for class use				
Library student staff (mounting photos, etc.)	310	930		
Teaching Fellows (selecting photos)	980	2,940		
Teaching Fellows (selecting slides)	1,120	3,360	1,120	3,360
Preservation of images				
Library student staff	45	271		
Collection shelving space (capital)	70	417		
Collection shelving space (maintenance)	19	113		
Digital storage and access			470	2,049
Study space				
Photo study gallery (capital)	2,986	8,959		
Photo study gallery (maintenance)	812	2,436		
Network connections			3,000	9,000
Totals	$7,149	$21,849	$21,290	$34,149
Film/photo less digital			($14,141)	($12,300)
Productive (unproductive) use of resources				−36%
Funding source				
Library	1,163	3,624	17,170	21,789
Art history department	2,100	6,300	1,120	3,360
University space costs	3,887	11,925	3,000	9,000
Totals	$7,149	$21,849	$21,290	$34,149

Along with the amortization period, the number of images digitized is another major variable that can be used to lower the total cost of digital provision and so move toward a productive use of resources. For years, it has been possible to mount no more than 400 photos in the study gallery. As Table 4.2 shows, if the Scully Web site had contained 400 digital images rather than 1,250 images, conversion costs

TABLE 4.2. "What If" Condition #1:
400 Images Used Primarily for Memory Training

1st Year and Cumulative 6-Year Expenses	*400 Photos*		*400 Digital Images*	
	1st Year	6-Year Total	1st Year	6-Year Total
Preparation of images				
Full-time library staff for photo collection	797	2,392	*2,067*	*2,480*
Library student staff	10	30		
Selection of digital images for digitizing			*2,067*	*2,480*
Digitization of images			*933*	*1,120*
Web site design			1,500	1,500
Selection of images for class use				
Library student staff (mounting photos, etc.)	310	930		
Teaching Fellows (selecting photos)	980	2,940		
Teaching Fellows (selecting slides)	1,120	3,360	1,120	3,360
Preservation of images				
Library student staff	45	271		
Collection shelving space (capital)	70	417		
Collection shelving space (maintenance)	19	113		
Digital storage and access			157	682
Study space				
Photo study gallery (capital)	2,986	8,959		
Photo study gallery (maintenance)	812	2,436		
Network connections			3,000	9,000
Totals	$7,149	$21,849	$10,843	$20,622
Film/photo less digital			($3,694)	$1,227
Productive (unproductive) use of resources				6%
Funding source				
Library	1,163	3,624	6,723	8,262
Art history department	2,100	6,300	1,120	3,360
University space costs	3,887	11,925	3,000	9,000
Totals	$7,149	$21,849	$10,843	$20,622

(italicized to isolate the changes from Table 4.1) would drop significantly, and the six-year cost of digital provision ($20,500) would be just under the cost of analog provision ($22,000). There is a 6% productivity gain over six years favoring digital provision.

The choice between 400 and 1,250 images has a dramatic impact on costs and productivity. That being so, one must ask what motivates the choice and what impact it has on student learning. Further consideration of this "what if" case is best deferred to the discussion of student productivity .

Speculation about another "what if" case is worthwhile. Professor Scully and his Teaching Fellows made no use of the Web site in the lecture hall or discussion sessions.[20] What if they had been able to depend on the Web site instead of traditional slides for their face-to-face teaching? There is of course a warm debate on whether digital images can match film images in quality or ease of classroom use. The question posed here speculatively assumes no technological reason to favor either analog or digital media and focuses solely on what happens to costs when classroom teaching is factored in.

Two changes are identified (in italics) in Table 4.3. They are (1) the cost savings when Teaching Fellows no longer need to assemble slides for the three classroom discussion sessions that each conducts during the term and (2) the added cost of equipping a classroom for digital instruction.

This "what if" modeling of the Scully Project shows an $11,000 negative balance, or a 34% loss in productivity. While digital provision in this scenario is not productive within six years, the significant comparison is with the 36% loss in productivity without using digital images in the classroom (Table 4.1). The conclusion is that substituting digital technology for the labor of selecting slides is itself productive and moves the overall results of digital provision modestly toward a productive use of university resources. This conclusion is strongly reinforced if one considers a variant "what if" condition in which the Teaching Fellows teach not just 3 of these discussion sessions in a classroom but all 14 of them, and in which each Fellow selects his or her own slides instead of depending in considerable measure on slides selected by the head Teaching Fellow. This scenario is modeled in Table 4.4. As a comparison of Tables 4.3 and 4.4 indicates, the weekly cost of selecting slides in this new scenario increases 12-fold, while the use of the electronic classroom increases fivefold. That the classroom costs are absolutely the lower number to begin with also helps drive this scenario to the highly favorable result of a 44% increase in productivity.

It is important to emphasize that these scenarios all assume that funds for Teaching Fellows are fungible in the same way that the library's operating and capital budgets are assumed to be fungible. Faculty and graduate students are most unlikely to make that assumption. Graduate education is one of the core products of a research university. The funds that support it will not be traded about in the way one imagines trades between the operating and capital funds being made for a unit, like the library, that supports education but does not constitute its core product.

TABLE 4.3.   "What If" Condition #2:
1,250 Images Used for Memorization and Instruction

1st Year and Cumulative 6-Year Expenses	400 Photos		1,250 Digital Images	
	1st Year	6-Year Total	1st Year	6-Year Total
Preparation of images				
Full-time library staff for photo collection	797	2,392	6,200	7,440
Library student staff	10	30		
Selection of digital images for digitizing			6,200	7,440
Digitization of images			2,800	3,360
Web site design			1,500	1,500
Selection of images for class use				
Library student staff (mounting photos, etc.)	310	930		
Teaching Fellows (selecting photos)	980	2,940		
Teaching Fellows (selecting slides)	1,120	3,360	*0*	*0*
Preservation of images				
Library student staff	45	271		
Collection shelving space (capital)	70	417		
Collection shelving space (maintenance)	19	113		
Digital storage and access			470	2,049
Study space				
Photo study gallery (capital)	2,986	8,959		
Photo study gallery (maintenance)	812	2,436		
Digitally equipped classroom (capital)			*692*	*2,075*
Digitally equipped classroom (maintenance)			*69*	*208*
Network connections			3,000	9,000
Totals	$7,149	$21,849	$20,931	$33,071
Film/photo less digital			($13,782)	($11,222)
Productive (unproductive) use of resources				−34%
Funding source				
Library	1,163	3,624	17,170	21,789
Art history department	2,100	6,300	0	0
University space costs	3,887	11,925	3,761	11,283
Totals	$7,149	$21,849	$20,931	$33,071

TABLE 4.4. "What If" Condition #3:
1,250 Images Used for Memorization and Instruction

1st Year and Cumulative 6-Year Expenses	400 Photos		1,250 Digital Images	
	1st Year	6-Year Total	1st Year	6-Year Total
Preparation of images				
Full-time library staff for photo collection	797	2,392	6,200	7,440
Library student staff	10	30		
Selection of digital images for digitizing			6,200	7,440
Digitization of images			2,800	3,360
Web site design			1,500	1,500
Selection of images for class use				
Library student staff (mounting photos, etc.)	310	930		
Teaching Fellows (selecting photos)	980	2,940		
Teaching Fellows (selecting slides, 700 hours)	14,000	42,000	*0*	*0*
Preservation of images				
Library student staff	45	271		
Collection shelving space (capital)	70	417		
Collection shelving space (maintenance)	19	113		
Digital storage and access			470	2,049
Study space				
Photo study gallery (capital)	2,986	8,959		
Photo study gallery (maintenance)	812	2,436		
Digitally equipped classroom (capital)			*3,358*	*10,075*
Digitally equipped classroom (maintenance)			*336*	*1,008*
Network connections			3,000	9,000
Totals	$20,029	$60,489	$23,864	$41,871
Film/photo less digital			($3,835)	$18,618
Productive (unproductive) use of resources				44%
Funding source				
Library	1,163	3,624	17,170	21,789
Art history department	14,980	44,940	0	0
University space costs	3,887	11,925	6,694	20,083
Totals	$20,029	$60,489	$23,864	$41,871

Productivity Gains Subject to Reader Control

Having accounted for the costs and potential productivity gains that are substantially under the university's administrative control, I will look briefly at potential productivity gains that lie beyond such control—the productivity of readers. In doing this we must consider the value of the qualitative differences between film and digital technologies for supporting Professor Scully's course. The availability of the images throughout the semester at all times of day and night, rather than just before exams, and the large increase in the number of images available for study constitute improvements in quality that make any discussion of increased productivity difficult—but interesting and important as well.

Students were enthusiastic about the convenience of the Web site. They could examine the images more closely, without competing for limited viewing space, at any time they wished. Without question this availability made their study time more efficient and possibly—though the evidence is inconclusive—more effective.

Let us focus first on the possibility that, as one of the Teaching Fellows observed, students learned more easily but did not learn more. Let us imagine, arbitrarily, that on average students were able to spend two hours less on memory training over the course of the semester because of easy and effective access to digital images. What is the value of this productivity gain for each of Professor Scully's 500 students? It would probably be possible to develop a dollar value for it, related to the direct cost and the short-term opportunity cost of attending Yale. Otherwise, there is no obvious way to answer the question, because each student will appropriately treat the time as a trivial consideration and use it with no regard for the resources needed to provide it. Whether the time is used for having coffee with friends, for sleeping, for volunteer community work, for additional study and a better term paper, or in some other way, the student alone will decide about the productive use of this time. And because there is no administrative means to cumulate the time saved or bring the student's increased productivity to bear on the creation of the information systems that enable the increase, there is no way to use the values created for the student in the calculation of how productive it was to spend library resources on creating the Scully Project.

The possibility that students would use the time they gain to prepare better for tests or to write a better paper raises the issue of quality improvements. How are we to think about the possibility that the teaching and learning that libraries support with digital information might become not only more efficient and productive, but also just *better*? What are the measures of better, and how were better educational results actually achieved? Was it, for instance, better to have 1,250 images for study rather than 400? The head Teaching Fellow answered with an unequivocal yes, affirming that she saw richer, more thoughtful comparisons among objects being made in student papers. But some student responses suggested they wanted to have on the Web site only those images they were directly responsible for memorizing—many fewer than 1,250. Do more images create new burdens or new opportunities for learning? Which objectives and what standards should guide decisions about enhancing instructional support? In the absence of some economically viable way to support additional costs, how does one decide on quality enhancements?

Such questions about quality traditionally mark the boundary of productivity studies. Considerations of quality drive us to acknowledge that, for education, we generally do not have the two essential features needed to measure productivity: clear measures of outputs and a well-understood production technology that allows one to convert inputs into outputs.[21] In such an environment, we have generally avoided talking about productivity for fear that doing so would distort goals—as when competency-based evaluation produces students who only take tests well.[22] Moreover, the rhetoric of productivity can undermine socially rather than empirically validated beliefs among students, parents, and the public about how higher education achieves its purposes. All institutions of higher education depend fundamentally on the maintenance of such socially validated beliefs.

So I end this account of the Scully Project by observing that what we actually did was not productive, but could be made so by extending the amortization period for the project or by reducing the number of images provided to students.[23] It also appears that the project made study much more convenient for students and may well have enhanced their learning. Such quality improvement, even without measurable productivity gain, is one of the fundamental objectives of the library.

These are conditionally positive findings about the economic productivity and educational value of a shift from photographs to digital images to support instruction in the history of art. Such findings should be tested in other courses and, if confirmed, should guide further investment in digital imaging. The soft finding that the use of digital images in the classroom may be productive is heartening, given that digital images may support improvements in the quality of teaching by simplifying the probing of image details and by enabling much more spontaneity in classroom instruction.[24]

All of my arguments about the Scully Project posit that new investment in digital technology would be supported by reduced spending elsewhere. However, such reductions would be difficult, forcing us to regard capital and operating budgets—especially the funds that support both "real" and "virtual" space—as fungible. Other possible cost shifts involve even more fundamental difficulties. It is, for instance, a degree requirement at Yale that graduate students in the History of Art participate in undergraduate instruction. Teaching discussion sections in Professor Scully's course are often the first opportunity graduate students take for meeting this academic requirement. For this reason and others, none of the shifts imagined in the scenarios described above would be easily achieved, and some would challenge us to revisit strongly embedded administrative practices and academic values. Funds rarely flow across such organizational boundaries. Failing to make at least some of these shifts would, however, imperil our ability to improve the quality and productivity of higher education.

PRODUCTIVITY AS AN URGENT CONCERN OF HIGHER EDUCATION

For a long time, higher education has behaved as if compelling opportunities for improving student learning should be pursued without much attention to productivity issues. Our community has focused on desirable results, on the outputs of the productivity formula, without disciplined attention to the inputs part of the equation.[25] One result has been that expenditures per student at public universities in the United States grew between 1979 and 1989 at an average annual rate of 1.82% *above* inflation. The annual growth rate for private universities was a much higher 3.36%.[26]

It is hard to believe that such patterns of cost increase can be sustained much longer or that we can continue simply to increase the price of higher education as the principal means for improving it and especially for meeting apparently insatiable demands for information technology. We must seriously engage with issues of productivity. Otherwise, there will be little to determine the pace of technology innovation except the squeaky wheel of student or faculty demand or, less commonly, an institutional vision for technology-enhanced education. In neither case is there economically cogent guidance for the right level of investment in information technology. We are left to invest as much as we can, with nothing but socially validated political and educational ideas about what the phrase "as much as we can" actually means. Because we so rarely close the economic loop between the productivity value we create for users and our investment in technology, the language for decision making almost never reaches beyond that of improving convenience and enhancing quality. I believe it is vitally important for managers of information technology to understand the fundamental economic disconnect in the language of convenience and service we primarily use and to add the language of productivity to our deliberations about investing in information technology.

In connecting productivity gains with technology investment, we may find—as analysis of the Scully Project suggests—that some improvements can be justified while others cannot. Productivity measures should not be the sole guide to investment in information technology. But by insisting on securing productivity gains where we can, we will at least identify appropriate if sometimes only partial sources for funding new investments and thereby lower the rate at which overall costs rise in higher education above those in the rest of the economy.[27]

The stakes for higher education in acting on the productivity problems confronting it are immense. Today, it is regularly asserted that administrative activities are wasteful and should be made more productive. But turning to core academic activities, especially teaching, we feel that no productivity gains can be made without compromising quality. Teaching is rather like playing in a string quartet. A string quartet required four musicians in Mozart's day, and it still does. To talk about making the performance of a string quartet more productive is to talk patent nonsense. To talk about making classroom teaching more productive seems to many almost as objectionable. The observable result is that higher education has had to live off the productivity gains of other sectors of the economy. The extreme pressure on all of higher education's income sources suggests that we are coming to the end of the time when people are willing uncritically to transfer wealth to higher education. Socially validated beliefs about the effectiveness of higher education are in serious jeopardy.[28] If our community continues to stare blindly at these facts, if we refuse to engage seriously with productivity issues on an institutional and community-wide basis, we will bring disaster upon the enterprise of teaching and learning to which we have devoted our professional lives.

If this seems alarmist, consider the work of 10 governors in the western United States intent on creating a high-tech, virtual university, the Western Governors' University.[29] Faced with growing populations and burgeoning demand for higher education, but strong taxpayer resistance to meeting that demand through the traditional cost structures of higher education, state officials are determined to create a much more productive regional system of higher education. That productivity is the key issue is evident in the statement of Alvin Meiklejohn, the chairman of the State Senate Education Committee in Colorado. "Many students in Colorado," he said, "are now taking six years to get an A.B. degree. If we could reduce that by just one year . . . it would reduce the cost to the student by one-sixth and also free up some seats in the classrooms for the tidal wave we see coming our way."[30]

Senator Meiklejohn is looking for a 17% increase in productivity. I think library and information technology managers know where some of that gain may be found. If, however, we scoff at the idea of increasing student productivity through the use of information technologies, if we insist that the job of measuring and redirecting the productivity gains we create with information technology is impossible, if we trap ourselves in the language of convenience and fail to engage with issues of productivity, then the consequences—at least in the West—are clear. Major new investment in higher education will be directed not to established institutions but to new organizations that can meet the productivity standards insisted on by Senator Meiklejohn and the taxpayers he represents.

A second and larger groundswell in American life is also instructive on the question of productivity. Health care reform and managed care are both driven by the idea that the high cost and poor delivery of health care must change, that costs must be controlled—that health care services must become much more productive.[31] Arguments about the incompatibility of higher productivity and the maintenance of quality care resonate strongly with parallel arguments about the impossibility of making higher education more productive without compromising quality. What makes the health care debate so instructive is that we already know which side will prevail. Everywhere we turn, medical institutions and the practitioners who lead them are scrambling to find ways to survive within a managed care environment. Survival means the preservation of quality care, to be sure, but the ineluctable reality is that quality will now be defined within terms set by managed care. We are beginning to find ways to talk about increased productivity and quality as complementary rather than as antithetical ideas.

Given the current state of public opinion about higher education, it is impossible for me to believe we will not soon follow health care. We will almost certainly find ourselves embroiled in divisive, rancorous debates about higher education reform. I hope we will avail ourselves in these debates of a language about information technology that continues to embrace ideas of convenience but reaches strongly beyond them. We will need to talk meaningfully about productivity and link our ability to create productivity gains with investment in information technology. And I hope we will follow the medical community in working to make productivity and quality regularly cognate rather than always antagonistic ideas.

For the past 150 years or so, libraries have been the guardians in the Western world of socially equitable access to information. Libraries have become public institutions instead of institutions serving powerful elites, as they once were. This is a noble heritage and a worthy ongoing mission for our profession. And information technology will play a key role in advancing it. As Richard Lanham argues in a landmark essay, "if our business is general literacy, as some of us think, then electronic instructional systems offer the only hope for the radically leveraged mass instruction the problems of general literacy pose."[32] But unless information technologies are employed productively, they will not offer the leverage on information access and literacy for which Lanham and others of us hope. Indeed, unless those who manage libraries and other instruments of scholarly discourse are prepared to embrace the language of productivity, we will find our ability to provide socially equitable access to information weakened as decisions are made about where investments for democratic education will be directed. I look at managed health care and the Western Governors' University and fear that traditional universities and their libraries will lose ground, not because we have failed to embrace information technology, but because we have failed to embrace it productively. I fear that outcome most because it imperils the wonderful accomplishment of libraries and because it could significantly weaken the public good that free libraries have been creating for the past 150 years.

APPENDIX

Cost Model for the Scully Project

The cost model uses the following facts, estimates, and assumptions:

Introduction to the History of Art, 112a
— Course offered once every two years; three times in six years
— Number of students enrolled in Scully course = 500/term
— Number of weeks Scully photos available in study space = 9 weeks per term
— Length of term = 14 weeks
— Number of Teaching Fellows for Scully course = 25
— Approximate value/hour of Teaching Fellow time = $20
— Hourly wage for library student staff = $6.46

Staff costs for selection, maintenance, and display of slide and photo images
— 1 FTE permanent staff devoted to photo collection = $xx,xxx for salary and benefits
— % of permanent library staff effort devoted to Scully course = x%
— Library student staff devoted to photo collection = 40% of $11,500 = $4,600 at $6.46/hr = 712 hrs
— Library student staff devoted to exhibiting Scully photos = 48 hrs/year
— Time spent by Teaching Fellows assembling photo study = 3.5 hr/wk × 14 wks = 49 hrs
— Time spent by Teaching Fellows assembling slides for review classes = 56 hrs

Cost to prepare digital images for instructional use
— Number of images in Scully Project = 1,250
— Digitization of images (outsourced) = $2,800
— Change in Scully Project Web site content over 6 years = 20%
— Selection and creation of images (by 2 Teaching Fellows) = $6,200
— Web site design = $1,500

Preservation and access costs for slide, photo, and digital images
— Library student staff hours spent on mending and maintenance of photos = 7 hrs/year
— Disk space required for Scully Project = .855 GB
— Disk space required per volume for Project Open Book = .015 GB
— Scully Project images = 57 Open Book vols
— Digital Storage costs = $2.58/year/Open Book vol

— Digital access costs = \$5.67/year/Open Book vol
— Storage and access cost inflation = -13%/year

Study and other space costs
— Number of items in photo collection = 182,432
— Number of Scully photos mounted in study space = 200 for midterm; 400 for final
— NSF of photo collection in Street Hall = 1,733
— NSF collection shelving for Scully photos = $400/182,432 \times (1,733 - 500)$ = 2.7
— NSF of photo study space = $2,019 + .25 \times 1500 = 2,394$
— % of photo study space devoted to Scully photos per term = 20%
— NSF of photo study space available for Scully photos = $2,394 \times .2 \times (9/28) = 154$
— NSF of photo study space utilized during term = $154 \times 75\% = 116$
— Annual cost of space maintenance = \$7 NSF
— Cost of new construction = \$300 NSF
— Amortization of capital costs at 8% over 35 yrs = \$85.81 per \$1,000
— Capital cost of converting existing classroom for digital display = \$50,000 depreciated over 6 years
— Maintenance of digital classroom hardware and software = 10% of capital cost/year = \$5,000/year
— Availability of digital classroom = 8 class hours $\times$ 5 days/wk $\times$ 28 wks $\times$ .8 efficiency factor = 896 sessions/yr
— Need by Scully grad assistants for digital classroom sessions = 25×3 = 75 sessions/yr = 8.3% of available sessions
— Annual cost of maintaining a network connection = \$300
— % use of network connection for study of Scully Web site = 2%

NOTES

1. See, for instance, Tefko Saracevic and Paul Kantor, "Studying the Value of Library and Information Services," *Journal of the American Society for Information Science* 48 (June 1997): 527–563. The terms used by readers to describe values attributed to the use of libraries include "convenience" and closely related concepts, such as "effort required" and "frustration." Saracevic and Kantor observe that users rarely assign monetary value to library services but often refer to their time saved.

2. "How Libraries Can Help to Pay Their Way in the Future," *Logos* 7, no. 3 (1996): 238. See also Bowen's paper, "JSTOR and the Economics of Scholarly Communication," presented at the Council on Library Resources conference held in October 1995 (available at *http://www.mellon.org/jstor.html*).

3. *The Andrew W. Mellon Foundation Report, from January 1, 1994 through December 31, 1994* (New York, 1995), 19; *The Andrew W. Mellon Foundation Report, from January 1, 1995 through December 31, 1995* (New York, 1996), 48.

4. A good general account of productivity is provided by the National Research Council, Panel to Review Productivity Statistics, *Measurement and Interpretation of Productivity* (Washington, D.C., 1979).

5. The productivity gains expected of information technology have sometimes been slow to appear, creating the so-called productivity paradox. Federal Reserve Board economist William Wascher argues we have had unrealistic expectations of information technology, which accounted for less than 8% of equipment expenditure in 1994 and was a "relatively minor input in the production process" (BNA Daily Report for Executives, 10 September 1996, p. C3).

6. For a fuller account of the difficulties, see Morton Owen Schapiro, "The Concept of Productivity as Applied to U.S. Higher Education," in *Paying the Piper: Productivity, Incentives, and Financing in U.S. Higher Education*, by Michael S. McPherson, Morton Owen Schapiro, and Gordon C. Winston (Ann Arbor, 1993), 37–68.

7. Libraries are no strangers to concerns about productivity. Indeed, the successful application of information technology to library cataloging is one of the great if not widely acknowledged productivity success stories of higher education. At Yale, the largest library investments we are now making—ranging from preserving and shelving the collections to the retrospective conversion of catalog records and the on-line delivery of information—are fundamentally motivated by productivity issues. The productivity issues that inform decisions to build off-campus shelving are particularly interesting. They involve productivity trade-offs between traditionally impermeable operating and capital budgets and appear to put the productivity of library operations in competition with reader productivity needs.

8. See, for instance, Frank Guliuzza III, "Asking Professor Jones to Fix the Crisis in Higher Education is Getting More and More Expensive," *Academe* (September/October 1996): 29–32.

9. See, for instance, Robert Zemsky and William F. Massy, "Expanding Perimeters, Melting Cores, and Sticky Functions: Toward an Understanding of Our Current Predicaments," *Change* (November/December 1995): 41–49; William F. Massy, *Resource Allocation in Higher Education* (Ann Arbor, 1996); and Charles T. Clotfelter, *Buying the Best: Cost Escalation in Elite Higher Education* (Princeton, 1996).

10. Arthur Levine, "Higher Education's New Status as a Mature Industry," *Chronicle of Higher Education*, 31 January 1997, A48.

11. This description of the Scully Project and parts of my commentary on it draw heavily on Max Marmor's Preliminary Report on the project of 6 September 1996. I am much indebted to Mr. Marmor, Christine de Vallet, and Donald J. Waters for their collegial and critical review of the ideas advanced in this paper and to Elizabeth Owen for her neverfailing and generous willingness to describe the practices of the Teaching Fellows in Professor Scully's course.

12. To achieve these results, the project managers enlisted the help of a senior administrator and two Webmasters at Yale's Information Technology Services, a graphic designer from University Printing Service, and student assistants for HTML markup and image manipulation. For copyright reasons, access to this Web site is restricted to members of the Yale community.

13. Mistakes in the administration of a survey left us without statistically meaningful measures of student use of the Web site or opinions about it.

14. Some, but not all, of the Teaching Fellows made use of the Web site in preparing for their classes and in making assignments. The e-mail addresses for Teaching Fellows provided at the Web site encouraged some exchanges with instructors outside of class sessions.

15. Dr. Carl Jaffe is director of the Center for Advanced Instructional Media at the Yale School of Medicine. The center was founded in 1987 to explore the educational and communications potential of new interactive multimedia computing technology. Through the center, the Yale University School of Medicine is one of the leading developers and publishers of multimedia medical education programs. The center is a recognized leader in information design, medical illustration, and interface design for networked information. Center projects have won many national and international awards for excellence in educational design and technological leadership. More information about the center is available on the Web at *http://info.med.yale.edu/caim/*.

16. Absent from the cost model is any consideration of copyright management costs. This is a significant and unsettled matter in the use of digital images for instructional support. The presence or absence of such costs in a full-scale digital image database would have a significant impact on the bottom-line results of the cost model.

17. However, estimating the cost of maintaining the Scully Project data over time does deserve some discussion. The primary experience of universities in doing this estimating lies in maintaining on-line catalog data and—more recently—in maintaining institutional business data as we adopt new administrative software to solve the Year 2000 and other problems. We have learned that it is very expensive to maintain bibliographic and business data over time as we move from one computing environment to another. Institutions generally do not budget for these costs. Recognizing that past practice is an unacceptable model for the preservation of library materials, Yale's Open Book Project endeavored to model the cost of reliably preserving large bodies of full-text library material in digital form over long periods of time. The Open Book cost model, applied to the Scully Project, suggests that the cost of maintaining a small Web site is $470 a year or $2,049 for six years. Focused attention to preservation is required because digital media are inherently the most unstable of information storage media, and hardware and software have high obsolescence rates. If we do not heed *Preserving Digital Information: Report of the Task Force on Archiving of Digital Information*, with its sobering account of the technical difficulties and significant costs involved in the long-term preservation of digital information, we will find the wonders of our silicon-based technologies to be houses built on sand. The *Report* was commissioned by the Commission on Preservation and Access and the Research Libraries Group, Inc., and published by the commission in May 1996; its work was led by Donald J. Waters and John Garrett.

18. This comparison assumes these are alternative means of support rather than duplicative. In fact, both means of support were provided in the fall 1996 term, and students made use of both.

19. That is, the cost model shows a −$703 balance over 16 years, or essentially break-even performance on 16-year expenditures of $59,000. Of course, it is quite unlikely that the facts, estimates, and assumptions used in the cost model would remain static for as long as 16 years.

20. Teaching Fellows conduct most of their discussion sessions in the Yale University Art Gallery, to relate Professor Scully's lectures to actual museum objects. They conduct conventional classroom discussions, supported by slides, only three times each during the

term. For the sake of simplicity, the cost model deals only with these conventional class-room sessions and does not try to model the cost of bringing digital images to locations throughout the gallery. Teaching Fellows often bring photographs to the gallery to enrich the discussions, so access to digital images there would actually be quite valuable.

21. See National Research Council, *Measurement and Interpretation of Productivity*, 33–34.

22. See, for instance, Kenneth H. Ashworth, "Virtual Universities Could Produce Only Virtual Learning," *Chronicle of Higher Education*, 6 September 1996, A88.

23. Another "what if" scenario, not developed here, for increasing the productivity of the investment in digital images is to imagine Professor Scully's Introduction to the History of Art being *taught* on the Web, with a large increase in enrollments beyond the 500 that the lecture hall now permits. This distance learning scenario raises a host of questions, not least that of how the rights to the image content of such a course would be secured and managed.

24. This finding is most tentative, given that the cost model is sensitive to the highly variable costs of equipping a classroom for digitally supported instruction.

25. This lack of attention is evident in the *Chronicle of Higher Education* account of Professor Stephen Murray's use of video media to teach architecture at Columbia University (see "Video Technology Transforms the Teaching of Art History," *Chronicle of Higher Education*, 14 February 1997, A20–22). Having described Murray's remarkable video presentation of Amiens Cathedral that cost some hundreds of thousands of dollars, the *Chronicle* reporter Lisa Guernsey describes Murray as insisting "the projects are worth it. 'What really convinces us is how they inspire students in the classroom,' [Murray] says. 'They are captivated to study further'" (A22).

26. Scott W. Blasdell, Michael S. McPherson, and Morton Owen Schapiro, "Trends in Revenues and Expenditures in U.S. Higher Education: Where Does the Money Come From? Where Does It Go?" in McPherson, Schapiro, and Winston, *Paying the Piper*, 17. A recent General Accounting Office report found that tuition at four-year public colleges has risen nearly three times as much as median household income over the past 15 years; see *Chronicle of Higher Education*, 6 September 1996, A59.

27. And in observing comparative measures of productivity gain in libraries and other operations of the university, we will also have created a powerful tool for helping to decide among competing technology investment strategies.

28. See "Why Colleges Cost Too Much," a so-called investigative report on higher education costs (as exemplified by those at the University of Pennsylvania) by Erik Larson in *Time*, 17 March 1997.

29. The Western Governors' University has been widely reported over the past two years. See, for instance, the account in the *New York Times*, 25 September 1996, B9. The *Chronicle of Higher Education* for 27 September 1996, A35–36, reports a similar initiative among twelve Scandinavian institutions.

30. *New York Times*, 25 Sept. 1996, B9.

31. See, for instance, Theodore Marmor and Mark Goldberg, "American Health Care Reform: Separating Sense from Nonsense," in *Understanding Health Care Reform* by Theodore Marmor (New Haven, 1994), 15–18.

32. Richard Lanham, "The Electronic Word: Literary Study and the Digital Revolution," in Richard Lanham, *The Electronic Word: Democracy, Technology, and the Arts* (Chicago, 1993), 23.

CHAPTER 5

Comparing Electronic Journals
to Print Journals
Are There Savings?

Janet H. Fisher

Three years ago the rhetoric of academics and librarians alike urged publishers to get on with it—to move their publications from print to electronic formats. The relentless pressure on library budgets from annual increases of 10 to 20% in serials prices made many academics and librarians look to electronic publication as the savior that would allow librarians to retain their role in the scholarly communication chain. Academics and university administrators were urged to start their own publications and take back ownership of their own research. The future role of the publisher was questioned: What did they do after all? Since so many scholars were now creating their own works on computer, why couldn't they just put them up on the Net? Who needs proofreading, copyediting, and design anymore? And since technology has made it possible for everyone to become a publisher, surely electronic publication would be cheaper than print.

Quite a few experiments in the last three years have tried to answer some of the questions posed by the emergence of the Internet, but few have yielded hard numbers to date. Most experiments have been focused on developing electronic versions of print products. MIT Press took a piece of the puzzle that we saw as important in the long run and within the capabilities of a university-based journal publisher with space and staff constraints. Many of our authors had been using e-mail, mailing lists, discussion groups, and so on, for 10 years or more, and we wanted to be visible on the Internet early.

We decided it was easier, cheaper, and less of a financial risk to try publishing a purely electronic journal rather than reengineering our production and delivery process for our print journals when we had so little feedback about what authors and customers really wanted. Starting with *Chicago Journal of Theoretical Computer Science* (CJTCS), which was announced in late 1994 and which began publication in June of 1995, we began publishing our first purely electronic journals. CJTCS, as well as *Journal of Functional and Logic Programming* (JFLP) and *Journal of Contem-*

porary Neurology (JCN), are published article-by-article. We ask subscribers to pay an annual subscription fee, but we have not yet installed elaborate mechanisms to ensure that only those who pay have access to the full text. *Studies in Nonlinear Dynamics and Econometrics* (SNDE), begun in 1996, is published quarterly in issues with the full text password protected. Another issue-based electronic journal—*Videre: Journal of Computer Vision Research*—began publishing in the fall of 1997. You can view these publications at our Web site *(http://mitpress.mit.edu/)*.

The lack of one format for all material available in electronic format has been a problem for these electronic journals and our production staff. The publication format varies from journal to journal based on several criteria:

- the format most often received from authors
- the content of the material (particularly math, tables, special characters)
- the cost to implement
- the availability of appropriate browser technology

CJTCS and JFLP are published in LaTeX and PostScript in addition to PDF (Adobe's Portable Document Format), which was added in 1997. JCN is published in PDF and HTML (Hypertext Markup Language, the language of the World Wide Web) because the PostScript files were too large to be practical. SNDE is published in PostScript and PDF. *Videre* is published in PDF.

Here I will present our preliminary results on the costs of electronic-only journals and compare them to the costs of traditional print journals. I will use *Chicago Journal of Theoretical Computer Science* as the model but will include relevant information from our experience with our other electronic journals.

BACKGROUND ON THE PROJECT

CJTCS was announced in fall of 1994 and began publication in June of 1995. Material is forwarded to us from the journal editor once the review process and revisions have been completed. Four articles were published from June through December of 1995, and six articles were published in 1996. The Web site is hosted at the University of Chicago, with entry from the MIT Press Web site. The production process includes the following steps:

1. manuscript is copyedited
2. copyedited manuscript is returned to author
3. author's response goes back to copyeditor
4. final copyedited article goes to "typesetter"
5. typesetter enters edits/tagging/formatting
6. article is proofread
7. author sees formatted version
8. typesetter makes final corrections
9. article is published (i.e., posted on the site)

Tagging and "typesetting" has been done by Michael J. O'Donnell, managing editor of CJTCS, who is a professor at University of Chicago.

The subscription price is $30 per year for individuals and $125 per year for institutions. When an article is published, subscribers receive an e-mail message announcing its publication. Included is the title, the author, the abstract, the location of the file, and the articles published to date in the volume. Articles are numbered sequentially in the volume (e.g., 1996–1, 1996–2). Individuals and institutions are allowed to use the content liberally, with permission to do the following:

- read articles directly from the official journal servers or from any other server that grants them access
- copy articles to their own file space for temporary use
- form a permanent archive of articles, which they may keep even after their subscription lapses
- display articles in the ways they find most convenient (on computer, printed on paper, converted to spoken form, etc.)
- apply agreeable typographical styles from any source to lay out and display articles
- apply any information retrieval, information processing, and browsing software from any source to aid their study of articles
- convert articles to other formats from the LaTeX and PostScript forms on the official servers
- share copies of articles with other subscribers
- share copies of articles with nonsubscribing collaborators as a direct part of their collaborative study or research

Library subscribers may also

- print individual articles and other items for inclusion in their periodical collection or for placing on reserve at the request of a faculty member
- place articles on their campus network for access by local users, or post article listings and notices on the network
- share print or electronic copy of articles with other libraries under standard interlibrary loan procedures

In February 1996, Michael O'Donnell installed a HyperNews feature to accompany each article, which allows readers to give feedback on articles. Forward pointers, which were planned to update the articles with appropriate citations to other material published later, have not yet been instituted.

Archiving arrangements were made with (1) the MIT Libraries, which is creating archival microfiche and archiving the PostScript form of the files; (2) MIT Information Systems, which is storing the LaTeX source on magnetic tape and refreshing it periodically; and (3) the Virginia Polytechnic Institute Scholarly Communications Project, which is mirroring the site *(http://scholar.lib.vt.edu)*.

DIRECT COSTS OF PUBLICATION

To date, CJTCS has published ten articles with a total of 244 pages. I have chosen to compare the direct costs we have incurred in publishing those 244 pages with the direct costs we incurred for a 244-page issue (Volume 8, Number 5, July 1996) of one of our print journals, *Neural Computation* (NC). NC has a print run of approximately 2,000 copies, and typesetting is done from LaTeX files supplied by the authors (as is the case for CJTCS) (Table 5.1). Several important differences in production processes affect these costs:

1. The number of articles published is different (10 in CJTCS, 12 in NC).
2. The copyeditor handles author queries for NC and bills us hourly. This contributed $100 to its copyediting bill.
3. Composition for CJTCS is done on a flat fee basis of $200 per article. Tagging and formatting has been done by Michael O'Donnell, the journal's managing editor at University of Chicago, because we were unable to find a traditional vendor willing to tag on the basis of content rather than format. The $200 figure was developed in conjunction with a LaTeX coding house that we planned to use initially but that was unable to meet the journal's schedule requirements. In comparison, the typesetting cost per article for NC is approximately $326, which includes a $58 per article charge for producing repro pages to send to the printer and a $21 per article charge for author alteration charges. These items are not included on the CJTCS composition bills.

For comparison, Table 5.2 shows the direct costs associated with three other electronic journals to date: *Journal of Contemporary Neurology* (JCN), *Journal of Functional and Logic Programming* (JFLP), and *Studies in Nonlinear Dynamics and Econometrics* (SNDE). JCN's cost per page is much higher than the other e-journals because the typesetter produces PDF and HTML formats and deals with complex images.

The issue-based electronic journal *Studies in Nonlinear Dynamics and Econometrics* (SNDE) is comparable in direct costs with a standard print journal, with the only difference being the lack of printing and binding costs. Table 5.3 is a comparison of the direct costs incurred for SNDE, Volume 1, Number 1, April 1996 (76 pages) and an 80-page issue (Volume 8, Number 4, Fall 1995) of one of our print journals, *Computing Systems* (COSY), that follows a similar production path.

Composition cost per page is comparable in these journals, but the total pro-

TABLE 5.1.   Production Costs by Article of Electronic
and Print Journals

	CJTCS	*NC*	*% Difference*
Copyediting/proofreading	$1,114	$1,577	+42%
Composition	$2,070	$3,914	+89%
Printing and binding	—	$6,965	—
Total production cost	$3,184	$12,456	+291%
Composition cost per page	$8.48	$16.24	+92%
Total production cost per page	$13.05	$51.05	+291%

TABLE 5.2.   Cost per Page Comparison of Electronic Journals

	# Pages	*# Articles/Issues*	*Direct Costs*	*Cost/Pg*
JCN	34	6 articles	$1,666	$49.00
JFLP	280	7 articles	$2,204	$7.87
SNDE	152	2 issues	$4,184	$27.53

TABLE 5.3.   Cost per Issue Comparison of Electronic
and Print Journals

	SNDE 1:1	*COSY 8:4*
Copyediting/proofreading	$551	$554
Composition	$1,383	$1,371
Printing and binding	—	$6,501
Total production cost	$1,934	$8,426
Composition cost per page	$18.20	$17.57
Total production cost per page	$25.44	$105.33

duction cost per page of SNDE is only 24% of that of COSY, which includes the printing and binding costs associated with a 6,000-copy print run.

INDIRECT COSTS

The overhead costs associated with CJTCS and the comparable issue of NC vary greatly. Overhead for our print journals is allocated on the following basis:

- Production—charged to each journal based on the number of issues published

- Circulation—charged to each journal based on the number of subscribers, the number of issues published, whether the journal has staggered or non-staggered renewals, and whether copies are sold to bookstores and news-stands

- Marketing/General and Administrative—divided evenly among all journals

For CJTCS, MIT Press incurs additional overhead costs associated with the Digital Projects Lab (DPL). These include the cost of staff, and the cost of hardware and software associated with the Press's World Wide Web server. These costs are allocated to each electronic publication on the following basis:

- Costs of hardware and software for the file server, network drops, staff time spent maintaining the server, and so on, are allocated to each e-journal based on the percentage of disk space that the journal files occupy as a function of all Web-related files on our server

- Amount of time per issue or article that DPL staff work on the journal is multiplied by the rate per hour of staff

Table 5.4 shows a comparison of overhead costs associated with CJTCS and the comparable issue of NC. CJTCS's production overhead is much higher than NC's because it is almost the same amount of work to traffic individual articles as it is an entire issue. Even though each batch of material was much smaller in terms of pages than an issue of NC would have been, it still required virtually the same tracking and oversight. Correspondingly, the general and administrative overhead from the journals division for CJTCS is dramatically higher than NC because of the small amount of content published in CJTCS. The overhead costs associated with publishing CJTCS for 1½ years had to be allocated to only 244 pages published, whereas NC published 2,320 pages in the same period of time.

JCN takes additional time from our DPL staff because of the HTML coding and linking of illustrations, which adds an additional $7 per page to its costs. The total of direct and indirect costs per page for JCN is, therefore, in line with our print journals even though there is no printing and binding expense. SNDE incurs an additional $1,400 per issue in indirect costs for the staff, hardware, and software in the DPL.

MARKET DIFFERENCES

The other side of the picture is whether the market reacts similarly to electronic-only products. Since this question is outside the scope of this paper, I will only generalize here from our experience to date. For the four electronic journals we have started, the average paid circulation to date is approximately 100, with 20 to 40 of those being institutional subscriptions. For the two print journals we started in 1996 (both in the social sciences), the average circulation at the end of their first volumes (1996) was 550, with an average of 475 individuals and 75 institutions.

TABLE 5.4.   Indirect Cost Comparison by Article
of Electronic and Print Journals

	CJTCS	*NC 8:5*
Journals department		
Production	$8,000	$1,000
Fulfillment cost per subscriber	$108	$1
General and administrative	$31,050	$2,300
Digital projects lab		
Staff	$200	—
Hardware and software	$5,000	—
Total overhead per subscriber	$44,358	$3,301
OH costs per page published	$182	$14

There appears to be a substantial difference in the readiness of the market to accept electronic-only journals at this point as well as reluctance on the part of the author community to submit material. It is, therefore, more difficult for the publisher to reach break even with only one-fifth of the market willing to purchase, unless subscription prices are increased substantially. Doing this would likely dampen the paid subscriptions even more.

CONCLUSION

From the comparison between CJTCS and NC, it seems that the direct costs of publishing an electronic journal are substantially below that of a print journal with comparable pages. The overhead costs, however, are much higher—1,240% higher in this case—but that figure is adversely affected by the small amount of content published in CJTCS over the course of 18 months of overhead costs compared with NC which published 12 issues over the same period of time. The disparity in the markets for electronic products and print products is, at this point in time, a very big obstacle to their financial viability, as is also the conservatism of the author community.

CHAPTER 6

Electronic Publishing in Academia
An Economic Perspective

Malcolm Getz

The Library at Washington University reports 150,000 hits per year on its electronic, networked *Encyclopedia Britannica* at a cost to the library of $.04 per hit.[1] This use rate seems to be an order of magnitude larger than the use rate of the print version of the document in the library. At the same time, the volunteer Project Gutenberg, whose goal was to build an electronic file of 10,000 classic, public domain texts on the Internet, has failed to sustain itself.[2] The University of Illinois decided it could no longer afford to provide the electronic storage space and no other entity stepped forward to sustain the venture.[3]

A first lesson here is that production values, the quality of indexing and presentation, the packaging and marketing of the work, matter. Those ventures that take the approach of unrestricted free access don't necessarily dominate ventures that collect revenues. When a shopper asks, "What does it cost?" we can naturally respond, "What is it worth to you?" Electronic communication among academics is growing when it is valuable. In contemplating investments in electronic publishing, the publishers', and indeed academia's, goal is to create the most value for the funds invested. Generally, the freebie culture that launched the Internet represents only a subset of a much wider range of possible uses. Many quality information products that flow through the Net will be generating revenue flows sufficient to sustain them.

The *Encyclopedia* gives a second lesson, namely, that the costs of electronic distribution may be significantly less than print. Serviceable home encyclopedias on CD now cost about $50 and *Britannica CD '98 Multimedia Edition* is $125, a small fraction of the $1,500 price for the 32-volume print edition of the same *Encyclopedia*. *Britannica* also offers a World Wide Web subscription at $85 per year or $8.50 per month with a discount to purchasers of the print or CD product. The World Wide Web service is updated thrice annually and offers more articles than the print edition. Of course, the price charged for a given format may reflect differences in the price elasticities of demand. Nevertheless, the lower price for the electronic product is consistent with a considerable cost advantage.

Indeed, the latest word processing software includes tools that will allow anyone who uses word processing to create documents tagged for posting on the World Wide Web. Essentially, anyone who owns a current vintage computer with sufficient network connection can make formatted text with tables and graphics available instantly to everyone on the Net. The cost of such communication is a small fraction of the cost of photocopying and mailing documents.

An important consequence of the dramatic decline in the cost of sharing documents is the likelihood of a dramatic increase in the quantity of material available. Everyone who writes may post the whole history of their work on the Web at little incremental cost. Availability is then hardly an issue.

The challenge to academia is to invest in services that will turn the ocean of data into sound, useful, compelling information products. The process of filtering, labeling, refining, and packaging, that is, the process of editing and publishing, takes resources and will be shaped by the electronic world in significant ways. This essay is concerned with this process.

SCHOLAR

Begin with first principles. Academia may become more useful to our society at large by communicating electronically. When electronic scholarship is more valuable, our institutions will invest more.

Scholarship plays three roles in our society. First, academia educates the next generation of professionals, managers, and leaders. Second, it makes formal knowledge available to society at large, stimulating the development of new products, informing debates on public policy, and improving understanding of our culture. Third, it develops new knowledge. Digital communication ought ultimately to be judged by how well it serves these three activities, teaching, service, and research. Consider each in turn.

Access to networked, digital information is already enhancing education. More students at more institutions have access to more information because of the World Wide Web. About 60% of high school graduates now pursue some college, and President Clinton has called for universal access to two years of college.[4] The importance of the educational mission is growing. Of course, today networked information is sporadic and poorly organized relative to what it might someday become. Still, the available search services, rapid access, and the wide availability of the network are sufficient to demonstrate the power of the tool. Contrast the service with a conventional two-year college library whose size depends on the budget of the institution, when access often depends on personal interaction with a librarian, and where a student must plan a visit and sometimes even queue for service. Access to well-designed and supported Web-based information gives promise of promoting a more active style of education. Students may have greater success with more open-ended assignments, may participate in on-line discussion with others pursuing similar topics, and may get faster feedback from more colorful, more interactive materials. Integrating academic information into the wider universe of Web information seems likely to have important benefits for students when it is done well.

Similarly, many audiences for academic information outside the walls of the academy already use the World Wide Web. Engineering Information, Inc. (EI), for example, maintains a subscription Web site for both academic and nonacademic engineers.[5] A core feature of the service is access to the premier index to the academic engineering literature with a fulfillment service. But EI's Village offers on-line access to professional advisers, conversations with authors, and services for practicing engineers. Higher quality, more immediate access to academic information seems likely to play an increasing role in the information sectors of our society, including nearly every career in which some college is a common prerequisite. Higher education seems likely to find wider audiences by moving its best materials to the networked, digital arena.

In the business of generating new knowledge, the use of networked information is already accelerating the pace. Working papers in physics, for example, are more rapidly and widely accessible from the automated posting service at Los Alamos than could possibly be achieved by print.[6] In text-oriented fields, scholars are able to build concordances and find patterns in ways impossible with print. Duke University's digital papyrus, for example, offers images of papyri with rich, searchable descriptive information in text.[7] In economics, the Web gives the possibility of mounting data sets and algorithmic information and so allows scholars to interact with the work of others at a deeper level than is possible in print. For example, Ray Fair maintains his 130-equation model of the U.S. economy on the Web with data sets and a solution method.[8] Any scholar who wants to experiment with alternative estimations and forecasting assumptions in a fully developed simulation model may do so with modest effort. In biology, the Human Genome Project is only feasible because of the ease of electronic communication, the sharing of databases, and the availability of other on-line tools.[9] In visually oriented fields, digital communication offers substantial benefits, as video and sound may be embedded in digital documents. Animated graphics with sound may have significant value in simulation models in science. In art and drama, digital files may allow comparative studies previously unimaginable. Digital communication, then, may have its most significant consequence in accelerating the development of new knowledge.

The pace of investment in digital communication within academia may well be led by its value in education, service broadly defined, and research. In each case, institutional revenues and success may depend on effective deployment of appropriate digital communication. Of course, individual scholars face a significant challenge in mastering the new tools and employing them in appropriate ways. It is also worth emphasizing that not all things digital are valuable. However, when digital tools are well used, they are often significantly more valuable than print.

PUBLISHER

The evolution of the digital arena will be strongly influenced by cost and by pricing policies. Cost is always a two-way street, a reflection, on the one hand, of the choices of authors and publishers who commit resources to publication and, on the other, of the choices of readers and libraries who perceive value. Publishers are challenged to harvest raw materials from the digital ocean and fashion valuable information products. Universities and their libraries must evaluate the possible ways of using digital materials and restructure budgets to deploy their limited resources to best advantage. Between publisher and library stands the electronic agent who may broker the exchange in new ways. Consider first the publisher.

The opportunity to distribute journals electronically has implications for the publishers' costs and revenues. On the cost side, the digital documents can be distributed at lower cost than paper. The network may also reduce some editorial costs. However, sustaining high production values will continue to involve considerable cost because quality editing and presentation are costly. On the revenue side, sale of individual subscriptions may, to some degree, yield to licenses for access via campus intranets and to pay-per-look services.

Publisher Costs

The central fact of the publishing business is the presence of substantial fixed cost with modest variable cost. The cost of gathering, filtering, refining, and packaging shapes the quality of the publication but does not relate to distribution. The cost of copying and distributing the publication is a modest share of the total expense. A publication with high production values will have high fixed costs. Of course, with larger sale, the fixed costs are spread more widely. Thus, popular publications have lower cost per copy because each copy need carry only a bit of the fixed cost. In thinking about a digital product, the publisher is concerned to invest sufficiently in fixed costs to generate a readership that will pay prices that cover the total cost.

There is a continuum of publications, from widely distributed products with high fixed costs but lower prices to narrowly distributed products with low fixed costs but higher prices. We might expect an even wider range of products in the digital arena.

To understand one end of the publishing spectrum, consider a publisher who reports full financial accounts and is willing to share internal financial records, namely, the American Economic Association (AEA). The AEA is headquartered in Nashville but maintains editorial offices for each of its three major journals in other locations. The AEA has 21,000 members plus 5,500 additional journal subscribers. Membership costs between $52 and $73 per year (students $26), and members get all three journals. The library rate is $140 per year for the bundle of three journals. The association had revenues and expenditures of $3.7 million in 1995.

The AEA prints and distributes nearly 29,000 copies of the *American Economic Review* (AER), the premier journal in economics. The AER receives nearly 900 manuscripts per year and publishes about 90 of them in quarterly issues. A *Papers and Proceedings* issue adds another 80 or so papers from the association's annual meeting. The second journal, the *Journal of Economic Perspectives* (JEP), invites authors to contribute essays and publishes more topical, less technical essays, with 56 essays in four issues in 1995. The third journal, the *Journal of Economic Literature* (JEL), contains an index to the literature in economics that indexes and abstracts several hundred journals, lists all new English-language books in economics, and reviews nearly 200 books per year. The JEL publishes more than 20 review essays each year in four quarterly issues. The three journals together yield about 5,000 pages, about 10 inches of linear shelf space, per year. The index to the economic literature published in JEL is cumulated and published as an *Index of Economic Articles in Journals* in 34 volumes back to 1886 and is distributed electronically as *EconLit* with coverage from 1969. The *Index* and *EconLit* are sold separately from the journals.

This publisher's costs are summarized in Figure 6.1. Some costs seem unlikely to be affected by the digital medium, while others may change significantly. The headquarters function accounts for 27% of the AEA's budget. The headquarters maintains the mailing lists, handles the receipts, and does the accounting and legal work. It conducts an annual mail ballot to elect new officers and organizes an annual meeting that typically draws 8,000 persons.[10] The headquarters function seems likely to continue in about its current size as long as the AEA continues as a membership organization, a successful publisher, and a coordinator of an annual meeting.[11] Declining membership or new modes of serving members might lead to reduction in headquarters costs. In the short run, headquarters costs are not closely tied to the number of members or sale of journals.

The AEA's second function is editing, the second block in Figure 6.1. Thirty-six percent of the AEA's annual expenditures goes to the editorial function of its three journals. Eighty-eight percent of the editorial cost is for salaries. The editorial function is essential to maintaining the high production values that are necessary for successful information products.

Operating digitally may provide some cost saving in the editorial function for the *American Economic Review*. The editors could allow manuscripts to be posted on the Internet, and referees could access network copies and dispatch their comments via the network. The flow of some 1,600 referee reports that the AER manages each year might occur faster and at lower cost to both the journals and the referees if the network were used in an effective way.[12] However, the editorial cost

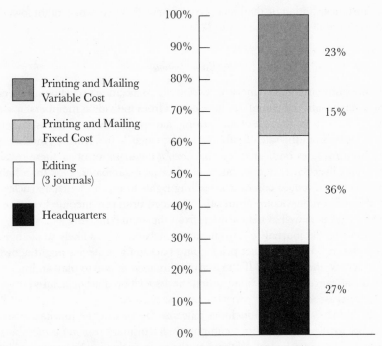

Figure 6.1. American Economic Association Expenses 1995
SOURCE: Elton Hinshaw, "Treasurer's Report," *American Economic Review*, May 1996, and unpublished reports.
NOTE: Percentages do not sum to 100% due to rounding.

will continue to be a significant and essential cost of bringing successful intellectual products to market. Top quality products are likely to have higher editorial costs than are lower quality products.

The top two blocks shown in Figure 6.1 describe the 38% of the AEA's total budget that goes to printing and mailing. These functions are contracted out and have recently gone through a competitive bid process. The costs are likely to be near industry lows. The total printing and mailing costs split into two parts. One part doesn't vary with the size of the print run and is labeled as fixed cost. It includes design and typesetting and thus will remain, to a significant degree, as a necessary function in bringing high quality products to market.[13] The variable-cost part of printing and mailing reflects the extra cost of paper, printing, and mailing individual paper issues. This 23% of total association expenditures, $800,000 out of $3.7 million total, might be reduced considerably by using distribution by network. However, as long as some part of the journal is distributed in print, the association will continue to incur significant fixed costs in printing.

In short, distribution of the journals electronically by network might lower the AEA's expenditures by as much as 23%.[14]

Publisher Revenue

Figure 6.2 summarizes the American Economic Association's revenues in six categories. Thirty-eight percent of revenue comes from individual memberships. Another 5% comes from the sale of advertising that appears in the journals. Nineteen percent comes from the sale of subscriptions, primarily to libraries. Another 19% comes from royalties on licenses of the *EconLit* database; most of these royalties come from SilverPlatter, a distributor of electronic databases. Less than half of one percent of revenues comes from selling rights to reprint journal articles. Finally, 18% of revenues come from other sources, primarily income from the cumulated reserves as well as net earnings from the annual meeting.[15]

Distributing the journals electronically by network seems likely to change the revenue streams. What product pricing and packaging strategies might allow the AEA to sustain the journals? If the journals are to continue to play an important role in the advance of the discipline, then the association must be assured that revenue streams are sufficient to carry the necessary costs.

If the library subscription includes a license for making the journals available by network to all persons within a campus, then a primary reason for membership in the association may be lost. With print, the main distinction between the library subscription and the membership subscription is that the member's copy can be kept at hand while the library copy is at a distance and may be in use or lost. With electronic delivery, access may be the same everywhere on the campus network. The license for electronic network distribution may then undercut revenues from memberships, a core 38% of AEA revenues.

The demand for advertising in the journals is probably motivated by distribution of journals to individual members. If individual subscriptions lag, then advertising revenue may fall as well. Indeed, one may ask the deeper question of whether ads associated with electronic journals will be salient when the journals are distributed electronically? The potential for advertising may be particularly limited if the electronic journals are distributed through intermediaries. If a database intermediary provides an index to hundreds of journals and provides links to individual articles on demand, advertising revenue may accrue to the database vendor rather than to the publisher of the individual journal.

The AEA might see 43% of its revenues (the 38% from member fees plus the 5% from advertising) as vulnerable to being cannibalized by network licensure of its journals. With only a potential 23% saving in cost, the association will be concerned to increase revenues from other sources so as to sustain its journals. The 20% shortfall is about $750,000 for the AEA. Here are three strategies: (1) charge libraries more for campus-use licenses, (2) increase revenues from pay-per-look services, (3) enhance services for members so as to sustain member revenues. Each

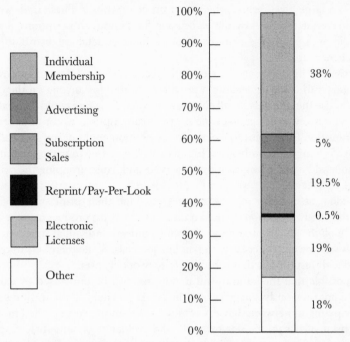

Figure 6.2. American Economic Association Revenues 1995
SOURCE: Elton Hinshaw, "Treasurer's Report," *American Economic Review*, May 1996, and unpublished reports.

of these strategies may provide new ways of generating revenue from existing readers, but importantly, may attract new readers.

The Campus License   The association could charge a higher price to libraries for the right to distribute the electronic journals on campus networks. There are about four memberships for each library or other subscription. If membership went to zero because the subscriptions all became campus intranet licenses, then the AEA would need to recoup the revenues from four memberships from each campus license to sustain current revenues. If network distribution lowered AEA costs by 20%, then the campus intranet license need only recoup the equivalent of two memberships. Libraries currently pay double the rate of memberships, so the campus intranet license need be only double the current library subscription rate. That is, the current library rate of $140 would need to go to about $280 for a campus-wide intranet license for the three journals.[16] Of course, many campuses have more than one library subscription, say one each in the social science, management, law, and agriculture libraries. The association might then set a sliding scale of rates from $280 for a small (one library print subscription) campus to

$1,400 for a large (five library print subscription) campus.[17] These rates would be the total revenue required by the association for campus subscriptions, assuming that the library's print subscriptions are abandoned. A database distributor would add some markup.

The campus intranet rate for electronic access is easily differentiated from the print library subscription because it provides a license for anyone on the campus intranet to use the journals in full electronic format. This rate could be established as a price for a new product, allowing the print subscriptions to continue at library rates. Transition from print to electronic distribution could occur gradually with the pace of change set by libraries. Libraries would be free to make separate decisions about adding the campus intranet service and, later, dropping the print subscription.

Individual association members could continue their print subscriptions as long as they wish, reflecting their own tastes for the print product and the quality of service of the electronic one as delivered. Indeed, individual members might get passwords for direct access to the on-line journals. Some members may not be affiliated with institutions that subscribe to network licenses.

It is possible that the campus intranet license will be purchased by campuses that have not previously subscribed to the AEA's journals. If the institution's cost of participating in network delivery is much less than the cost entailed in sustaining the print subscription—for example, the avoidance of added shelf space as will be discussed below—then more campuses might sign on. This effect may be small for the AEA because it is the premier publisher in economics, but might be significant for other journal publishers.

Pay-Per-Look   The AEA has had minimal revenues from reprints and royalties on copies. Indeed, it pioneered in guaranteeing in each issue of its journals a limited right to copy for academic purposes without charge.[18] The association adopted the view that the cost of processing the requests to make copies for class purposes (which it routinely granted without charge) was not worth incurring. By publishing a limited, no-charge right to copy, it saved itself the cost of managing the granting of permissions and saved campuses the cost of seeking them.

With electronic distribution, the campus intranet license will automatically grant permission for the journals to be used in course reserves and in print-on-demand services for classes.

On campuses with too little commitment to instruction in economics to justify a library subscription or a campus intranet license, there may still be occasional interest in use of journal articles. There may be law firms, businesses, consulting enterprises, and public interest groups who occasionally seek information and would value the intensity of exploration found in academic journals. With the ubiquitous Internet, they should be able to search a database on-line for a modest usage fee, identify articles of interest, and then call up such articles in full-image format on a pay-per-look basis. Suppose the Internet reaches a million people who are either on campuses without print library subscriptions today or are not on campuses at all but who would have interest in some occasional use of the academic material. This market represents a new potential source of revenue for the AEA that could be reached by an Internet-based pay-per-look price.

What rate should the association set per page to serve the pay-per-look market without unduly cannibalizing the sale of campus intranet licenses? Let's take a one print library subscription campus rate at $280 per year for access to about 3,500 published pages of journal articles (leaving aside the index and abstracts). One look at each published article page per year at $.08 per page would equal the $280 license. A campus that had a distribution of users that averaged one look at each page would break even with the campus intranet license with a pay-per-look rate of $.08 per page. This rate is the rate of net revenue to the association; the database distributor may add a markup. For discussion, suppose the database distributor's markup is 100%. If the Internet users beyond the campus intranet licenses looked at 2 million pages per year at $.16 per page including fees to the Internet service provider, the association would recoup nearly a quarter of its lost membership revenue from the intranet licenses from this source.

A critical issue for the emergence of a pay-per-look market is the ability to account for and collect the charges with a low cost per transaction. If accounting and billing costs $10 per hit with hits averaging 20 pages, then the charge might be $14 per hit ($10 to the agent, $4 to the AEA). Such a rate compares well with the $30-per-exchange cost incurred in conventional interlibrary loan. Yet such high transaction costs will surely limit the pay-per-look market.

A number of enterprises are offering or plan to offer electronic payment mechanisms on the Internet.[19] In the library world, RLG's WebDOC system may have some of the necessary features. These systems depend on users being registered in advance with the Web bank. As registered users, they have accounts and encrypted "keys" that electronically establish their identity to a computer on the Net. To make a transaction, users need only identify themselves to the electronic database vendor's computer using the "key" for authentication. The vendor's computer checks the authentication and debits the readers' account at the Web bank. In this fashion, secure transactions may occur over the network without human intervention at costs of a few cents per hit. If such Web banks become a general feature of the Internet, Web money will be used for a variety of purposes. The incremental cost of using Web banks for access to information should be modest and should allow the pay-per-look market to gain in importance. Markups per transaction might then be quite modest, with gross charges per page in the vicinity of $.10 to $.20. This rate compares with the $.04-per-hit cost of the *Britannica* mentioned in the opening sentence of this essay.

The core idea here is that individual readers make the decisions about when to look at a document under a pay-per-look regime. The reader must face a budget constraint, that is, have a limited set of funds for use in buying information products or other services. The fund might be subsidized by the reader's institution, but the core choices about when to pay and look are made individually. When the core decision is made by the reader with limited funds, then the price elasticity of demand for such services may be high. With a highly elastic demand, even for-profit publishers will find that low prices dominate.

Current article fulfillment rates of $10 to $20 could fall greatly. The MIT Press offers to deliver individual articles from its electronic journals for $12. EI Village delivers reprints of articles by fax or other electronic means for fees in this range.

Enhanced Member Services   A third strategy for responding to the possible revenue shortfall from the loss of memberships at the AEA would be to enhance membership services. One approach, proposed by Hal Varian, would be to offer superior access to the electronic journals to members only.[20] The electronic database of journal articles might be easily adapted to provide a personal notification to each member as articles of interest are posted. The association's database service for members might then have individual passwords for members and store profiles of member interests so as to send e-mail notices of appropriate new postings. The members' database might also contain ancillary materials, appendices to the published articles with detailed derivations of mathematical results offered in software code (for example, as *Mathematica* notebooks), copies of the numerical data sets used in empirical estimation, or extended bibliographies. The members' database might support monitored discussions of the published essays, allowing members to post questions and comments and allowing an opportunity for authors to respond if they wish. These enhancements generally take advantage of the personal relationship a member may want to have with the published literature, a service not necessarily practical or appropriate for libraries.

Indeed, one divide in the effort to distinguish member from library access to the journal database is whether the enhancement would have value to libraries if offered. Libraries will be asked to pay a premium price for a campus intranet license. They serve many students and faculty who are not currently members of the AEA and who are unlikely to become members in any event, for example, faculty from disciplines other than economics. Deliberately crippling the library version of the electronic journals by offering lower resolution pages, limited searching strategies, a delay in access, or only a subset of the content will be undesirable for libraries and inconsistent with the association's goal of promoting discussion of economics. However, there may be some demand for lower quality access at reduced prices. The important point is that for membership to be sustained, it must carry worthwhile value when compared to the service provided by the campus license.

Another approach is simply to develop new products that will have a higher appeal to members than to libraries. Such products could be included in the membership fee, but offered to libraries at an added extra cost. One such product would be systematic access to working papers in economics. Indexes, abstracts, and in some cases, the full text of working papers are available without charge at some sites on the World Wide Web today. The association might ally itself with one of these sites, give the service an official status, and invest in the features of the working paper service to make it more robust and useful. Although freebie working paper services are useful, an enhanced working paper service for a fee (or as part of membership) might be much better.[21]

To the extent that enhanced services can sustain memberships in the face of readily available campus intranet access to journals, the premium for campus intranet access could be lower.

The AEA might offer a discount membership rate to those who opt to use the on-line version of the journals in lieu of receiving print copies. Such a discounted rate would reflect not only the association's cost saving with reduced print distribution but also the diminished value of membership given the increased prospect of campus intranet licenses.

To the extent that the pay-per-look market generates new revenue, then the campus intranet rate could also be less. The total of the association's revenues need only cover its fixed and variable costs. (The variable cost may approach zero with electronic distribution.) If membership revenues dropped by two-thirds and pay-per-look generated one-quarter of the gap, then the premium rate for the campus intranet license need be only one-third to one-half above current rates, say, $200 for a one library print subscription campus to $1,000 for a five library print subscription campus (net revenue to the association after the net distributor's markup).

Other Publishers

At the other end of the publishing spectrum from the AEA are those publishers who produce low-volume publications. Some titles have few personal subscriptions and depend primarily on library subscriptions that are already at premium rates. For these titles, replacing the print subscription with an intranet license will simply lower costs. The Johns Hopkins University Press offers its journals electronically at a discount in substitution for the print.

Some titles may have mostly personal subscriptions with no library rate, including popular magazines like the *Economist*. Such publications might simply be offered as personal subscriptions on the Internet with an individual password for each subscriber. The distribution by network would lower distribution costs and so ought to cause the profit-maximizing publisher to offer network access to individuals at a discount from the print subscription rate. Such a publication may not be available by campus intranet license.

The *Journal of Statistics Education* (JSE) is distributed via the Internet without charge. It began with an NSF/FIPSE grant to the North Carolina State University in 1993. The JSE receives about 40 manuscripts per year and, after a peer review, publishes about 20 of them.[22] The published essays are posted on a Web site and a table of contents and brief summaries are dispatched by e-mail to a list of about 2,000 interested persons. JSE's costs amount to about $25,000 per year to sustain the clerical work necessary to receive manuscripts, dispatch them to suitable referees, receive referee reports, and return them to the author with the editor's judgment. The JSE also requires a part-time system support person to maintain the server that houses the journal. The JSE has not charged for subscriptions, receives no continuing revenue, and needs about $50,000 per year to survive. Merger with a publisher of other statistics journals may make sense, allowing the JSE to be bundled in a larger member service package. Alternatively, it might begin to charge a subscription fee for individuals and a campus license rate for libraries. Making the transformation from a no-fee to a fee-based publication may prove difficult. A critical issue is how much fixed cost is necessary to maintain reasonable production values in a low-volume publication. At present, JSE is seeking a continuing source of finance.

In general, a publisher will consider three potential markets: (1) the campus intranet license/library sale, (2) the individual subscription, and (3) the pay-per-look/individual article sale. These three markets might be served by one title with shared fixed costs. The issue of whether to offer the title in each market and at what price will reflect the incremental cost of making the title available in that market, the elasticity of demand in each market, and the cross price elasticities between markets. For example, the price of the campus license will have an effect on individual subscription sales and vice versa, and the price of the individual subscriptions will have an effect on the sale of individual articles and vice versa. The more elastic the demands, the lower the prices, even for for-profit publishers. With higher substitution between the three forms, the closer the prices will be across the three forms.[23]

Economies of Scope

To this point, the analysis applies essentially to one journal at a time, as though the journal were the only size package that counted. In fact, of course, the choice of size of package for information could change. Two centuries ago, the book was the package of choice. Authors generally wrote books. Libraries bought books. Readers read books. In the past 50 years, the size of package shifted to the journal in most disciplines. Authors write smaller packages, that is, articles, and get their work to market more quickly in journals. The elemental information product has become more granular. Libraries commit to journals and so receive information faster and at lower cost per unit. In deciding what to read, readers depend on the editors' judgment in publishing articles. In short, libraries buy bigger packages, the journals, while authors and readers work with smaller units, the articles.

With electronic distribution, the library will prefer to buy a still larger package, a database of many journals. A single, large transaction is much less expensive for a library to handle than are multiple, small transactions. Managing many journal titles individually is expensive. Similarly, readers may prefer access to packages smaller than journal articles. They are often satisfied with abstracts. The electronic encyclopedia is attractive because it allows one to zip directly to a short, focused package of information with links to more. Authors, then, will be drawn to package their products in small bundles embedded in a large database with links to other elements of the database with related information. Information will become still more granular.

If the database becomes the dominant unit of trade in academic information, then publishers with better databases may thrive. The JSTOR enterprise appears to have recognized the economies of scope in building a database with a large quantity of related journal titles. JSTOR is a venture spawned by the Mellon Foundation to store archival copies of the full historic backfiles of journals and make them available by network. The core motive is to save libraries the cost of storing old journals. JSTOR plans to offer 100 journal titles within a few years. Some of the professional societies, for example, psychology and chemistry, exploit economies of scope in the print arena by offering dozens of journal titles in their disciplines. Elsevier's dominance in a number of fields is based in part on the exploitation of scope with many titles in related subdisciplines. The emergence of economies of scope in the electronic arena is illustrated by Academic Press's offer to libraries in Ohio LINK. For 10% more than the cost of the print subscriptions the library had held, it could buy electronic access to the full suite of Academic Press journals electronically on Ohio LINK.

To take advantage of the economies of scope, the electronic journal might begin to include hot links to other materials in the database. The electronic product would then deliver more than the print version. Links to other Web sites is one of the attractive features of the Web version of the *Encyclopedia Britannica*. An academic journal database could invite authors to include the electronic addresses of references and links to ancillary files. Higher quality databases will have more such links.

The American Economic Association eschews scope in the print arena, preferring instead to let a hundred flowers bloom and to rely on competition to limit prices. Its collection of three journals does not constitute a critical mass of journal articles for an economics database, and so it must depend on integration with other economics journals at the database level. The Johns Hopkins University Press's MUSE enterprise suffers similar lack of scope. Although it has 45 journal titles, they are scattered among many disciplines and do not, collectively, reach critical mass in any field.

The emergence of more powerful, network-based working paper services seems likely to lower the cost of the editorial process, as mentioned above. A common, well-managed electronic working paper service might make the cost of adding a journal title much lower than starting a title from scratch without access to electronic working papers. The enterprise that controls a capable working paper service may well control a significant part of the discipline and reap many of the advantages of scope in academic publishing.

In fact, a capable electronic working paper service could support multiple editors of a common literature. One editor might encourage an author to develop a work for a very sophisticated audience and publish the resulting work in a top academic journal. Another editor might invite the author to develop the same ideas in a less technical form for a wider audience. Both essays might appear in a common database of articles and link to longer versions of the work, numerical data sets, bibliographies, and other related material. The published essays will then be front ends to a deeper literature available on the Net.

Rents

In addition to limiting the number of journals it produces, the American Economic Association differs from many publishers by emphasizing low cost. The price of its journals is less than half the industry average for economics journals, and the differential between library and individual rates is low.[24] If the AEA's goal were to maximize profit, it could charge authors more, charge members and libraries more, make more revenue from its meetings, and launch more products to take advantage of its reputation by extending its scope. The rents available in this marketplace are then left to the authors, members, libraries, and competing publishers. The AEA is not maximizing its institutional rents.

Other nonprofit publishers may seek higher revenues to capture more of the available rents and use the proceeds to generate more products and association services. Lobbying activities, professional certification and accreditation, more meetings, and more journals are common among professional societies.

Many for-profit publishers seek to maximize the rents they can extract from the marketplace for the benefit of their shareholders. In considering how to package and price electronic products, the for-profit publishers will continue to be concerned with finding and exploiting the available rents. The profit-maximizing price for a journal is determined by the price elasticity of demand for the title and the marginal cost of producing it. With convenient network access, there may be an increase in demand that would allow a higher price, other things being equal. How the price elasticity of demand might change with network access is unknown. The fall in marginal cost with electronic distribution need not lead to a lower price.

One might then ask how a shift to electronic publishing may affect the size of the rents and their distribution. A shift to the database as the optimal size package with falling marginal costs would seem both to increase the size of potential rents and to make easier their exploitation for profit. Suppose control of a powerful working paper service gives a significant cost advantage to journal publishers. Suppose further that academic institutions find major advantages in subscribing to large databases of information rather than making decisions about individual journal titles. The enterprise that controls the working paper service and the database of journals may then have considerable rent-capturing ability. The price elasticities of demand for such large packages may be low and the substitutes poor, and so the markups over costs may be substantial. The possibility of a significant pay-per-look market with high price elasticity of demand might cause the profit-maximizing price to be lower. The possibility of self-publication at personal or small-scale Web sites offers a poor substitute to integration in a database because Web search engines are unlike to point to those sites appropriately.

LIBRARY

In contemplating how to take advantage of electronic publications, universities and their libraries face two problems. First, they face decisions about scaling back costly conventional operations so as to make resources available for acquiring electronic licenses. Second, the cost savings occur in a variety of ways, each with its own history, culture, and revenue sources. Although many boards of trustees and their presidents might like all the funds within their institutions to be fungible, in fact they face limitations on their ability to reduce expenditures in one area so as to spend more in another. If donors or legislatures are more willing to provide funds for buildings than for electronic subscriptions, then the dollar cost of a building may not be strictly comparable to the dollar cost of electronic subscriptions. Universities are investing more in campus networks and computer systems and are pruning elsewhere as the campuses become more digital. The following paragraphs consider how conventional operations might be pruned so as to allow more expenditure on electronic information products.

Conventional Library Costs

It is possible that some universities will view electronic access to quality academic journals as sufficiently attractive to justify increasing their library budget to accommodate the electronic subscriptions when publishers seek premium prices for electronic access. Some universities place particular emphasis on being electronic pioneers and seem willing to commit surprising amounts of resources to such activities. Other universities owe a debt to these pathfinders for sorting out what works. For most institutions, however, the value of the electronic journals will be tested by middle management's willingness to prune other activities so as to acquire more electronic journals. The library director is at the front line for such choices, and an understanding of the basic structure of the library's expenditures will help define the library director's choices.

Figure 6.3 provides a summary picture of the pattern of costs in conventional academic libraries. The top four blocks correspond to the operating budgets of the libraries. Acquisitions account for about a third of the operating budget. To give a complete picture, the bottom section of the figure also accounts for the costs of library buildings. The cost of space is treated as the annual lease value of the space including utilities and janitorial services. The total of the operating budget plus

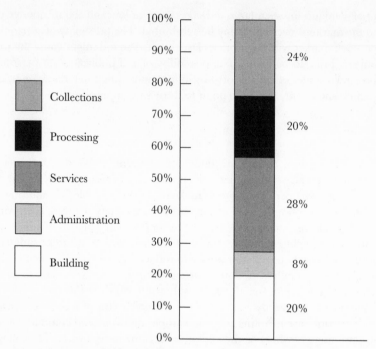

Figure 6.3. Conventional Library Costs
SOURCE: Heuristic characterization based on Association of Research Libraries Annual
Statistical Survey on expenditures on materials and operating budgets and on the author's
own studies of library space and technical service costs.

the annualized cost of the building space represents a measure of the total institutional financial commitment to the library.

Library management typically has control only of the operating budget. Let's
suppose that, on average, campus intranet licenses to electronic journals come at
a premium price, reflecting both the electronic database distributor's costs as well
as adjustments in publishers' pricing behavior as discussed above. The library,
then, confronts a desire to increase its acquisition expenditure, possibly as much as
doubling it.

A first choice is to prune expenditures on print so as to commit resources to digital materials. Some publishers offer lower prices for swapping digital for paper
and in this case, swapping improves the library's budget. Some publishers may
simply offer to swap digital for print at no change in price. However, many publishers may expect a premium gross price for digital access on the campus intranet.
The library manager may seek to trim other acquisition expenditures so as to
commit to more digital access. For several decades, academic libraries have been
reducing the quantity of materials acquired so as to adjust to increases in prices.

The possibility of substantial cuts in the quantity of acquisitions so as to afford a smaller suite of products in electronic access seems unappealing and so may have limited effect.

A second possible budget adjustment is to prune technical service costs. The costs of processing arise from the necessity of tracking the arrival of each issue, claiming those that are overdue, making payments, adjusting catalog records, and periodically binding the volumes. If the electronic journal comes embedded in a database of many journals, the library can make one acquisition decision and one payment. It need have little concern for check-in and the claiming of issues. Testing the reliability of the database will be a concern, but presumably large database providers have a substantial incentive to build in considerable redundancy and reliability and will carefully track and claim individual issues. The library will avoid binding costs. The library will likely have some interest in building references to the electronic database into its catalog. Perhaps the database vendor will provide suitable machine readable records to automate this process.

A third possibility is the library's public service operations. Until a substantial quantity of materials are available and widely used via network, the demand for conventional library hours, reference, and circulation services may change only modestly. In 1996, one-third to one-half of the references in my students' essays were to World Wide Web sources. However, these sources generally were complements of conventional sources rather than substitutes for them. As frontline journals become commonly accessible by campus networks, the demand for conventional library services may decline. For example, campuses that operate departmental and small branch libraries primarily to provide convenient access to current journals for faculty might be more likely to consolidate such facilities into a master library when a significant number of the relevant journals are available on the Net. These changes are likely to take a number of years to evolve.

A fourth possibility concerns the cost of library buildings. When journals are used digitally by network, the need for added library space declines. Libraries will need less stack space to hold the addition of current volumes. In many larger libraries, lesser used, older volumes are currently held in less expensive, off-site facilities, with new volumes going into the prime space. The marginal stack space, then, is off-site, with costs of perhaps $.30 per volume per year for sustaining the perpetual storage of the added volumes.[25] Replacing a 100-year run of a journal with an electronic backfile ought to save about $30 per year in continuing storage costs at a low-cost, remote storage facility. Reductions in the extent of processing and in public services will also reduce requirements for space.

The library building expenses typically do not appear in operating budgets, so saving space has no direct effect on the library budget. The capital costs of buildings are frequently raised philanthropically or paid through a state capital budget, keeping the costs out of the university current accounts. Even utilities and janitorial services may appear in a general university operating budget rather than within the library account. Savings in building costs will accrue to those who fund capital projects and to university general budgets but often not to the library operating budget. University presidents and boards may redirect their institutions' capital funds to more productive uses. Of course, the interests of philanthropy and the enthusiasm of state legislators may pose some limit on the ability to make such reallocations. Moreover, library building projects occur relatively infrequently, say every 25 years or so. The savings in capital may not be apparent for some time or, indeed, ever if capital budgets are considered independently of operating budgets. Library buildings, particularly the big ones in the middle of campuses, come to play a symbolic role, an expression of the university's importance, a place of interdisciplinary interaction, a grand presence. Because symbols are important, the master library facility will continue to be important. The marginal savings in building expense will probably be in compact or remote storage facilities and in departmental and smaller branch libraries. Digital access ought then to save the larger campus community some future commitment of capital, but the savings will be visible mostly to the president and board.

A fifth possibility is savings in faculty subscriptions. In law, business, and other schools in which faculty have university expense accounts, faculty may be accustomed to paying for personal subscriptions to core journals from the accounts. If the university acquires a campuswide network license for such journals, the faculty members may rely on the campus license and deploy their expense accounts for other purposes. By adjusting the expense account downward in light of the offering of campus licenses for journals, the university may reclaim some of the cost of the journals. On those campuses and in those departments in which faculty members do not have expense accounts and in which personal copies of core journals are necessary for scholarly success, the faculty salaries might be adjusted downward over a course of time to reflect the fact that faculty may use the campus license rather than pay for personal subscriptions. Indeed, when the personal subscriptions are not deductible under federal and state income taxes, the cost of subscriptions to the faculty in after-tax dollars may be greater than the cost to the university using before-tax dollars. As a result, a shift to university site licenses for core journals should be financially advantageous for faculty and the university.

In sum, the university may find a number of ways to economize by shifting to digital journals distributed by network. Although direct subscription prices may go up in some cases, the university may trim technical and public services, save space, and offer more perquisites to faculty at some saving in cost.

ELECTRONIC AGENT

Publishers could establish their own digital distribution function by creating a Uniform Resource Locator (URL) for each title. The publisher would deal directly with libraries and individual readers. For a number of reasons, the publisher is likely to prefer to work with an agent for electronic distribution. Just as the typesetting and printing is usually performed by contractors, so the design and distribution of electronic products is likely to involve specialized agents. However, the role of electronic distribution agent is becoming more important than that of the printer for two important reasons. The first arises because of economies of scale in managing access to electronic services. The second concerns the potential advantages of integrating individual journals into a wider database of academic information. The electronic agent accepts materials, say journal titles, from publishers and mounts them on electronic services to be accessed by the Internet. The agent captures economies of scale in maintaining the service and in supporting a common payment mechanism and a common search interface and search engine, and may take other steps to integrate articles and journal titles so that the whole is greater than the sum of the parts.

OCLC was an early entrant in the market for electronic distribution of academic journals with *Online Clinical Trials. Online Clinical Trials* was priced at $220 for institutions and $120 for individuals.[26] OCLC shifted to a World Wide Web interface in January 1997. In 1998, OCLC's *First Search Electronic Collections Online* offers access to hundreds of titles from many publishers. Most of the journals deliver page images using Adobe's PDF. OCLC's new approach offers publishers the opportunity to sell electronic access to journals by both subscription and pay-per-look.[27] It charges libraries an access fee based on the number of simultaneous users to be supported and the number of electronic journals to which the library subscribes. Libraries buy subscriptions from publishers. Publishers may package multiple titles together and set whatever rates they choose. The following discussion puts the strategies of OCLC and other electronic agents in a broader context.

Storage and Networks

With electronic documents, there is a basic logistical choice. A storage-intensive strategy involves using local storage everywhere. In this case, the network need not be used to read the journal. At the other extreme, the document might be stored once-for-the-world at a single site with network access used each time a journal is read. Between these two extremes is a range of choices. With the cost saving of fewer storage sites comes the extra cost of increased reliance on data communication networks.

Data storage is an important cost. Although the unit costs of digital storage have fallen and will continue to fall sharply through time, there is still a considerable advantage to using less storage. Data storage systems involve not simply the storage medium itself, but a range of services to keep the data on-line. A data center typically involves sophisticated personnel, backup and archiving activities, and software and hardware upgrades. If 10 campuses share a data storage facility, the storage cost per campus should be much less than if each provides its own. Having one storage site for the world might be the lowest storage cost per campus overall.

To use a remote storage facility involves data communication. The more remote the storage, the greater the reliance on data networks. A central problem for data communication is congestion. Data networks typically do not involve traffic-based fees. Indeed, the cost of monitoring traffic so as to impose fees may be cost-prohibitive. Monitoring network traffic so as to bill to individuals on the basis of use would require keeping track of the origin of each packet of data and accounting for it by tallying a register that notes source, time, and date. Because even simple mail messages may be broken into numerous packets for network shipment, the quantity of items to be tracked is much more numerous than tracking telephone calls. If every packet must go through the toll plaza, the opportunity for delay and single points of failure may be substantial. Because each packet may follow a different route, tracking backbone use with a tally on each leg would multiply the complexity. Traffic-based fees seem to be impractical for the Internet. Without traffic-based fees, individual users do not face the cost of their access. Like a driver on an urban highway at rush hour, each individual sees only his or her own trip, not the adverse effect of his or her trip in slowing others down. An engineering response to highway congestion is often to build more highways. Yet the added highways are often congested as well. In data networking, an engineering solution is to invent a faster network. Yet individuals deciding to use the network will see only their personal costs and so will have little incentive to economize. The demand for bandwidth on networks will surely grow with the pace of faster networks, for example, with personal videophones and other video-intensive applications. Without traffic-based pricing, congestion will be endemic in data networks.

Another response to network congestion is to build private networks with controlled access. Building networks dedicated to specific functions seems relatively expensive, but may be necessary to maintain a sufficient level of performance. Campus networks are private, and so access can be controlled. Perhaps investments in networking and technical change can proceed fast enough on individual campuses so as to allow the campus network to be reliable enough for access to journals and other academic information.

Because the telephone companies have launched data network services, they seem likely to introduce time-of-day pricing. Higher rates in prime time and higher rates for faster access speeds are first steps in giving incentives to economize the use of the network and so to reduce congestion. America Online (AOL) ran into serious difficulty when, in late 1996, it shifted from a per hour pricing strategy to a flat monthly rate to match other Internet service providers. AOL was swamped with peak period demand, demand it could not easily manage. The long distance telephone services seem to be moving to simpler pricing regimes, dime-a-minute, for example. The possibility of peak period congestion, however, likely means that some use of peak period pricing in telephones and in network services will remain desirable. In the end, higher education's ability to economize on data storage will depend on the success of the networks in limiting congestion.

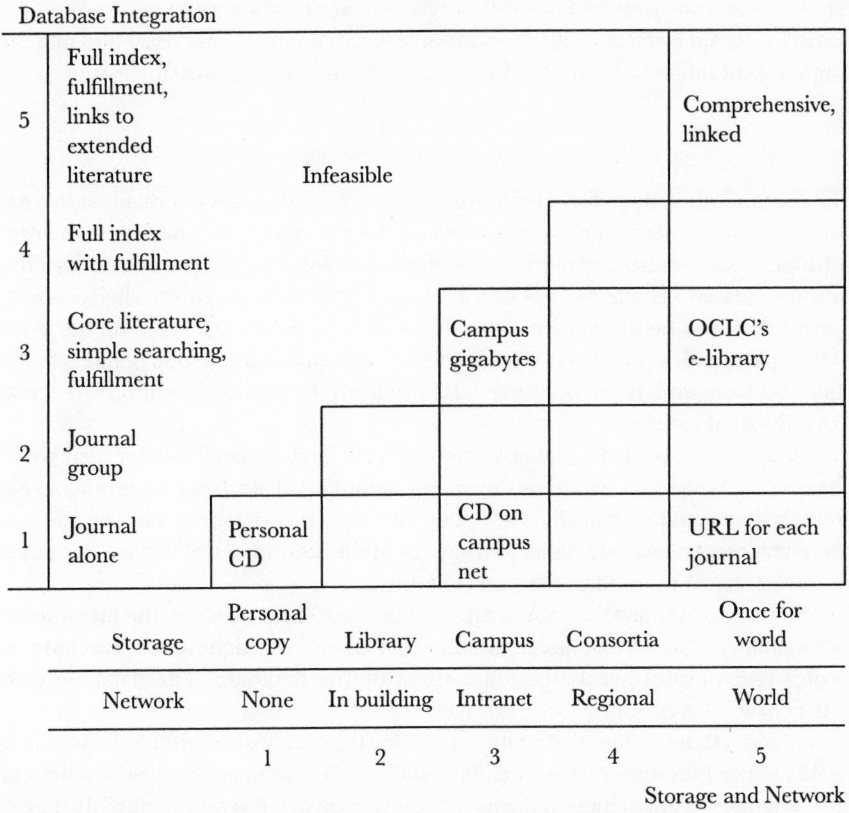

Database Integration

Database Integration	Personal copy / None	Library / In building	Campus / Intranet	Consortia / Regional	Once for world / World
5 Full index, fulfillment, links to extended literature	Infeasible				Comprehensive, linked
4 Full index with fulfillment					
3 Core literature, simple searching, fulfillment			Campus gigabytes		OCLC's e-library
2 Journal group					
1 Journal alone	Personal CD		CD on campus net		URL for each journal
Storage	Personal copy	Library	Campus	Consortia	Once for world
Network	None	In building	Intranet	Regional	World
	1	2	3	4	5

Storage and Network

Figure 6.4. Network Intensity and Database Integration

Some milestones in the choice of storage and networks are illustrated along the horizontal margin of Figure 6.4. The rapid growth of the World Wide Web in the last couple of years has represented a shift toward the right along this margin, with fewer storage sites and more dependence on data communication. The World Wide Web allows a common interface to serve many computer platforms, replacing proprietary tools. Adobe's Portable Document Format (PDF) seems to offer an effective vehicle to present documents in original printed format with equations, tables, and graphics, yet allow text searching and hypertext links to other Web sites. The software for reading PDF documents is available without charge, is compatible with many Web browsers, and allows local printing. Some of the inconveniences of older network-based tools are disappearing.

That rightward shift may offer the electronic agent an advantage over either the publisher or the library. That is, the electronic agent may acquire rights from publishers and sell access to libraries, while taking responsibility for an optimal choice of storage sites and network access. Storage might end up in a low-cost location with the electronic agent responsible for archiving the material and migrating the digital files to future hardware and software environments.

Integration into a Database

The second advantage for an electronic agent is in integrating individual journal titles and other electronic materials into a coherent database. The vertical margin of Figure 6.4 sketches a range of possibilities. At root, a journal title stands as a relatively isolated vehicle for the distribution of information. In the digital world, each title could be distributed on its own CD or have its own URL on the Web. Third party index publishers would index the contents and provide pointers to the title and issue and, perhaps, to the URL. Indeed, the pointer might go directly to an individual article.

However, relatively few scholars depend on a single journal title for their work. Indeed, looking at the citations shown in a sampling of articles of a given journal reveals that scholars typically use a range of sources. A database that provides coherent access to several related journals, as in the second tier of Figure 6.4, offers a service that is more than the sum of its parts.

At yet a higher level, an agent might offer a significant core of the literature in a discipline. The core of journals and other materials might allow searching by words and phrases across the full content of the database. The database then offers new ways of establishing linkages.

At a fourth level, the organizing engine for the database might be the standard index to the literature of the discipline, such as *EconLit* in economics. A search of the database might achieve a degree of comprehensiveness for the published literature. A significant fraction of the published essays might be delivered on demand by hitting a "fulfill" button. Fulfillment might mean delivery of an electronic image file via network within a few seconds or delivery of a facsimile within a few minutes or hours.

At a fifth level, the database might include hot links from citations in one essay to other elements of the database. The database might include the published works from journals with links to ancillary materials, numeric data sets, computer algorithms, and an author's appendices discussing methods and other matters. The database might invite commentary, and so formal publications might link to suitably moderated on-line discussions.

In integrating materials from a variety of sources into a coherent database, the electronic agent may have an advantage over publishers who offer only individual journal titles. The agent might set standards for inclusion of material that specifies metatags and formats. The agent might manage the index function; indeed, the index might be a basis for forward integration with database distribution, as EI has done. This issue is discussed more fully below.

Integration of diverse materials into a database is likely to come with remote storage and use of networks for access. Integrating the material into a database by achieving higher levels of coherence and interaction among diverse parts may be at lower cost for an electronic agent than for publishers of individual journals or for individual libraries. The agent is able to incur the cost of integration and storage once for the world.

Agent's Strategy

Given the interest of publishers in licensing their products for campus intranets and the universities' interest in securing such licenses, there is opportunity for enterprises to act as brokers, to package the electronic versions of the journals in databases and make them accessible, under suitable licenses, to campus intranets. The brokers may add a markup to reflect their cost of mounting the database. The size of the markup will reflect the extent of integration as well as the choice of storage strategy.

SilverPlatter became the most successful vendor of electronic index databases by making them available on CDs for use on campus intranets with proprietary software. OCLC plays an important role in offering such databases from its master center in Ohio. Ovid, a third vendor, supports sophisticated indexing that integrates full text with Standard Generalized Markup Language (SGML) and Hypertext Markup Language (HTML) tagging. A number of other vendors have also participated in the index market and are likely to seek to be brokers for the electronic distribution of journals.

A core strategy will probably be to mount the database of journals on one or more servers on the World Wide Web, with access limited to persons authorized for use from licensed campuses or through other fee-paid arrangements. This strategy has three important parts: (1) the database server, (2) the Internet communication system, and (3) the campus network.

The advantage of the World Wide Web approach is that the data can be made accessible to many campuses with no server support on any campus. A campus intranet license can be served remotely, saving the university the expense of software, hardware, and system support for the service.

The risk of the Web strategy is with the Internet itself and its inherent congestion. OCLC used a private data communication network so as to achieve a higher level of reliability than the Internet and will do the same to ensure high-quality TCP/IP (the Internet Protocol) access. Some campuses may prefer to mount database files locally, using CD-ROMs and disk servers on the campus network. Some high-intensity campuses may prefer to continue to mount the most used parts of databases locally, even at extra cost, as a method of ensuring against deficiencies in Internet services.

The third element, after storage and the Internet, is the campus network. Campus networks continue to evolve. Among the hundred universities seeking to be top-ten universities, early investment in sophisticated networking may play a strategic role in the quest for rank. On such campuses, network distribution of journals should be well supported and popular. Other campuses will follow with some lag, particularly where funding depends primarily on the public sector. Adoption within 10 years might be expected.[28]

The electronic agent, then, must choose a strategy with two elements: (1) a storage and network choice and (2) an approach to database integration.

Journal publishers generally start at the bottom left of Figure 6.4, the closest to print. They could make a CD and offer it as an alternative to print for current subscribers. The AEA offers the *Journal of Economic Literature* on CD instead of print for the same price.

Moves to the upper left seem to be economically infeasible. Integrating more materials together increases local storage costs and so tilts the storage-network balance toward less storage and more network. With more data integration, the agent's strategy will shift to the right.

Moves to the lower right, with reduced storage costs and more dependence on networks, should involve considerable cost savings but run risks. One risk is of network congestion. A second is of loss of revenues because traditional subscribers drop purchases in favor of shared network access. The viability of these strategies depends on the level of fees that may be earned from network licenses or pay-per-look.

Moves along the diagonal up and to the right involve greater database integration with cost savings from lower storage costs and more dependence on networks. The advantage of moves upward and to the right is the possibility that integration creates services of significantly more value than the replication of print journals on the Internet. When database integration creates significantly more value, subscribers will be willing to pay premium prices for using products with remote storage with networks. Of course, network congestion will remain a concern.

A move toward more database integration raises a number of interesting questions. The answers to these questions will determine the size of the markup by the electronic agent. How much should information from a variety of sources be integrated into a database with common structure, tags, and linkages? For a large database, more effort at integration and coherence may be more valuable. Just how much effort, particularly how much hand effort, remains an open question. If the electronic agent passively accepts publications from publishers, the level of integration of materials may be relatively low. The publisher may provide an abstract and metatags and might provide URLs for linking to other network sites. The higher level of integration associated with controlled vocabulary indexing and a more systematic structure for the database than comes from journal titles would seem to require either a higher level of handwork by an indexer or the imposition of standard protocols for defining data elements. Is a higher level of integration of journal material from a variety of sources sufficiently valuable to justify its cost? The index function might be centralized with storage of individual journals distributed around the Net. Physical integration of the database is not necessary to logical integration, but will common ownership be necessary to achieve the control and commonality necessary for high levels of integration?

A second question concerns how an agent might generate a net revenue stream from its initial electronic offerings sufficient to allow it to grow. The new regime will not be borne as a whole entity; rather, it will evolve in relatively small steps. Each step must generate a surplus to be used to finance the next step. Early steps that generate larger surpluses will probably define paths that are more likely to be followed. Experimentation with products and prices is already under way. Those agents finding early financial success are likely to attract publishers and libraries and to be imitated by competitors.

JSTOR has captured the full historic run of a significant number of journals, making the promise of 100 titles in suites from major disciplines within three years. However, it does not yet have a program for access to current journals. Its program is primarily to replace archival storage of materials that libraries may or may not have already acquired in print.

OCLC's approach is to sell libraries access services while publishers sell subscriptions to the information. The publisher can avoid the cost of the distribution in print, a saving if the electronic subscriptions generate sufficient revenue. The unbundling of access from subscription sales allows the access to be priced on the basis of simultaneous users, that is, akin to the rate of use, while the information is priced on the basis of quantity and quality of material made available. Of course, the information may also be priced on a pay-per-look basis and so earn revenue as it is used. What mix of pay-per-look and subscription sales will ultimately prevail is an open question.

A third question is whether publishers will establish exclusive arrangements with electronic agents or whether they will offer nonexclusive licenses so as to sustain competition among agents. Some publishers may prefer to be their own electronic agents, retaining control of the distribution channels. If database integration is important, this strategy may be economic only for relatively large publishers with suites of journals in given disciplines. Many publishers may choose to distribute their products through multiple channels, to both capture the advantages of more integration with other sources and promote innovation and cost savings among competing distributors.

As the electronic agents gain experience and build their title lists, competition among them should drive down the markups for electronic access. If the store-once-and-network strategy bears fruit, the cost savings in access should be apparent. If higher levels of database integration prove to be important, the cost savings may be modest. Cost savings here are in terms of units of access. As the cost of access falls, the quantity of information products used may increase. The effect on total expenditure, the product of unit cost and number of units used, is hard to predict. If the demand for information proves to be price elastic, then as unit costs and unit prices fall, expenditures on information will increase.

The electronic agents will gather academic journals from publishers and distribute them in electronic formats to libraries and others. They will offer all available advantages of scale in managing electronic storage, optimize the use of networks for distribution, offer superior search interfaces and engines, and take steps to integrate materials from disparate sources into a coherent whole. The agent will be able to offer campus intranet licenses, personal subscriptions, and pay-per-look access from a common source. The agent may manage sales, accounting, billing, and technical support. Today, agents are experimenting with both technical and pricing strategies. It remains to be seen whether single agents will dominate given content areas, whether major publishers can remain apart, or whether publishers and universities can or should sustain a competitive market among agents.

CONCLUSION

Higher education faces a significant challenge in discovering what academic information will succeed on the Net. In 1996, the MIT Press launched *Studies in Nonlinear Dynamics and Econometrics* (SNDE), one of six titles that the Press distributes by network. The price per year is $40 for individuals and $130 for libraries.[29] MIT's strategy seems to be to launch titles in disciplines in which an electronic journal has some extra value, for example, links to computer code and data sets. The rates for the journals seem to be well below those quoted by OCLC's electronic journal program and lower than at least some new print journals. The cost of launching a new journal electronically seems to be falling. It remains to be seen whether the electronic journals will attract successful editors and valued manuscripts from authors, but the venture shows promise. The number and quality of electronic journals continues to grow. MIT has decided to forgo the use of an electronic agent and to depend only on conventional, independent indexing services for database integration, an incremental approach. Yet, the potential seems greater than an individual journal title reveals.

When Henry Ford launched the first mass-produced automobile, he chose a design that carried double the load, traveled three times farther, and went four times faster than the one-horse buggy it replaced, and yet was modestly priced. Successful digital information products for academia seem likely to exploit the inherent advantages of the digital arena, the timeliness, the sophisticated integration of new essays into the existing stock, the links from brief front-end items to more elaborate treatment, and the opportunity to interact with the material by asking for "fulfillment," "discussion," and the "underlying data." Network delivery will make possible both the campus intranet license and the sale of information on a pay-per-look basis. It will allow the material to be more readily consulted in circles beyond the academy.

Electronic agents will play significant new roles as intermediaries between publishers and campuses by handling the electronic storage and distribution and by integrating material into a more coherent whole. Universities and their libraries will make adjustments in operations so as to expend less on conventional activities and more on digital communication.

Of course, there are unknowns. Agents and publishers will experiment to discover optimal pricing strategies. Agents will explore different ways of storing and delivering electronic products and different approaches to integration. Campuses and libraries will consider just what extra dimensions of service are worth their price. The process here is one of bringing order, meaning, and reliability to the emerging world of the Internet, of discovering what sells and what doesn't.

In the end, universities should be drawn to the electronic information services because of their superiority in instruction, their reach beyond the academy, and their power in the creation of new ideas. American higher education is largely shaped by competitive forces—the competition for faculty, students, research funding, and public and philanthropic support. In different ways, the private and public sector, the large institutions and the small, the two-year and four-year institutions all share the goal of doing a better, more cost-effective job of expanding the human potential. When artfully done, the digital sharing of ideas seems likely to expand that potential significantly.

NOTES

I appreciate the help of Elton Hinshaw and the American Economic Association in understanding its operations, and the comments of Paul Gherman, David Lucking-Reiley, and Flo Wilson on an earlier draft of this essay.

1. Shirley Baker, talk at Washington University, November, 1996.

2. Robin Frost, "The Electronic Gutenberg Fails to Win Mass Appeal," *Wall Street Journal*, 21 November 1996, B6. Project Gutenberg was a 25-year effort led by Michael S. Hart at the University of Illinois to create, store, and make accessible ASCII files of public domain materials from the Constitution, the Bible, Shakespeare, and beyond.

3. A large part of the Project Gutenberg files were moved to the library at the University of Maryland after this essay was written. See *http://www.inform.umd.edu/EdRes/ReadingRoom/*.

4. Stephen Burd, "President Pushes Tax Breaks to Help Families Afford College," *Chronicle of Higher Education*, 17 January 1997, A33.

5. *www.ei.org*

6. *http://xxx.lanl.gov/*

7. *http://scriptorium.lib.duke.edu/papyrus/* offers 1,373 images of Egyptian papyri with a significant database of descriptive textual material.

8. *http://fairmodel.econ.yale.edu/*

9. *http://gdbwww.gdb.org/*

10. The headquarters publishes *Job Openings in Economics* (JOE) seven times a year with nearly 1,500 job announcements. In 1995, JOE had about 4,000 subscribers and generated about $41,000 of revenue with a base rate of $15.00 per year ($7.50 for students, $25.00 for nonmembers and institutions). The sum of monthly printing and mailing costs was associated with the number of copies produced and the number of pages per copy for 1995 and 1996 as follows (with t-ratios in parenthesis):

$$\text{print \& mail} = -1,129.57 + 0.875 \text{ \# of copies} + 76.725 \text{ pages per issue}$$
$$(-2.83) \quad (7.35) \quad\quad\quad (17.2)$$

This relationship is estimated from data on each of 14 issues over the two years and has an adjusted R-square of 0.957. During this period of time, JOE averaged 25 pages per issue (the range was from 11 to 51). With seven issues per year, this equation forecasts total printing and mailing costs of $30,019 for 4,000 copies.

JOE became available without charge in 1994 *(http://www.eco.utexas.edu/joe/)*. The JOE site generated about 25,000 hits per month in 1996, and the subscription list of the printed JOE dropped to 1,000. The print and mail relationship estimated above forecasts a cost of $11,645 for 1,000 copies. The association will move from a net revenue position of $11,000 ($41,000 − $30,019) in the all-print regime to about a zero net ($15,000 − $11,645) with print subscription sales at about 1,000. Of course, the association incurs fixed costs in producing JOE that may be similar under both regimes.

The headquarters also publishes a directory of membership biennially. The directory became available on-line at the University of Texas in 1995 and is getting about 4,600 hits per month. Because the directory comes with membership, we have no measure of the rate of decline in the demand for the print version.

11. At some point in the future, membership ballots might be solicited and received by the Internet.

12. The AER's reviewing process is double-blind, with author's names withheld from reviewers and reviewer's names kept from authors. When nearly all working papers are posted on the World Wide Web, the refereeing may become single-blind de facto. Anyone who wants might search the title listing in the working paper file and so identify the author. When working papers are generally accessible on the Net, they would seem to be usable in the editorial process with some saving in cost but with some loss in anonymity.

13. The fixed costs of a print run (but not typography) would be eliminated entirely if print were abandoned completely. The fixed costs of electronic distribution would replace them in part. Presumably, the more sophisticated the electronic files submitted by authors, the lower the fixed cost of production at the publisher.

14. Since 1995, the association has made the JEL available in CD-ROM format instead of print for the same price. The CD-ROM costs about the same to produce on the margin per subscriber as a printed issue of a large journal. The CD-ROM contains the page images of the published journal and is distributed by mail. Its advantage is not reduced cost but increased subscriber benefit: it adds the power of electronic searching. Therefore, this version is gaining popularity. More than 10% of the AEA's members opted for the CD-ROM version of JEL in 1996.

15. The annual meeting contributed a net of about $125,000 in 1995.

16. Assume the current library subscription rate of $140 from 5,500 subscribers yields 20% of the AEA's gross and that membership plus ads from 21,000 members yields $70, about 40%. Assume the shift to electronic distribution lowers total expenditures by 20%. Doubling the library rate to $280, if all libraries subscribed, would keep AEA revenues constant.

17. The notion of doubling the library subscription rate in setting a rate for the campus intranet license is meant to define the association's probable revenue goals, but not to define the rate structure. The rate structure will need to be tied to something more substantial, like

enrollment and total research dollars. Alternatively, the rate could be set on the basis of a forecast of the hit rate. OCLC's electronic journal service sets rates on the basis of the number of simultaneous users. The level of rates would likely be set so as to yield about double the current library print subscriptions unless other revenue is forthcoming as discussed in subsequent paragraphs.

18. Here is part of the language the AEA prints on the copyright page: "Permission to make digital or hard copies of part or all of this work for personal or classroom use is granted without fee provided that copies are not made or distributed for profit or direct commercial advantage and that copies show this notice on the first page or initial screen of a display along with the full citation, including the name of the author."

19. Jared Sandberg ("Cash Advances Aid Electronic Commerce," *Wall Street Journal*, 30 September 1996, B8) reports an offering from CyberCash, a firm working with Visa and several banks. Cybercash put the cost of a transaction between $.08 and $.31 for purchases between $.25 and $10.

http://www.millicent.digital.com describes the protocols and tools developed by Digital Equipment Corporation to facilitate Web transactions in fractions of cents. "The key innovations of Millicent are its use of brokers and of scrip. Brokers take care of account management, billing, connection maintenance, and establishing accounts with vendors. Scrip is microcurrency that is only valid within the Millicent-enabled world."

20. Draft essay at *ftp://alfred.sims.berkeley.edu/pub/Papers/dlib.html*.

21. See Malcolm Getz, "Petabytes of Information," in *Advances in Library Administration and Organization*, XII (JAI Press, 1994), 203–37. Here are some features that might be added to the network working paper service: Each association member might receive a private password and encryption key. When the member submits a paper with the password and key, the service would return a time-stamped digital authentication message. This message and the posting would establish ownership to the working paper at the time of submission. The working paper service might include a more elaborate system of tagging papers, including the author's sense of the target audience, degree of originality, sophistication, empirical content, and revision number. The service might include links to comments.

22. E. Jacquelin Dietz, "The Future of the Journal of Statistics Education," North Carolina State University, mimeo, 1996.

23. The issue of optimal pricing for three products that share a fixed cost and in which cross elasticities are not zero should be explored formally.

24. David Carpenter and Malcolm Getz, "Evaluation of Library Resources in the Field of Economics: A Case Study," *Collection Management* 20, no. 1/2 (1995), 49–89.

25. See Malcolm Getz, "Information Storage," *Encyclopedia of Library and Information Science* 52, supplement 15 (1993), 201–39. High-density off-site storage might yield an annual cost of $.30 per volume and so about $3.00 of capital cost.

26. OCLC's Electronic Journals Online (EJO) preceded the Web-based program. With EJO, OCLC charged publishers for mounting their journals, much like printers charge for printing. This approach did not attract many publishers. The OCLC Web site *(www.OCLC.org)* lists several titles. Here is a sample of subscription rates.

The Online Journal of Current Clinic Trials from Chapman & Hall, distributed by OCLC: Institutional, $220; Individual, $120; Student (with ID), $49; Network (unlimited access), $3,000.

Online Journal of Knowledge Synthesis for Nursing from Sigma Theta Tau International, distributed by OCLC: Individuals, $60; Institutions, $250.

27. OCLC, "Bringing Your Publications Online With OCLC" (Dublin, Ohio, ca. 1996) and OCLC, "A Complete Electronic Journals Solution for Your Library" (Dublin, Ohio, ca. 1996).

28. Malcolm Getz, John J. Siegfried, and Kathryn H. Anderson, "Adoption of Innovations in Higher Education," *The Quarterly Review of Economics and Finance* 37(3) (Fall 1997): 605–31.

29. *http://mitpress.mit.edu/journals.tcl.* SNDE is one of six electronic journals offered by the MIT Press in 1996. The library rate includes a license to store the journal on a campus facility and make it available in library reserve services. The MIT Press puts the subscription rate at $30 for individuals and $125 for libraries, with a $12 fee for downloading an individual article.

CHAPTER 7

JSTOR

The Development of a
Cost-Driven, Value-Based Pricing Model

Kevin M. Guthrie

In the spring of 1996, when I was first asked for this contribution and was informed that my topic was pricing and user acceptance, I remember thinking it was quite a leap of faith, since JSTOR had neither a business model with prices, nor users. And we surely did not have user acceptance. Much has happened in a relatively short period of time, most notably the fact that JSTOR signed up 199 charter participants during the first three months of 1997. Our original projections were to have 50 to 75 participating institutions, so we are very encouraged to be off to such a good start.

The purpose of this brief case report is to summarize how JSTOR's economic model was developed, what we have learned along the way, and what we think the future challenges are likely to be. JSTOR is a work-in-progress, so it is not possible, nor would it be wise, to try to assert that we have done things "right." The jury is out and will be for quite some time. My goal is only to describe our approach to this point in the hope that doing so will provide useful experience for others working in the field of scholarly communication. In providing this summary I will try not to stray far from the organizing topic assigned to me—pricing and user acceptance—but I think it is impossible to separate these issues from more general aspects of a not-for-profit's organizational strategy and particularly its mission.

HISTORY

JSTOR began as a project of The Andrew W. Mellon Foundation designed to help libraries address growing and persistent space problems. Couldn't advances in technology help reduce the systemwide costs associated with storing commonly held materials like core academic journals? A decision was made to test a prototype system that would make the backfiles of core journals available in electronic form. Mellon Foundation staff signed up journal publishers in history and economics and, working through a grant to the University of Michigan, began to create a database with associated controlling software that was made available to several test site libraries. It became evident very soon both that the concept was extremely complicated to implement and that it held great promise.

JSTOR was established as an independent not-for-profit organization with its own board of trustees in August 1995. From the outset, JSTOR was given the charge to develop a financial plan that would allow it to become self-sustaining—the Mellon Foundation was not going to subsidize the concept indefinitely. At the same time, JSTOR is fortunate to have had Mellon's initial support because enormous resources have been invested in getting the entity launched that never have to be paid back. Apart from the direct investments of funds in the development of software, production capacity, and mirror sites through grants to Michigan and Princeton, there were large investments of time and effort by Mellon Foundation staff. JSTOR has received, in effect, venture capital for which it need not produce an economic return. We have tried to translate these initial grants into lower prices for the services that we provide to JSTOR participants.

DEFINING THE "PRODUCT"

Although JSTOR does not have to repay initial investments, it must have a mechanism to recover its ongoing costs. In developing a plan for cost recovery, our first step was to define exactly what it is that our "customers" would pay for—what is the "product"? On the face of it, this step sounds simple, but it is anything but that, especially given the rate of change of technology affecting the Internet and World Wide Web. For example, those publishers reading this paper who are working to put current issues in electronic form will know that even choosing the display format can be extremely difficult. Should the display files be images or text? If text, should they be SGML, PDF, HTML, SGML-to-HTML converted in advance, SGML-to-HTML converted on the fly, or some combination of these or other choices? The format that is chosen has far-reaching implications for present and future software capabilities, charging mechanisms, and user acceptance. It is easy to imagine how this decision alone can be paralyzing.

For nonprofit institutions like JSTOR, a key guidepost for making decisions of this type is the organization's mission. Nonprofits do not set out to maximize profits or shareholder wealth. In fact, they have been created to provide products or services that would not typically be made available by firms focused on maximizing profit. Consequently, not-for-profits cannot rely solely on quantitative approaches for decision making, even when such decisions are quantitative or financial in nature. Without such tools, having a clearly defined mission and using it to inform decisions is essential.

A good example of how JSTOR has relied on its mission for decision making is the question mentioned briefly above—choosing an appropriate display format.

We have decided to use a combination of images and text for delivery of the journal pages. We provide the images for display—so a user reads and can print a perfect replication of the original published page—and in the background we allow users to search the full text. This decision has been criticized by some people, but it is an appropriate approach for us, given the fact that our goal is to be a trusted archive and because JSTOR is now chiefly concerned with replicating previously published pages. There would be benefits to tagging the full text with SGML and delivering 100% corrected text files to our users, but because we also are committed to covering our costs, that approach is not practical. We are building a database of millions of pages and the effort required to do so is enormous. Digitizing even a single JSTOR title is a substantial undertaking. I have heard some people wonder why JSTOR is including "only" 100 journals in its first phase when other electronic journal initiatives are projecting hundreds, even thousands of journals. Presently, the 20 JSTOR journals that are available on-line have an average run of more than 50 years. So any calculation about the effort required for converting a single title needs to be multiplied 30 to 50 times to be comparable to the effort required to publish an electronic version of a single year of a journal. That imposes very real constraints.

Having a clear understanding of our fundamental mission has also allowed us to remain flexible as we confront a rapidly evolving environment. Trying to keep up with the technology is a never-ending task. We work hard to remain open to change, and at the same time we are committed to using the appropriate technology to fulfill our objective—no more, no less. Progress can grind to a halt quickly when so much is unknown and so much is changing, but our simple goal is to keep making progress. We recognize that by pushing forward relentlessly we will make some mistakes, but we are convinced that we cannot afford to stop moving if we are to build something meaningful in this dynamic environment.

So we established goals consistent with our mission and have made adjustments as we have gained experience. As mentioned previously, one of our fundamental goals is to serve as a trusted archive of the printed record. That means that output produced by the database has to be at least as good as the printed journals. A key determining factor in the quality of JSTOR printouts is the initial resolution at which the journal pages are scanned. Our original inclination was to scan pages at a resolution of 300 dots per inch (dpi). Anne Kenney[1] was a key advocate for scanning at 600 dpi when most people advised that 300 dpi was adequate and 600 dpi too expensive. Kenney made a strong case that scanning at 600 dpi is not just better than scanning at 300 dpi, but that, for pages comprised mainly of black-and-white text, there are rapidly diminishing perceivable improvements in the appearance of images scanned at resolutions greater than 600 dpi. It made sense, given the predominance of text in our database, to make the additional investment to gain the assurance that the images we were creating would continue to be acceptable even as technologies continued to improve. We are pleased that we made this choice; the quality of output now available from the JSTOR database is generally superior to a copy made from the original.

Another illustration of how it has been important for us to remain flexible concerns delivery of current issues. In the early days of JSTOR, several scholarly associations approached us with the idea that perhaps we could publish their current issues. The notion of providing scholars with access to the complete run of the journal—from the current issue back to the first issue—had (and has) enormous appeal. On the face of it, it seemed to make sense for JSTOR also to mount current issues in the database, and we began to encourage associations to think about working with us to provide both current issues and the backfiles. It was soon evident, however, that this direction was not going to work for multi-title publishers. These publishers, some of which publish journals owned by other entities such as scholarly associations, justifiably regarded a JSTOR initiative on current issues to be competition. They were not about to provide the backfile of a journal to us only to risk that journal's owners turning to JSTOR for electronic publication of current and future issues. Again, we had to make adjustments. We are now committed to working with publishers of current issues to create linkages that will allow seamless searches between their data and the JSTOR archive, but we will not ourselves publish current issues.[2] If we are to have maximum positive impact on the scholarly community, we must provide a service that benefits not only libraries and scholars but also publishers of all types, commercial and not-for-profit, multi-title and single-title. It is part of having a systemwide perspective, something that has been a central component of our approach from JSTOR's first days.

DETERMINING VIABILITY

Once we had framed the basic parameters of what we were going to offer, the key question we had to ask ourselves was whether the organization could be economically viable. Unfortunately, definitive answers to this question are probably never known in advance. The fact of the matter is that during their earliest phase, projects like JSTOR, even though they are not-for-profit, are still entrepreneurial ventures. They face almost all the same risks as for-profit start-ups, and the same tough questions must be asked before moving forward. Is there a revenue-generating "market" for the service to be provided?[3] Does the enterprise have sufficient capital to fund up-front costs that will be incurred before adequate revenue can be generated? Is the market large enough to support the growth required to keep the entity vibrant?

Pursuing this analysis requires a complicated assessment of interrelated factors. What are the costs for operating the entity? That depends on how much "product" is sold. How much product can be sold, and what are the potential revenues? That depends on how it is priced. What should be the product's price? That depends on the costs of providing it. Because these factors are so closely related, none of them can be analyzed in isolation from the others; however, it is natural for a not-for-profit project focused on cost recovery to begin its assessment with the expense side of the ledger.

DEFINING THE COSTS

When the product or service is one that has not previously been offered, projecting potential costs is more art than science. Even if one has some experience providing a version of the product, as JSTOR had because of the Mellon initiative, one finds that the costs that have been incurred during the initial start-up period are irregular and unstable and thus not reliable for projecting beyond that phase. Even now, with nearly 200 paying participants, we still have much to learn about what our stable running costs are likely to be.

What we have learned is that our costs fall into six categories:

1. *Production:* identifying, finding, and preparing the complete run; defining indexing guidelines to inform a scanning subcontractor; and performing quality control on the work of the scanning subcontractor.
2. *Conversion:* scanning, OCR, and inputting of index information to serve as the electronic table of contents (performed by a scanning subcontractor).
3. *Storage and access:* maintaining the database (at a number of mirror sites), which involves continuous updating of hardware and systems software.
4. *Software development:* migrating the data to new platforms and systems and providing new capabilities and features to maximize its usefulness to scholars as technological capabilities evolve.
5. *User support:* providing adequate user help desk services for a growing user base.
6. *Administration and oversight:* managing the overall operations of the enterprise.

Some of these costs are one-time (capital) expenditures and some of them are ongoing (operating) costs. For the most part, production and conversion (#1 and #2 above) are one-time costs. We hope that we are digitizing from the paper to the digital equivalent only once.[4] The costs in the other categories will be incurred regardless of whether new journals are added to the database and are thus a reflection of the ongoing costs of the enterprise.[5]

Because the most visible element of what JSTOR provides is the database of page images, many people tend to think that the cost of scanning is the only cost factor that needs to be considered. Although the scanning cost is relevant, it does not reflect the total cost of conversion for a database like JSTOR. In fact, scanning is not even the most expensive factor in the work done by our scanning contractor. During the conversion process, JSTOR's scanning vendor creates an electronic table of contents, which is just as costly as the scanning. In addition, because creating a text file suitable for searching requires manual intervention after running OCR software, that step has proven to be even more expensive than scanning. All told, the direct incremental costs of creating the three-part representation of a journal page in the JSTOR database (page image, electronic table of contents entry, and text file) is approximately $.75 to $1.00 per page.

Payments to the scanning bureau do not represent the complete production cost picture. Converting 100,000 pages per month requires a full-time staff to prepare the journals and to give the scanning bureau instructions to ensure that table of contents and indexing entries are made correctly. At present production levels, these costs are approximately equal to the outlays made to the scanning bureau. On average then, JSTOR production costs approach $2.00 per page.

Other costs of operating JSTOR are less easily segregated into their respective functional "departments." Our present estimates are that once all of the 100 Phase I journals are available in the database, operating costs (independent of the one-time costs associated with production) will be approximately $2.5 million annually.

DEFINING PRICING

On the one hand, the obvious goal is to develop a pricing plan that will cover the $2.5 million in projected annual expenses plus whatever one-time production-related expenses are incurred in converting the journals. These production costs, of course, depend on the rate at which the content is being digitized. For projects designed to recover costs by collecting fees from users, it is also important to assess whether the value of the service to be provided justifies the level of expenditures being projected.

In JSTOR's case, we evaluated the benefits to participants of providing a new and more convenient level of access to important scholarly material while also attempting to calculate costs that might be saved by participants if JSTOR allowed them to free expensive shelf space. A central part of the reason for our founding was to provide a service to the scholarly community that would be both better and cheaper. That goal is one that remains to be tested with real data, but it can and will be tested as JSTOR and its participating institutions gain more experience.

Our initial survey of the research indicated that the cost of library shelf space filled by long runs of core journals was substantial. Using a methodology devised by Malcolm Getz at Vanderbilt and cost data assembled by Michael Cooper at UC-Berkeley, we estimated that the capital cost for storing a single volume ranged between $24 and $41.[6] It follows that storing the complete run of a journal published for 100 years costs the holding institution between $2,400 and $4,100. In addition, operating costs associated with the circulation of volumes are also significant, and resources could be saved by substituting centrally managed electronic access to the material. Estimates of these costs for some of our original test site libraries indicated that costs in staff time for reshelving and other maintenance functions ranged from $45 annually for a core journal at a small college to $180 per title at a large research library with heavy use. These estimates of savings do not take into account the long-term costs of preservation or the time saved by users in finding articles of interest to them.

Although these estimates were not used to set prices, they did give us confidence that a pricing strategy could be developed that would offer good value for participating institutions. We set out to define more specifically the key components of the service we would offer and attempted to evaluate them both in the context of our mission and our cost framework. We found that deciding how to price an electronic product was extraordinarily complex, and it was clear that there was no correct answer. This list is by no means exhaustive, but here are some of the key factors that we weighed in our development of a pricing approach:

- Will access be offered on pay-per-use model, or by subscription, or both?
- If by subscription, will the resource be delivered to individuals directly or via a campus site license?
- If by site license, how is the authorized community of users defined?
- Will there be price differentiation or a single price?
- If the price varies in some way for different types of licensees, what classifying approach will be used to make the determinations?

In making decisions, we weighed the merits of various options by evaluating which seemed most consistent with JSTOR's fundamental objectives. For example, we wanted to provide the broadest possible access to JSTOR for the academic community. Because pricing on a pay-per-use model usually yields prices higher than the marginal cost of providing the product, we determined that this approach was not consistent with our goal. We did not want to force students and scholars to have to decide whether it would really be "worth it" to download and print an article. We wanted to encourage liberal searching, displaying, and printing of the resource. In a similar vein, we concluded that it would be better to begin by offering institutional site licenses to participating institutions. We defined the site license broadly by establishing that authorized users would consist of all faculty staff and students of the institution, plus any walk-up patrons using library facilities.[7]

Another decision made to encourage broad access was our determination that different types of users should pay different prices for access. This approach is called price differentiation, which is very common in industries with high fixed costs and low marginal costs (like airlines, telecommunications, etc.). We decided to pursue a value-based pricing approach that seeks to match the amount that institutions would contribute with the value they would receive from participation. By offering different prices to different classes of institutions, we hoped to distribute the costs of operating JSTOR over as many institutions as possible and in a fair way.

Once we had decided to offer a range of price levels, we had to select an objective method to place institutions into different price categories. We chose the Carnegie Classification of Institutions of Higher Education for pricing purposes. Our reason for choosing the Carnegie Classes was that these groupings reflect the degree to which academic institutions are committed to research. Because the JSTOR database includes journals primarily used for scholarly research and would therefore be most highly valued by research institutions, the Carnegie Classes offered a rubric consistent with our aims. In addition to the Carnegie Classes, JSTOR factors in the FTE enrollment of each institution, making adjustments that move institutions with smaller enrollments into classes with lower price levels. We decided to break higher education institutions into four JSTOR sizes: Large, Medium, Small, and Very Small.

Having established four pricing classes and a means for determining what institutions would fill them, we still had to set the prices themselves. In doing so, we thought about both the nature of our cost structure and the potential for revenue generation from the likely community of participants. We noted immediately that the nature of JSTOR's cost structure for converting a journal—a large one-time conversion cost followed by smaller annual maintenance costs—was matched by the nature of the costs incurred by libraries to hold the paper volumes. In the case of libraries holding journals, one-time or capital costs are reflected in the cost of land, building, and shelves, while annual outlays are made for such items as circulation/reshelving, heat, light, and electricity. We decided, therefore, to establish a pricing approach with two components: a one-time fee (which we called the Database Development Fee, or DDF) and a recurring fee (which we called the Annual Access Fee, or AAF).

But what should those prices be? As mentioned previously, the long-term goal was to recover $2.5 million in annual fees while also paying the one-time costs of converting the journals to digital formats. Because it was impossible to model potential international interest in JSTOR, we limited our plan to U.S. higher education institutions. We conducted an assessment of the potential number of participants in each of our four pricing classifications. The number of U.S. higher education institutions in each category is shown in Table 7.1.

After thorough analysis of various combinations of prices, participation levels, and cost assumptions, we arrived at a pricing plan that we felt offered a reasonable chance of success. One other complicating aspect that arose as we developed the plan was how to offer a one-time price for a resource that was constantly growing. To deal with that problem, we defined our initial product, JSTOR–Phase I, as a database with the complete runs of a minimum of 100 titles in 10 to 15 fields. We promised that this database would be complete within three years. Prices for participation in JSTOR–Phase I are shown in Table 7.2.

These prices reflect the availability of the complete runs of 100 titles. For a Large institution, perpetual access to 80 years of the *American Economic Review* (1911–1991) would cost just $400 one-time and $50 per year. For a Small institution,

TABLE 7.1.   Number of U.S. Higher
Education Institutions by JSTOR Class

JSTOR Class	Number of Institutions
Large	176
Medium	589
Small	166
Very small	471
Total	1,402

TABLE 7.2.   JSTOR Prices—Phase I

JSTOR Class	One-Time Database Development Fee (DDF)	Annual Access Fee (AAF)
Large	$40,000	$5,000
Medium	30,000	4,000
Small	20,000	3,000
Very small	10,000	2,000

the cost would be only $200 one-time and $30 per year. For comparison, consider that purchasing microfilm costs more but offers far less convenient access. Also, institutions that find it possible to move print copies to less expensive warehouses or even to remove duplicate copies from library shelves will capture savings that consists of some or all of the shelving and circulation costs outlined earlier in this paper. (For 80 volumes, that analysis projected capital costs between $24 and $41 per volume, or $1,920 to $3,280 for an 80-volume run. Also, annual circulation costs were estimated as $180 per year for a Large institution.)

We purposely set our prices low in an effort to involve a maximum number of institutions in the endeavor. We are often asked how many participating institutions are needed for JSTOR to reach "breakeven." Because the total revenue generated will depend upon the distribution of participants in the various class sizes, there is no single number of libraries that must participate for JSTOR to reach a self-sustaining level of operations. Further, since our pricing has both one-time and recurring components, breakeven could be defined in a number of ways. One estimate would be to say that breakeven will be reached when revenues from annual access fees match non-production-related annual operating expenditures (since the production-related costs are primarily one-time). Although this guide is useful, it is not totally accurate because, as mentioned previously, there are costs related to production that are very difficult to segregate from other expenses. Another approach would be to try to build an archiving endowment and to set a target endowment size that would support the continuing costs of maintaining and migrating the Phase I archive, even if no additional journals or participants were added after the Phase I period. Our plan combines these two approaches. We believe it is important to match the sources of annual revenues to the nature of the purposes for which they will be used. We require sufficient levels of annual inflows to cover the costs of making JSTOR available to users (user help desk, training, instruction, etc.). These inflows should be collected by way of annual access fees from participants. There is also, however, the archiving function that JSTOR provides, which is not directly attributable to any particular user. Like the role that libraries fill by keeping books on the shelves just in case they are needed, JSTOR's archiving is a public good. We must build a capital base to support the technological migration and other costs associated with this archiving function.

Like our approach to other aspects of our organizational plan, we remain open to making adjustments in pricing when it is fair and appropriate and it does not put our viability at risk. One step we took was to offer a special charter discount for institutions that chose to participate in JSTOR prior to April 1, 1997. We felt it was appropriate to offer this discount in recognition of participants' willingness to support JSTOR in its earliest days. We also have made minor adjustments in the definitions of how Carnegie Classes are slotted into the JSTOR pricing categories. In our initial plan, for example, we included all Carnegie Research (I and II) and Doctoral (I and II) institutions in the Large JSTOR category. Subsequent conversations with librarians and administrators made it clear that including Doctoral II institutions in this category was not appropriate. There proved to be a significant difference in the nature of these institutions and in the resources they invest in research, and so an adjustment was made to place them in the Medium class. Any such adjustments that we have made have not been for a single institution, but for all institutions that share a definable characteristic. We strive to be fair; therefore, we do not negotiate special deals.

There is a component of our pricing strategy that needs some explanation because it has been a disappointment to some people, that is, JSTOR's policy toward consortia. JSTOR's pricing plan was developed to distribute the costs of providing a shared resource among as many institutions as possible. The same forces that have encouraged the growth of consortia—namely, the development of technologies to distribute information over networks—are also what make JSTOR possible. It is not necessary to have materials shelved nearby in order to read them. A consequence of this fact is that marginal costs of distribution are low and economies of scale substantial. Those benefits have already been taken into account in JSTOR's economic model. In effect, JSTOR is itself a consortial enterprise that has attempted to spread its costs over as much of the community as possible. Offering further discounts to large groups of institutions would put at risk JSTOR's viability and with it the potential benefits to the scholarly community.

A second significant factor that prevents JSTOR from offering access through consortia at deep discounts is that the distribution of organizations in consortia is uneven and unstable. Many institutions are members of several consortia, while some are in none at all (although there are increasingly few of those remaining). If the consortial arrangements were more mature and if there was a one-to-one relationship between the institutions in JSTOR's community and consortial groups, it might have been possible for JSTOR to build a plan that would distribute costs fairly across those groups. If, for example, every institution in the United States was a member of one of five separate consortia, a project like JSTOR could divide its costs by five and a fair contribution could be made by all. But there are not five consortia; there are hundreds. The patchwork of consortial affiliations is so complex that it is extremely difficult, if not impossible, to establish prices that will be regarded as fair by participants. JSTOR's commitment to share as much of what it learns with the scholarly community as possible requires that there be no special deals, that we be open about the contributions that institutions make and their reasons for making them. Our economic model would not be sustainable if two very similar institutions contributed different amounts simply because one was a member of a consortium that drove a harder bargain. Instead, we rely on a pricing unit that is easily defined and understood—the individual institution. And we rely on a pricing gradient, the Carnegie Classification, which distributes those institutions objectively into groupings that are consistent with the nature and value of our resource.

CONCLUSION

The initial response to JSTOR's charter offer in the first three months of this year is a strong signal that JSTOR will be a valued resource for the research community; however, it is still far too early to comment further on "user acceptance." Tom Finholt and JoAnn Brooks's research (see chapter 11) into usage at the test site libraries provides a first snapshot, but this picture was taken prior to there being any effort to increase awareness of JSTOR in the community and on the specific campuses. There is much to learn. JSTOR is committed to tracking usage data both for libraries and publishers and to providing special software tools to enable users to create usage reports tailored to their own needs and interests. We will continue to keep the academic community informed as we learn more.

While we are encouraged by the positive reaction of the library community to JSTOR, we recognize that this good start has raised expectations and has created new challenges. In addition to the challenges of reaching our 100-title goal before the end of 1999, trying to encourage the next 200 libraries to participate, and keeping up with changing technologies, we face other complex challenges, including how to make JSTOR available outside the United States and how to define future phases of JSTOR. Addressing these issues will require the development of new strategic plans and new economic and pricing models. In creating those plans, we know that we will continue to confront complicated choices. As we make decisions, we will remain focused on our mission, making adjustments to our plans as required to keep making progress in appropriate ways.

NOTES

1. Anne Kenney is the associate director of preservation at the Cornell University Library. She has also contributed to this work; see chapter 2, "Digital Image Quality: From Conversion to Presentation and Beyond."

2. We did agree to work with three scholarly associations—the Ecological Society of America, the American Economic Association, and the American Political Science Association—to provide access to current issues through JSTOR. We stand by our commitments to these organizations, but our goal is to learn more about the technology required to make linkages between current issues and the archive, not to build the capability for JSTOR to become a publisher of current issues.

3. In the not-for-profit context, a revenue-generating market need not consist solely of paying customers; it could include other types of indirect funders like government agencies or foundations.

4. To refer to these costs as one-time costs is not precisely accurate. Not all of the production costs are one-time. We add another volume of each journal title to the database as each year passes, so there is an ongoing element of the production costs, but that element represents a small fraction of total production expenditures.

5. There is a caveat here as well. Some of the administrative and overhead costs are higher because JSTOR is adding titles. Negotiating agreements with publishers is a time-consuming task, as is overseeing the production operation converting 100,000 pages per month. It is not practical, however, to allocate exactly the portion of general administrative and other costs that pertain directly to production.

6. For a more complete description of these estimates, see "JSTOR and the Economics of Scholarly Communication," a paper by William G. Bowen, which is available at *http://www.mellon.org/jsesc.html*.

7. For a more complete description of the evolution in the development of JSTOR's library license terms, see Sarah E. Sully, "JSTOR: An IP Practitioner's Perspective," *D-Lib*, January 1997.

CHAPTER 8

The Effect of Price
Early Observations

Karen Hunter

INTRODUCTION

Scientific journal publishers have very little commercial experience with electronic full text distribution, and it is hard, if not impossible, to segregate the effect of pricing on user acceptance and behavior. Most experiments or trial offers have been without charge to the user. Most paid services have targeted institutional rather than individual buyers. Nevertheless, we can look at some of the known experiences and at ongoing and proposed experiments to get some sense of the interaction of pricing and acceptance and of the other factors that seem to affect user behavior. We can also look at institutional buying concerns and pricing considerations.

IN THE BASIC PAPER WORLD

Many journals have offered reduced prices to individuals. In the case of journals owned by societies or other organizations, there are generally further reductions in the prices for members. It is important to the society that members not only receive the lowest price but can clearly see that price as a benefit of membership. The price for members may be at marginal cost, particularly if (1) the size of the membership is large, (2) subscriptions are included as a part of the membership dues, and (3) there is advertising income to be gained from the presence of a large individual subscription base. This third factor is commonly seen in clinical medical journals, where the presence of 15,000 or 30,000 or more individual subscribers leads to more than $1 million in advertising income—income that would be near zero without the individual subscription base. Publishers can "afford" to sell the subscriptions at cost because of the advertising.

For many other journals, including most published by my company, there either are no individual rates or the number of individual subscribers is trivial. This is largely because the size of the journals, and therefore their prices, are sufficiently high (average $1,600) that it is difficult to set a price for individuals that would be attractive. Giving even a 50% reduction in price does not bring the journal into the price range that attracts individual purchasers.

One alternative is to offer a reduced rate for personal subscriptions to individuals affiliated with an institution that has a library subscription. This permits the individual rate to be lower, but it is still not a large source of subscriptions in paper. The price is still seen as high (e.g., the journal *Gene* has an institutional price of $6,144 in 1997 and an associated personal rate of $533; the ratio is similar for *Earth and Planetary Sciences Letters*—$2,333 for an institutional subscription, $150 for individuals affiliated with that institution.) This alternative still draws only a very limited number of subscribers.

We have not recently (this decade) rigorously tested alternative pricing strategies for this type of paper arrangement nor talked with scientists to learn specifically why they have or have not responded to an offer. This decision not to do market research reflects a view that there is only limited growth potential in paper distribution and that the take-up by individuals (if it is to happen) will be in an electronic world.

ALTERING SERVICES

There is some experience with free distribution, which may be relevant. Over the last decade we have developed a fairly large number of electronic and paper services designed to "alert" our readers to newly published or soon-to-be-published information. These services take many forms, including lists of papers accepted for publication; current tables of contents; groupings of several journals in a discipline; journal-specific alerts; and inclusion of additional discipline-specific news items. Some are mailed. Some are electronically broadcast. Others are electronically profiled and targeted to a specific individual's expressed interest. Finally, some are simply on our server and "pulled" on demand.

All are popular and all are sent only to users who have specifically said they want to receive these services. The electronic services are growing rapidly, but the desire for those that are paper-based continues. We even see "claims" for missing issues should a copy fail to arrive in the mail. What we conclude from this response is that there is a demand for information about our publications—the earlier the better—and that so long as it is free *and* perceived as valuable, it will be welcomed. Note, however, that in the one case where, together with another publisher, we tried to increase the perceived value of an alerting service by adding more titles to the discipline cluster and adding some other services, there was noticeable resistance to paying a subscription for the service.

ELECTRONIC PRICING

In developing and pricing new electronic products and services, journal publishers may consider many factors, including (in random order):

- the cost of creating and maintaining the service;
- the possible effect of this product or service on other things you sell ("cannibalization" or substitution);
- the ability to actually implement the pricing (site or user community definitions, estimates of the anticipated usage or number of users, security systems);
- provision for price changes in future years;
- what competitors are doing;
- the functionality actually being offered;
- the perceived value of the content and of the functionality;
- the planned product development path (in markets, functionality, content);
- the ability of the market to pay for the product or service;
- the values that the market will find attractive (e.g., price predictability or stability);
- the anticipated market penetration and growth in sales over time;
- the market behavior that you want to encourage;
- and, not inconsequentially, the effect on your total business if you fail with this product or service.

To make informed judgments, you have to build up experience and expertise. Pricing has long been an important strategic variable in the marketing mix for more mature electronic information players. They have more knowledge of how a market will react to new pricing models. For example, more than five years ago, you would see at an Information Industry Association meeting staff from business, financial, and legal on-line services with titles such as Vice President, Pricing. Nothing comparable existed within the journal publishing industry. A price was set, take it or leave it, and there was little room for nuance or negotiation.

This situation is now changing. Many large journal publishers are actively involved in either negotiating pricing agreements or, under fixed terms, negotiating other aspects of the licensed arrangement that relate to the effective price being paid (such as number of users, number of simultaneous accesses, etc.). At Elsevier in 1996, we engaged consultants to make a rigorous study to assist us in developing pricing models for electronic subscriptions and other electronic services. What we found was that we could not construct algorithms to predict buying behavior in relation to price. That finding has not stopped us from trying to pursue more sophistication in pricing—and indeed, we have now hired our own first full-time Director of Pricing—but until we build up more experience, our pricing decisions are still often a combination of tradition, strategic principle, gut feeling, and trial and error. We do have, however, a view on the desired long-term position and how we want to get there.

Too often, some buyers argue that pricing should be based solely on cost (and often without understanding what goes into the cost). They sometimes express the simplistic view that electronic journals are paper journals without the paper and postage and should therefore be priced at a discount. That view clearly is naive because it overlooks all of the new, additional costs that go into creating innovative electronic products (as well as maintaining two product lines simultaneously). Indeed, if you were to price right now on simply the basis of cost, the price for electronic products would likely be prohibitively high.

It is equally doubtful whether you can accurately determine the value added from electronic functionality and set prices based *exclusively* on the value, with the notion that as more functionality is added, the value—therefore, the price—can be automatically increased. Some value-based pricing is to be expected and is justified, but in this new electronic market there are also limited budgets and highly competitive forces, which keep prices in check. At the same time, it is not likely that the "content" side of the information industry will totally follow the PC hardware side, in other words, that the prices will stay essentially flat, with more and more new goodies bundled in the product. Hardware is much more of a competitive commodity business.

Pricing components are now much more visible and subject to negotiation. In discussions with large accounts, it is assumed that there will be such negotiation. This trend is not necessarily a positive development for either publishers or libraries. I hope that collectively we won't wind up making the purchase of electronic journals the painful equivalent of buying a car ("How about some rust proofing and an extended warranty?").

There is and will continue to be active market feedback and participation on pricing. The most obvious feedback is a refusal to buy, either because the price is too high (the price-value trade-off is not there) or because of other terms and conditions associated with the deal. Other feedback will come via negotiation and public market debates. Over time, electronic journal pricing will begin to settle into well-understood patterns and principles. At the moment, however, there are almost as many definitions and models as there are publishers and intermediaries. One need only note the recent discussions on the e-list on library licensing moderated by Ann Okerson of Yale University to understand that we are all in the early stages of these processes. An early 1997 posting gave a rather lengthy list of pricing permutations.

END USER PURCHASING

If we talk of pricing and "user acceptance," an immediate question is: who is the user? Is it the end user or is it the person paying the bill, if they are not one and the same? We presume that the intention was to reflect the judgments made by end users when those end users are also the ones bearing the economic consequences of their decisions. In academic information purchasing (as with consumer purchasing), the end user has traditionally been shielded from the full cost (often any cost) of information. Just as newspapers and magazine costs are heavily subsidized by advertising, and radio and television revenues (excluding cable) are totally paid by advertisers, so do academic journal users benefit from the library as the purchasing agent.

In connection with the design of its new Web journal database and host service, *ScienceDirect*, Elsevier Science in 1996 held a number of focus groups with scientists in the United States and the United Kingdom. Among the questions asked was the amount of money currently spent personally (including from grant funds) annually on the acquisition of information resources. The number was consistently below $500 and was generally between $250 and $400, often including society dues, which provided journal subscriptions as part of the dues. There was almost no willingness to spend more money, and there was a consistent expectation that the library would continue to be the provider of services, including new electronic services.

This finding is consistent with the results of several years of direct sales of documents through the (now) Knight-Ridder CARL UnCover service. When it introduced its service a few years ago, UnCover had expected to have about 50% of the orders coming directly from individuals, billed to their credit cards. In fact, as reported by Martha Whitaker of CARL during the 1997 annual meeting of the Association of American Publishers, Professional/Scholarly Publishing Division in February, the number has stayed at about 20% (of a modestly growing total business).

From their side, libraries are concerned that the user has little or no appreciation of the cost to the library of fulfilling their users' requests. In two private discussions in February of 1997, academic librarians told me of their frustration when interlibrary loan requests are made, the articles procured, and the requesters notified, but then the articles are not picked up. There is a sense that this service is "free," even though it is well-documented (via a Mellon study) that the cost is now more than $30 per ILL transaction.

In this context, discussions with some academic librarians about the introduction of electronic journal services have not always brought the expected reactions. It had been our starting premise that electronic journals should mimic paper journals in certain ways, most notably that once you have paid the subscription, then you have unlimited use within the authorized user community. However, one large library consortium negotiator has taken the position that such an approach may not be desirable, that it may be better to start educating users that information has a cost attached to it.

Similarly, other librarians have expressed concern about on-line facilities that permit users to acquire individual articles on a transactional basis from nonsubscribed titles (e.g., in a service such as *ScienceDirect*). While the facilities may be in place to bill the end user directly, the librarians believe the users will not be willing to pay the likely prices ($15–25). Yet, if the library is billed for everything, either the cost will run up quickly or any prepaid quota of articles will be used equally rapidly. The notion that was suggested was to find some way to make a nominal personal charge of perhaps $1 or $2 or $3 per transaction. It was the librarians' belief that such a charge would be enough to make the user stop and think before ordering something that would result in a much larger ultimate charge to the library.

The concern that demand could swamp the system if unregulated is one that would be interesting to test on a large scale. While there have been some experiments, which I will describe further below, we have not yet had sufficient experience to generalize. Journal users are, presumably, different from America Online customers, who so infamously swamped the network in December 1996 when pricing was changed from time-based to unlimited use for $19.95 per month. Students, faculty, and other researchers read journals for professional business purposes and generally try to read as little as possible. They want to be efficient in combing and reviewing the literature and not to read more and more without restraint. The job of a good electronic system is to increase that efficiency by providing tools to sift the relevant from the rest.

It is interesting to note that in a paper environment, the self-described "king of cancellations," Chuck Hamaker, formerly of Louisiana State University, reported during the 1997 mid-winter ALA meeting that he had canceled $738,885 worth of subscriptions between 1986 and 1996 and substituted free, library-sanctioned, commercial document delivery services. The cost to the library has been a fraction of what the subscription cost would have been. He now has about 900 faculty and students who have profiles with the document deliverer (UnCover) and who order directly, on an unmediated basis, with the library getting the bill. He would like to see that number increase (there are 5,000 faculty and students who would qualify). It will be interesting to see if the same pattern will occur if the article is physically available on the network and the charge is incurred as a result of viewing or downloading. Will the decision to print be greater (because it is immediate and easy) than to order from a document delivery service?

This question highlights one of the issues surrounding transactional selling: how much information is sufficient to ensure that the article being ordered will be useful? Within the *ScienceDirect* environment we hope to answer this question by creating services specifically for individual purchase that offer the user an article snapshot or summary (SummaryPlus), which includes much more than the usual information about the article (e.g., it includes all tables and graphs and all references). The summary allows the user to make a more informed decision about whether to purchase the full article.

TULIP (THE UNIVERSITY LICENSING PROGRAM)

Elsevier Science has been working toward the electronic delivery of its journals for nearly two decades. Its early discussions with other publishers about what became

ADONIS started in 1979. Throughout the 1990s there have been a number of large and small programs, some experimental, some commercial. Each has given us some knowledge of user behavior in response to price, although in some cases the "user" is the institution rather than the end user. The largest experimental program was TULIP (The University LIcensing Program).

TULIP was a five-year experimental program (1991–1995) in which Elsevier partnered with nine leading U.S. universities (including all the universities within the University of California system) to test desktop delivery of electronic journals. The core of the experiment was the delivery of initially 43, later an additional optional 40, journals in materials science. The files were bitmapped (TIFF) format, with searchable ASCII headers and unedited, OCR-generated ASCII full text. The universities received the files and mounted them locally, using a variety of hardware and software configurations. The notion was to integrate or otherwise present the journals consistently with the way other information was offered on campus networks. No two institutions used the same approach, and the extensive learning that was gained has been summarized in a final report (available at *http://www.elsevier.com/locate/TULIP*).

These are a few relevant observations from this report. First, the libraries (through whom the experiment was managed) generally chose a conservative approach in a number of discretionary areas. For example, while there was a document delivery option for titles not subscribed to (each library received the electronic counterparts of their paper subscriptions), no one opted to do this. Similarly, the full electronic versions of nonsubscribed titles were offered at a highly discounted rate (30% of list) but essentially found no takers. The most frequently expressed view was that a decision had been made at some time not to subscribe to the title, so its availability even at a reduced rate was not a good purchasing decision.

Second, one of the initial goals of this experiment was to explore economic issues. Whereas the other goals (technology testing and evaluating user behavior) were well explored, the economic goal was less developed. That resulted perhaps from a failure in the initial expectations and in the experimental design. From our side as publisher, we were anxious to try out different distribution models on campus, including models where there would be at least some charge for access. However, the charging of a fee was never set as a requirement, nor were individual institutions assigned to different economic tests. And, in the end, all opted to make no charges for access. This decision was entirely understandable, because of both the local campus cultures and the other issues to be dealt with in simply getting the service up and running and promoting it to users. However, it did mean that we never gathered any data in this area.

From the universities' side, there was a hope that more progress would be made toward developing new subscription models. We did have a number of serious discussions, but again, not as much was achieved as might have been hoped for if the notion was to test a radical change in the paradigm. I think everyone is now more experienced and realizes that these issues are complex and take time to evolve.

Finally, the other relevant finding from the TULIP experiment is that use was very heavily related to the (lack of) perceived critical mass. Offering journals to the desktop is only valuable if they are the right journals and if they are supplied on a timely basis. Timeliness was compromised because the electronic files were produced after the paper—a necessity at the time but not how we (or other publishers) are currently proceeding. Critical mass was also compromised because, although there was a great deal of material delivered (11 GB per year), materials science is a very broad discipline and the number of journals relevant for any one researcher was still limited. If the set included "the" journal or one of the key journals that a researcher (or more likely, graduate student) needed, use was high. Otherwise, users did not return regularly to the system. And use was infrequent even when there was no charge for it.

ELSEVIER SCIENCE EXPERIENCES
WITH COMMERCIAL ELECTRONIC JOURNALS
Elsevier Electronic Subscriptions

The single largest Elsevier program of commercial electronic delivery is the Elsevier Electronic Subscriptions (EES) program. This is the commercial extension of the TULIP program to all 1,100 Elsevier primary and review journals. The licensing negotiations are exclusively with institutions, which receive the journal files and mount them on their local network. The license gives the library unlimited use of the files within their authorized user community. As far as we are aware, academic libraries are not charging their patrons for their use of the files, so there is no data relating user acceptance to price. At least one corporate library charges use back to departments, but this practice is consistent for all of its services and has not affected use as far as is known.

If you broaden the term *user* to include the paying institution, as discussed above, then there is clearly a relation between pricing and user acceptance. If we can't reach an agreement on price in license negotiations, there is no deal. And it is a negotiation. The desire from the libraries is often for price predictability over a multiyear period. Because prices are subject to both annual price increases and the fluctuation of the dollar, there can be dramatic changes from year to year. For many institutions, the deal is much more "acceptable" if these increases are fixed in advance.

The absolute price is also, of course, an issue. There is little money available, and high pricing of electronic products will result in a reluctant end to discussions. Discussions are both easier and more complicated with consortia. It is easier to make the deal a winning situation for the members of the consortium (with virtually all members getting access to some titles that they previously did not have), but it is more complicated because of the number of parties who have to sign off on the transaction.

Finally, for a product such as EES, the total cost to the subscribing institution goes beyond what is paid to Elsevier as publisher. There is the cost of the hardware and software to store and run the system locally, the staff needed to update and maintain the system, local marketing and training time, and so on. It is part of Elsevier's sales process to explain these costs to the subscribing institution, because it is not in our interest or theirs to underestimate the necessary effort only to have it become clear during implementation. To date, our library customers have appreciated that approach.

Immunology Today Online (ITO)

Immunology Today is one of the world's leading review journals, with an ISI impact factor of more than 24. It is a monthly magazine–like title, with a wide individual and institutional subscription base. (The Elsevier review magazines are the exception to the rule in that they have significant individual subscriptions.) In 1994 *Immunology Today*'s publishing staff decided it was a good title to launch also in an electronic version. They worked with OCLC to make it a part of the OCLC Electronic Journals Online collection, initially offered via proprietary Guidon software and launched in January 1995.

As with other journals then and now making their initial on-line appearance, the first period of use was without charge. A test bed developed of about 5% of the individual subscribers to the paper version and 3% of the library subscribers. In time, there was a conversion to paid subscriptions, with the price for the combined paper and electronic personal subscriptions being 125% of the paper price. (Subscribers were not required to take both the paper and electronic versions— but only three people chose to take electronic only.) At the time that OCLC ended the service at the end of 1996 and we began the process of moving subscribers to a similar Web version of our own, the paid subscription level for individuals was up to about 7.0% of the individual subscribers and 0.3% of the institutional subscribers.

The poor take-up by libraries was not really a surprise. At the beginning, libraries did not know how to evaluate or offer to patrons a single electronic journal subscription as opposed to a database of journals. (There is a steady improvement in this area, provoked in part by the journals—notably *The Journal of Biological Chemistry*—offered via High Wire Press.) How do you let people know it is available? How and where is it available? And is a review journal—even a very popular review journal—the place to start? It apparently seemed like more trouble than it was worth to many librarians.

In talking with the individual subscribers—and those who did not subscribe— it was clear that price was not a significant factor in their decisions. The functionality of the electronic version was the selling point. It has features that are not in the paper version and is, of course, fully searchable. That means the value was, in part, in efficiency—the ease with which you find that article that you recalled reading six months ago but don't remember the author or precise month or the ease with which you search for information on a new topic of interest. The electronic version is a complement to the paper, not a substitute. Those individuals who chose not to subscribe either were deterred by the initial OCLC software (which had its problems) and may now be lured back via our Web version or they have not yet seen a value that will add to their satisfaction with paper. But their hesitation has not been a question of price.

Journal of the American College of Cardiology

A project involving the *Journal of the American College of Cardiology* (JACC) was somewhat different. This flagship journal is owned by a major society and has been published by Elsevier Science since its beginning in the early 1980s. In 1995, in consultation with the society, Elsevier developed a CD-ROM version. The electronic design—style, interface, and access tools—is quite good. The cost of the CD-ROM is relatively low ($295 for institutions, substantially less for members), and it includes not only the journal but also five years of JACC abstracts, the abstracts from the annual meeting, and one year (six issues) of another publication, entitled *ACC Current Reviews.*

But the CD-ROM has sold only modestly well. Libraries, again, resist CD-ROMs for individual journals (as opposed to journal collections). And the doctors have not found it a compelling purchase. Is it price per se? Or is it the notion of paying anything more, when the paper journal comes bundled as part of the membership dues? Or is there simply no set of well-defined benefits? Clearly, the perceived value to the user is not sufficient to cause many to reach for a credit card.

GeneCOMBIS and Earth and Planetary Sciences Letters Online

I mentioned above that for some paper journals we have personal rates for individuals at subscribing institutions. This model has been extended to Web products related to those paper journals. In addition to the basic journal *Gene*, mentioned earlier, we publish an electronic section called *GeneCOMBIS* (for *Computing for Molecular Biology Information Service*), which is an electronic-first publication devoted to the computing problems that arise in molecular biology. It publishes its own new papers. The papers are also published in hard copy, but the electronic version includes hypertext links to programs, data sets, genetics databases, and other software objects. *GeneCOMBIS* is sold to individuals for $75 per year, but only to those individuals whose institutions subscribe to *Gene*.

The same model is repeated with the electronic version of a leading earth sciences journal, *Earth and Planetary Sciences Letters.* The affiliated rate for the electronic version was introduced in 1997, with a nominal list price of $90 and a half-price offer for 1997 of $45. The electronic version provides on-line access to the journal and to extra material such as data sets for individuals affiliated with subscribing institutions.

It is too early to know whether this model will work. There certainly has been interest. In the case of *GeneCOMBIS*, its success will ultimately depend on the quality and volume of the papers it attracts. With *EPSL Online*, success will be determined by the perceived value of the electronic version and its added information. In neither case is price expected to have a significant effect on subscriptions. More likely, there will be pressure to extend the subscriptions to individuals working outside institutions that have the underlying paper subscriptions.

EXPERIENCES OF OTHERS

It is perhaps useful to note also some of the experiences of other publishers.

Red Sage Experiment

The Red Sage experiment started in 1992 and ran through 1996. It was initially started by Springer-Verlag, the University of California at San Francisco, and AT&T Bell Labs. Ultimately, several other publishers joined in, and more than 70 biomedical journals were delivered to the desktops of medical students and faculty at UCSF. As with TULIP, the experiment proved much harder to implement than had been originally hoped for. To the best of my knowledge, there were no user charges, so no data is available on the interplay of price and user acceptance. But what is notable is that there was greater critical mass of user-preferred titles among the Red Sage titles and, as a result, usage was very high. The horse will drink if brought to the right water.

Society CD-ROM Options

A second anecdote comes from discussions last year with a member of the staff of the American Institute of Physics. At least one of their affiliated member societies decided to offer members an option to receive their member subscriptions on CD-ROM rather than on paper, at the same price (i.e., the amount allocated from their member dues). The numbers I recall are that more than 1,500 members of the society took the option, finding the CD-ROM a more attractive alternative. I suspect that had they tried to sell the CD-ROM on top of the cost of the basic subscription, there would have been few takers. However, in this case, if you ignore the initial investment to develop the CD, the CD option saved the society money because it was cheaper on the incremental cost basis to make and ship the CDs rather than print and mail the paper version. In this case, the economics favored everyone.

BioMedNet

The final observation relates to an electronic service that started last year called BioMedNet. It is a "club" for life scientists, offering some full text journals, Medline, classified ads (the most frequently used service), marketplace features, news, and other items. To date, membership is free. There are more than 55,000 members, and another 1,000 or more come in each week. The site is totally underwritten at the moment by its investors, with an expectation of charging for membership at some later date but with the plan that principal revenues will come from advertising and a share of marketplace transactions. The observation here is that while the membership is growing steadily, usage is not yet high per registered member. There is a core of heavy users, but it is rather small (2–3%). So, again, behavior and acceptance is not a function of price but of perceived value. Is it worth my time to visit the site?

PEAK: THE NEXT EXPERIMENT

As was mentioned above, the aspect of the TULIP experiment that produced the least data was the economic evaluation. One of the TULIP partners was the University of Michigan, which is now also an EES subscriber for all Elsevier journal titles. As part of our discussions with Michigan, we agreed to further controlled experimentation in pricing. Jeffrey MacKie-Mason, an associate professor of economics and information, has designed the experiment at the University of Michigan. MacKie-Mason is also the project director for the economic aspects of the experiment.

This pricing field trial is called Pricing Electronic Access to Knowledge (PEAK). Michigan will create a variety of access models and administer a pricing system. The university will apply these models to other institutions, which will be serviced from Michigan as the host facility. Some institutions will purchase access on a more or less standard subscription model. Others will buy a generalized or virtual subscription, which allows for prepaid access to a set of N articles, where the articles can be selected from across the database. Finally, a third group will acquire articles strictly on a transactional basis. Careful thought has, of course, gone into the relationship among the unit prices under these three schemes, the absolute level of the prices, and the relationship among the pricing, the concepts of value, and the publishers' need for a return.

The experiment should begin in early 1998 and run at least through August 1999. We are all looking forward to the results of this research.

IN CONCLUSION

Journal publishers have relatively little experience with offering electronic full text to end users for a fee. Most new Web products either are free or have a free introductory period. Many are now in the process of starting to charge (*Science*, for example, instituted its first subscription fees as of January 1997 and sells electronic subscriptions only to paper personal subscribers). However, it is already clear that a price perceived as fair is a necessary but not sufficient factor in gaining users. Freely available information will not be used if it is not seen as being a productive use of time. Novelty fades quickly. If a Web site or other electronic offering does not offer more (job leads, competitive information, early reporting of research results, discussion forums, simple convenience of bringing key journals to the desktop), it will not be heavily used. In designing electronic services, publishers have to deal with issues of speed, quality control, comprehensiveness—and then price. The evaluation of acceptance by the user will be on the total package.

CHAPTER 9

Electronic Publishing Is Cheaper

Willis G. Regier

Electronic publishing is cheaper than many kinds of publishing. Cheap electronic publishing proliferates newsletters, fanzines, vanity publishing, testimonials, political sniping, and frantic Chicken Littles eager to get the word out. Cheaper publishing has always meant more publishing. But students, scholars, and libraries complain that there is already an overproduction of academic writing. Electronic publishing would just make matters worse, unless it comes with additional features to manage its quantity. Scholarly publishing is prepared to enter electronic publishing, but will not let go of print. Why? Because the demands of scholars and libraries for *enhanced* electronic publishing make it *more* expensive.

Electronic publishing comes with a long menu of choices: differing speeds of access, adjustable breadth and depth of content, higher or lower visibility, flexibility, durability, dependability, differentiation, and ease of use. In such a field of choices, there is not a basic cost or an optimum one or an upper limit. Until the wish for more and the desire to pay less find equilibrium, there will be discomfort and hesitation in the shift from paper to ether.

At present, most mainstream digital publications remain dependent on print, either as a publication of record, as with most scholarly journals, or as a nexus for electronic sites, as with the Web sites for *Wired,* numerous newspapers and magazines, publishers of all stripes, book clubs, and booksellers. In this parallel-publishing environment, print costs remain in place; the costs of mounting and maintaining a digital presence are added on.

Some publishers have established Web sites, with little expectation of recovering those added costs, in order to maintain an up-to-date profile, to market directly to customers, and to be sure that when and if the Web market matures, they will be ready to compete for it.

Those who declare that electronic publishing is cheaper than print focus chiefly on perceived savings in reproduction and distribution. Once the first copy is prepared, its reproduction and transmission reduce or eliminate the costs of printing, paper, ink, packaging, shipping, spoilage, and inventory. The manufacturing cost of a typical print journal in the humanities, for example, consumes about 50% of the journal's operating budget, and shipping and warehousing can eat up another 10%. Such costs are incidental in the electronic environment.

But electronic publishing adds numerous new costs to preparation of the first copy. Further, the savings enjoyed by the publisher are made possible only if the end user, whether a library or an individual, has also invested a hefty sum in making it possible to receive the publication. Both the scholarly publisher and the end user alike are dependent upon even greater costs being born by colleges and universities.

As costs became more routine for Project MUSE, Marie Hansen calculated that the additional costs for preparing parallel print and electronic journals is about 130% of the cost of print only. Even if print versions were dropped, the costs to produce the first copy ready for mounting on a server would be as high as 90% of the cost of a paper journal.[1] The cost savings for printing, storage, shipping, and spoilage are substantial, but in the digital realm they are replaced by the costs of system administration, content cataloging, tagging, translating codes, checking codes, inserting links, checking links, network charges, computer and peripherals charges, and additional customer service. The susceptibility of the Internet for revision and its vulnerability to piracy impose still other additional costs.[2]

There are also high costs for acquisitions. It has taken longer than expected to negotiate contracts with journal sponsors, to obtain permissions, and to acclimate journal editors to the steps required for realizing the efficiencies of the digital environment. Electronic editors play fast and loose with copyright, always waving the banner of "fair use" while blithely removing copyright notices from texts and images. Explaining to electronic editors why copyright is in their best interest, and thus worthy of observance, has been just one time-consuming task. As Project MUSE matures, we see more clearly the costs of rearing it.

THE SUPRA OF THE INFRA

The costs of building a university infrastructure are enormous. The Homewood campus at Johns Hopkins is home to 5,200 students, faculty, and staff who want connections to the Internet. The start-up costs for rewiring the campus for UTPs (Unshielded Twisted Pairs)—at a rate of about $150 per connection—would have been impossibly high for the university if not for $1 million in help from the Pew Trust. According to Bill Winn, formerly associate director for academic computing at the Hopkins, it costs $20 per person per month to connect to the campus network. The network itself costs $1 million per year to maintain and an additional $200,000 to support PPP (point-to-point protocol) connections. The annual bill to provide Internet access to the 900 students who live off-campus is an additional $200,000. The fee to the campus's Internet service provider for a 4-megabit-per-second Internet link, plus maintenance and management, costs the university about $50,000 per year.

Students, Winn says, require high maintenance: if their connections are insecure, it is often because the connections have been ripped from the wall. Last year, students in engineering attempted to install a software upgrade for a switch that exceeded their wildest dreams: it shut down the university's system for more than a week. That adds up to about $20,000 of lost Internet access, not to mention the costs of repair.

In 1996, Johns Hopkins University budgeted $70,000 for hardware maintenance and $175,000 for hardware upgrades, chiefly to handle rapidly increasing traffic. The million-dollar budget supports a staff of three technicians, an engineer, a software analyst, and a director for networking. Their skills are in high demand, the salaries they can command are rising rapidly, and they are notoriously hard to retain.

A $15- to $20-per-month access charge is comparable to other campuses elsewhere in the United States. When it costs $180 to $240 per person per year to link a computer to the Internet, a university's administration confronts a huge recurring cost. And the costs go deeper: it is typical for each academic department to bear most of the costs for its own infrastructure, and often some department systems are incompatible with others. In order to make an initial investment worthwhile, expensive investments must be made regularly: upgrades, peripherals, database access fees, consultants, and specialized software. It is no wonder that many colleges have second thoughts about their level of commitment to Internet access.

To some extent, electronic publishers are stymied by the lag between the Internet's ability to produce and its readers' ability to receive. The lag bears a price tag, and so does any effort to close it. Some institutions cannot or will not pay, most state governments cannot pick up the bill, and the federal government is increasingly reluctant to reserve space or investment for scholarly networking. It becomes a matter for the publisher and the market to decide.

OPTIMUM OPTIMISM

Digital prophets soothsay that electronic publishing will exacerbate monopolies and class divisions, or that a slow, steady spread of access will lower costs and promote democratization. In 1951 a new technology led Theodor Adorno to predict a publishing revolution: "In a world where books have long lost all likeness to books, the real book can no longer be one. If the invention of the printing press inaugurated the bourgeois era, the time is at hand for its repeal by the mimeograph, the only fitting, the unobtrusive means of dissemination."[3] By contrast, Mario Morino, founder of the Legent Corporation, electrifies campus audiences by asking, "Which corporation will be the first to acquire a university?"[4] Costs are not everything. Even if they were, the Internet is full of threads on the inconsistent costs of access from place to place. If the digital revolution is a revolution rather than a colossal marketing scheme, it is because so many people and institutions are involved and invested.[5]

It may be that computers will be as ubiquitous as television sets and an Internet connection as cheap as a telephone,[6] but when I look at the role of the Internet in higher education, I see higher costs and foresee only more differentiation between universities based upon their ability to pay those costs. The conversion from print to pixels is not merely an expensive change of clothes: it is an enormous expansion of capability. The chief reason that scholarly electronic publishing costs more than print is that it offers more, much more, and students, faculty, and libraries want all of it.

Under the domain plan that Project MUSE, JSTOR, ARTFL, and other experiments are refining, electronic publishing achieves no less than seven advances in scholarly transmission: (1) instead of a library maintaining one copy of a work that can be read by one person at one time, the work can now be read by an entire campus simultaneously; (2) instead of having to search for a location and hope that a work is not checked out or misshelved, a user can find the full text at the instant it is identified; (3) the work can be read in the context of a large and extensible compilation of books and journals, including back issues, each as easily accessible as the first; (4) the work is capable of being transformed without disturbing an original copy; pages can be copied without being ripped out; copies can be made even if a photocopier is jammed or out of toner; (5) the work can be electronically searched; (6) there is no worry about misplacing the work or returning it by a due date; and (7) the electronic library can be open all night every day of the year. The increased value, if offered by a corresponding increase in price, permits libraries to spend a little more to be able to acquire much more: more content, more access, more use. Librarians pay close attention to what they pay for and many are willing to purchase ambitious electronic publishing projects. Project MUSE has already attracted 100 library subscribers who previously subscribed to no Johns Hopkins print journals, including libraries in museums and community colleges (see Figure 9.1).

If some claims for the digital revolution are laughably inflated, it is not for lack of information: the revolution has occurred with unprecedented self-consciousness and organizational care. That care comes from many sources. Foundation support has proved essential. The Association of American Publishers has led the way for standardization, defense of copyright, vigilance against piracy, and scrutiny of current and pending legislation. At Hopkins, Stanford, Chicago, and many other places, frank and frequent discussions between publishers and librarians have focused on the price and appeal of potential projects. Conversations with Jim Neal remind me that libraries are the original multimedium. For multiple reasons, librarians' reactions to the systemic costs of digitalization are immediately relevant

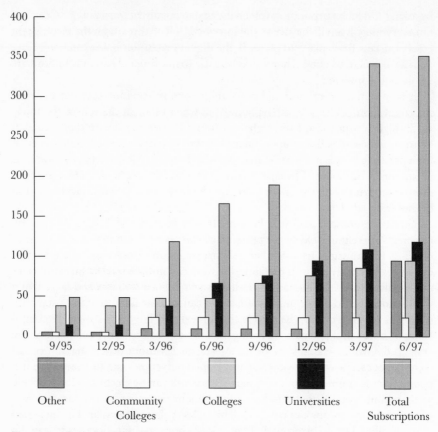

Figure 9.1. Project MUSE Subscription Base

to publishing decisions. Many libraries are asked to acquire extraordinarily expensive databases without a clue about the relationship between price and actual costs, but partnering libraries know better.

For Project MUSE, the greatest cost is for personnel. For decades, it has been possible to maintain a journals program staffed by literate and dedicated people; MUSE employees also have to be adept with computers, software, protocols, and platforms. To raise MUSE from infancy, its employees must also be creative, patient, resourceful, and endowed with heroic stamina. Because their jobs require higher and higher levels of education and technical skill, starting positions are more expensive. Disregarding administrative costs, the staff of MUSE cost about 20% more per capita per month than the staff of print journals, and the differential is rising.

We are just beginning to understand the costs of hiring, training, and retaining qualified staff. Because the skills of the Project MUSE team are pioneering, those who succeed are subject to recruitment raiding for higher salaries. Due to the inordinate pressures put upon them—the stress of tight schedules, the frustrations of downtime, the frictions of incompatible programming and opposed ideas—these young people are prone to rapid burnout.

Excluding independent contractor costs, personnel costs account for 46% of the start-up and maintenance costs for Project MUSE. Including independent contractor costs, which are themselves chiefly a matter of personnel, that percentage rises to 59%.

The second-largest expense has been hardware, accounting for 12% of total costs. Third is rent, at 3.3%. Fourth, surprisingly, has been travel, requiring 2.9% of investment. The travel budget is a consequence of the need to parlay and negotiate on every frontier: with the learned societies and editorial boards that run the journals, with the librarians who buy them, and with editors who contemplate moving their journals to MUSE. In the first two years of MUSE's development, our efforts to build MUSE were distracted by the novelties of the Internet—training staff, dealing with journal sponsors, conversing with libraries—each a task as vital as the selection of software or the conversion of codes. Marketing was kept to a minimum until MUSE had a complete package to deliver. With the completion of the 40-journal base in December 1996, Hopkins is now in high gear marketing MUSE. Travel and exhibits will have higher costs as MUSE strives to attract a subscription base strong enough to become self-supporting.

THE ELECTRONIC MARKET

Marketing on the Web is a different creature than marketing via print or radio, because it must contend with misinformation and with building an audience. Misinformation about an electronic site shows up in the same search that finds the site itself and may require quick response. MUSE responds readily enough to the Internet's search engines, but only if the person is searching. Even then, the searcher can read text only if the searcher's library has already subscribed. At the December 1996 Modern Language Association exhibit, about half the persons who expressed their wish that they could subscribe to MUSE belonged to universities that already did, but the scholars didn't know it. With usage data looming as a subscription criterion, we cannot rest after a subscription is sold; we still have to reach the end user and solicit use. Otherwise scholars and libraries alike will be unable to determine the value of what is available on-line.

The marketplace itself is changing. Most conspicuously, the unexpected formation of library consortia has reshaped many a business plan. Expectations of library sales have often hung fire while libraries consorted, but in the long run it is likely that by stimulating these consortia, electronic publishing will have served an important catalytic function for discovering and implementing many kinds of efficiencies.

The Net market is enormous and enormously fragmented.[7] In the next year there will be numerous marketing experiments on the Web. New and improved tools emerge every month that will help us reply to scholars with specific requests, complaints, and inquiries. Publishers are cautiously optimistic that electronic marketing will prove more advantageous than bulk mail, and it will certainly be cheaper. Already most university presses have their catalogs on-line and many are establishing on-line ordering services.

Customer service is another high cost—at present, much higher than for print journals. Today it takes one customer service agent to attend to 400 Project MUSE subscriptions, while a customer service agent for print journals manages about 10,000 subscriptions. But the future offers bright hope. In February 1997, our customer service agent for Project MUSE sent an e-mail message to 39 past-due subscribers to MUSE who were not with a consortium. Within 24 hours of sending the message, she received 29 responses to it, and 4 more arrived the next day. Each thanked her for sending the letter, and all 33 renewed for the year. Here the advantages of on-line communication are obvious and immediate.

There are also costs that are difficult or impossible to track or quantify, like intellectual costs. It is these costs that have emerged as the next vexed problem in the development of electronic scholarly resources. The problem has three prongs.

One is scholarly skepticism about the value of electronic publishing for tenure and promotion. Rutgers University has put a policy in place; the University of Illinois and Arizona University are in the process of setting their policies. Like everything else in the digital environment, these policies will likely need frequent change.

The fluidity of the Web, gushing with nautical metaphors, often seems a murky sea. Journal editors are anxious about the futures of their journals and hesitant about entrusting them to a medium as fleeting as electricity. Well aware of past losses to flood and fire, scholars prefer durable media. This preference is firmly based: scholarship studies its own history, its history is full of ideas that took years to hatch, and the Web seems unstable, engulfing, and founded on a premise of perpetual replacement. Scholars care about speed, but they care more that their work endures; that it is a heritage; that if they care for it well, it will live longer than they do. Scholars who use the Net frequently encounter defunct URLs, obsolete references, nonsense, wretched writing, and mistakes of every kind. Ephemera appear more ephemeral on-screen. Chief among the concerns expressed by librarians interested in purchasing an electronic publication is whether the publication is likely to be around next year and the year after.

The third prong is the sharpest: will electronic publishing be able to recover the operating costs of producing it, the costs of editing, of maintaining a membership, of defending a niche? If journals are to migrate to electronic formats, they will have to be able to survive there and survive the transition, too: the current competition is part endurance, part sprint. Since parallel publishing in print and on-line costs more, library budgets will either have to pay more to sustain dual-format journals, choose between them, or cut other purchases.

In the short term, there is reassurance in numbers. Rather than erode reader

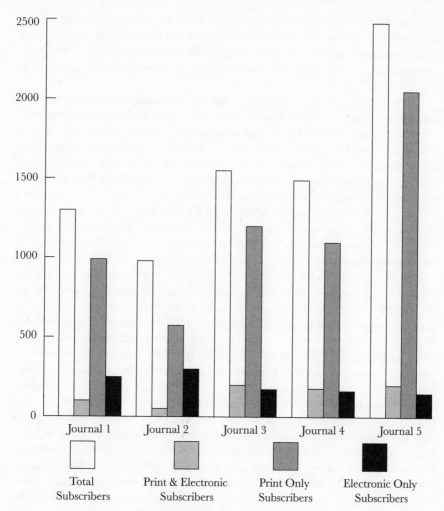

Figure 9.2. Types of Journal Subscriptions 1997

and subscription base, electronic versions of journals may increase them (see Figure 9.2). Even if paper subscriptions dwindle, the increase in subscriptions and readership may last. Perhaps, perhaps. Means for cost recovery for each journal must also last, which is why different publishers are trying different pricing strategies.

Competition in the electronic environment is expensive and aggressive (a favorite book for Netizens is Sun Tzu's *Art of War*).[8] Foundation assistance was essential for enabling university presses and libraries to enter the competition, but it is uncertain whether their publications can compete for very long when foundation support ends. Scholarship has deep reservoirs of learning and goodwill, but next to no savings; one year of red ink could wipe out a hundred-year-old journal. Unless journal publishers and editors migrate quickly and establish a system to recover costs successfully, the razzle-dazzle of paper-thin monitors will cover a casualty list as thick as a tomb.

The risks of migration increase the costs of acquisition. Publishers and their partners are trying to determine what costs must be paid to attract scholars to contribute to their sites. It is obvious that a moment after a scholar has completed a work, a few more keystrokes can put the work on the Web without bothering a publisher, librarian, faculty committee, or foundation officer. Electronic publishing is cheaper than print, *if* you rule out development, refereeing, editing, design, coding, updating, marketing, accounting, and interlinking. Further, there are numerous scholars who believe they should be well paid for their scholarship or their editing. Stipends paid by commercial publishers have raised their editors' financial expectations, which in turn exacerbate the current crisis in sci-tech-med journals. Retention of such stipends will devour savings otherwise achieved by digitalization.

How much added value is worthwhile? Competitive programs are now testing the academic market to see whether scanned page images are preferable to HTML, whether pricing should sequester electronic versions or bundle them into an omnibus price, what degree of cataloging and linking and tagging are desired, what screen features make sense, and a realm of other differentia, not least of which is the filtering of the true from the spew. We expect to see the differences between the costs and prices of scientific and humanities journals to grow larger; with library partners scrutinizing real usage and comparative costs, we expect these differences will be less and less defensible. We expect to see gradual but salutary changes in scholarship itself as different disciplines come to terms with the high visibility of electronic media. We expect to see shifts in reformation of publishers' reputation, with all that a reputation is worth, as professionally managed electronic media distance their offerings from the Web sites of hobbyists, amateurs, and cranks. Finally, we expect to see increasing academic collaboration between and within disciplines. As electronic publishing increases its pressure on hiring, evaluation, tenure, and promotion, the certification and prestige functions of publishers will increasingly depend on their attention to the emerging criteria of e-publishing, in which costs are measured against benefits that print could never offer. Because students, faculty, and libraries want these benefits, scholarly electronic publishing is not cheaper.

NOTES

1. Marie Hansen, "Pricing Issues for Electronic Journals," unpublished, 1996.

2. Piracy is a real threat. According to the Software Publishers Association, about $13 billion in sales was lost due to piracy in 1996. See the SPA home page against piracy: *http://www.spa.org/piracy/homepage.htm.*

3. Adorno, *Minima Moralia,* translated by E. F. N. Jephcott (London: New Left Books, 1974), section 30.

4. *The Gazette* (Johns Hopkins), February 24, 1997, 9.

5. Skeptics of electronic communication are not convinced that digitization will lead to Utopia with a spell checker. See, for example, Kurt Andersen, "The Digital Bubble: Waking Up from the New-Media Pipe Dream," *New Yorker,* January 19, 1998, 30.

6. An article in *Upside* forecast that Internet customer services could save businesses 25% to 50% of the cost of traditional telephonic customer support (David Kline, "Reshaping the Way America Does Business," *Upside Online,* August 5, 1996). But in 1998, mailing lists carry alerts that the telephone companies are seeking ways to add new charges for Internet use.

7. The size of the Web market has grown as rapidly as the Web itself. In 1997 CyberAtlas estimated between 5.8 million and 35 million users. The CyberAtlas estimate in October 1998 is 100 million users. See *http://www.cyberatlas.com/market/size/index.html.*

8. See, for instance, *http://www.stud.ifi.uio.no/~vebjornk/bookmarks/aow.html; http://www.geocities.com/Athens/4884/;* and *http://www.kimsoft.com/polwar.htm.*

CHAPTER 10

Economics of Electronic Publishing—
Cost Issues
Comments on Part Two

Robert Shirrell

I have a few brief comments on the very interesting and stimulating chapters prepared by Janet Fisher (chapter 5), Malcolm Getz (chapter 6), and Bill Regier (chapter 9). I'll focus on their presentations of publisher costs. I'll add a few words about the electronic publishing efforts we have undertaken at the University of Chicago Press and contrast the model we have adopted with the ones that have been mentioned earlier.

Janet Fisher, from the MIT Press, gave us costs related both to the electronic journals that they are publishing and to two of MIT's print journals. In Table 10.1, I've reworked the numbers and computed "first-copy" costs on a per-page basis. What I mean by first-copy cost is simply the cost for editing, typesetting, and producing materials that can subsequently be duplicated and distributed to several hundred or several thousand subscribers. The total first-copy costs for electronic journals at MIT Press range from approximately $15 to $56 per page, and the total first-copy costs for the print journals are $22 and $24 per page. In computing these costs, I did not include what Janet labeled as the G&A costs, the general and administrative costs, but I did include the portion of the cost of the Digital Projects Lab (DPL) that is related to first-copy production.

Several things here are important and worth comment. First, the DPL cost, that is, the cost of preparing an electronic edition after editing and typesetting, is a significant portion of the total. Although the percentage varies between 13% and 62% (as indicated in Table 10.1), the cost is close to 50% of the total first-copy costs of publishing these particular electronic journals.

This breakdown raises the questions, why are these costs so high? and, will they decline over time? I think the expense reflects the fact that there are handcrafted aspects of electronic production, which are expensive, and substantial hardware costs that need to be allocated among a relatively small number of publications and pages. As for the future, the per-page costs at the DPL can be expected to go

TABLE 10.1.   MIT Press First-Copy Cost per Page

	Electronic Journals			
	JFLP	SNDE	CJTCS	JCN
MS editing		7.25	4.57	
Composition		18.20	8.48	
Subtotal	7.87	25.45	13.05	49.00
Lab	7.68	18.42	21.31	7.00
Total	15.55	43.87	34.36	56.00
Lab %	49%	42%	62%	13%

	Print Journals	
	NC	COSY
MS editing	6.46	6.93
Composition	16.04	17.57
Subtotal	22.50	24.50
Lab		
Total	22.50	24.50

down as pages increase and new processing techniques are developed, but even if they do go down to 40%, the totals for digital production are going to be a significant portion of the publisher's total cost. This is important.

Another point about these costs. Note that the total first-copy costs of the electronic journals average $40–$43 per page, whereas those for the print journals average about $23 per page—roughly a $20 difference in the costs. For a 200-page issue, that would amount to about $4,000. That is, it is $4,000 more expensive to produce materials for the reproduction and distribution of 200 pages in electronic form than for the reproduction and distribution of 200 pages in hard-copy form.

If $4,000 will pay for printing and distribution of a 200-page issue to 500 subscribers, which is a reasonable estimate, then MIT can produce a print edition less expensively than an electronic edition when the distribution is under 500. That conclusion is important: at this point, for the MIT Press, it's cheaper to produce journals in paper than to do them electronically, if the circulation is small, i.e., less than 500. That situation may evolve over time, but right now, the additional costs of electronic processing are not offset by sufficiently large reductions in printing and distribution costs.

Now let me turn to the paper by Malcolm Getz. Malcolm presented some numbers from the American Economic Association (AEA), and the numbers in Table 10.2 are approximately the same as the ones he presented. I have also presented numbers from the University of Chicago Press for 37 of our titles. That

TABLE 10.2.   Cost Breakdown by Percentage for AEA
(3 Journals) and University of Chicago Press (37 Journals)

	AEA	Press
Edit	36%	32%
Typeset	13%	10% (to 18%)
Print and mail	23%	24%
Other	27%	34%

NOTE: Percentages may not sum to 100% due to rounding.

figure is not the total of our serial publications; we publish 54 in all. The figure excludes *The Astrophysical Journal*, our largest single title, and a number of journals that we publish in cooperation with other not-for-profit organizations. The journals that are included are principally titles in the humanities and social sciences, with some in medicine and biology.

The breakdown of costs for the Press and for the AEA is quite similar. Editorial costs are 36% for AEA and 32% for the Press. Typesetting is 13% for AEA and 10% at the Press, though it varies substantially by journal. Distribution costs are similar. Overall, these numbers are very close, and they are, it seems to me, reasonable numbers industry-wide.

It is possible to provide a more detailed breakdown of the numbers for the Press, and in Table 10.3, I have broken down the 32% that is related to editorial into the portion that is related to the peer review of manuscripts, which is 22% of the total, and the portion that is related to manuscript editing, which is 10% of the total. Because of the manner in which some of the Press's costs are recorded, the number I have shown for manuscript editing may be somewhat higher, but the breakdown between peer review and manuscript editing is a reasonably accurate division of costs in traditional journal publishing. I think this revised breakdown of costs provides an interesting context for reviewing the way in which costs evolve in an electronic publishing environment, and I would like to turn now to make a few remarks about the possibilities for cost restructuring and cost reduction.

The electronic publishing model we have been discussing is structured so that, basically, electronic costs are add-on costs: you do everything you do in print, and then you do some more. I have outlined the process in Table 10.4. The process includes the traditional functions of peer review, manuscript editing, typesetting, and printing and mailing and adds new functions and new costs for the derivation of electronic materials from the typesetting process and for the management of electronic services.

In this model, as for the vast majority of journals, so long as we continue to produce both print and electronic editions, the total cost is not going to decrease. The reason is that, even if a significant portion of the subscribers convert from paper to electronic editions, the additional costs for electronic processing are not offset by reductions in the printing and distribution costs. As we all know, the marginal

TABLE 10.3.   Cost Breakdown by Percentage
for University of Chicago Press (37 Journals)

Edit	
Peer review	22%
MS edit	10%
Typeset	10% (to 18%)
Print and mail	24%
Other	34%

TABLE 10.4.   Cost Breakdown for
Electronic Publishing, Model One

Edit		
Peer review	22%	
MS edit	10%	
Typeset	10%–18%	
Derive e-materials		*New cost*
Print and mail	24%	
Other	34%	
Manage e-services		*New cost*

cost of printing and mailing is small, much smaller than the average cost, and the additional costs for electronic processing are substantial. The consequence is that, in this model, electronic costs turn out to be added costs, costs in addition to the total that would exist if only a print edition were being produced.

This is exactly what is argued by Regier. He reported that for Project MUSE, the electronic publishing venture of the Johns Hopkins University Press, the total costs for both print and electronic editions were about 130% of the print-only costs. This increase is significant, and I believe it is representative of efforts that are based on deriving electronic materials from typesetting files, as a separate stage of production, undertaken subsequent to the typesetting process.

I would now like to discuss another approach to electronic publishing, another way to obtain electronic materials and to do electronic dissemination. This process is quite different from the one I have just described, with different cost structures and different total costs. The process is outlined in Table 10.5. In this process, data are converted to SGML form in the earliest stages of editing. Then the SGML database is used to derive both the typeset output for hard copy printing and the electronic materials for electronic dissemination.

This process generates costs quite different than those for the model we looked at before. The costs are summarized in Table 10.6. Most important, there is a substantial increase in the cost at the beginning of the process, that is, in the conversion of data to SGML form and the editing of it in that format. SGML editing is not easy and it is not cheap. However, because manuscripts are extensively marked

TABLE 10.5.   Process Analysis for
Electronic Publishing, Model Two

Edit
   Peer review
   Data conversion to SGML
   MS edit in SGML
   Derive e-materials from SGML
Typeset from SGML
Print and mail
Other
Manage e-services

TABLE 10.6.   Cost Analysis for Electronic Publishing,
Model Two

Edit	
Peer review	
Data conversion to SGML	*Additional cost*
MS edit in SGML	*Additional cost*
Derive e-materials from SGML	*New cost, less than for Model One*
Typeset from SGML	*Reduced cost*
Print and mail	
Other	
Manage e-services	*New cost*

up and formatted in this process, a typeset version can be derived from the SGML database inexpensively, and of course, the electronic files for distribution in electronic form are also straightforward and inexpensive to derive. Overall, the additional costs for conversion and editing are being offset in large part by reductions in typesetting costs.

This process is the approach that we have undertaken with *The Astrophysical Journal* at the University of Chicago Press and are now implementing for other publications. *The Astrophysical Journal,* sponsored by the American Astronomical Society, is the world's leading publication in astronomy, issuing some 25,000 pages each year, in both print and on-line editions. The conclusions we have reached in our efforts for that journal are that a reduction in the typesetting costs can offset other additional costs and that this method of producing the journal is less expensive than any alternative way of generating the electronic materials that we want to obtain for the on-line edition.

These general conclusions are probably applicable to most scientific and technical journals, because this method, based on processing in SGML form, results in substantial reductions in the cost of typesetting tabular and mathematical matter. For those publications, we will be able to produce electronic editions for, at most,

10% more than the cost of producing print editions alone. In some cases it may be possible to produce electronic versions in addition to the print versions at no additional total cost.

Let me add one other point. Because we are converting manuscripts to SGML immediately and editing in SGML, we can obtain materials for electronic distribution much faster than in the traditional print model. In 1997 we published papers in the on-line edition of *The Astrophysical Journal Letters* 14 days after acceptance by the editor. That turnaround is possible because we obtain the electronic version immediately from our SGML database and do not derive it by postprocessing typesetting files.

In sum, this process will allow us, in certain circumstances, to publish complex scientific material in a sophisticated electronic version both less expensively and more rapidly than by employing alternative means. This sort of processing is an important alternative approach to electronic publishing.

PART THREE

Use of Electronic Journals and Books: Empirical Studies

CHAPTER 11

Analysis of JSTOR
The Impact on Scholarly Practice of Access to On-line Journal Archives

Thomas A. Finholt and JoAnn Brooks

Innovations introduced over the past thirty years, such as computerized library catalogs and on-line citation indexes, have transformed scholarly practice. Today, the dramatic growth of worldwide computer networks raises the possibility for further changes in how scholars work. For example, attention has focused on the Internet as an unprecedented mechanism for expanding access to scholarly documents through electronic journals (Olsen 1994; Odlyzko 1995), digital libraries (Fox et al. 1995), and archives of prepublication reports (Taubes 1993). Unfortunately, the rapid evolution of the Internet makes it difficult to accurately predict which of the many experiments in digital provision of scholarly content will succeed. As an illustration, electronic journals have received only modest acceptance by scholars (Kling and Covi 1996). Accurate assessment of the scholarly impact of the Internet requires attention to experiments that combine a high probability of success with the capacity for quick dissemination. According to these criteria, digital journal archives deserve further examination. A digital journal archive provides on-line access to the entire digitized back archive of a paper journal. Traditionally, scholars make heavy use of journal back archives in the form of bound periodicals. Therefore, providing back archive content on-line may significantly enhance access to a resource already in high demand. Further, studying the use of experimental digital journal archives may offer important insight into the design and functionality of a critical Internet-based research tool. This paper, then, reports on the experience of social scientists using JSTOR, a prototype World Wide Web application for viewing and printing the back archives of ten core journals in history and economics.

THE JSTOR SYSTEM

JSTOR represents an experiment in the technology, politics, and economics of on-line provision of journal content. Details of JSTOR's evolution and development are covered elsewhere in this volume (see chapter 7). At the time of this study, early 1996, the faculty audience for JSTOR consisted of economists, historians, and ecologists—reflecting the content of JSTOR at that time. This paper focuses on reports of JSTOR use shortly after the system became officially available at the test sites. Respondents included historians and economists at five private liberal arts colleges (Bryn Mawr College, Denison University, Haverford College, Swarthmore College, and Williams College) and one public research university (the University of Michigan). The core economics journals in JSTOR at the time of this study included *American Economic Review, Econometrica, Quarterly Journal of Economics, Journal of Political Economy,* and *Review of Economics and Statistics.* The core history journals included *American Historical Review, Journal of American History, Journal of Modern History, William and Mary Quarterly,* and *Speculum.* In the future, JSTOR will expand to include more than 150 journal titles covering dozens of disciplines.

JOURNAL USE IN THE SOCIAL SCIENCES

To understand JSTOR use requires a general sense of how social scientists seek and use scholarly information. In practice, social scientists apply five main search strategies. First, social scientists use library catalogs. Broadbent (1986) found that 69% of a sample of historians used a card catalog when seeking information, while Lougee, Sandler, and Parker (1990) found that 97% of a sample of social scientists used a card catalog. Second, journal articles are a primary mechanism for communication among social scientists (Garvey 1979; Garvey, Lin, and Nelson 1970). For example, in a study of social science faculty at a large state university, Stenstrom and McBride (1979) found that a majority of the social scientists used citations in articles to locate information. Third, social scientists use indexes and specialty publications to locate information. As an illustration, Stenstrom and McBride found that 55% of social scientists in their sample reported at least occasional use of subject bibliographies, and 50% reported at least occasional use of abstracting journals. Similarly, Olsen (1994) found that in a sample of sociologists, 37.5% reported regular use of annual reviews. Fourth, social scientists browse library shelves. For instance, Lougee et al. and Broadbent both found that social scientists preferred to locate materials by browsing shelves. Sabine and Sabine (1986) found that 20% of a sample of faculty library users reported locating their most recently accessed journal via browsing. On a related note, Stenstrom and McBride found that social scientists used departmental libraries more heavily than the general university library. Finally, social scientists rely on the advice of colleagues and students. For example, various studies show that colleagues have particular value when searching for a specific piece of information (Stenstrom and McBride; Broadbent; Simpson 1988). Also, students working on research projects often locate background material that social scientists find useful (Olsen; Simpson). Similarly, faculty report a valuable but infrequent role for librarians in seeking information (Stenstrom and McBride; Broadbent; Lougee et al.).

Computer-based tools do not figure prominently in the preceding description of how social scientists search for scholarly information. Results from previous studies show that the primary application of digital information technology for social scientists consists of computerized searching, which social scientists do at lower rates than physical scientists but at higher rates than humanists (Lougee et al. 1990; Olsen 1994; Broadbent 1986). Lougee et al. and Olsen both report sparse use of on-line catalogs by social scientists. Evidence of the impact of demographic characteristics on use of digital resources is mixed. For example, Lougee et al. found a negative correlation between age and use of digital information technology, while Stenstrom and McBride (1979) found no correlation. Finally, in a comparison of e-mail use by social scientists and humanists, Olsen found higher use rates among the social scientists, apparently correlated with superior access to technology.

In terms of journal access, previous studies indicate that economics faculty tend to subscribe to more journals than do faculty in other social science disciplines (Simpson 1988; Schuegraf and van Bommel 1994). Journal subscriptions are often associated with membership in a professional society. For example, in their analysis of a liberal arts faculty, Schuegraf and van Bommel found that 40.9% of faculty journal subscriptions—including 12 of the 15 most frequently subscribed-to journals—came with society memberships. Stenstrom and McBride (1979) found that membership-related subscriptions often overlapped with library holdings. However, according to Schuegraf and van Bommel, other personal subscriptions included journals not held in library collections. In terms of journal use, Sabine and Sabine (1986) found that only 4% of faculty in their sample reported reading the entire contents of journals, while 9% reported reading single articles, and 87% reported reading only small parts, such as abstracts. Similarly, at least among a sample of sociologists, Olsen (1994) found that all respondents reported using abstracts to determine whether to read an article. Having found a relevant article, faculty often make copies. For instance, Sabine and Sabine found that 47% of their respondents had photocopied the most recently read journal article, Simpson found that 60% of sampled faculty reported "always" making copies, and all the sociologists in Olsen's sample reported copying important articles.

GOALS OF THIS STUDY

The research described above consists of work conducted prior to the advent of the World Wide Web and widespread access to the Internet. Several recent studies suggest that Internet use can change scholarly practice (Finholt and Olson 1997; Hesse, Sproull, and Kiesler 1993; Walsh and Bayma 1997; Carley and Wendt 1991). However, most of these studies focused on physical scientists. A key goal of this study is to create a snapshot of the effect of Internet use on social scientists, specifically baseline use of JSTOR. Therefore, the sections that follow will address core questions about the behavior of JSTOR users, including: (1) how faculty searched for information; (2) which faculty used JSTOR; (3) how journals were used; (4) how the Internet was used; and (5) how journal use and Internet use correlated with JSTOR use.

METHOD

Participants

The population for this study consisted of the history and economics faculty at the University of Michigan and at five liberal arts colleges: Bryn Mawr College, Denison University, Haverford College, Swarthmore College, and Williams College. History and economics faculty were targeted because the initial JSTOR selections drew on ten journals, reflecting five core journals in each of these disciplines. The institutions were selected based on their status as Andrew W. Mellon Foundation grant recipients for the JSTOR project.

Potential respondents were identified from the roster of full-time history and economics faculty at each institution. With the permission of the respective department chairs at each school, faculty were invited to participate in the JSTOR study by completing a questionnaire. No incentives were offered for respondents, and participation was voluntary. Respondents were told that answers would be confidential, but not anonymous due to plans for matching responses longitudinally. The resulting sample contained 161 respondents representing a response rate of 61%. In this sample, 46% of the respondents were economists, 76% were male, and 48% worked at the University of Michigan. The average respondent was 47.4 years old and had a Ph.D. granted in 1979.

Design and Procedure

Respondents completed a 52-item questionnaire with questions on journal use, computer use, attitudes toward computing, information search behavior, demographic characteristics, and JSTOR use. Respondents had the choice of completing this questionnaire via a telephone interview, via the Web, or via a hard-copy version. Questionnaires were administered to faculty at the five liberal arts colleges and to the faculty at the University of Michigan in the spring of 1996.

Journal Use   Journal use was assessed in four ways. First, respondents reported how they traditionally accessed the journal titles held in JSTOR, choosing from: no use; at the library; through a paid subscription; or through a subscription received with membership in a professional society. Second, respondents ranked the journals they used in order of frequency of use for a maximum of ten journals. For each of these journals, respondents indicated whether they had a personal subscription to the journal. Third, respondents described their general use of journals in terms of the frequency of browsing journal contents, photocopying journal contents, saving journal contents, putting journal contents on reserve, or passing journal contents along to colleagues (measured on a 5-point scale, where 1 = never, 2 = rarely, 3 = sometimes, 4 = frequently, and 5 = always). Finally, respondents indicated the sections of journals they used, including the table of contents, article abstracts, articles, book reviews, reference lists, and editorials.

Computer Use   Computer use was assessed in three ways. First, respondents described their computer systems in terms of the type of computer (laptop versus desktop), the computer family (e.g., Apple versus DOS), the specific model (e.g., PowerPC), and the operating system (e.g., Windows 95). Second, respondents reported their level of use via a direct network connection (e.g., Ethernet) of the World Wide Web, e-mail, databases, on-line library catalogs, and FTP (measured on a 5-point scale, where 1 = never, 2 = 2–3 times per year, 3 = monthly, 4 = weekly, and 5 = daily). Finally, respondents reported their level of use via a modem connection of the Web, e-mail, databases, on-line library catalogs, and FTP (using the same scale as above).

Attitudes toward Computing   Attitudes toward computing were assessed by respondents' reported level of agreement with statements about personal computer literacy, computer literacy relative to others, interest in computers, the importance of computers, confusion experienced while using computers, and the importance of programming knowledge (measured on a 5-point scale, where 1 = strongly disagree, 2 = disagree, 3 = neutral, 4 = agree, and 5 = strongly agree).

Information Search Behavior   Information search behavior was assessed in three ways. First, respondents indicated their use of general search strategies, including: searching/browsing on-line library catalogs; searching/browsing paper library catalogs; browsing library shelves; searching/browsing on-line indexes; searching/browsing paper indexes; browsing departmental collections; reading citations from articles; and consulting colleagues. Second, respondents described the frequency of literature searches within their own field and the frequency of on-line literature searches within their own field (both measured on a 5-point scale, where 1 = never, 2 = 2–3 times per year, 3 = monthly, 4 = weekly, and 5 = daily). Finally, respondents described the frequency of literature searches outside their field and the frequency of on-line literature searches outside their field (measured on the same 5-point scale used above).

Demographic Characteristics   Respondents were asked to provide information on demographic characteristics, including age, sex, disciplinary affiliation, institutional affiliation, highest degree attained, and year of highest degree.

JSTOR Use   Finally, JSTOR use was assessed in two ways. First, respondents reported whether they had access to JSTOR. Second, respondents described the frequency of JSTOR use (measured on a 5-point scale, where 1 = never, 2 = 2–3 times per year, 3 = monthly, 4 = weekly, and 5 = daily).

RESULTS

The data were analyzed to address five core questions related to the impact of JSTOR: (1) how faculty searched for information; (2) which faculty used JSTOR; (3) how journals were used; (4) how the Internet was used; and (5) how journal use and Internet use correlated with JSTOR use.

Information Searching

Table 11.1 summarizes data on how faculty searched for information. The proportion of faculty using the search strategies did not differ significantly by institution or discipline, with the exception of three strategies. First, the proportion of Michigan economists who reported browsing library shelves (46%) was significantly less than the proportion of five-college historians who used this strategy (86%). Second, the proportion of Michigan economists who reported searching card catalogs (14%) was significantly less than the proportion of five-college historians who used this strategy (39%). And finally, the proportion of Michigan economists who reported browsing departmental collections (48%) was significantly greater than the proportion of five-college historians who used this strategy (4%).[1]

Who Used JSTOR

Overall, 67% of the faculty did not use JSTOR,[2] 14% used JSTOR once a year, 11% used JSTOR once a month, and 8% used JSTOR once a week. None of the faculty used JSTOR daily. Table 11.2 summarizes JSTOR frequency of use by type of institution and discipline. A comparison of use by type of institution shows a higher proportion of JSTOR users at the five colleges (42%) than at the University of Michigan (27%). A further breakdown by discipline shows that the five-college economists had the highest proportion of users (46%), followed by the Michigan economists (40%), the five-college historians (39%), and the Michigan historians (16%). One way to put JSTOR use into perspective is to compare this activity with similar, more familiar on-line activities, such as literature searching. Overall, 21% of the faculty did not do on-line searches, 25% searched once a year, 25% searched once a month, 25% searched once a week, and 4% searched daily. Table 11.3 summarizes data on the frequency of on-line searching by type of institution and discipline for the same faculty described in Table 11.2. A comparison of on-line searching by type of institution shows a higher proportion of on-line searchers at the five colleges (85%) than at the University of Michigan (76%). A further breakdown by discipline shows that the five-college economists had the highest proportion of searchers (89%), followed by the five-college historians (82%), and the Michigan economists and historians (both 76%).

TABLE 11.1.   Percentage of Faculty by Search Strategy,
Type of Institution, and Discipline ($n = 151^a$)

	University of Michigan		Five Colleges	
Search Strategies	Economics ($n = 44$)	History ($n = 54$)	Economics ($n = 25$)	History ($n = 28$)
Use citations from related publications	84%	96%	100%	100%
Consult a colleague	93%	85%	96%	89%
Search electronic catalogs for a known item	80%	89%	88%	89%
Browse library shelves	46%$_a$	83%	72%	86%$_b$
Browse electronic catalogs	57%	56%	80%	79%
Use electronic indexes	59%	59%	84%	64%
Use printed indexes	34%	57%	64%	82%
Search card catalogs for a known item	14%$_a$	32%	17%	39%$_b$
Browse departmental collections	48%$_a$	11%	20%	4%$_b$
Browse card catalogs	2%	20%	24%	25%

Note: Means with different subscripts differ significantly at $p < .01$ in the Tukey honestly significant difference test.
[a]Nine cases were unusable due to incomplete data.

TABLE 11.2.   Percentage of Faculty by Frequency of JSTOR Use,
Type of Institution, and Discipline ($n = 147^a$)

	University of Michigan			Five Colleges		
Frequency of Use	Overall ($n = 93$)	Economics ($n = 43$)	History ($n = 50$)	Overall ($n = 54$)	Economics ($n = 26$)	History ($n = 28$)
never[b]	73%	60%	84%	58%	54%	61%
once a year	12%	17%	8%	17%	15%	18%
once a month	9%	14%	4%	14%	19%	10%
once a week	6%	9%	4%	11%	12%	11%
daily	0%	0%	0%	0%	0%	0%

[a]Thirteen cases were unusable due to incomplete data.
[b]The "never" category also includes faculty who were unaware of JSTOR.

Figure 11.1 shows a plot of the cumulative percentage of faculty per institution who used JSTOR and who did on-line searches versus the frequency of these activities. For example, looking at the values plotted on the y-axis against the "Monthly" category shows that over three times as many Michigan faculty searched once a month or more (51%) compared with those who used JSTOR at least once a month (15%). Similarly, over two times as many of the five-college faculty searched once a month or more (62%) compared with those who used JSTOR at least once a month (25%). A further breakdown by discipline shows that

TABLE 11.3. Percentage of Faculty by Frequency of On-Line Searching, Type of Institution, and Discipline ($n = 147^a$)

Frequency of Searches	University of Michigan			Five Colleges		
	Overall ($n = 93$)	Economics ($n = 43$)	History ($n = 50$)	Overall ($n = 54$)	Economics ($n = 26$)	History ($n = 28$)
never	24%	24%	24%	15%	11%	18%
once a year	25%	28%	22%	24%	16%	32%
once a month	25%	22%	28%	26%	34%	18%
once a week	23%	19%	26%	30%	35%	25%
daily	3%	7%	0%	6%	4%	7%

[a]Thirteen cases were unusable due to incomplete data.

over twice as many of the five-college economists searched once a month or more (73%) than used JSTOR at least once a month (31%), that over six times as many of the Michigan historians searched once a month or more (54%) than used JSTOR at least once a month (8%), that over twice as many of the five-college historians searched once a month or more (50%) than used JSTOR at least once a month (21%), and that over twice as many of the Michigan economists searched once a month or more (48%) than used JSTOR at least once a month (23%).

Journal Use

Table 11.4 summarizes how faculty used features of journals. Across all journal features, patterns of use were similar except in two areas. First, the proportion of Michigan historians who used article abstracts (31%) was significantly smaller than the proportion of Michigan economists (81%), five-college economists (89%), and five-college historians (61%) who used abstracts. Second, the proportion of Michigan economists who used book reviews (49%) was significantly smaller than the proportion of five-college historians (100%), Michigan historians (98%), and five-college economists (85%) who used book reviews.

Overall, faculty in the sample reported that they regularly used 8.7 journals, that they subscribed to 4.1 of these journals, and that 2.2 of these journals were also in JSTOR. Table 11.5 summarizes journal use by institution and discipline. There were no significant differences in the number of journals used across institution and discipline, although Michigan historians reported using the most journals (8.9). There were also no significant differences across institution and discipline in the number of paid journal subscriptions among the journals used, although again Michigan historians reported having the most paid subscriptions (4.6). There was a significant difference in the number of journals used regularly by the economists that were also titles in JSTOR ($M = 2.9$) compared with those used by the historians ($[M = 1.7]$, t [158] = 5.71, $p < .01$).

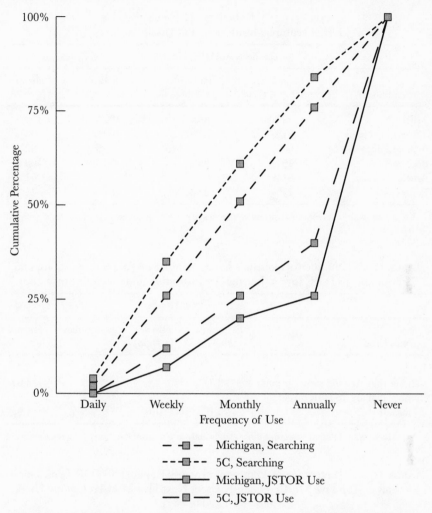

Figure 11.1. Cumulative percentage of on-line searchers versus JSTOR users, by frequency of use and type of institution (*n* = 147)

Further examination of differences in use of journals shows a much greater consensus among the economists about the importance of the economics journals in JSTOR than among the historians about the history journals in JSTOR. For example, Table 11.6 shows the economists' ranking in order of use of the five economics journals chosen for JSTOR. The *American Economic Review* was cited among the top ten most frequently used journals by over 75% of both the Michigan and the five-college economists; the *Journal of Political Economy* was cited

TABLE 11.4. Percentage of Faculty by Use of Journal Features, Institution, and Discipline ($n = 159^a$)

Journal Feature	University of Michigan		Five Colleges	
	Economics ($n = 47$)	History ($n = 58$)	Economics ($n = 26$)	History ($n = 28$)
Articles	96%	98%	100%	100%
Tables of contents	81%	86%	100%	96%
Bibliographies	60%	71%	89%	82%
Book reviews	49%$_b$	98%$_a$	85%$_a$	100%$_a$
Article abstracts	81%$_a$	31%$_b$	89%$_a$	61%$_a$
Editorials	13%	24%	35%	43%

Note: Means with different subscripts differ significantly at $p < .01$ in the Tukey honestly significant difference test.

[a]One case was unusable due to incomplete data.

TABLE 11.5. Number of Journals Used, Number of Paid Subscriptions, and Number of JSTOR Target Journals by Institution and Discipline ($n = 160$)

Journals Used	University of Michigan		Five Colleges	
	Economics ($n = 48$)	History ($n = 58$)	Economics ($n = 26$)	History ($n = 28$)
Total	8.6	8.9	8.4	8.7
Number that are paid subscriptions	3.7	4.6	4.0	3.6
Number that are JSTOR target journals	3.1$_a$	1.6$_b$	2.5	1.9$_b$

Note: Means with different subscripts differ significantly at $p < .01$ in the Tukey honestly significant difference test.

TABLE 11.6. Percentage of Economics Faculty Ranking JSTOR Economics Journals as Top Five Most Frequently Used, Next Five Most Frequently Used, and Not Used ($n = 74$)

Journal	University of Michigan ($n = 48$)			Five Colleges ($n = 26$)		
	Top Five	Next Five	Not Used	Top Five	Next Five	Not Used
American Economic Review	79%	6%	15%	66%	15%	19%
Journal of Political Economy	52%	10%	38%	32%	26%	42%
Quarterly Journal of Economics	41%	15%	44%	16%	26%	58%
Econometrica	26%	30%	44%	8%	15%	77%
Review of Economics and Statistics	18%	28%	54%	12%	34%	54%

among the top ten by over 60% of both the Michigan and the five-college economists; and the *Quarterly Journal of Economics* and the *Review of Economics and Statistics*
were cited among the top ten by over 50% of the Michigan economists and by
over 40% of the five-college economists. By contrast, Table 11.7 shows the historians' ranking in order of use of the five history journals chosen for JSTOR. The
American Historical Review was cited among the top ten most frequently used journals by over 60% of both the Michigan and the five-college historians. However,
none of the other four journals were used by a majority of the historians at Michigan or at the five colleges.

Internet Use

Overall, faculty reported weekly use of e-mail ($M = 4.3$), monthly use of on-line
catalogs ($M = 3.2$) and the Web ($M = 3.0$), and two or three uses per year of FTP
($M = 2.3$) and on-line database ($M = 2.1$). Table 11.8 summarizes the use of these
Internet applications by institution and discipline. In terms of e-mail use, Michigan historians ($M = 3.3$) were significantly lower than the Michigan economists ($M
= 4.9$), the five-college economists ($M = 5.0$), and the five-college historians ($M =
4.7$). In terms of World Wide Web use, Michigan historians ($M = 1.8$) were
significantly lower than everyone, while the five-college historians ($M = 2.9$) were
significantly lower than the five-college economists ($M = 4.2$) and the Michigan
economists ($M = 3.9$). In terms of FTP use, the Michigan historians ($M = 1.4$) and
the five-college historians ($M = 1.7$) differed significantly from the Michigan economists ($M = 3.4$) and the five-college economists ($M = 2.7$). In terms of on-line
database use, the Michigan historians ($M = 1.6$) were significantly lower than the
five-college economists ($M = 2.9$). Faculty did not differ significantly in terms of
on-line catalog use.

The Relationship of Journal and Internet Use to JSTOR Use

Examination of the frequency of JSTOR use among faculty aware of JSTOR ($n
= 78$) showed that 58% of the respondents had varying levels of use, while 42%
reported no use. Using the frequency of JSTOR use as the dependent variable,
the faculty who reported no use were censored on the dependent variable. The
standard zero, lower-bound tobit model was designed for this circumstance (Tobin
1958). Most important, by adjusting for censoring, the tobit model allows inclusion
of negative cases in the analysis of variation in frequency of use among positive
cases, which greatly enhances degrees of freedom. Therefore, hierarchical tobit
regression analyses were used to examine the influence of demographic characteristics, journal use, search preferences, Internet use, and attitude toward computing on the frequency of JSTOR use. Independent variables used in these
analyses were selected on the basis of significance in univariate tobit regressions

TABLE 11.7.   Percentage of History Faculty Ranking JSTOR History Journals
as Top Five Most Frequently Used, Next Five Most Frequently Used,
and Not Used (*n* = 86)

Journal	University of Michigan (n = 58)			Five Colleges (n = 28)		
	Top Five	Next Five	Not Used	Top Five	Next Five	Not Used
American Historical Review	44%	19%	37%	58%	24%	18%
Journal of American History	31%	6%	63%	39%	4%	57%
Journal of Modern History	15%	10%	75%	18%	11%	71%
William and Mary Quarterly	13%	6%	81%	15%	3%	82%
Speculum	9%	3%	88%	11%	10%	79%

TABLE 11.8.   Mean Frequency of Computer Application Use over Direct
Connection (High-Speed Network) by Institution and Discipline (*n* = 158[a])

Computer Application	University of Michigan		Five Colleges	
	Economics (n = 47)	History (n = 57)	Economics (n = 26)	History (n = 28)
E-mail	4.9_a	3.3_b	5.0_a	4.7_a
On-line catalogs	3.3	2.8	3.6	3.7
On-line databases	2.3	1.6_a	2.9_b	2.1
World Wide Web	3.9_a	1.8_b	4.2_a	2.9_c
File Transfer Protocol (FTP)	3.4_a	1.4_b	2.7_a	1.7_b

Note: Frequency of use was reported on a 5-point scale (1 = never; 2 = 2–3 times per year; 3 = monthly; 4 = weekly; 5 = daily).

Note: Means with different subscripts differ significantly at $p < .01$ in the Tukey honestly significant difference test.

[a]Two cases were unusable due to incomplete data.

on the frequency of use variable. Table 11.9 summarizes the independent variables used in the multiple tobit regression analyses.

Table 11.10 summarizes the results of the hierarchical tobit regression of demographic, journal use, search preference, Internet use, and computing attitude variables on frequency of JSTOR use. The line second from the bottom in Table 11.10 summarizes the log likelihood score for each model. Analysis of the change in log likelihood score between adjacent models gives a measure of the significance of independent variables added to the model. For example, in Model 1, the addition of the demographic variables failed to produce a significant change in the log likelihood score compared to the null model. By contrast, in Model 2, the addition of journal use variables produced a significant change in the log likelihood score compared to Model 1—suggesting that the addition of the journal

TABLE 11.9.   Descriptive Statistics for Faculty
Aware of JSTOR ($n = 78$)

Variable	Mean	Std
At Michigan	49%	—
In economics	54%	—
Male	82%	—
Years since degree	17.2	11.5
Copies articles	3.09	0.91
Puts articles on reserve	2.73	1.15
Reads abstracts	68%	—
Total # subs., JSTOR	2.5	1.5
Total # subs., all	8.8	1.96
# paid subs.	4.04	2.43
Uses on-line indexes	60%	—
Searches on-line catalog	85%	—
Browses on-line catalog	65%	—
Frequency of on-line catalog use	3.47	1.25
Frequency of on-line database use	2.33	1.31
Frequency of WWW use	3.47	1.62
Frequency of FTP use	2.39	1.42
Attitude toward computing	3.52	0.70
Frequency of JSTOR use	2.05	2.09

use variables improved the fit in Model 2 over Model 1. Similarly, the addition of search variables in Model 3 and of Internet use variables in Model 4 both produced significant improvements in fit, but the addition of the computer attitude variable in Model 5 did not. Therefore, Model 4 was selected as the best model. From Model 4, the coefficients for gender, article copying, abstract reading, and searching on-line catalogs are all positive and significant. These results suggest that, controlling for other factors, men were 0.77 points higher on frequency of JSTOR use than were women, that there was a 0.29-point increase in the frequency of JSTOR use for every point increase in the frequency of article copying, that faculty who read article abstracts were 0.82 points higher on frequency of JSTOR use than were faculty who didn't read abstracts, and that there was a 1.13-point increase in the frequency of JSTOR use for every point increase in the frequency of on-line catalog searching. From Model 4, the coefficients for affiliation with an economics department and the number of paid journal subscriptions are both negative and significant. These results suggest that, controlling for other factors, economists were 0.88 points lower on frequency of JSTOR use than were historians and that there was a 0.18-point decrease in frequency of JSTOR use for every unit increase in the number of paid journal subscriptions.

TABLE 11.10. Tobit Regression on Frequency of JSTOR Use
among Faculty Aware of JSTOR ($n = 78$)

Variable	Model 1	Model 2	Model 3	Model 4	Model 5
Constant	0.56	−2.45*	−3.89***	−3.86***	−4.63***
At Michigan	−0.11	.28	.47	.47	.47
In economics	0.20	−.73	−.48	−.88*	−.94**
Male	.77	.82*	.91**	.77*	.77*
Years since degree	−0.04**	−0.02	−0.00	0.00	0.00
Copies articles		.29	.28	.29*	.29*
Puts articles on reserve		.28*	.33**	.24	.22
Reads abstracts		1.38***	1.22***	.82**	.86**
Total # subs., JSTOR		.27*	.26*	.21	.23
Total # subs., all		0.03	−0.02	−0.02	−0.03
# paid subs.		−.17**	−.16**	−.18**	−.19**
Uses on-line indexes			.37	.22	.25
Searches on-line catalog			1.34**	1.13*	1.17*
Browses on-line catalog			−0.02	−.15	−.25
Frequency of on-line catalog use				0.02	0.01
Frequency of on-line database use				0.02	−0.00
Frequency of WWW use				.22	.19
Frequency of FTP use				.20	.15
Attitude toward computing					.31
−Log likelihood	111.94	98.08	93.56	89.31	88.70
Chi-square	6.72	27.72***	9.04**	8.5*	1.2

Note: −Log likelihood for the null model = 115.30.
* = $p < .10$; ** = $p < .05$; *** = $p < .01$.

DISCUSSION

This study addressed five questions related to the preliminary impact of JSTOR: (1) how faculty searched for information; (2) which faculty used JSTOR; (3) how journals were used; (4) how the Internet was used; and (5) how journal use and Internet use correlated with JSTOR use.

Summary of Findings

In terms of how faculty searched for information, results were consistent with earlier findings reported in the literature. Specifically, a strong majority of the faculty reported relying on citations from related publications, on colleagues, on electronic catalogs, and on browsing library shelves when seeking information. Faculty did not differ dramatically in selection of search strategies, except that Michigan economists were less likely to browse library shelves and less likely to search card catalogs.

In terms of JSTOR use, Michigan faculty were less likely to know about JSTOR than were the five-college faculty, and Michigan faculty were less likely to use JSTOR than were the five-college faculty. These results probably reflected the delayed rollout and availability of JSTOR at Michigan. Economists were more likely to use JSTOR than historians were. Of the faculty who reported JSTOR use, frequency of use did not differ dramatically from frequency of use of a related, more traditional technology: on-line searching. That is, 58% of the faculty who used JSTOR said they used JSTOR once a month or more, while 69% of the faculty who did on-line searches reported doing searches once a month or more. Note, however, that over twice as many faculty reported doing on-line searches (75%) as reported use of JSTOR (33%).

In terms of journal use, faculty did not vary greatly in their use of journal features, except that Michigan historians were less likely to use article abstracts and that Michigan economists were less likely to use book reviews. Economists and historians did not differ in the total number of journals used; however, there was greater consensus among the economists about core journals. Specifically, two of the five economics titles included in JSTOR (the *American Economic Review* and the *Journal of Political Economy*) were cited among the top 10 most frequently used journals by a majority of the economists, while four of the five titles (the two mentioned above plus the *Quarterly Journal of Economics* and the *Review of Economics and Statistics*) were cited among the top 10 most frequently used journals by a majority of the Michigan economists. By contrast, only one of the five history titles included in JSTOR (the *American Historical Review*) was cited among the top 10 most frequently used journals by a majority of the historians.

In terms of Internet use, the Michigan historians lagged their colleagues in economics at Michigan and the five-college faculty. For example, the Michigan historians reported less use of e-mail, the World Wide Web, FTP, and on-line databases than did the other faculty. The economists were more likely to use FTP and more likely to use the World Wide Web than the historians were. Faculty used on-line catalogs at similar rates.

In terms of factors correlated with JSTOR use, the tobit regressions showed that a model including demographic factors, journal use factors, search factors, and Internet use factors offered the best fit to the data on frequency of JSTOR use. The addition of the computer attitude variable did not improve the fit of this model. In the best fit model, gender, article copying, abstract reading, and searching on-line catalogs were all positively and significantly related to frequency of JSTOR use. Also from the best fit model, affiliation with an economics department and greater numbers of journal subscriptions were negatively and significantly related to frequency of JSTOR use.

Limitations of the Study

These data represent a snapshot of faculty response to JSTOR at an extremely early stage in the evolution of the JSTOR system. In the spring of 1996, JSTOR had been available to the five-college faculty for less than six months, while at Michigan, the system had not yet been officially announced to faculty. Therefore, the results probably underestimate eventual use of the mature JSTOR system. Further, as a survey study, self-reports of use were crude compared to measures that could have been derived from actual behavior. For example, it was intended to match use reports with automated usage statistics from the JSTOR Web servers, but the usage statistics proved too unreliable. Another problem was that the survey contained no items on the frequency of traditional journal use. Therefore, it is unknown whether the low use of JSTOR reported by the faculty reflected dissatisfaction with the technology or simply a low base rate for journal use. Finally, the faculty at Michigan and at the five colleges were atypical in the extent of their access to the Internet and in the modernity of their computing equipment. Faculty with older computers and slower network links would probably be even less likely to use JSTOR.

Implications for the JSTOR Experiment

Although extremely preliminary, these early data suggest trends that merit further exploration as JSTOR expands. First, it is encouraging to discover that among faculty who have used JSTOR, rates of use are already comparable to rates for use of on-line searching—a technology that predates JSTOR by two decades. It will be interesting to see if JSTOR use grows beyond this modest level to equal the use of key Internet applications, like e-mail and Web browsing. Second, there appear to be clear differences in journal use across disciplinary lines. For example, economists focus attention on a smaller set of journals than is the case in history. Therefore, it may be easier to satisfy demand for on-line access to back archives in fields that have one or two flagship journals than in more diverse fields where scholarly attention is divided among dozens of journals. This conclusion may lead commercial providers of back archive content to ignore more diverse disciplines at the expense of easier-to-service, focused disciplines. Finally, the negative correlation between the number of journal subscriptions and JSTOR use suggests the possibility of a substitution effect (i.e., JSTOR for paper). However, the significance of this correlation is difficult to determine, since there is no way to know the direction of causality in a cross-sectional study.

NOTES

Preparation of this article was supported by a grant to the University of Michigan from the Andrew W. Mellon Foundation. JSTOR is the proprietary product of JSTOR, a nonprofit corporation dedicated to provision of digital access to the back archives of scholarly journals. For more information, please consult *www.jstor.org.*

We gratefully acknowledge the assistance of Kristin Garlock, Marcia Heringa, Christina Maresca, William Mott, Sherry Piontek, Tony Ratanaproeksa, Blake Sloan, and Melissa Stucki in gathering the data for this study. Also, we thank Ann Bishop, Joan Durrance, Kristin Garlock, Kevin Guthrie, Wendy Lougee, Sherry Piontek, Sarah Sully, and the participants of The Andrew W. Mellon Foundation Scholarly Communication and Technology Conference for comments on earlier drafts. Finally, we thank the history and economics faculty of Bryn Mawr College, Denison University, Haverford College, Swarthmore College, the University of Michigan, and Williams College for their patience and cooperation as participants in this research.

Requests for copies should be sent to: (1) Thomas Finholt, Collaboratory for Research on Electronic Work, C-2420 701 Tappan Street, Ann Arbor, MI 48109–1234; or (2) *finholt@umich.edu.*

1. At the time of this study, the Department of Economics at the University of Michigan maintained an extensive departmental library with support from the central library. This departmental collection is no longer supported.

2. This figure combines the 44% of the faculty who were unaware of JSTOR with the 23% of the faculty who were aware of JSTOR, but did not use it.

REFERENCES

Broadbent, E. A. (1986). Study of humanities faculty library information seeking behavior. *Cataloging and Classification Quarterly, 6,* 23–37.

Carley, K., & Wendt, K. (1991). Electronic mail and scientific communication: A study of the SOAR extended research group. *Knowledge: Creation, Diffusion, Utilization, 12,* 406–440.

Finholt, T. A., & Olson, G. M. (1997). From laboratories to collaboratories: A new organizational form for scientific collaboration. *Psychological Science, 8,* 28–36.

Fox, E. A., Akscyn, R. M., Furuta, R. K., & Leggett, J. J. (Eds.). (1995). Digital libraries [Special issue]. *Communications of the ACM, 38(4).*

Garvey, W. D. (1979). *Communication: The essence of science.* Toronto: Pergamon Press.

Garvey, W. D., Lin, N., & Nelson, C. E. (1970). Communication in the physical social sciences. *Science, 170,* 1166–1173.

Hesse, Bradford W., Sproull, Lee S., & Kiesler, Sara B. (1993). Returns to science: Computer network in oceanography. *Communications of the ACM, 26(8)* (August), 90–101.

Kling, R., & Covi, L. (1996). Electronic journals and legitimate media. *The Information Society, 11,* 261–271.

Lougee, W. P., Sandler, M. S., & Parker, L.L. (1990). The Humanistic Scholars Project: A study of attitudes and behavior concerning collection storage and technology. *College and Research Libraries, 51,* 231–240.

Odlyzko, A. (1995). Tragic loss or good riddance? The impending demise of traditional scholarly journals. *International Journal of Human-Computer Studies, 42,* 71–122.

Olsen, J. (1994). *Electronic journal literature: Implications for scholars.* Westport, CT: Mecklermedia.

Sabine, G. A., & Sabine, P. L. (1986). How people use books and journals. *Library Quarterly, 56,* 399–408.

Schuegraf, E. J., & van Bommel, M. F. (1994). An analysis of personal journal subscriptions of university faculty. Part II: Arts and professional programs. *Journal of the American Society of Information Science, 45,* 477–482.

Simpson, A. (1988). Academic journal usage. *British Journal of Academic Librarianship, 3,* 25–36.

Stenstrom, P., & McBride, R. B. (1979). Serial use by social science faculty: A survey. *College and Research Libraries, 40,* 426–431.

Taubes, G. (1993). Publication by electronic mail takes physics by storm. *Science, 259,* 1246–1248.

Tobin, J. (1958). Estimation of relationship for limited dependent variables. *Econometrica, 26,* 24–36.

Walsh, J. P., & Bayma, T. (1997). Computer networks and scientific work. In S. B. Kiesler (Ed.), *Culture of the Internet.* Hillsdale, NJ: Lawrence Erlbaum Associates.

CHAPTER 12

Patterns of Use for the Bryn Mawr Reviews

Richard Hamilton

HISTORICAL BACKGROUND

Bryn Mawr Classical Review (BMCR), one of the first electronic journals in the humanities, was started in 1990 to provide timely reviews of books in the classics. To lend solidity, a paper version was produced as well, and the two were issued simultaneously until late 1995, when the electronic reviews began to be published individually more or less as they were received and the paper versions issued four times a year. In 1993 a sister journal, *Bryn Mawr Medieval Review* (BMMR), was created to review books in medieval studies, and the two journals were combined to form the *Bryn Mawr Reviews* (BMR). After about two years of activity BMMR became dormant, and toward the end of 1996 both location and management were shifted.[1] Since then it has become tremendously active, at one point even surpassing BMCR in its monthly output.[2] Comparisons should be considered with this history in mind. (For more detail, see chapter 24.)

DATA

We have two sets of users: subscribers and gopher hitters.[3] For data from the former we have subscription lists, which are constantly updated, and periodic surveys that we have conducted; for the latter we have monthly reports of gopher hits and gopher hitters (but not what the hitters hit). In considering this data our two main questions have been (1) how are we doing? and (2) how can we afford to keep doing it?

Gopher Reports

Our analysis of the monthly gopher reports has concentrated on the hitters rather than the hits. After experimenting rather fruitlessly in 1995 with microanalysis of the data from the Netherlands and Germany hitter by hitter month by month for a year, we decided to collect only the following monthly figures:

- total number of users
- total by address (country, domain, etc.)
- list of top hits (those reviews that received 15+ hits/month and are over a year old[4])
- list of top hitters (those who use the system 30+/month)

Analysis shows that use has leveled off at a peak of about 3,800 users a month. With a second full year of gopher use to study we can see the seasonal fluctuation more easily. The one area of growth seems to be non-English foreign sites. If we compare the top hitters in the first ten months of 1995 with the comparable period in 1996, we find that the total increased only 5% but the total number of non-English heavy users increased 120% (Table 12.1). Three countries were among the heavy users in both 1995 and 1996 (France, Germany, Netherlands); two appeared only in 1995 (South Africa, Taiwan), and eight only in 1996 (Brazil, Italy, Ireland, Poland, Portugal, Russia, Spain, Venezuela).

In terms of total number of users from 1995 to 1996 there was an overall increase of 10.8%, although the increase among U.S. users was only 9.1%. Conversely, most foreign countries showed a marked increase in total use over the ten months of 1996 versus 1995: Argentina, 16 to 27; Australia, 542 to 684; Brazil, 64 to 165; Denmark, 80 to 102; Spain, 107 to 197; Greece, 41 to 80; Ireland, 50 to 69; Israel, 89 to 108; Italy, 257 to 359; Japan, 167 to 241; Korea, 26 to 40; Netherlands, 273 to 315; Portugal, 16 to 26; Russia, 9 to 27; (former) USSR, 13 to 20; and South Africa, 63 to 88. On the other hand, Iceland went from 22 to 8, Malaysia from 30 to 21, Mexico from 68 to 56, Sweden from 307 to 250, and Taiwan from 24 to 14. Also, among U.S. users there was a large drop in the .edu domain, from 7,073 to 5,962, and a corresponding rise in the .net domain, from 1,570 to 4,118, perhaps because faculty members are now using commercial providers for home access.[5]

In the analysis of top hits (Table 12.2), a curious pattern emerges: BMMR starts out with many more top hits despite offering a much smaller number of reviews (about 15% of BMCR's number), but toward the end of 1995 the pattern shifts. BMMR dominates at the beginning but drops when BMMR becomes inactive.

The shift is easily explained because it occurs about the time BMMR was becoming inactive, but the original high density is still surprising.[6] Also surprising is that medieval books receive noticeably more attention: 32 medieval titles made the top hits list 116 times (avg 3.6), while 81 classical titles made the list only 219 times (avg 2.7), despite including two blockbuster titles, Amy Richlin's *Pornography and Representation* (10 times) and John Riddle's *Contraception and Abortion* (14 times).[7] My guess is that medievalists, being more widely dispersed in interests and location, have found the Net more important than have classicists, who are mostly located

TABLE 12.1.   BMCR/BMMR Top Hitters
(30+ hits a month)

	U.S.	English	Non-English	Total
1995	47	8	5	60
1996	42	10	11	63

TABLE 12.2.   Top Hits (averaging 15+ hits per month for at least one year)

Month	1/95	2/95	3/95	4/95	5/95	6/95	7/95	8/95	9/95	10/95
BMMR	2	15	10	2	5	16	3	12	41	46
BMCR	1	11	6	3	5	20	1	14	116	170

Month	1/96	2/96	3/96	4/96	5/96	6/96	7/96	8/96	9/96	10/96
BMMR	38	14	15	19	6	9	7	8	20	14
BMCR	81	69	74	50	25	13	16	19	48	54

in a classics department and whose professional work is more circumscribed (and has a longer history).

Subscriptions

Subscriptions to the e-journals continue to grow at a rate of 5% per quarter, although there is considerable seasonal fluctuation (see Table 12.3). Looking more broadly we see a steady slowdown in growth of all but the joint subscriptions (see Table 12.4).

If we look at the individual locations (Table 12.5), we find again that while the U.S. subscriptions continue to grow, they are becoming steadily fewer of the whole, going from 77% of the total in 1993 to 68% in 1996. English-speaking foreign countries have remained about the same percentage of the whole; it is non-English speaking foreign countries that have shown the greatest increase, going from 4% of the total in 1993 to 13% of the total in 1996.

Subscriber Surveys

As opposed to the gopher statistics, which give breadth but little depth, our surveys offer the opportunity for deeper study of our users but at the expense of breadth. We cannot survey our subscribers too often or they will not respond.[8] A further limitation is that we felt we could not survey those who take both BMCR and BMMR, a significant number, without skewing the results, since many subscribers lean heavily toward one journal or the other and the journals are significantly different in some ways. So far we have conducted five surveys:

TABLE 12.3. Subscriptions over Two Years

	3/95	6/95	9/95	3/96	6/96	10/96	3/97
BMCR	1,072	1,067	1,135	1,253	1,273	1,317	1,420
		(−.4%)	(+6%)	(+10%)	(+2%)	(+3%)	(+8%)
BMMR	711	755	865	931	964	995	1,091
		(+6%)	(+13%)	(+8%)	(+4%)	(+3%)	(+10%)
Joint	568	562	599	672	685	770	844
		(−1%)	(+7%)	(+12%)	(+2%)	(+12%)	(+10%)
Total	2,351	2,384	2,599	2,856	2,922	3,082	3,355
		(+1%)	(+9%)	(+10%)	(+2%)	(+5%)	(+9%)

TABLE 12.4. Subscriptions over Three Years

	9/93	9/94	9/95	10/96
BMCR	651	882	1,135	1,317
		(+35%)	(+29%)	(+16%)
BMMR	257	498	865	995
		(+94%)	(+74%)	(+15%)
Joint	261	460	599	770
		(+76%)	(+30%)	(+29%)

1. a 20-question survey in November 1995 to BMCR subscribers
2. a 21-question survey in February 1996 to BMMR subscribers
3. a 2-question survey in October 1996 to all subscribers[9]
4. a 15-question survey in January 1997 to all BMCR reviewers whose e-mail addresses we knew
5. a 2-question survey in March 1997 to those who have canceled subscriptions in the past year

Table 12.6 presents the subscriber profile as revealed in the surveys. Many of the differences are easily explained by the checkered history of BMMR or by the differing natures of the two readerships.[10] I doubt many readers will be surprised to learn that medievalists are more often female and less often faculty. The paucity of reader-reviewers of BMMR reflects the paucity of BMMR reviews. To me, the most surprising statistic is the low use of gopher by subscribers to either journal.

The key question, of course, is willingness to pay for subscriptions. With that in mind, we did some correlation studies for the BMCR survey, first seeing what variables correlated with a willingness to pay $5 for a subscription.[11] We found posi-

TABLE 12.5. BMCR Subscribers

	1993	1994	1995	1996
Total	730	1,019	1,130	1,349
.edu	529	701	703	779
.com	22	44	72	103
.gov	3	6	4	4
.mil	2	2	2	2
.org	5	6	7	12
.net	3	5	8	17
U.S. Total	564 (77%)	764 (75%)	796 (70%)	917 (68%)
Foreign Total	154	254	332	428
.ca	58	87	106	114
.uk	31	45	57	77
.au	21	33	38	43
.nz	4	6	7	6
.za	8	12	14	18
.ca/.uk/.au/.nz/.za	122 (17%)	183 (18%)	222 (20%)	258 (19%)
Non-English	32 (4%)	71 (7%)	110 (10%)	170 (13%)
.de	5	11	16	27
.nl	7	10	16	24
.ie	1	4	5	5
.fi	3	8	9	12
.br	0	2	2	2
.fr	1	4	7	9
.es	0	0	1	3
.it	2	4	7	17
.hu	0	2	2	2
.ve	1	1	1	1
.se	3	4	6	7
.gr	0	1	3	8
.il	2	6	11	14
.dk	1	1	1	0
.no	3	4	4	4
.kr	0	0	1	1
.be	0	2	5	7
.us	0	2	2	4
.jp	1	2	3	4
.ch	1	2	4	12
.pt	0	0	1	1
.at	0	0	1	2
.hk	0	1	1	1
.my	0	0	1	1
.tr	0	0	1	1
.pl	0	0	0	2

TABLE 12.6. Subscriber Profiles

	BMCR (%)	BMMR (%)
Male	74.1	52.8
Female	25.9	47.2
High school degree	.5	2.6
A.B.	5.6	9.8
M.A.	11.1	15.9
ABD	13.0	18.5
Ph.D.	67.7	50.6
M.D., etc.	2.1	2.6
No academic affiliation	4.7	9.7
Faculty	65.5	45.0
Adjunct, research	7.1	6.6
Grad student	15.3	24.1
Undergrad	.8	2.3
Other	6.6	12.3
Check e-mail daily	90.8	87.4
Read review on-screen	68.2	65.8
Print immediately	6.7	6.1
Read on-screen to decide	25.1	27.3
Never/rarely delete without reading	83.7	86.3
Make printed copy sometimes/often	57.2	52.5
Copy on disk sometimes/often	52.0	51.6
Have used gopher	42.5	16.0
Reviewed for this journal	25.1	9.6
Heard reference to this journal	71.5	31.0
Start no/a few reviews	20.2	20.7
Start many/most reviews	70.5	65.8
Start almost all reviews	9.3	13.5
Finish no/a few reviews	43.1	42.2
Finish many/most reviews	53.8	54.6
Finish almost all reviews	3.1	3.2
Review useful for teaching	56.9	45.5
Review useful for research	88.1	81.2
Willing to pay $5 subscription	69.8	53.8

tive correlation (Pearson product-moment correlation) with the following categories:

- ever found review useful for teaching ($r = .19$, .00037 likelihood of a chance correlation)
- ever found review useful for research ($r = .21$, .00005)
- ever hear a reference to BMCR ($r = .23$, .00001)
- ever written a review for BMCR ($r = .17$, .00084)

Further correlations were found, some not at all surprising:

- start to read many / most reviews // heard a reference to BMCR (r = .20, .00014)
- willing to review // heard a reference to BMCR (r = .22, .00002)
- get paper BMCR // have written review (r = .22, .00002)
- have written review // will write in future (r = .24, .00000)
- will write in future // library gets BMCR (r = .21, .00005)
- Ph.D. // willing to review (r = .24, .00000)
- institutional affiliation // useful for teaching (r = .21, .00009)
- useful for teaching // useful for research (r = .25, .00000)
- heard a reference // willing to review (r = .22 , .00002)

A follow-up two-question survey done in October 1996 asked whether subscribers would prefer to pay for e-mail subscription, receive advertisements from publishers, or cancel. Fourteen percent preferred to pay, 82% to receive advertisements, and 4% to cancel.

Our most recent survey, of those who had for one reason or another dropped from the list of subscribers, revealed that almost a third were no longer valid addresses and so were not true cancellations. Of those who responded, almost half (40, 44%) of the unsubscriptions were only temporary (Table 12.7). The reason for cancellation was rarely the quality of the review.

CONCLUSIONS

If we return to our two questions—progress and cost recovery—we can see that our progress is satisfactory but that cost recovery is still uncertain.

BMCR is growing at the rate of 30% a year.[12] The major American classics organization (The American Philological Association) has about 3,000 members, and on that basis we estimate very roughly that the total world population of classicists is somewhere between 7,000 and 10,000. BMCR, then, presently reaches between 22% and 32% of its total market. Presumably, only half of that market has access to computers, so BMCR's real penetration may be over 50%. If so, at its present rate of growth, BMCR may saturate its market in as few as five years. It is much more difficult to estimate the total world market for BMMR, but it is certainly greater than that for BMCR. With BMMR's present growth rate of perhaps 30%,[13] it will take somewhat longer to reach saturation.

BMCR unrecovered costs are about $4,000 per year for over 700 pages of reviews.[14] About half the cost goes for producing the paper version, and we anticipate costs of between $1,500 and $2,000 per year for preparing reviews for the Web.[15] Uncompensated editorial time averages 34 hours per month. Therefore, total out-of-pocket expenses could be as high as $6,000 if the paper version con-

TABLE 12.7. BMCR Unsubscriber Survey
(January 1996 through February 1997)

317 total: 103 address no longer valid; 91 responses

Identity of Respondents

15 unaffiliated with academic institution	46 faculty (4 retired, 9 adjunct or research)
7 librarians	8 students (2 undergraduates)
7 other	

Reason Given for Unsubscribing	No. Giving Reason	No. of Those Who Are Faculty
Never subscribed	2	1
Never meant to unsubscribe	2	1
Unsubscribed from old, subscribed to new address	16	14
Suspended subscription while away	15	9+1
Decided reviews not sufficiently relevant to interests	22	6+2
Decided review quality not high enough	2	+1
Too much e-mail	11+3	6+3
No longer have time to read reviews	7+1	+2
Other (5 shifted to BMR, 1 to BMCR, mistake)	7+1	4+1

Question	Unaffiliated	Faculty	Librarian	Student	Other
Not relevant	8	6+2	1	2	2
Too much mail	2	7	—	2	—
No time	4	+2	—	—	1
Total	14	13+4	1	4	3

"+" numbers signify those who marked more than one category

tinues and if markup continues to be done by hand. A third possible reduction in costs besides elimination of the paper version and automatic markup is a "fast-track" system whereby the review never leaves the Net: it is e-mailed to the editor, who sends it to a member of the editorial board; when the two have made changes, it is sent back to the reviewer for approval and then published on the Net. The great advantage for the reviewer is that this system cuts publication time by a month; the disadvantage is that the reviewer is asked to do some simple markup on the text before sending it.[16]

Possible revenue sources include advertising, subscriptions, and institutional support. As we have seen, our subscribers much prefer receiving advertising to paying for a subscription, but we have no idea how successful we will be in attracting advertising.[17] Hal Varian has suggested that we try to arrange something with Amazon Books, and we have made a tentative agreement to list their URL on our Web reviews.[18] We will not consider charging for subscriptions until BMCR is on the Web; at that point we could charge for timely delivery of the review, perhaps several months before universal access. We also want to wait for wide acceptance of a simple electronic cash transfer system. Institutional support seems to us the most obvious way to cover costs, since the college gets considerable exposure for what seems to us a small cost.

NOTES

1. BMMR has, as of May 7, 1997, become *The Medieval Review* (TMR).

2. The output by month (4/95–3/97) is as follows:

Month	4/95	5/95	6/95	7/95	8/95	9/95	10/95	11/95	12/95	1/96	2/96	3/96
BMMR	10	17	5	8	4	3	5	11	6	7	4	6
BMCR	15	14	19	13	11	29	26	17	27	12	14	15

Month	4/96	5/96	6/96	7/96	8/96	9/96	10/96	11/96	12/96	1/97	2/97	3/97
BMMR	1	4	1	6	6	9	8	11	16	6	16	12
BMCR	37	7	12	19	17	28	14	8	13	7	30	40

3. Since May 7, 1997, BMMR (that is, TMR) has been on the Web, which will eventually provide valuable data to compare with the BMCR gopher data.

4. Naturally, new reviews are visited often; we are trying to isolate those of enduring value.

5. Likewise, the .mil domain dropped from 310 to 186; the .gov domain, from 819 to 409.

6. The explosive growth in 9/95 and 10/95 was only temporary.

7. The difference would be even more pronounced had I not excluded books that appeared on the list only once. In 1996 the gap virtually disappears: 31 medieval titles (total number of titles 53) made the list 126 times (avg. 4.1) while 93 classical titles (total number of titles 169) made the list 360 times (avg. 3.9).

8. As is, our response rate is only in the 30–40% range.

9. Unfortunately the survey was worded as if only for BMCR subscribers, but even so the response rate was about 35%.

10. We found similar results in a pilot comparison of qualitative differences between the two journals that was done by two advanced graduate students (one a classicist, one a medievalist) in the summer of 1995. The students concluded that the major differences stem from the scholarly orientation of either discipline, not from their media (i.e., classicists criticize at a microscopic level, assuming in-depth acquaintance with a given text). The reviews are longer and the number of typographical errors is much greater in BMMR, but other differences seemed to be personal (tone of the review, footnotes and additional bibliography, organization, amount of direct quotation).

11. The values given are those of the Pearson chi-square test, but we also ran Continuity Correction, Likelihood Ratio, Mantel-Haenszel test for linear association among the chi-square tests, and also Pearson's R and Spearman Correlation.

12. Combined BMCR and joint figures are 912 for 1993, 1,342 for 1994 (+47%), 1,734 for 1995 (+29%), and 2,264 for 1996 (+30%).

13. Combined BMMR and joint figures are 518 for 1993, 958 for 1994 (+85%), 1,464 for 1995 (+53%), and 1,765 for 1996 (+21%). We have already seen an increase since BMMR relocated (3/97 = 1,985, about 30% annually), and we may expect a considerable bump

after official unveiling of TMR at the annual conference in May 1997 (and the introduction of the Web site).

14. Printing and mailing costs are about $5,000 and are covered by the subscription price of the paper version.

15. BMMR has found that it takes 35 minutes on average to code a review in SGML.

16. We received our first fast-track reviews in June and now find that well over half are submitted in this form.

17. So far only Princeton and Michigan (of the eight university presses contacted) have signed up for e-advertising.

18. Unfortunately, the University of Michigan, where our Web site is located, does not at present allow any advertising.

CHAPTER 13

The Crosscurrents of Technology Transfer
The Czech and Slovak Library Information Network

Andrew Lass

INTRODUCTION

> One would have no great difficulty in estimating the demand function, i.e., the rela-
> tionship between the price and the quantity that can be sold at that price for, say,
> tomatoes. But one would have considerable problems in making sales predictions at
> various hypothetical alternative prices for a new product that looks like a blue
> tomato and tastes like a peach. (Quandt 1996, 20)

This vivid image of an odd-looking vegetable that tastes like a fruit is meant to
highlight the difficulty of estimating the demand side in the overall cost picture of
producing and distributing new products, such as electronic publications. Compared to the traditional printed material, electronic products *are* new, from their
internal architecture to the mechanisms of production, distribution, and access
that stem from it. After all, the world of readers is not a homogeneous social
group, a market with a simple set of specific needs. Yet we assume that a segment
of this market—the scholarly community—takes easily and more or less quickly to
supplementing their long established habits (of associating the printed text with a
paper object) with different habits, experienced as equally convenient, of searching for and reading electronic texts. While this observation may be correct, it
should be emphasized at this point that precisely in the expression "more or less"
is where the opportunity lies—for those of us interested in transitions—to see
what is involved in this change of habit and why it is not just a "matter of time."
As anyone who has tried to explain the possibilities of electronic text delivery to an
educated friend will attest, the idea can be viewed with anxiety and taken to mean
the end of the book. The Minister of Culture of the Czech Republic, a well-
known author and dissident, looked at me with surprise as I tried to explain the
need for library automation (and therefore for his ministerial support): he held
both hands clasped together as if in prayer and then opened them up like a book

close to his face. He took a deep breath, exhaled, and explained how much the scent of books meant to him. His jump from on-line cataloging and microfilm preservation to the demise of his personal library was a rather daring leap of the imagination but not an uncommon one, even among those who should know better. It is not just the community of scholars, then, but of politicians and even librarians who must change their attitudes and habits. The problem is further compounded if we consider that in the case of Eastern Europe this new product is being introduced into a setting where the very notion of a market is itself unsettled. The question of demand is quite different in a society that had been dominated by a political economy of command.

In the pages that follow I will give a brief account of an extensive interlibrary automation and networking project that The Andrew W. Mellon Foundation initiated and funded abroad, in the Czech and Slovak republics.[1] While most of the papers in this volume deal with digital libraries, this one points to the complexities that affect the ability of any library to change its ways and expand its mandate to include access to digitized materials. My aim is critical rather than comprehensive. By telling the reader about some of the obstacles that were confronted along the way, I hope to draw attention to the kinds of issues that need to be kept in mind when we think of establishing library consortia—the seemingly natural setting for the new technologies—in other countries.

THE CASLIN PROJECTS

The Mellon-funded proposal to establish the Czech and Slovak Library Information Network (CASLIN) commenced in January 1993. In its original stage it involved four libraries in what has now become two countries: the National Library of the Czech Republic (in Prague), the Moravian Regional Library (in Brno), the Slovak National Library (in Martin), and the University Library of Bratislava. These four libraries had signed an agreement (a Letter of Intent) that they would cooperate in all matters that pertained to fully automating their technical services and, eventually, in developing and maintaining a single on-line Union Catalogue. They also committed themselves to introducing and upholding formats and rules that would enable a "seamless" integration into the growing international library community. For example, compliance with the UNIMARC format was crucial in choosing the library system vendor (the bid went to ExLibris's ALEPH). Similarly, Anglo-American cataloging rules (AACR2) have been introduced, and most recently, there is discussion of adopting the LC subject headings. Needless to say, the implementation was difficult and the fine-tuning of the system is not over yet, though most if not all of the modules are up and running in all four libraries. The first on-line OPAC terminals were made available to readers during 1996. At present, these electronic catalogs reflect only the library's own collection—there are no links to the other libraries, let alone to a CASLIN Union Catalogue—though they do contain a variety of other databases (for example, a periodicals distribution list is available on the National Library OPAC that lists the location of journals and periodicals in different libraries in Prague, including the years and numbers held). A record includes the call number—a point of no small significance—but does not indicate the loan status, nor does the system allow users to "Get" or "Renew" a book.[2] In spite of these shortcomings, the number of users of these terminals has grown sharply, especially among university students, and librarians are looking for ways to finance more (including some graphics terminals with access to the WWW).

In the period between 1994 and 1996, several additional projects (conceived as extensions of the original CASLIN project) were presented to The Mellon Foundation for funding. It was agreed that the new partners would adopt the same cataloging rules as well as any other standards and that they would (eventually) participate in the CASLIN Union Catalogue. Each one of these projects poses a unique opportunity to use information technology as an integrator of disparate and incongruous institutional settings.

The Library Information Network of the Czech Academy of Science (LINCA) was projected as a two-tiered effort that would (1) introduce library automation to the central library of the Czech Academy of Sciences and thereby (2) set the stage for the building of an integrated library-information network that would connect the specialized libraries of all the 60 scientific institutes into a single web with the central library as their hub. At the time of this writing the central library's LAN has been completed and most of the hardware installed, including the high-capacity CD-ROM (UltraNet) server. The ideal of connecting all the institutes will be tested against reality as the modular library system (BIBIS by Square Co., Holland) is introduced together with workstations and/or miniservers in the many locations in and outside the city of Prague.[3]

The Košice Library Information Network (KOLIN) is an attempt to draw together three different institutions (two universities and one research library) into a single library consortium. If successful, this consortium in eastern Slovakia would comprise the largest on-line university and research library group in that country. The challenge lies in the fact that the two different types of institutions come under two different government oversight ministries (of education and of culture), which further complicates the already strained budgetary and legislative setup. Furthermore, one of the universities—the University of Pavel Josef Šafárik (UPJS)—at that time had two campuses (in two cities 40 km apart) and its libraries dispersed among thirteen locations. UPJS is also the Slovak partner in the Slovak-Hungarian CD-ROM network (Mellon-funded HUSLONET) that shares in the usage and the costs of purchasing database licenses.[4]

Finally, the last of the CASLIN "add-ons" involves an attempt to bridge incompatibilities between two established library software systems by linking two university and two state scientific libraries in two cities (Brno and Olomouc) into a single regional network, the Moravian Library Information Network (MOLIN). The two universities—Masaryk University in Brno and Palacký University in Olomouc—have already completed their university-wide library network with TinLib (of the United Kingdom) as their system of choice. Since TinLib records do not recognize the MARC structure (the CASLIN standard adopted by the two state scientific libraries), a conversion engine has been developed to guarantee full import and export of bibliographic records. Though it is too soon to know how well the solution will actually work, it is clear already that its usefulness goes beyond MOLIN, because TinLib has been installed in many Czech universities.[5]

Fortunately, storage, document preservation, retrospective conversion, and connectivity have all undergone substantial changes over the past few years. They are worth a brief comment:

1. Up until the end of the Communist era, access to holdings was limited not only by the increasingly ridiculous yet strict rules of censorship but also by the worsening condition of the physical plant and, in the case of special collections, the actual poor condition of the documents. The National Library in Prague was the most striking example of this situation; it was in a state of de facto paralysis. Of its close to 4 million volumes, only a small percentage was accessible. The rest were literally "out of reach" because they were either in milk crates and unshelved or in poorly maintained depositories in different locations around the country.[6] This critical situation turned the corner in January 1996 when the new book depository of the NL was officially opened in the Prague suburb of Hostivar. Designed by the Hillier Group (Princeton, N.J.) and built by a Czech contractor, it is meant to house 4.5 million volumes and contains a rare book preservation department (including chemical labs) and a large microfilm department. Because more than 2 million volumes were cleaned, moved, and reshelved by the end of 1996, it is now possible to receive the books ordered at the main building (a book shuttle guarantees overnight delivery).[7] Other library construction has been under way, or is planned, for other major scientific and university libraries in the Czech Republic.[8] There is no comparable library construction going on in Slovakia.

2. The original CASLIN Mellon project included a small investment in microfilm preservation equipment, including a couple of high-end cameras (GRATEK) with specialized book cradles—one for each of the National Libraries—as well as developers, reader-printers, and densitometers. The idea was to (1) preserve the rare collection of nineteenth- and twentieth-century periodicals (that are turning to dust), (2) significantly decrease the turnaround time that it takes to process a microfilm request (from several weeks to a few days), and (3) make it technically possible to meet the highest international standards in microfilm preservation. The program has since evolved to a full-scale digitalization project (funded by the Ministry of Culture) that includes the collections of other libraries.[9]

3. The most technologically ambitious undertaking, and one that also has the most immediate and direct impact on document accessibility, is the project for the retrospective conversion of the general catalog of the National Library in Prague. Known under the acronym RETROCON, it involves a laboratory-like setup of hardware and software (covered by a Mellon Foundation grant) that would—in an assembly-line fashion—convert the card catalog into ALEPH-ready electronic form (UNIMARC). RETROCON is designed around the idea of using a sophisticated OCR in combination with a specially designed software that semiautomatically breaks down the converted ASCII record into logical segments and places them into the appropriate MARC field. This software, developed by a Czech company (COMDAT) in cooperation with the National Library, operates in a Windows environment and allows the librarian to focus on the "editing" of the converted record (using a mouse and keyboard, if necessary) instead of laboriously typing in the whole record. As an added benefit, the complete scanned catalog has now been made available for limited searching (under author and title in a Windows environment), thereby replacing the original card catalog. One of the most interesting aspects of this project has been the outsourcing of the final step in the conversion to other libraries, a sort of division of labor (funded in part by the Ministry of Culture) that increases the pool of available expert catalogers.[10]

4. For the most part, all installations of the LAN have proceeded with minimal problems, and the library automation projects, especially those involving technical services, are finally up and running. Unfortunately, this achievement cannot be said for the statewide infrastructure, especially not the phone system. Up until the end of 1997, the on-line connections between libraries were so poor that it was difficult to imagine, let alone test, what an on-line library network would have to offer. Needless to say, this holdback has had an adverse effect on library management, especially of the CASLIN consortium as a whole.[11]

CROSSCURRENTS

A comparison of the present condition and on-line readiness of research and university libraries in Central Europe with the status quo as it arrived at the doorstep of the post-1989 era leaves no doubt that dramatic improvements have taken place. But even though the once empty (if not broken) glass is now half filled, it also remains half empty. Certainly that is how most of the participants tend to see the situation, perhaps because they are too close to it and because chronic dissatisfaction is a common attitude. Yet the fact remains that throughout the implementation and in all of the projects, obstacles appeared nearly every step of the way. While most of the obstacles were resolved, although not without some cost, all of them can be traced to three basic sources of friction: (1) those best attributed

to external constraints—the budgetary, legal, political, and for the most part, bureaucratic ties that directly affect a library's ability to function and implement
change; (2) those caused by cultural misunderstandings—the different habits, values, and expectations that inform the activity of localization; and (3) the internal
problems of the libraries themselves, no doubt the most important locus of micropolitical frictions and therefore of problems and delays.[12] In what follows, I will
focus on the first source of friction (with some attention paid to the second), since
my emphasis here is on the changing relations *between* what are taken to be separate institutional domains (particularly between libraries and other government
organizations or the market) as I try to make sense of the persistently problematic
relationships between libraries (particularly within the CASLIN group). Obviously, while these analytical distinctions are heuristically valuable, in reality, these
sources of friction are intertwined and further complicated by the fact that the two
countries are undergoing post-Communist aftershocks and an endless series of
corrections. Not only are the libraries being transformed, but so is the world of
which they form a part. To make sense of this double transition and to describe
the multifaceted process that the library projects have moved through may pose
some difficulties. But the task also offers a unique opportunity to observe whether,
and if so how, the friction points move over time. What could have been predicted
when the initial project commenced—that implementation and system localization would also mean giving in to a variety of constraints—is only beginning to
take on the hard contours of reality four years later. In several instances, the results
differ from our initial conception, but I don't think it would be fair to assume that
the final outcome will be a compromise. Instead, the success of the Mellon library
projects in Eastern Europe (of which CASLIN is only one) should be judged by
the extent to which they have been accepted and have taken on a life of their own,
initially distinguishable but finally inseparable from the library traditions already
in place. After all, if the projects were designed to affect a change in the library
system—and by "system," we must understand a complex of organizational structures, a real culture, and an actually existing social network—then we must also
expect that the library system will respond that way, that is, as a complex sociocul-
tural system. What appeared at first as a series of stages (goals) that were to follow
one another in logical progression and in a "reasonable" amount of time may still
turn out to have been the right series. It's just that the progression will have followed another (cultural) logic, one in which other players—individuals and the organizational rules that they play by—must have their part. As a result, the time it
actually takes to get things done seems "unreasonable," and some things even appear to have failed because they have not taken place as and when expected. What
is the meaning of these apparent problems? A seemingly philosophical issue takes
on a very real quality as we wonder, for example, about the future of the CASLIN
consortium. If establishing a network of library consortia was one of the central
aims of the Mellon project, then it is precisely this goal that we have failed to
reach, at least now, when it was supposed to be long in place according to our

scheme of things. There is no legal body, no formal association of participating libraries in place. This deficiency is particularly important and, needless to say, frustrating for those of us who take for granted the central role that networking and institutional cooperation play in education and scholarly research. But behind this frustration another one hides: it is probably impossible to say whether what is experienced as the status quo, in this case as a failure or shortcoming, is not just another unexpected curve in a process that follows an uncharted trajectory.[13]

As I have noted above, in 1992 a Letter of Intent had been signed by the four founding CASLIN members. It was a principal condition of the project proposal. In January 1996, when this part of the project was—for all intents and purposes—brought to a close, there was still no formally established and registered CASLIN association with a statute, membership rules, and a governing body in place. Although the four libraries had initially worked together to choose the hardware and software, the work groups that had been formed to decide on specific standards (such as cataloging rules, language localization, or the structure of the Union Catalogue record) had trouble cooperating and their members often lacked the authority to represent their institution. Tasks were accomplished more because of the enthusiasm of individuals and the friendly relations that developed among them than because of a planned, concerted effort on the part of the library leadership guided by a shared vision. The initial stages of the implementation process were characterized by an uneven commitment to the shifting of priorities that would be necessary in order to carry the intent through. There was even a sense, in some instances, that the prestige of the project was more important than its execution or, more exactly, that while the funding for library automation was more than welcome, so was the political capital that came with being associated with this U.S.-funded project, even if such an attitude meant using this political capital at a cost to the consortium. As is well documented from many examples of outside assistance in economic development, well-intentioned technology transfer is a prime target for subversion by other, local intentions; it can be transformed with ease into a pawn in another party's game. Potential rivalries and long-standing animosities that existed among some of the libraries, instead of being bridged by the project, seemed to be exacerbated by it. In one instance, for example, affiliation with the Mellon project was used by a library to gain attention of high government officials (such as the cultural minister) responsible for policies affecting their funding and, most important, their mandate. The aim, as it now turns out, was to gain the status of a national library. This library's target, that is, the library that already had this status, was the Slovak National Library, its primary CASLIN partner. While both libraries participated in the CASLIN project's implementation and even cooperated in crucial ways at the technical level (as agreed), their future library cooperation was being undermined by a parallel, semiclandestine, political plot. Needless to say, this situation has left the CASLIN partnership weakened and the managements of both libraries dysfunctional.[14]

As the additional library projects mentioned earlier were funded and the new libraries joined the original CASLIN group, it became clear that the new, larger group existed more in rhetoric than in fact. From the newcomer's point of view there was not much "there" to join. "What is in this for us, and at what cost?" seemed to be the crucial question at the January 1996 meeting at which a written proposal for a CASLIN association was introduced by the National Library in Prague. This meeting was not the first time that an initiative had been presented but failed to take hold. Nor was it the last. The discussion about the proposal resulted in a squabble. An e-mail discussion group was established to continue the discussion but nothing came of it nor of several other attempts.

If the point of a consortium is for libraries to cooperate in order to benefit (individually) from the sharing of resources so as to provide better on-line service, then a situation such as this one must be considered counterproductive. How does one explain the chronic inability of CASLIN to get off the ground as a real existing organization? Where does the sense of apathy, reluctance, or even antagonism come from? Most of the answers (and there are many) lie hidden within the subtleties of society and history. But of these answers, a few stand out clearly: the fact that all the original CASLIN libraries come under the administrative oversight of the Ministry of Culture is one key piece of the puzzle. The dramatic cuts in the ministries' overall budgets are passed down to the beneficiaries who find themselves competing for limited goods. Another answer is in the lingering nature of the relationship: if the difference from the previous setup (under the "planned" socialist economy) lies with the fact that the library has the status of a legal subject that designs and presents its own budget, its relationship to the ministry—very tense and marked by victimization—seems more like the "same old thing." In other words, certain aspects of organizational behavior continue not only by force of habit (a not insignificant factor in itself), but also because these aspects are reinforced by a continuing culture of codependency and increased pressure to compete over a single source of attention. The situation appears as if, from our point of view, the formal command economy has been transformed into a market economy only to the extent that strategic and self-serving positioning is now more obvious and potentially more disruptive. So-called healthy competition (so called by those whose voices dominate in the present government and who believe in the self-regulating spirit of "free market forces") seems to show only its ugly side: we see the Mellon project embraced with eagerness *in part* because of the way its prestige could be used to gain a competitive advantage over other libraries. In the case of CASLIN partners, we see it take the form of suspicion, envy, and even bad-mouthing expressed directly to the Mellon grants administrator (myself).[15]

What are the constraints under which a research or national library operates, and in what way is the present situation different from the "socialist" era [1948–1989]? An answer to these questions will give us a better sense of the circumstances under which attempts to bring these institutions up to international standards—and get them to actively cooperate—must unfold.

Figures 13.1 and 13.2 illustrate the external ties between a library and other important domains of society that affect its functioning and co-define its purpose before and after 1989 (while keeping in mind that economic, legal, and regulatory conditions have been in something of a flux in the years since 1989 and, therefore, that the rules under which a library operates continue to change).

1. Under "party" rule the library, like all other organizations, came under direct control of its ministry, in this case the Ministry of Culture [MK]. One could even say, by comparison with the present situation, that the library was an extension of the ministry. However, the ministry was itself an extension of the centralized political rule (the Communist party), including the watchful eye of the secret police [STB]. The director was appointed "from above" [PARTY] and the budget arrived from there as well. While requests for funding were entertained, it was hard to tell what would be funded and under what ideological disguise.[16] For the most part the library was funded "just in order to keep it alive," though if the institution ran out of money in any fiscal year, more could be secured to "bail it out" [hence "Soft" Budget]. In addition to bureaucratic constraints (regarding job descriptions and corresponding wage tables, building maintenance and repairs, or the purchase of monographs and periodicals), many of which remain in place, there were political directives regarding employability[17] and, of course, the ever-changing and continuously growing list of prohibited materials to which access was to be denied [Index]. In contrast, the library is now an independent legal body that can more or less decide on its priorities and is free to establish working relationships with other (including foreign) organizations. The decision making, including organizational changes, now resides within the library. While the budget is presented to the ministry and is public knowledge, it is also a "hard" budget that is set at the ministerial level as it matches its cultural policies against those of the Ministry of Finance [MF] (and therefore of the ruling government coalition). After an initial surge in funds (all marked for capital investment only), the annual budgets of the libraries have been cut consistently over the past five years (i.e., they are not even adjusted for inflation but each year are actually lower than the previous one). These cuts have seriously affected the ability of the libraries to carry out their essential functions, let alone purchase documents or be in the position to hire qualified personnel.[18] For this reason, I prefer to speak of a relationship of codependence. The Ministry of Culture still maintains direct control over the library's ability to actualize its "independence"—though it has gradually shifted from an antagonistic attitude to one of genuine concern. The point is that whereas the Ministry of Culture is supposed to oversee the well-being of its institutions, it is, as is usually the case in situations of government supervision, perceived as the powerful enemy.

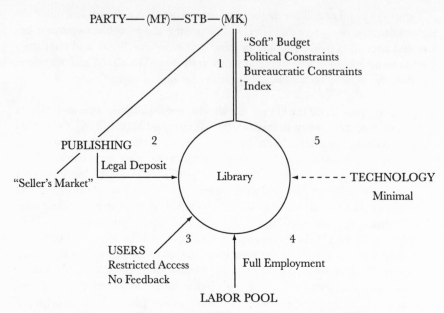

Figure 13.1. Czech Research Library *before* 1990: External Ties

2. The publishing world was strictly regulated under the previous regime: all publishing houses were state enterprises (any other attempt at publishing was punishable by law), and all materials had to pass the scrutiny of the state (political) censor. Not everything that was published was necessarily political trash, and editions were limited; the resulting economy of shortage created a high demand for printed material, particularly modern fiction, translations from foreign languages, and the literary weekly [hence "Seller's Market"]. Libraries benefited from this situation. Because all state scientific and research libraries were recipients of the legal deposit, their (domestic) acquisitions were, de facto, guaranteed. At present the number of libraries covered by the deposit requirement has been reduced from some three dozen to half a dozen. This change was meant to ease the burden on publishers and give the libraries a freer hand in building their collection in a "competitive marketplace." But considering the severe cuts in the budget, many of the libraries cannot begin to fulfill even the most Spartan acquisitions policy. For the same reason publishers, of whom there are many and all of whom are private and competing for the readers' attention, do not consider libraries as important parts of their market. Furthermore, many of the small and often short-lived houses do not bother to apply for the ISBN or to send at least one copy (the legal deposit law is impossible to enforce) to the National Library, which, in turn, cannot fulfill its mandate of maintaining the national bibliographic record.

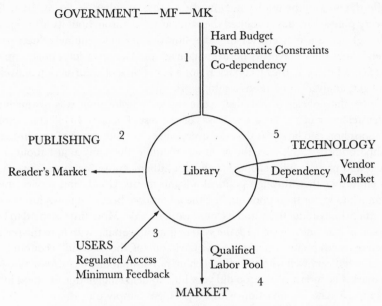

Figure 13.2. Czech Research Library *after* 1990: External Ties

3. During the Communist era, access to materials was limited for several obvious reasons: political control (books on the Index, limited number of books
from Western countries, theft) or deliberate neglect (the progressively deteriorating storage conditions eventually made it impossible to retrieve materials). Over the years there was less and less correspondence between the
card catalogs in the circulation room and the actual holdings, and as a result, students and scholars stopped using the National Library in Prague because it was increasingly unlikely that their requests would be filled. This
situation was also true for current Czech or Slovak publications because of
an incredible backlog in cataloging or because the books remained unshelved. Of course, in such a system there was no place for user feedback.
Since then, some notable improvements—many of them due to Mellon and
other initiatives—have been made in public services, such as self-service
photocopying machines and, to remain with the example of the National
Library, quick retrieval of those volumes that have been reshelved in the
new depository. Also, readers are now used to searching the electronic
OPACs or using the CD-ROM databases in the reference room. On the
other hand, the backlog of uncataloged books is said to be worse than before and, with acquisitions cut back and the legal deposit not observed, the
reader continues to leave the circulation desk empty-handed. The paradoxical situation is not lost on the reader: if the books are out of print or, as is
more often the case these days, their price beyond what readers could

afford, going to the library may not be a solution either. So far the basic library philosophy has remained the same as it has throughout its history: although there is concern for the user, libraries are not genuinely "user driven" (only a few university libraries have adopted an open stack policy) and, as far as I can tell, user feedback is not a key source of information actively sought, analyzed, and used in setting priorities.

4. Under the policies of socialist economy, full employment was as much a characteristic of the library as it was of the rest of society. In effect, organizations hoarded labor (as they did everything else) with a sort of just-in-case philosophy in mind, since the point was to fulfill "the plan" at just about any cost and provide full benefits for all with little incentive for career development (other than through political advancement). Goods and services became known for their poor quality; the labor force became known for its extremely low productivity and its lousy work morale. More time seemed to be spent in learning how to trick the system than in working with it, to the point where micro political intrigue—the backbone of the "second" economy—competed very well with the official chain of command. The introduction of a market economy after 1990 did very little to help change this situation in a library, a state organization with no prestige. Simply put, the novelty and promise of the private sector, coupled by its high employment rate and good wages, has literally cut the library out of the competitive market for qualified labor. Between the budget cuts and the wage tables still in place, there is little space left for the new management to negotiate contracts that would attract and keep talented people in the library, certainly not those people with an interest in information technologies and data management.[19]

5. As mentioned above, the first information technologies arrived in the state scientific and national libraries in the late 1980s. Their impact on budgets was minimal (UNESCO's ISIS is freeware) as was their effect on technical services. On the other hand, the introduction of information technologies into these libraries, in particular the CASLIN group, was the single most visible *and disruptive* change—a sort of wedge that split the library organizations open—that has occurred since 1990 (or, according to some, during the last century). The dust has not yet settled, but in view of our present discussion, one thing is clear already: between the Mellon funds and the initial capital investment that followed, libraries have become a significant market for the local distributors of hardware and for the library software vendors (in contrast to the relationship with publishers). But as we all know, these purchases are not one-time purchases but only the first investments into a new kind of dependency, a new external tie that the library must continue to support and at no small cost. And the cost is not just financial. The ongoing complications with the technology and the chronic delays in systems localization only

contribute to the present sluggish state of affairs and thus lend support to the ever cynical factions within the organization that knew "all along" that "the whole automation project was a mistake." Obviously, the inability to attract qualified professionals doesn't help.

What I have painted here is but part of the picture (the other part would be made up of a detailed analysis of the micropolitics that actually go on, both inside the organization and in relation to other organizations, particularly other libraries). But the above discussion should help us see how and why the libraries feel trapped in a vicious circle from which they perceive little or no way out other than continuing to battle for their place in the sun. Of course, their tactics and battle cries only reinforce the relationship of codependency as well as their internal organizational problems. And that is exactly what the public and government officials see: that these institutions need to grow up and learn what real work is before more money is poured down the drain. Needless to say, a sizable portion of the blame must be carried by a government that has made a conscious choice against long-term investment into the educational, scientific, and information sectors.

If the long-standing administrative ties between libraries and the Ministry of Culture inform and override the building of new, potentially powerful ties to other libraries, then the flip side of this codependency, its result, is a lack of experience with building and envisioning the practical outcome of a horizontally integrated (i.e., nonhierarchical) association of independent organizations. The libraries had only limited exposure to automation, and the importance of long-term strategic planning was lost on some of them.[20] At least two other factors further reinforced this situation: the slow progress (the notorious delays mentioned above) in the implementation of the new system, which had involved what seemed like impractical and costly steps (such as working in UNIMARC), and the sluggish Internet connection. These factors suggest that at the present, a traditional understanding of basic library needs (which themselves are overwhelming) tends to take precedent over scenarios that appear much too radical and not grounded in a familiar reality. Since the on-line potential is not fully actualized, its impact is hard to imagine, and so the running of the organization in related areas continues to be predominantly reactive rather than proactive. In other words, in-house needs are not related to network solutions, especially when such solutions appear to be counterintuitive for the established (and more competitive) relationship between the libraries.

Cooperation among the libraries exists at the level of system librarians and other technical experts. Without this cooperation, the system would not have been installed, certainly not as an identical system in all four libraries. In addition (and, I should say, ironically) the CASLIN project has now received enough publicity to make it a household name among librarians. The acronym has a life of its own, and there is a growing interest among other scientific libraries to join this "prestigious" group (that both does and does not exist).[21] But are we waiting for a moment at which the confluence of de facto advances in technical services and a growing interest of other libraries in logistical support (involving technology and technical services) will create a palpable *need* for a social organization that would exist (1) above and beyond the informal network of cooperation and (2) without association with the name and funds of The Andrew W. Mellon Foundation (its original reason for existence)? I have heard it said that "nothing more is needed," because the fundamentals of CASLIN are now embedded in the library process itself (reference here, I gather, was to cataloging) and in the existing agreements between individual libraries on the importing and exporting of records into and from the CASLIN Union Catalogue that is to be serviced by the two national libraries. In fact, as the most recent meeting (June 1997) of the Union Catalogue group made clear, such processes are indeed where the seed of an association of CASLIN libraries lies. The import and export of records and the beginning of the Union Catalogue database have yet to materialize, but they did bring together these individuals who represented individual libraries. If these people figure out a way to run their own show and stick to it, then there is a fair chance that an organization of CASLIN libraries will take off after all.[22]

CONCLUDING REMARKS

The above discussion raises three very important points. The first point regards cultural misunderstanding. The problem with the "misbehaving consortium" may lie to some extent with *our* (e.g., U.S.) expectations of what cooperation looks like and what basic fundamentals an on-line library consortium must embrace in order to do its job well. In the Czech and Slovak case, not only were the conditions not in place, they were counterindicative. While our naïveté caused no harm (the opposite is the case, I am repeatedly told!), it remains to be seen what the final result will look like. And in the final result resides the really intriguing lesson: maybe it is not so much that we should have or even could have thought differently and therefore ended up doing "this" rather than "that." Perhaps it is in the (information) technology itself—in its very organization—that the source of our (mis)understanding lies. After all, these technologies were developed in one place and not another. Our library automation systems obviously embody a particular understanding of technical and public services and an organization of work that share the same culture as a whole tradition of other technologies that emphasize speed, volume (just think of the history of railroads or the development of the "American system" of manufacturing), and finally, access. Every single paper in this volume exemplifies and assumes this world. In transferring a technology from one place to another, an implied set of attitudes and habits is being marketed as well. The intriguing question is whether the latter emerges logically from the former in the new location. To this possibility, my second point lends some support: technology transfer involves a time lag, the duration of which is impossible to predict and that is accounted for by a complex series of micropolitical adjustments. It is this human factor that transforms the logical progression in the *projected* implementation process into a much less logical but essentially social act. Thanks to this human factor, the whole effort may fail. Without it, the effort will not exist. Only after certain problems and not others arise will certain solutions and not others seem logical. It is no secret that much social change is technology driven. It is less clear, ethnographically speaking, what exactly this process means, and even less is known about it when technology travels across cultural boundaries. There is much to be gained from looking carefully at the different points in the difficult process of implementing projects such as CASLIN. Apparently the ripple effect reaches far deeper (inside the institutions) and far wider (other libraries, the government, the market, and the users) than anyone would have anticipated. Before it is even delivering fully on its promise, the original Mellon project is demanding changes in library organization and management. Such changes are disruptive, even counterproductive, long before they "settle in." Nevertheless, and this is my third point, internal organizational change involves a gradual but, in consequence, quite radical realignment of ties with the outside, that is, with the Ministry of Culture (which—at least on the Czech side—has taken a keen interest in supporting library automation throughout the country; on the Slovak side, unfortunately, the situation is rather different), with other libraries (there has been a slow but palpable increase in interlibrary cooperation on specific projects that involve the use of information technologies, e.g., retrospective conversion, newspaper preservation, and, I hope, the CASLIN Union Catalogue), and most important, with the public. How far reaching and permanent these shifts are is difficult to say, especially when any accomplishments have been accompanied by a nagging feeling that they were done on a shoestring and against all odds. The persistent inability of the governments to pass legislation and appropriate funding that would support the newly emerging democracies' entrance into the global, information age in a sustainable manner highlights a serious lack of vision as well as of political savvy.

At the beginning of this paper I argued that in discussing the introduction of new technologies, specifically information technologies, it is important to pay attention to the point of transition, to see all that is involved in this change of habit and why it is not just a "matter of time." The body of this paper, I hope, provided at least a glimpse of some of the friction points involved. For the time being, the last word, like the first, belongs to an economist, in this case to Václav Klaus, the prime minister of the Czech Republic (1993–1997), whose opinions expressed in a recent op-ed piece on "Science and our Economic Future" make him sound like someone who has just bitten into a blue tomato only to find that it tastes like a peach.

> Science is not about information, but about knowing, about thinking, about the ability to generalize thoughts, make models of them and then testable hypotheses that

are to be tested. Science is not about the Internet and certainly not about its compulsory introduction. (Klaus 1997)

NOTES

1. Unless otherwise noted, the following discussion pertains to the situation as it appeared in the latter part of 1996 and the first part of 1997. Understandably, a year or two later many of the issues raised will have taken on a new significance.

2. These and other features should be available shortly. As for the size of the database, of the total collection only a fragment is presently on-line. Prior to the introduction of the new system, libraries had been cataloging in ISIS. These records have been converted with little or no loss to the UNIMARC format, which meant—in the case of the National Library—that, from the outset, several hundred thousand records were ALEPH-ready. New acquisitions are cataloged directly into the new system and more records are made available through retrospective conversion.

The Web addresses (with access to the catalogs) are as follows: National Library of the Czech Republic (Prague), *www.nkp.cz;* the Moravian Regional Library (Brno), *www.mzk.cz;* the Slovak National Library (Martin), *www.matica.sk/snk/snk.html;* the University Library in Bratislava, *www.ulib.sk.*

3. For additional details on this project, see the LINCA proposal presented to The Mellon Foundation (LINCA 1994).

4. As of January 1997, the two campuses of UPJS have been turned into two universities. The move was political (divide and conquer), playing off existing institutional rivalry. What the consequence of this division will be on the project is not yet clear. The details of the original project can be found in the KOLIN proposal to The Mellon Foundation (KOLIN 1995).

5. For a more detailed account of the compatibility and conversion problem as well as of the solution, see Appendix H of the MOLIN proposal (MOLIN 1996). TinLib is the most widely used library system among Czech universities (the Czech vendor is located at Charles University in Prague).

6. More precisely, out of the approximately 1.5 million volumes deposited in the central library (the Klementinum), about one-fifth were unshelved. Because these volumes were new acquisitions—most in demand by users—most requests went unfulfilled.

7. Hence also the symbolic significance of including the call number on the electronic record—it actually corresponds to a retrievable object! What a treat!

8. With the series of austerity measures introduced by the Czech government in spring 1997, it remains unclear how the plans will be realized.

9. Equally important in the area of rare book and manuscript preservation is the direct digitalization project at the National Library in Prague, in which early medieval illuminated manuscripts are being scanned and made available on CD-ROM (in 1995/96: *Antiphonarium Sedlecense* and *Chronicon Concilii Constantiniensis*). This project is a UNESCO-sponsored *Memory of the World* project. For more on this project and its latest developments, see A. Knoll (1997), *http://digit.nkp.cz/Structure_Proposal/navrhiii.htm.*

10. There is much more to this fascinating and complex project, well worth a separate study. The interested reader may wish to look at the original text of the project as it was pre-

sented to The Mellon Foundation for Funding (RETROCON 1994) and at a special publication of the National Library devoted to this topic (Bareš and Stoklasová 1995).

11. With the proliferation of the cellular phone network in Eastern Europe, it is possible that many connections—such as user access—will take the wireless route.

12. "External" constraints are often found embedded inside the organization. I wish to exercise caution in using this term since it is often quite difficult to pinpoint where an organization ends and the external world begins.

13. The role of time management and, in particular, of delays in the implementation of the library project is a topic of a separate study (Lass 1997).

14. According to a recent document (issued by the Slovak Ministry of Culture), the library's new mandate would include, among other things, the issuing of ISBNs and the development of the national bibliographic records. This mandate has put the library in the situation, apparently desired, of having to demand from the Slovak National Library the transfer of positions, computer hardware (mostly CASLIN Mellon purchases), and existing databases, without which it cannot do the job, although how it would gain the expertise remains unclear. While there are other examples in which institutional rivalries have adversely affected the CASLIN project, in only some of them does the rivalry reside with the libraries themselves. In several instances it is the libraries that are caught in the middle of a battle. Such is the case in the KOLIN project discussed above (see also footnote 4).

15. On several occasions, librarians of one institution would express concern that "the other" library received more funds than they did. The symbolic significance of foreign (Western) funds is not to be underestimated nor should the role that this phenomenon has on the actual implementation of the project (covered best by the anthropological studies of cargo cults or witchcraft). As for the politics of institutional positioning, the situation under review was made transparent (and more complicated) by the breakup of Czechoslovakia and, following that, by the surfacing of other regional tensions. As a result, the relationship across the border is more amicable (there is nothing to compete over), while the relationship between the two libraries in each of the countries is much less so.

16. One of the surprises was the funding of automation at the National (then University or State) Library during the 1980s in Prague, which resulted in the development of a local machine-readable record format (MAKS) that became the accepted system among a majority of Czech and Slovak libraries. The grounds for technology transfer were therefore prepared (contrary to some who maintained that there was no expertise in place) when automation arrived in earnest after 1990.

17. Ironically, the library became one of the safe places to hide politically discredited intellectuals (from the post-1968 purges).

18. If the purchase of foreign (especially Western) books and periodicals was restricted for mostly political reasons, it is now actually stopped altogether due to zero (!) funding.

19. As a result, organizational behavior retains its characteristic sluggishness. It is reasonable to predict that as the constraints on the budget continue to increase, so will the familiar ability to trick the system. Under these conditions, teaching new management skills has been close to impossible, and introducing a new record structure and cataloging rules has been very slow. These conditions account, to a large extent, for the continued backlog of uncataloged books.

20. The fact that "planning" is a discredited term doesn't help. And trying to explain that socialist planning and strategic planning may be quite different things doesn't seem to work.

21. On the Czech side, the Ministry of Culture has decided to support library automation projects throughout the country, in the form of capital investment grants (no funds for salaries) that meet CASLIN standards.

22. As of early fall 1997, the prospects for a functioning CASLIN Union Catalogue look promising. With the purchase of an Oracle software license and access to a Digital Alpha server, the plan is to make access to the database available to participating libraries by early 1998.

REFERENCES

Bareš, Miroslav, and Stoklasová, Bohdana. 1995. *Retrospective Conversion in Czech Libraries.* Praha: Narodní knihovna.

KOLIN. 1995. *Kosice Library Information Network.* A proposal presented to The Andrew W. Mellon Foundation, South Hadley, Mass.

Klaus, Václav. 1997. "Věda a naše hospodářská budoucnost." In *Lidové noviny,* May 31.

Knoll, Adolf. 1997. "Dissemination and Archival Storage of Old Materials as Electronic Documents." Paper presented at The Mellon Foundation Conference on Library Automation, Warsaw, October 16–18, 1997.

Lass, Andrew. 1997. "Managing Delay: The Micropolitics of Time in the Czech and Slovak Library Automation Projects." Paper presented at Mellon Foundation Conference on Library Automation, Warsaw, October 16–18, 1997.

LINCA. 1994. *Library Information Network of the Czech Academy of Science.* A proposal presented to The Andrew W. Mellon Foundation, South Hadley, Mass.

MOLIN. 1996. *Moravian Libarary Information Network.* A proposal presented to The Andrew W. Mellon Foundation, South Hadley, Mass.

RETROCON. 1994. *National Library in Prague: Retrospective catalogue conversion.* A proposal presented to The Andrew W. Mellon Foundation, South Hadley, Mass.

Quandt, Richard. 1996. "Electronic Publishing and Virtual Libraries: Issues and an Agenda for The Andrew W. Mellon Foundation." *Serials Review* (summer): 9–24.

CHAPTER 14

Consortial Access versus Ownership

Richard W. Meyer

INTRODUCTION

This chapter reports on a consortial attempt to overcome the high costs of scholarly journals and to study the roots of the cost problem with the advent of high-speed telecommunication networks throughout the world. The literature on the problem of journal costs includes both proposals for new ways of communicating research results and many studies on pricing.

Prominent members of the library profession have written proposals on how to disengage from print publishers.[1] Others have suggested that electronic publications soon will emerge and bring an end to print-based scholarship.[2] Another scientist proposes that libraries solve the problem by publishing journals themselves.[3] These proposals, however, tend not to accommodate the argument that loosely coupled systems cannot be easily restructured.[4] While access rather than ownership promises cost savings to libraries, the inflation problem requires further analysis of the factors that establish journal prices before it is solved.

Many efforts to explain the problem occupy the literature of the library profession and elsewhere. The most exhaustive effort to explain journal price inflation, published by the Association of Research Libraries for The Andrew W. Mellon Foundation, provides ample data, but no solution.[5] Examples of the problem appear frequently in the *Newsletter on Serials Pricing Issues*, which was developed expressly to focus discussion of the issue.[6] Searches for answers appear to have started seriously with Hamaker and Astle, who provided an explanation based on currency exchange rates.[7] Other analyses propose means to escape inflation by securing federal subsidies, complaining to publishers, raising photocopying charges, and convincing institutional administrators to increase budgets.[8]

Many analyses attempt to isolate factors that determine prices and the difference in prices between libraries and individuals. Some studies look at the statistical relevance of sundry variables, but especially publisher type.[9] They confirm the belief that certain publishers, notably in Europe, practice price discrimination.[10] They also show that prices are driven by cost of production, which is related to frequency of issue, number of pages, and presence of graphics. Alternative revenue from advertising and exchange rate risk for foreign publishers also affects price.[11] Quality measures on the content, such as number of times a periodical is cited, affects demand that then impacts price. Economies of scale that are available to some journals with large circulation affects price.[12] These articles help explain differentials between individual and library prices.[13] Revenues lost to photocopying also account for some difference.[14] Also, differences in the way electronic journals may be produced compared to print provides a point on which some cost savings could be based.

The costs of production and the speed of communication may be driving forces that determine whether new publications emerge in the electronic domain to replace print. However, in a framework shaped by copyright law, the broader issue of interaction of demand and supply more likely determines the price of any given journal. Periodical prices remain quite low over time when magazine publishers sell advertising as the principal generator of revenue. When for political or similar reasons, publication costs are borne by organizations, usually not scholarly societies, periodical prices tend to be lower. Prices inflate in markets with high demand such as the sciences, where multiple users include practicing physicians, pharmaceutical firms, national laboratories, and so forth.

Unfortunately for libraries, the demand *from users* for any given journal is usually inelastic. Libraries *tend* to retain subscriptions regardless of price increases, because the demand originates with nonpaying users. In turn, price increases charged to individual subscribers to scholarly journals drive user demands. Therefore, it might be expected that as publishers offer currently existing print publications in an electronic form, they will retain both their price as well as inelastic demand. Commercial publishers, who are profit maximizers, will seek to retain or improve their profits when expanding into the electronic market. However, there are some properties associated with electronic journals that could relax the inelasticity of prices.

This chapter describes a multidisciplinary study of the impact of electronic publishing on the pricing of scholarly periodicals. A brief overview of the pricing issue comparing print and electronic publishing is followed by a summary of the access approach to cost containment. A preliminary report on an attempt at this technique by a consortium and on an associated econometric study also is included.[15]

OVERVIEW OF PRICING RELEVANT TO ELECTRONIC JOURNALS

The industry of scholarly print publishing falls into the category of monopolistic competition, which is characterized by the presence of many firms with differentiated products and by no barriers to entry of new firms.[16] As a result of product differentiation, scholarly publishers do not encounter elastic aggregate demand typically associated with competitive markets. Rather, each publisher perceives a negatively sloped individual demand curve. Therefore, each supplier has the opportunity to partially control the price of its product, even though barriers to entry of new, competing periodical titles may be quite low. Given this control, publishers have raised their prices to libraries with some loss of sales but with consequent increases in profits that overwhelm those losses. They segment their market between individuals and libraries and charge higher prices to the latter in order to extract consumer surplus.

As publishers lose sales to individuals, scholars increase their dependency on libraries, which then increases interlibrary borrowing to secure the needed articles. Photocopies supplied via library collections constitute revenue lost to publishers, but is recaptured in the price differential. Additional revenue might accrue if publishers could offer their products in electronic databases where they could monitor all duplication. This potential may rest on the ability of publishers to retain control in the electronic domain of the values they have traditionally added to scholarship.

Scholars need two services from scholarly literature: (1) input in the form of documentation of the latest knowledge and/or information on scholarly subjects and (2) outlets for their contributions to this pool of scholarship. Partly in exchange for their trade of copyright, scholars receive value in four areas. First, scholars secure value in communication when every individual's contribution to knowledge is conveyed to others, thus impacting the reputation of each author. Second, although not provided by publishers directly, archiving provides value by preserving historically relevant scholarship and fixing it in time. Third, value accrues from filtering of articles into levels of quality, which improves search costs allocation and establishes or enhances reputation. Fourth, segmenting of scholarship into disciplines reduces input search costs to scholars. The exchange of copyright ownership for value could be affected with the emergence of electronic journals.

Electronic journals emerge as either new titles exclusively in electronic form or existing print titles transformed to electronic counterparts. Some new journals have begun exclusively as electronic publications with mixed success. The directory published by the Association of Research Libraries listed approximately 27 new electronic journals in 1991. By 1995 that figure had risen to over 300, of which some 200 claim to be peer reviewed.[17] Since then hundreds more electronic journals have been added, but the bulk of these additions appear to be electronic counterparts of previously existing print journals.[18] In fact, empirical work indicates that exclusively electronic publications have had little impact on scholarship.[19]

The infrastructure of scholarly print publishing evolved over a long time. In order for a parallel structure to emerge in the electronic domain, publishers have to add as much value to electronic journals as they do print. Value must be added in archiving, filtering, and segmenting in addition to communication. Establishing brand quality requires tremendous energy and commitment. Some electronic titles are sponsored by individuals who are fervent in their efforts to demonstrate that the scholarly community can control the process of communicating scholarship. However, it is unrealistic to expect an instantaneous, successful emergence of a full-blown infrastructure in the electronic domain that overcomes the obstacles to providing the values required by scholars. The advantage of higher communication speed is insufficient to drive the transformation of scholarship; thus traditional publishing retains an edge in the electronic domain.

A transformation is being achieved effectively by duplicating existing print journals in the electronic sphere, where publishers face less imposing investments to provide electronic counterparts to their product lines. For example, the Adonis collection on CD-ROM contains over 600 long-standing journals in medicine, biology, and related areas covering about seven years.[20] Furthermore, EBSCO, University Microfilms (UMI), Information Access Company (IAC), Johns Hopkins University Press, OCLC, and other companies are implementing similar products. OCLC now offers libraries access to the full text of journal collections of more than 24 publishers. Johns Hopkins University Press has made all 46 plus titles that it publishes available on-line through Project MUSE.

During the past 15 years, libraries have experienced a remarkable shift from acquiring secondary sources in print to accessing them through a variety of electronic venues, which suggests that many scholarly periodicals will become available electronically as an automatic response to the economies available there. However, some monopoly power of publishers could be lost if barriers to the entry of new journals are lower in the electronic domain than in the print domain. With full text on-line, libraries may take advantage of the economies of sharing access when a group of libraries contracts for shared access to a core collection. Sharing a given number of access ports allows economies of scale to take effect. Were one access port provided to each member of a consortium of 15 libraries, the vendor would tie up a total of 15 ports, but any given library in the group would have difficulty servicing a user population with one port. Whereas by combining access, 15 libraries together might get by with as few as 10 ports collectively. The statistical likelihood is small that all 10 ports would be needed collectively by the consortium at any given moment. This saves the vendor some computer resources that can then lead to a discount for the consortium that nets out less cost to the libraries.

Numerous models for marketing exist, but publishers can price their products in the electronic domain fundamentally only two ways. Either they will offer their products on *subscription* to each title or group of titles, or they will price the content on an article-by-article *transaction* basis. Vendor collections of journals for one flat fee based on the size of the user population represents a variant on the subscription fee approach. Commercial publishers, who are profit maximizers, will choose the method with the higher potential to increase their profit. Transaction-based pricing offers the possibility of capturing revenue lost to interlibrary lending. Also, demand for content could increase because of the ease of access afforded on-line. On the risk side, print subscription losses would occur where the cumulative expenditure for transactions from a given title is less than its subscription price.

Potentially, two mechanisms could flatten demand functions in the electronic domain. First, by making articles available individually to consumers, the separation of items of specific interest to given scholars creates quality competition that increases the elasticity of demand, because quality varies from article to article. Presumably, like individual grocery items, the elasticity of demand for particular articles is more elastic than that of periodical titles. Economists argue that the demand for tortillas is more elastic than for groceries in general because other bakery goods can be substituted, whereas there is no substitute for groceries in general except higher priced restaurant eating. Similarly, when faced with buying individual articles, price increases will dampen demand more quickly than would be the case for a bundle of articles that are of interest to a group of consumers.

Second, by offering articles in an environment where the consuming scholar is required to pay directly (or at least observe the cost to the library), the effect of separation of payer and demander common with library collections resulting in high inelasticity will be diminished. This mechanism will increase elasticity because scholars will no longer be faced with a zero price. Even if the scholar is not required to pay directly for the article, increased awareness of price will have a dampening effect on inelasticity. However, publishers may find it possible to price individual articles so that the sum of individual article fees paid by consumers exceeds the bundled subscription price experienced by libraries formerly forced to purchase a whole title to get articles in print.

For a product like Adonis, which is a sizable collection of periodicals in the narrow area of biomedicine, transaction-based pricing works out in favor of the consumer versus the provider, since there will likely be only a small number of articles of interest to consumers from each periodical title. This result makes purchasing one article at a time more attractive than buying a subscription, because less total expenditure will normally result. In the case of a product composed of a cross section of general purpose periodicals, such as the UMI Periodical Abstracts, the opposite will be true. The probability is higher that a user population at a college may collectively be interested in every single article in general purpose journals. This probability makes subscription-based pricing more favorable for libraries, since the cumulative cost of numerous transactions could easily exceed the subscription price. Publishers will seek to offer journals in accordance with whichever of these two scenarios results in the higher profit. Scientific publishers will tend to bundle their articles together and make products available as subscriptions to either individual journals or groups. Scholarly publishers with titles of general interest will be drawn toward article-by-article marketing.

An Elsevier effort to make 1,100 scientific titles available electronically will be priced on a title-by-title subscription basis and at prices higher than the print version when only the electronic version is purchased.[21] On the other hand, the general purpose titles included in UMI's Periodical Abstracts full text (or in the similar products of EBSCO and IAC), as an alternative interface to their periodicals, are available on a transaction basis by article. These two approaches seek to maximize profit in accordance with the nature of the products.

Currently, UMI, EBSCO, and IAC, which function as the aggregators, have negotiated arrangements that allow site licenses for unlimited purchasing. These companies are operating as vendors who make collections of general purpose titles available under arrangements that pay the publishers royalties for each copy of their articles printed by library users. UMI, IAC, and EBSCO have established license arrangements with libraries for unlimited printing with license fees based on expected printing activity, thus offering some libraries a solution to the fundamental pricing problem created by the monopoly power of publishers.

New research could test whether publishers are able to retain monopoly power with electronic counterparts to their journals. Theory predicts that in a competitive market, even when it is characterized as monopolistic competition, the price offered to individuals will tend to remain elastic. Faced with a change in price of the subscriptions purchased from their own pockets, scholars will act discriminately. Raise the price to individuals and some will cancel their subscriptions in favor of access to a library. In other words, the price of periodicals to individuals is a determinant of demand for library access. By exercising a measure of monopoly power in place of price, publishers have some ability to influence their earnings through price discrimination.[22]

In contrast, publishers can set prices to libraries higher than the price to individuals as a means to extract consumer surplus. The difference in prices provides a reasonable measure of the extent of monopoly power, assuming that the individual subscription price is an acceptable proxy for the marginal cost of production.[23] Even if not perfect, the difference in prices represents some measure of monopoly power. Extending this line of research may show that monopoly power is affected by the medium.

In monopolistic competition, anything that differentiates a product may increase monopoly power. Historically, tremendous amounts of advertising money are expended to create the impression that one product is qualitatively distinguishable from others. It may be that electronic availability of specific titles will create an impression of superior quality that could lead to higher prices. However, the prices of journals across disciplines also may be driven by different factors. In general, prices are higher in the sciences and technical areas and lower in the humanities. This price differential is understandable considering that there is essentially no market for scholarly publications in the humanities outside of academe, whereas scientific publications are used heavily in corporate research. As a result, monopoly power will likely be stronger in the sciences than in other areas. This power would reflect additional price discrimination in the electronic environment by publishers who are able to capture revenue lost to photocopying.

ACCESS VERSUS OWNERSHIP STRATEGY

Clearly, if commercial publishers continue to retain or enhance their monopoly power with electronic counterparts of their journals, the academic marketplace must adjust or react more effectively than it has in the past. The reaction of universities could lead to erosion of previous success achieved with price discrimination if an appropriate strategy is followed. Instead of owning the periodicals needed by their patrons, some libraries have experimented with replacing subscriptions with document delivery services. Louisiana State University reports canceling a major portion of their print journals.[24] They replaced these cancellations by offering faculty and students unlimited subsidized use of a document delivery service. The first-year cost for all the articles delivered through this service was much less than the total cost to the library for the former subscriptions. Major savings for the library budget via this approach would appeal to library directors and university administrators as a fruitful solution. However, it may turn out to be a short-term solution at best.

Carried to its logical conclusion, this approach produces a world in which each journal is reduced to one subscription shared by all libraries. This situation is equivalent to every existing journal having migrated to single copies in on-line files accessible to all interested libraries. Some libraries will pay a license fee in advance to allow users unlimited printing access to the on-line title, while others will require users to pay for each article individually. Individual article payment requires the entire fixed-cost-plus-profit components of a publisher's revenue to be distributed over article prints only, whereas with print publications, the purchase of subscriptions of physical artifacts that included many articles not needed immediately brought with it a bonus. The library acquired and retained many articles with future potential use. Transaction-based purchasing sacrifices this bonus and increases the marginal cost of articles in the long run. In sum, the marginal cost of a journal article in the print domain was suppressed by the spread of expenditure over many items never read. In the electronic domain under transaction-based pricing, users face a higher, more direct price and therefore are more likely to forego access. While the marginal benefit to the user may be equivalent, the higher marginal cost makes it less likely that users will ask for any given article. The result may show up in diminished scholarly output or notably higher prices per article.

In the long term, should a majority of libraries take this approach, it carries a benefit for publishers. There has been no means available in the past for publishers to count the actual number of photocopies made in libraries and thus to set their price accordingly. The electronic domain could make all those hidden transactions readily apparent. As a result, publishers could effectively maintain their corporate control of prices and do so with more accurate information with which to calculate license fees. Given this attempted solution, publishers would be able to regain and strengthen their monopoly position.

A more promising approach lies in consortial projects such as that conducted by the Associated Colleges of the South (ACS).[25] Accompanying the *Periodical Abstracts* and *ABI/Inform* indexes of UMI that are made available on-line from the vendor or through OCLC are collections in full text of over 1,000 existing journals with backfiles. The ACS contracted an annual license for these two products (*ABI/Inform* and *Periodical Abstracts*) for the 13 schools represented. Trinity University pays $11,000 per year for the electronic periodicals in the UMI databases, a cost that is similar to that paid by each ACS library. Coincidentally, Trinity subscribes to the print version of about 375 titles covered by these products. Trinity could cancel its subscriptions to the print counterparts of the journals provided and save $25,000. Even considering that Trinity's library will subsidize user printing for paper, toner, and so forth at an expected cost of several thousand dollars per year to service its 230 faculty and 2,500 students, it appears likely that favorable economies accrue from switching to these electronic products. Of course, these savings will be accompanied by a significant decrease in nondollar user cost to patrons, so unmet demand will emerge to offset some of the savings. Moreover, there is a substantial bonus for Trinity users inherent in this arrangement.

There are a number of titles made available in the UMI product for which subscriptions would be desirable at Trinity but have not been purchased in the past because of budget limitations. From some of these titles, users would have acquired articles through the normal channels of interlibrary loan. However, the interlibrary loan process imposes costs in the form of staff time and user labor and is sufficiently cumbersome, causing many users to avoid it for marginally relevant articles. However, if marginal articles could be easily viewed on screen as a result of electronic access, users would consider the labor cost of acquiring them to have been sufficiently reduced to encourage printing the articles from the system. Therefore, the net number of article copies delivered to users will be significantly increased simultaneous with a substantial net decrease in the cost of subscriptions delivered to libraries.

Included in this equation are savings that accrue to the consortial libraries by sharing access to electronic subscriptions. Shared access will result in a specific number of print cancellations, which will decrease publisher profit from subscriptions. Publishers offering their journals in the electronic domain will be confronted by a change in the economic infrastructure that will flatten the scholar's demand functions for their titles while simultaneously increasing the availability of articles to the direct consumers. By lowering the user's nondollar cost of accessing individual articles, demand will increase for those items. Scholars, therefore, will be more likely to print an article from an electronic library than they would be to request it through interlibrary loan. However, depending on library policy, those scholars may be confronted with a pay-per-print fee, which will affect their demand function. If publishers raise the price to scholars for an article, they are more likely to lose a sale. Users will be more cautious with their own money than with a library's. That is, in the electronic domain, where scholars may be paying directly for their consumption, demand functions will be more elastic. This elasticity will occur to some extent even when users do not pay for articles but merely note the article price paid by their subsidizing library. Therefore, price discrimination may be more difficult to apply and monopoly power will be temporarily lost.

The loss might be temporary because this strategy is functionally the same as merging several libraries into one large library and providing transaction-based access versus ownership. This super library could ultimately face price discrimination similar to that currently existing in the print domain. This discrimination will lead, in turn, to the same kind of inflation that has been suffered for many years.

PRELIMINARY ANALYSIS OF FINANCIAL IMPACT

This paper reports on the early stages of a three-year study funded by The Andrew W. Mellon Foundation. The study includes analysis directed at testing the viability of consortial access versus ownership for cost savings as well as the potential long-term solution that would derive from emergence of a new core of electronic titles. A complete financial analysis of the impact of consortial, electronic access to a core collection of general purpose periodicals and an econometric analysis of over 2,000 titles on the impact of electronic availability on pricing policy will issue from the study conducted under this grant. Some interesting issues have emerged with preliminary results of the study.

Financial Analysis

The Palladian Alliance is a project of the Associated Colleges of the South funded by The Andrew W. Mellon Foundation. This consortium of 13 liberal arts colleges—not just libraries—has a full-time staff and organizational structure. The Palladian Alliance came about as result of discussions among the library directors who were concerned about the problem described in this paper. As the project emerged, it combined the goals of several entities, which are shown in Table 14.1 along with the specific objectives of the project.

The Andrew W. Mellon Foundation awarded a grant of $1.2 million in December 1995 to the ACS. During the first half of 1996, the librarians upgraded hardware, selected a vendor to provide a core collection of electronic full-text titles, and conducted appropriate training sessions. Public and Ariel workstations were installed in libraries by July 1996 and necessary improvements were made to the campus networks to provide access for using World Wide Web technology. Training workshops were developed under contract with Amigos and SOLINET on technical aspects and were conducted in May 1996. During that same time, an analysis was conducted to isolate an appropriate full-text vendor.

TABLE 14.1.   Goals and Objectives of the ACS Consortial Access Project

---

Goals of the ACS libraries:
  • Improve the quality of access to current information
  • Make the most efficient use of resources
Goals of the ACS deans:
  • Cost containment
Goals of The Andrew W. Mellon Foundation:
  • Relieve the economic pressure from periodical price inflation
  • Evaluate the impact of electronic access on publisher pricing practices
Objectives of the project:
  • Improve the hardware available within the libraries for electronic access
  • Provide on-line access to important undergraduate periodical indexes
  • Provide on-line access to core undergraduate periodicals in full text
  • Provide campuswide access through Internet browsers
  • Determine the financial impact on the ACS libraries
  • Test the pricing practices of publishers and their monopoly power

---

After comparison of the merged print subscription list of all institutions with three products—IAC's InfoTrac, EBSCO's EBSCOHOST, and UMI's Periodical Abstracts and ABI/Inform—the project team selected UMI with access through OCLC. A contract with OCLC was signed in June for July 1, 1996, start-up of FirstSearch for the nine core databases: WorldCat, FastDoc, ERIC, Medline, GPO Catalog, ArticleFirst, PapersFirst, ContentsFirst, and ProceedingsFirst; and for UMI's two core indexes, Periodical Abstracts and ABI/Inform, along with their associated full-text databases. This arrangement for the UMI products provides a general core collection with indexing for 2,600 titles, of which approximately 1,000 are full-text titles.

The UMI via OCLC FirstSearch subscription was chosen because it offered several advantages including the potential for a reliable, proprietary backup to the Internet, additional valuable databases at little cost, and easy means to add other databases. The UMI databases offered the best combination of cost and match with existing holdings. UMI also offered the future potential of full-image as well as ASCII text. After the first academic year, the project switched to access via Pro-Quest Direct in order to provide full image when available.

Students have had access to the core electronic titles since the fall semester in 1996. As experience builds, it is apparent that the libraries do have some opportunity to cancel print subscriptions with financial advantages. The potential costs, savings, and added value are revealed in Tables 14.2 through 14.4. Specific financial impact on the institutions during the first year is shown in Tables 14.5 and 14.6. It should be noted that the financial impact is based on preliminary data that has been extremely difficult to gather. Publisher and vendor invoices vary considerably between schools on both descriptive information and prices. Therefore, these results will be updated continually throughout the project.

At the outset, the project benefits the libraries in a significant way because of the power of consortial purchasing. Only a few of the larger libraries might be able to afford to purchase access to both full-text databases were they constrained to individual purchases. Added together, individual subscriptions to ABI/Inform and Periodical Abstracts accompanied with the full text would collectively cost the 13 libraries $413,590 for 1997/98. By arranging consortial purchase, the total cost to the ACS is $129,645 for this second year. Because the libraries can then afford their share of the collective purchase, the vendor benefits from added sales otherwise not available and the libraries add numerous articles to the resources provided their students. More detailed accounting of the benefits are determined in the accompanying tables.

These tables are based on actual financial information for the consortium. Table 14.2 summarizes the project costs. These calculations will be corrected to reflect revised enrollment figures immediately prior to renewal for the third year. The project was designed to use grant funds exclusively the first year, then gradually shift to full support on the library accounts by the fourth year.

As the project started, the ACS libraries collectively subscribed through EBSCO, FAXON, and Readmore to approximately 14,600 subscriptions as shown in Table 14.3. Of these subscriptions, 6,117 are unique titles; the rest are duplicates of these unique titles. Were the ACS libraries collectively merged into one collection, it would therefore be possible to cancel more than 8,000 duplications and save over $1,000,000. Since this merger was not possible, the libraries contracted for electronic access to nearly 1,000 full-text titles from UMI. Over 600 of these UMI titles match the print subscriptions collectively held by the libraries. As Table 14.3 indicates, canceling all but one subscription to the print counterparts of the UMI titles could save the libraries about $137,000 for calendar year 1996. Canceling all the print counterparts to the electronic versions would save nearly $185,000, which is about equal to the licensing costs for the first year per Table 14.2.

For calendar year 1996, the libraries canceled very few titles. In part, this came about because of reluctance to depend upon an untested product. There was no existing evidence that UMI (or any other aggregator) could maintain a consistent list of offerings. To date, cancellations for 1997 have also been fewer than expected at the outset. Furthermore, the project has begun to show that products such as ProQuest Direct come closer to offering a large pool of journal articles than they do to offering full electronic counterparts to print subscriptions. However, these products do provide significant benefits to the libraries.

The project adds considerable value to the institutional resources. The schools had not previously subscribed to many of the titles available through UMI. As an

TABLE 14.2.   Cost Sharing between the Grant and the Institutions
for License to UMI Products Plus OCLC Base Package

Institution	First Year Enrollment	% of Total Enrollment	First Year	Second Year	Third Year
Mellon Grant			$184,295	$120,705	$45,000
Atlanta	13,174	38.70%		$19,423	$52,231
Birmingham	1,406	4.13%		$2,073	$5,574
Centenary	821	2.41%		$1,210	$3,255
Centre	968	2.84%		$1,427	$3,838
Furman	2,673	7.85%		$3,941	$10,598
Hendrix	978	2.87%		$1,442	$3,877
Millsaps	1,278	3.75%		$1,884	$5,067
Rhodes	1,407	4.13%		$2,074	$5,578
Richmond	3,820	11.22%		$5,632	$15,145
Rollins	2,632	7.73%		$3,880	$10,435
Southwestern	1,199	3.52%		$1,768	$4,754
Trinity	2,430	7.14%		$3,583	$9,634
Sewanee	1,257	3.69%		$1,853	$4,984
Totals	34,043		$184,295	$170,895	$179,970

TABLE 14.3.   1996 Potential Savings from Substitution
of UMI Full-Text for Print Subscriptions

	No. Titles	Costs / Savings
Cost total for all ACS print subscriptions	14,613	$2,716,480
Number of unique titles	6,117	$1,466,862
Number of duplicate titles	8,496	$1,249,618
Canceling of all overlapping duplicates	2,680	$184,862
Number of unique titles overlapping UMI	606	$47,579
Canceling of all but one overlapping duplicates	2,074	$137,283

illustration, Table 14.4 lists the number of print subscriptions carried by each institution and indicates how many of those are available in the UMI databases electronically. The fourth column reveals the potential savings available to each school
were the print counterparts of all these electronic journals to be canceled. The
column labeled Added E-Titles shows the number of new journals made available
to each institution through the grant. The final column indicates the total titles
now available at each institution as a result of the consortial arrangement. Comparison of the final column with the first reveals that the electronic project nearly
doubles the journal resources available to students.

Table 14.5 details the preliminary financial impact on the ACS institutions for
the first and second calendar year of the project. While the opening premise of

TABLE 14.4.   1996 Savings Potential for Each Institution
and Value Added by Electronic Subscriptions

Institution	No. Print Subscriptions in 1996	Overlap with UMI	Potential Cancellation Savings	Added E-Titles	Total Subscriptions
Atlanta	1,085	112	$8,689	1,004	2,089
Birmingham	659	181	$18,141	935	1,594
Centenary	558	163	$12,974	953	1,511
Centre	701	152	$4,913	964	1,665
Furman	1,685	229	$13,856	887	2,572
Hendrix	599	145	$7,976	971	1,570
Millsaps	686	167	$10,485	949	1,635
Rhodes	964	187	$9,617	929	1,893
Richmond	1,827	358	$28,640	758	2,585
Rollins	1,017	210	$14,932	906	1,923
Southwestern	1,309	272	$16,648	844	2,153
Trinity	2,739	384	$27,373	732	3,471
Sewanee	784	120	$10,618	996	1,780
Totals	14,613	2,680	$184,862	11,828	26,441

the project suggests that canceling print subscriptions would pay for consortial access to UMI's aggregated collections, actual practice shows otherwise. The data is still being collected in the form of invoices, but preliminary summaries of cancellations show meager savings. Total savings across the 13 campuses is little more than $50,000 per year. This savings is not enough to pay for the first two years of the project, which is over $350,000. However, the added value to the combined collections exceeds $2,000,000 per year as measured by the cost of print counterparts to the UMI titles. Furthermore, additional action by some institutions, as shown in Table 14.6, reveals better outcomes.

Comparing the savings shown in Table 14.6 with the subsidized cost reveals that in the cases of Trinity and Millsaps, even without Mellon support, the consortial provision of the OCLC/UMI databases could be paid for by canceling indexes along with a few print subscriptions. In Trinity's case, two indexes previously purchased as CD-ROMs or direct links to another on-line source were canceled for savings of over $5,000 in the first year. Trinity canceled a CD-ROM subscription to a site license of ABI/Inform, which saved expenditures totaling over $6,000 per year, and an on-line general purpose index that previously cost over $12,000. The Trinity share to the Palladian Alliance project would have been just over $13,000 per year for the first three years. Similarly, Millsaps canceled one index and 74 periodical titles that overlapped the UMI content for net first-year savings of nearly $9,000. On this basis, the project more than pays for itself.

Added interesting outcomes of the project at this point include a couple of new

TABLE 14.5. Preliminary Financial Impact on Each Institution by the Palladian Project

1996 Savings and Added Value	Atlanta	Birmingham	Centenary	Centre	Furman	Hendrix
Number of print subscriptions	1,085	659	558	701	1,685	599
Number of subscriptions canceled	0	1	0	0	5	0
Canceled title overlapping Palladian	0	0	0	0	0	0
Total invoices for periodical titles	$297,717	$94,416	$72,567	$117,947	$327,910	$82,112
Total Palladian expenditure	$0	$0	$0	$0	$0	$0
Total expenditures	$297,717	$94,416	$72,567	$117,947	$327,910	$82,112
Total invoice for canceled periodical titles	$0	$0	$0	$0	$11,022	$0
Total invoice for canceled Palladian overlap	$0	$0	$0	$0	$0	$0
Net cost	$297,717	$94,416	$72,567	$117,947	$316,888	$82,112
Total expenditures	$297,717	$94,416	$72,567	$117,947	$327,910	$82,112
Net cost	$297,717	$94,416	$72,567	$117,947	$316,888	$82,112
Savings	$0	$0	$0	$0	$11,022	$0
Total value of Palladian titles	$160,796	$160,796	$160,796	$160,796	$160,796	$160,796
Overlap value of Palladian titles	$8,689	$18,141	$12,974	$4,913	$13,856	$7,976
Value of added net benefit from Palladian	$152,107	$142,655	$147,822	$155,883	$146,940	$152,820
Savings	$0	$0	$0	$0	$11,022	$0
Value of added net benefit from Palladian	$152,107	$142,655	$147,822	$155,883	$146,940	$152,820
Total savings and added value	$152,107	$142,655	$147,822	$155,883	$157,962	$152,820

1997 Savings and Added Value	Atlanta	Birmingham	Centenary	Centre	Furman	Hendrix
Number of print subscriptions	1,086	655	566	706	1,685	608
Number of subscriptions canceled	0	1	0	1	1	1
Canceled title overlapping Palladian	0	1	0	1	1	0
Number of subscriptions overlapping UMI	107	135	119	120	174	115
Total invoices for periodical titles	$328,049	$74,170	n/a	$140,851	$350,580	$89,613
Total Palladian expenditure	$19,423	$2,073	$1,210	$1,427	$3,941	$1,442
Total expenditures	$347,472	$76,243	n/a	$142,278	$354,521	$91,055

Millsaps	Rhodes	Richmond	Rollins	Southwestern	Trinity	Sewanee	TOTAL
686	964	1,827	1,017	1,309	2,739	784	14,613
3	1	7	0	0	79	0	96
0	1	3	0	0	11	0	15
$87,358	$140,431	$327,270	$134,659	$191,291	$659,080	$183,722	$2,716,480
$0	$0	$0	$0	$0	$0	$0	$0
$87,358	$140,431	$327,270	$134,659	$191,291	$659,080	$183,722	$2,716,480
$350	$0	$744	$0	$0	$41,640	$0	$53,756
$0	$60	$138	$0	$0	$30	$0	$228
$87,308	$140,371	$326,387	$134,659	$191,291	$617,410	$183,722	$2,662,795
$87,358	$140,431	$327,270	$134,659	$191,291	$659,080	$183,722	$2,716,480
$87,308	$140,371	$326,387	$134,659	$191,291	$617,410	$183,722	$2,662,795
$50	$60	$883	$0	$0	$41,670	$0	$53,685
$160,796	$160,796	$160,796	$160,796	$160,796	$160,796	$160,796	$2,090,348
$10,485	$9,617	$28,640	$14,932	$16,648	$27,373	$10,618	$184,862
$150,311	$151,179	$132,156	$145,864	$144,148	$133,423	$150,178	$1,905,486
$50	$60	$882	$0	$0	$41,670	$0	$53,984
$150,311	$151,239	$133,039	$145,864	$144,148	$133,423	$150,178	$1,906,429
$150,361	$151,299	$133,921	$145,864	$144,148	$175,093	$150,178	$1,960,113

Millsaps	Rhodes	Richmond	Rollins	Southwestern	Trinity	U of South	TOTAL
645	959	1,816	1,017	1,349	2,849	819	14,760
14	0	1	0	1	42	0	62
73	0	1	0	1	0	0	78
215	151	285	161	237	327	105	2,251
$74,095	$154,258	$358,417	$148,769	$195,075	$670,749	$202,079	$2,786,705
$1,884	$2,074	$5,632	$3,880	$1,768	$3,583	$1,853	$50,190
$75,979	$156,332	$364,049	$152,649	$196,843	$674,332	$203,932	$2,836,895

continued next page

TABLE 14.5.   *(continued)*

1997 Savings and Added Value	Atlanta	Birmingham	Centenary	Centre	Furman	Hendrix
Total invoice for canceled						
periodical titles	$0	$0	$0	$0	$270	$0
Total invoice for canceled						
Palladian overlap	$0	$24	$0	$120	$0	$0
Net cost	$347,472	$76,219	n/a	$142,158	$354,251	$91,055
Total expenditures	$347,472	$76,243	n/a	$142,278	$354,521	$91,055
Net cost	$347,472	$76,219	n/a	$142,158	$354,251	$91,055
Savings	$0	$24	$0	$120	$270	$0
Total value of Palladian titles	$183,772	$183,772	$183,772	$183,772	$183,772	$183,772
Overlap value of Palladian titles	$9,890	$9,373	$4,396	$7,927	$12,787	$7,505
Value of added net benefit from						
Palladian	$173,882	$174,399	$179,376	$175,845	$170,985	$176,267
Savings	$0	$24	$0	$120	$270	$0
Value of added net benefit from						
Palladian	$173,882	$174,399	$179,376	$175,845	$170,985	$176,267
Total savings and added value	$173,882	$174,423	$179,376	$175,965	$171,255	$176,267

pieces of important information. First, canceling individual subscriptions to indexes provides a viable means for consortial pricing to relieve campus budgets, at least in the short run. Were it necessary for Trinity to pay its full share of the cost, canceling indexes alone provided sufficient savings to pay for the project. Just considering trade-offs with indexes alone, Trinity's net savings over the project life span total nearly $18,000.

Second, on the down side, canceling journals and replacing them with an aggregator's collection of electronic subscriptions may not be very reliable. It is apparent that the aggregators suffer from the vagaries of publishers. In just the first few months of the project, UMI dropped and added a number of titles in both full-text databases. This readjustment means that instead of full runs of each title, the databases often contain only partial runs. Furthermore, in some cases the publisher provides only significant articles, not the full journal. Therefore, the substitution of UMI provides the libraries with essentially a collection of articles, not a collection of electronic subscription substitutes. This result diminishes reliability and discourages libraries from being able to secure really significant cost savings.

It should be noted however, that several of the libraries independently subscribed to the electronic access to Johns Hopkins Project MUSE. In contrast to an aggregated collection, this project provides full-image access to every page of the print counterparts and guarantees access indefinitely to any year of the subscription once it's paid for. This guarantee means that reliability of the product is substantially improved, and it provides reasonable incentives to the libraries to substitute access for

Millsaps	Rhodes	Richmond	Rollins	Southwestern	Trinity	U of South	TOTAL
$4,216	$0	$0	$0	$0	$46,345	$0	$50,831
$4,591	$0	$0	$0	$0	$0	$0	$4,735
$67,171	$156,332	$364,049	$152,649	$196,843	$627,987	$203,932	$2,780,118
$75,979	$156,332	$364,049	$152,649	$196,843	$674,332	$203,932	$2,835,686
$67,171	$156,332	$364,049	$152,649	$196,843	$627,987	$203,932	$2,780,119
$8,808	$0	$0	$0	$0	$46,345	$0	$55,567
$183,772	$183,772	$183,772	$183,772	$183,772	$183,772	$183,772	$2,389,039
$11,907	$9,741	$25,570	$14,303	$17,456	$28,145	$8,846	$167,846
$171,865	$174,031	$158,202	$169,469	$166,316	$155,627	$174,926	$2,221,193
$8,808	$0	$0	$0	$0	$46,345	$0	$55,567
$171,865	$174,031	$158,202	$169,469	$166,316	$155,627	$174,926	$2,221,193
$180,673	$174,031	$158,202	$169,469	$166,316	$201,972	$174,926	$2,276,760

TABLE 14.6. Total First Year Financial Impact on Selected Institutions

	Birmingham	Centre	Hendrix	Millsaps	Trinity
Periodical subscriptions					
Total 1996	659	701	599	686	2739
Total 1997	655	706	608	645	2849
Cancellations					
Total 1997	2	2	1	87	42
Overlap of UMI	1	1	0	73	0
Indexes	1	0	1	1	9
Savings					
Other periodicals	$24	$120	$0	$256	$20,049
Overlap of UMI	$0	$0	$0	$4,591	$0
Print indexes	$4,650	$0	$604	$3,960	$7,806
Electronic indexes	$0	$0	$0	$0	$18,491
Total savings	$4,674	$120	$604	$8,807	$46,346
Subsidized cost of project	$7,612	$5,240	$5,294	$6,919	$13,155
NET SAVINGS	($2,938)	($5,120)	($4,690)	$1,888	$33,191

collecting. While it may be acceptable to substitute access to a large file of general purpose articles for undergraduate students, Project MUSE promises better results than the initial project for scholarly journal collections. The final report of this project will include information on the impact of the Project MUSE approach as well as on the original concept.

Third, the impact of on-line full-text content may or may not have an impact on interlibrary loan activity. Table 14.7 summarizes the searching and article delivery statistics for the first six months of the project compared to the total interlibrary borrowing as well as nonreturn photocopies ordered through the campus interlibrary loan offices. The change in interlibrary loan statistics for the first six months of the project compared to the previous year show that in some cases interlibrary borrowing increased and in other cases it decreased. Several variables besides the availability of full-text seem to affect use of interlibrary loan services. For instance, some of the institutions had full-text databases available before the project started. Some made more successful efforts to promote the project services than others. It seems likely that improved access to citations from on-line indexes made users more aware of items that could be borrowed. That effect probably offset an expected decrease in interlibrary loans that the availability of full text makes predictable. Regardless, statistics on this issue yield inconclusive results early in the project.

Fourth, it is curious that secondary journals in many fields are published by commercial firms rather than by professional organizations and that their publications are sold at higher prices. Libraries typically pay more for Haworth publications than they do for ALA publications. Haworth sells largely to libraries responding not to demand for content but for publication outlets. Libraries are willing to pay for the Haworth publications. This fact helps explain why secondary titles cost more than primary ones. Demand may be more for exposure of the contributor than it is for reading of content by subscribers. The econometric analysis included in the project may confirm this unintended hypothesis.

Econometric Analysis

At this point, a meaningful econometric analysis is many months away. A model based on Lerner's definition of monopoly power will be used to examine pricing as journals shift into the electronic sphere. The model calls for regressing the price of individual titles on a variety of independent variables such as number of pages, advertising content, circulation, and publisher type, and for including a dummy variable for whether a journal is available electronically. Data is being collected on over 2,000 of the subscriptions held by Trinity for the calendar years 1995 through 1997. Difficulties with financial data coupled with the time-consuming nature of data gathering have delayed progress on the econometric analysis.

It would be desirable to conduct an analysis on time series data to observe the

TABLE 14.7.   UMI Articles Delivered to Users Compared to Change in Interlibrary Loans from 1995 to 1996

Institution	Enrollment	Search of Base Files	Total Searches	Searches per Student	ABI Documents Delivered	PA Documents Delivered	Total Documents Delivered
Birmingham	1,406	8,734	11,869	8.44	646	842	1,488
Centenary	821	948	1,819	2.22	—	8	8
Centre	968	6,713	15,003	15.50	309	4,134	4,44
Furman	2,673	8,666	18,068	6.76	998	863	1,861
Hendrix	978	1,481	5,117	5.23	301	1,600	1,901
Millsaps	1,278	5,994	22,455	17.57	4,583	4,424	9,007
Morehouse	13,174	3,642	12,305	0.93			
Rhodes	1,407	2,244	3,691	2.62	252	418	670
Richmond	3,820	33,490	83,477	21.85	6,104	11,900	18,004
Rollins	2,632	5,464	16,471	6.26	1,198	3,298	4,496
Southwestern	1,119	14,763	36,018	32.19	1,752	8,153	9,905
Sewanee	1,257	12,140	40,317	32.07	403	1,534	1,937
Trinity	2,430	30,601	134,693	55.43	16,317	37,838	54,155

Insitution	Total Documents per Student	Nonreturns 1995	Nonreturns 1996	Change in Nonreturns	Total Borrows 1995	Total Borrows 1996	Change in Total Borrowing
Birmingham	1.06	662	668	0.91%	928	380	−59.05%
Centenary	0.01	583	441	−24.36%	911	1,137	24.81%
Centre	4.59	409	351	−14.18%	872	758	−13.07%
Furman	0.70	246	246	0.00%	833	923	10.80%
Hendrix	1.94	146	192	31.51%	251	353	40.64%
Millsaps	7.05	568	352	−38.03%	710	887	24.93%
Morehouse	*	*	*	*	*	*	
Rhodes	0.48	255	198	−22.35%	601	471	−21.63%
Richmond	4.71	1,034	1,044	0.97%	1,892	1,831	−3.22%
Rollins	1.71	394	365	−7.36%	656	652	−0.61%
Southwestern	8.85	412	308	−25.24%	695	571	−17.84%
Sewanee	1.54	626	434	−30.67%	1,083	1,038	−4.16%
Trinity	22.29	706	711	0.71%	1,172	1,257	7.25%

*Data not available.

consequences in journal price changes as a shift is made to electronic products. This analysis would provide a forecast of how publishers react. Lacking the opportunity at the outset to examine prices over time, a straightforward model applying ordinary least squares (OLS) regression on cross section data, similar to the analyses reported by others, will form the basis of the analysis. Earlier models have typically regressed price on a number of variables to distinguish the statistical relevance of publisher type in determining price. By modifying the earlier models, this analysis seeks to determine whether monopoly power may be eroded in the electronic market. The methodology applied uses two specifications for an ordinary least squares regression model. The first regresses price on the characteristics of a set of journal titles held by the ACS libraries. This data set is considerably larger than those utilized in previous studies. Therefore, we propose to confirm the earlier works that concentrate on economic journals across a larger set of disciplines. This specification includes the variables established earlier: frequency of publication, circulation, pages per year, and several dummy variables to control for whether the journals contain advertising and to control for country of publication. Four dummy variables are included for type of publisher with the residual being commercial. A second specification regressing the difference in price for libraries compared to individuals will be regressed on the same set of variables with an additional dummy added to show whether given journals are available electronically.[26]

The ACS libraries collectively subscribe to approximately 14,000 titles. Where they duplicate, an electronic set has been substituted for shared access. We anticipate that at the margin, the impact on publishers would be minimal if ACS canceled subscriptions to the print counterparts of this set. However, the national availability of the electronic versions will precipitate cancellations among many institutions in favor of electronic access. Prices will be adjusted accordingly. Since most publishers will offer some products in print only and others within the described electronic set, we expect the prices of the electronic version will reflect an erosion of monopoly power. Thus the cross section data will capture the effect of electronic availability on monopoly power.

Since the data set is comprised of several thousand periodical titles representing general and more popular items, several concerns experienced by other investigators will be mitigated. The only study found in the literature so far that examines publishers from the standpoint of the exercise of monopoly power investigated price discrimination.[27] This project intends to extend that analysis in two ways. First, we will use a much broader database, since most of the previous work was completed on limited data sets of less than 100 titles narrowly focused in a single academic discipline. Second, we will extend the analysis by assuming the existence of price discrimination given the difference in price to individuals versus libraries for most scholarly journals. With controls in the model for previous discoveries regarding price discrimination, we will attempt to test the null hypothesis that monopoly power will not decrease in the electronic domain.

In the data set available, we were unable to distinguish the specific price of each journal for the electronic replacement, because UMI priced the entire set for a flat fee. This pricing scheme may reflect an attempt by publishers to capture revenue lost to interlibrary lending. Alternatively, it may reflect publisher expectations that article demand will increase when user nondollar costs decrease. Thus, monopoly power will be reflected back on to the subscription price of print versions. As a result we will use the price of print copies as a proxy for the specific electronic price of each title.

An alternative result could emerge. In monopolistic competition, anything that differentiates a product may increase its monopoly power. For example, firms selling products expend tremendous amounts of money on advertising to create the impression that their product is qualitatively distinguishable from others. Analogous electronic availability of specific titles may create an impression of superior quality.

The general model of the first specification is written:

$$y_j = \alpha + \beta_1 IPRICE_j + \beta_2 CIRC_j + \beta_3 FREQ_j + \beta_4 PAGES_j + \beta_5 AGE_j + \beta_6 QUAL\text{-}$$
$$ITY_j + \beta_7 PEERREV_j + \beta_8 CCCREG_j + \beta_9 ADV_j + \beta_{10} ASSOC_j + \beta_{11} GOVERN_j +$$
$$\beta_{12} FOUNDTN_j + \beta_{13} UNIVPR_j + \beta_{14} EUROPE_j + \beta_{15} GBRITAIN_j + \beta_{16} OTHER_j$$
$$+ \beta_{17} ELECTRN_j + \epsilon_j$$

where y equals the library price (LPRICE) for journal $j = 1, 2, 3, \ldots n$. The definitions of independent variables appear in Table 14.8 along with the expected signs on and calculations of the parameters b1 through b17 to be estimated by traditional single regression techniques.

The general model of the second specification is written:

$$y_{ij} = \alpha_i + \beta_{1i} RISK_j + \beta_{2i} CIRC_j + \beta_{3i} FREQ_j + \beta_{4i} PAGES_j + \beta_{5i} AGE_j +$$
$$\beta_{6i} QUALITY_j + \beta_{7i} PEERREV_j + \beta_{8i} CCCREG_j + \beta_{9i} ADV_j + \beta_{10i} ASSOC_j +$$
$$\beta_{11i} GOVERN_j + \beta_{12i} FOUNDTN_j + \beta_{13i} UNIVPR_j + \beta_{14i} EUROPE_j + \beta_{15i} GBRI\text{-}$$
$$TAIN_j + \beta_{16i} OTHER_j + \beta_{17i} ELECTRN_j + \epsilon_{ij}$$

where y equals two different forms of monopoly power (MPOWER1; MPOWER2) defined as measure $i = 1$ and 2 for journal $j = 1, 2, 3, \ldots n$. Again, the definitions of independent variables appear in Table 14.8 along with the expected signs on and calculations of the parameters b1 through b17 to be estimated by traditional single regression techniques.

The variables listed in Table 14.8 are suggested at this point based on previous studies that have demonstrated that they are appropriate. Testing with the regression model is required in order to determine those variables ultimately useful to this study. Additional variables will be introduced should experiments suggest them. A very brief rationale for the expected sign and the importance of the variables is in order. If the difference in price between what publishers charge libraries versus individuals represents price discrimination, then a variable for the individual price (IPRICE) will be a significant predictor of price to institutions (LPRICE). Higher individual prices will shift users toward the library, thus raising demand for library subscriptions, which will pull institutional prices higher. The sign on this variable is expected to be positive.

One group of variables deals with the issue of price discrimination based on

TABLE 14.8. List of Variables

Dependent variable	
LPRICE	The price for library subscriptions
MPOWER1	Monopoly power as represented by LPRICE − IPRICE
MPOWER2	Monopoly power as represented by the index: (LPRICE − IPRICE)/LPRICE

Independent variables	
IPRICE	Price for individuals (+, number)
GBRITAIN	1 if the journal is published in Great Britain, 0 otherwise (−, dummy variable)
EUROPE	1 if the journal is published in Europe, 0 otherwise (−, dummy variable)
OTHER	1 if the journal is published outside United States, Canada, Europe or Great Britain, 0 otherwise (−, dummy variable)
RISK	Standard deviation of the annual free market exchange rate between the currency of the home country of a foreign publisher to the U.S. dollar
ASSOC	1 if the journal is published by an association, 0 otherwise (−, dummy variable)
GOVERN	1 if the journal is published by a government agency, 0 otherwise (−, dummy variable)
FOUNDTN	1 if the journal is published by a foundation, 0 otherwise (−, dummy variable)
UNIVPR	1 if the journal is published by a university press, 0 otherwise (−, dummy variable)
FREQ	The number of issues per year (+, number)
PAGES	Number of pages printed per year (+, number)
PEERREV	1 if the article submissions are peer reviewed, 0 otherwise (+, dummy variable)
SUBMISSFEE	1 if the contributor is required to pay a fee with submission (−, dummy variable)
CCCREG	1 if the journal is registered with the CCC, 0 otherwise (+, dummy variable)
ILLUS	1 if the journal contains graphics or illustrations, 0 otherwise (+, dummy variable)
CIRC	The reported number of subscriptions to the journal (−, number)
ADV	1 if there is commercial advertising in the journal, 0 otherwise (−, dummy variable)
AGE	Current year minus the date the journal first published (−, number)
QUALITY	Sum of the Institute for Scientific Information citation measures (+, number)
HUMAN	1 if the journal is in the humanties, 0 otherwise (−, dummy variable)
SOCSCI	1 if the journal is in the social sciences, 0 otherwise (−, dummy variable)
ELECTRONIC	1 if the journal is available in electronic form, 0 otherwise (+, dummy variable)

the monopoly power that can be exercised by foreign publishers. Publishers in Great Britain (GBRITAIN), western Europe (EUROPE), and other countries outside the United States (OTHER) may have enough market power to influence price. Therefore these variables will carry a positive sign if a sizable market influence is exerted. Some of these publishers will also be concerned with currency exchange risks (RISK), which they will adjust for in prices. However, since they offer discounts through vendors for libraries who prepay subscriptions, this variable will carry a negative sign if the price to individuals captures most of the financial burden of risk adjustment.

It is expected that commercial publishers discriminate by price more than their nonprofit counterparts do. Therefore, in comparison to the commercial residual, associations (ASSOC), government agencies (GOVERN), university presses (UNIVPR) and foundations (FOUNDTN) will capture generally lower prices of these nonprofit publishers. Negative signs are expected on these.

All the publishers will experience production costs, which can be exposed through variables that control for frequency (FREQ), total pages printed per year (PAGES), peer review (PEERREV), submission fees (SUBMISSFEE), processing/communication expenses and copyright clearance registration expenses (CCCREG), and the presence of graphics, maps, and illustrations (ILLUS), all of which will positively affect price to the extent they are passed along through price discrimination. Circulation (CIRC) will capture the effects of economies of scale, which those publications that are distributed in larger quantities will experience. Thus this variable is expected to be negative. Similarly, the inclusion of advertising (ADV) will provide additional revenue to that of sales, so this variable is expected to be negative since journals that include ads will have less incentive to extract revenue through sales. New entries into the publishing arena are expected to experience costs for advertising to increase awareness of their products, which will be partially passed on to consumers. Therefore, age (AGE), which is the difference between the current date and the date the journal started, will be a negative predictor of price and monopoly power.

Previous studies have developed measures of quality based on rankings of publications compared to each other within a given discipline. Most of these comparisons work from information available from the Institute for Scientific Information. Data acquired from this source that shows the impact factor, immediacy index, half-life, total cites, and cites per year will be summarized in one variable to capture quality (QUALITY) of journals, which is expected to be positive with regard to both price and monopoly power.

The prices of journals across disciplines may be driven by different factors. In general, prices are higher in the sciences and technical areas and lower in the humanities. This discrepancy is understandable when we consider the market for science versus humanities. As stated earlier, there is essentially no market for scholarly publications in the humanities outside of academe, whereas scientific publications are used heavily in corporate research by pharmaceutical firms and other industries highly dependent on research. As a result, two additional dummies are included in the model to segment the specification along discipline lines. HUMAN and SOCSCI will control for differences in price among the humanities and social sciences as compared to the residual category of science. These variables are expected to be negative and strong predictors of price.

Finally, a dummy variable is included to determine whether availability of each journal electronically (ELECTRONIC) has a positive impact on ability to discriminate by price. Since we have predicted that monopoly power will erode in the electronic arena, ELECTRONIC should be statistically significant and a negative predictor of monopoly power. However, to the extent that availability of a journal electronically distinguishes it from print counterparts, there is some expectation that this variable could be positive. This would show additional price discrimination by publishers who are able to capture lost revenue in the electronic environment.

The data set will be assembled by enhancing the data on subscriptions gathered during the planning project. Most of the additional data set elements including prices will come from examination of the journals and invoices received by the libraries. Impact and related factors will be acquired from the Institute for Scientific Information. The number of subscriptions supplied in print by two major journal vendors, FAXON and EBSCO, will be used as a proxy for circulation. An alternative measure of circulation will be compiled from a serials bibliography. The rest of the variables were obtained by examination of the print subscriptions retained by the libraries or from a serials bibliography.

CONCLUSION

There may be other ways to attack the problem of price inflation of scholarly periodicals. Some hope arises from the production cost differences between print and electronic periodicals. The marginal cost of each added print copy diminishes steadily from the second to the nth copy, whereas for electronic publications, the marginal cost of the second and subsequent copies is approximately zero. Although distribution is not quite zero for each additional copy, since computer resources can be strained by volume of access, the marginal cost is so close to zero that technical solutions to the problem of unauthorized redistribution for free of pirated copies might provide an incentive for publishers in the electronic domain to distribute equitably the cost of the first copy across all consumers. If the total cost of production of the electronic publications is lower than it would be for printed publication, some publishers may share the savings with consumers. However, there is no certainty that they will, because profit maximizers will continue to be profit maximizers. Therefore, it is appropriate to look for a decoupled solution lying in the hands of consumers.

In the meantime, the outcomes of this research project will include a test of the benefits of consortial access versus ownership. In addition, earlier work on price discrimination will be extended with this cross-discipline study to determine whether electronic telecommunications offers hope of relief from monopoly power of publishers.

NOTES

The author wishes to acknowledge with thanks the financial support of The Andrew W. Mellon Foundation and the participation of several colleagues from libraries of the Associated Colleges of the South. Thanks also to my associate Tanya Pinedo for data gathering and analysis. All errors remain the responsibility of the author.

1. Richard M. Dougherty, "A 'Factory' for Scholarly Journals." *Chronicle of Higher Education* 38/41 (June 17, 1992): b1–b2; Bert R. Boyce, "Meeting the Serials Cost Problem: A Supply Side Proposal." *American Libraries* 24/3 (March 1993): 272–273.

2. Stevan Harnad, "Post-Gutenberg Galaxy: The Fourth Revolution in the Means of Production of Knowledge." *Public Access Computer Systems Review* 2/1 (1991): 39–53; Andrew M. Odlyzko, "Tragic Loss or Good Riddance? The Impending Demise of Traditional Scholarly Journals." *International Journal of Man-Machine Studies* 42/1 (January 1995): 71–122.

3. Frank Quinn, "A Role for Libraries in Electronic Publication." *Serials Review* 21/1 (1995): 27–30.

4. Charles A. Schwartz, "Scholarly Communication as a Loosely Structured System: Reassessing Prospects for Structural Reform." *College and Research Libraries* 55/2 (March 1994): 101–117.

5. Anthony W. Cummings, Marcia L. Witte, William G. Bowen, Laura O. Lazarus, and Richard H. Ekman, *University Libraries and Scholarly Communication: Study Prepared for The Andrew W. Mellon Foundation.* Washington, D.C.: Association of Research Libraries for The Andrew W. Mellon Foundation, 1992.

6. *Newsletter on Serials Pricing Issues.* Edited by Marcia Tuttle. Chapel Hill: University of North Carolina, 1989–1997. Available electronically by subscribing to PRICES from list-proc@unc.edu.

7. Deana Astle and Charles Hamaker, "Journal Publishing: Pricing and Structural Issues in the 1930s and the 1980s. *Advances in Serials Management* 2 (1988): 1–36; Charles Hamaker and Deana Astle, "Recent Price Patterns in British Journal Pricing." *Library Acquisitions: Practice and Theory* 8 (1984): 225–232; Deana Astle and Charles Hamaker, "Pricing by Geography: British Journal Pricing 1986 Including Developments in Other Countries." *Library Acquisitions: Practice and Theory* 10 (1986): 165–181.

8. David Lewis, "Economics of the Scholarly Journal." *College and Research Libraries* 50/6 (November 1989): 674–688; H. Craig Peterson, "Variations in Journal Prices: A Statistical Analysis." *Serials Librarian* 17/1&2 (1989): 1–9; Bruce Kingma and Philip Eppard, "Journal Price Escalation and the Market for Information: The Librarians' Solution." *College and Research Libraries* 53/6 (November 1992): 523–535; Michael A. Stoller, Robert Christopherson, and Michael Miranda, "The Economics of Professional Journal Pricing." *College and Research Libraries* 57/1 (January 1996): 9–21.

9. Henry H. Barshall, "The Cost Effectiveness of Physics Journals." *Physics Today* 41 (July 1988): 56–59; H. Craig Peterson, "The Economics of Economics Journals: A Statistical Analysis of Pricing Practices by Publishers." *College and Research Libraries* 53 (March 1992): 176–181; John O. Christensen, "Do We Know What We Are Paying For? A Comparison of Journal Subscription Costs." *Serials Review* 19/2 (Summer 1993): 39–61.

10. Edward A. Dyl, "A Note on Price Discrimination by Academic Journals." *Library Quarterly* 53/2 (1983): 161–169; Patrick Joyce and Thomas E. Merz, "Price Discrimination in Academic Journals." *Library Quarterly* 55/3 (1985): 273–283; Patrick Joyce, "Price Discrimination in 'Top' Scientific Journals." *Applied Economics* 22/8 (1990): 1127–1135.

11. George A. Chressanthis and June D. Chressanthis, "A General Econometric Model of the Determinants of Library Subscription Prices of Scholarly Journals: The Role of Exchange Rate Risk and Other Factors." *Library Quarterly* 64/3 (1994): 270–293; George A. Chressanthis and June D. Chressanthis, "The Relationship between Manuscript Submission Fees and Journal Quality." *Serials Librarian* 24/1 (1993): 71–85.

12. Roger Noll and W. Edward Steinmueller, "An Economic Analysis of Scientific Journal Prices: Preliminary Results." *Serials Review* 18 (Spring/Summer 1992): 32–37.

13. George A. Chressanthis and June D. Chressanthis, "The Determinants of Library Subscription Prices of the Top-Ranked Economics Journals: An Econometric Analysis." *Journal of Economic Education* 25/4 (Fall 1994): 367–382.

14. S. J. Liebowitz, "Copying and Indirect Appropriability: Photocopying of Journals." *Journal of Political Economy* 93/5 (1985): 945–957.

15. For a fuller exploration of the issues that prescribe the study reported here, see Richard W. Meyer, "Monopoly Power and Electronic Journals." *Library Quarterly* 67/4 (October 1997): 325–349.

16. Edward Chamberlin, *The Theory of Monopolistic Competition.* Cambridge: Harvard University Press, 1935; Jan Keppler, *Monopolistic Competition Theory: Origins, Results, and Implications.* Baltimore: Johns Hopkins University Press, 1994.

17. *Directory of Electronic Journals, Newsletters, and Academic Discussion List.* Washington, D.C.: Association of Research Libraries, 1991–1996.

18. Steve Hitchcock, Leslie Carr, and Wendy Hall, "A Survey of STM Online Journals 1990–1995: The Calm Before the Storm." In D. Mogge, editor, *Directory of Electronic Journals, Newsletters, and Academic Discussion List.* 6th Edition. Washington, D.C.: Association of Research Libraries, 1996, 7–32.

19. Stephen P. Harter, "The Impact of Electronic Journals on Scholarly Communication: A Citation Analysis." *The Public-Access Computer Systems Review* 7, no. 5 (1996): 5–34. URL: *http://info.lib.uh.edu/pr/v7/n5/hart7n5.html.*

20. Adonis is a product of Adonis USA, 238 Main St., 5th Floor, Cambridge, MA; a wholly owned subsidiary of Elsevier.

21. Personal conversation with Karen Hunter, vice president of Elsevier, 15 February 1997.

22. George A. Chressanthis and June D. Chressanthis, "Publisher Monopoly Power and Third-Degree Price Discrimination of Scholarly Journals." *Technical Services Quarterly* 11/2 (1993): 13–36.

23. This theory is based on the classic work by Abba Lerner, "The Concept of Monopoly and the Measurement of Monopoly Power." *Review of Economic Studies* (June 1934): 157–175.

24. John R. Hayes, "The Internet's First Victim?" Forbes 156/14 (December 18, 1995): 200–201.

25. The Associated Colleges of the South includes: Birmingham Southern, Centenary, Centre, Furman, Hendrix, Millsaps, Morehouse (Atlanta University Center), Rhodes, University of Richmond, Rollins, Southwestern, University of the South, and Trinity.

26. Two variations in the dependent variable will be used: the net difference and the index of monopoly power after the work of Lerner.

27. Chressanthis and Chressanthis, "Publisher Monopoly Power," 13–36.

CHAPTER 15

The Use of Electronic Scholarly Journals
Models of Analysis and Data Drawn from the Project MUSE Experience at Johns Hopkins University

James G. Neal

Project MUSE is a collaborative initiative between the Johns Hopkins University Press and the Milton S. Eisenhower Library at Johns Hopkins University to provide network-based access to scholarly journals including titles in the humanities, social sciences, and mathematics. Launched with electronic versions of 40 titles still published in print, Project MUSE coverage has now been expanded to include electronic-only publications. Funded initially by grants from The Mellon Foundation and the National Endowment for the Humanities, Project MUSE seeks to create a successful model for electronic scholarly publishing characterized by affordability and wide availability. It has been designed to take advantage of new technical capabilities in the creation and storage of electronic documents. It has been developed to provide a range of subscription options for individual libraries and consortia. It is based on a very liberal use and reuse approach that encourages any noncommercial activity within the bounds of the subscribing organization.

Project MUSE has been produced from the outset for usability, with a focus on user-centered features. This focus has evolved as a participative and interactive process, soliciting input and feedback from users and integrating user guidance components into the system. An on-line survey is available to all users, and libraries are providing information about the local implementation and the results of campus and community focus group discussions on Project MUSE. As the number of subscribing libraries expands and the activity grows, a valuable database of user experiences, attitudes, and behaviors will accumulate. A new feature will be the ability to track and analyze individual search sessions and to observe closely user activities. This feature will monitor the impact of new capabilities and the efficiency of searching practices.

Six models of use analysis are discussed in this paper that cover both the macro, or library-level, activity and the micro, or individual user–level, activity:

1. subscribing organizations—which libraries are subscribing to Project MUSE and how do they compare with the base of print journal customers?
2. subscriber behaviors—how do libraries respond as access to electronic journals is introduced and expanded, and in particular, how are acquisitions like Project MUSE accommodated in service and collection development programs and budgets?
3. user demography—what are the characteristics of the individual user population in such areas as status, background/experience, motivation, attitudes, and expectations?
4. user behaviors—how do individuals respond to the availability of scholarly materials in electronic format as they explore the capabilities of the system and execute requests for information?
5. user satisfaction—what objectives do users bring to network-based access to scholarly information, and how do users evaluate system design and performance and the quality of search results?
6. user impact—how are user research and information-seeking activities being shaped by access to full-text journal databases like Project MUSE?

One of the objectives of Project MUSE is to achieve full cost recovery status by the completion of the grant funding period in 1998. Therefore, it is important to monitor the growth in the base of subscribing libraries and to evaluate the impact on the print journal business of the Hopkins Press. An analysis of those libraries subscribing to the full Project MUSE database as of June 1997 (approximately 400 libraries) demonstrates a very significant expansion in the college, community college, and now public library settings with very low or no history of subscriptions to the print journals (see Table 15.1). The result is a noteworthy expansion in access to Hopkins Press titles, with 70% of the subscribing libraries currently purchasing less than 50% of the titles in print and over one-fourth acquiring no print journals from the Hopkins Press.

One explanation for these patterns of subscription activity is the purchase arrangement for Project MUSE. Over 90% of the libraries are subscribing to the full Project MUSE database of 43 titles. And due to very favorable group purchase rates, nearly 80% of Project MUSE subscribers are part of consortial contracts. The cooperative approach to providing access to electronic databases by libraries in a state or region is widely documented, and the Project MUSE experience further evidences this phenomenon.

Another objective of Project MUSE is to enable libraries to understand the use of collections and thus to make informed acquisitions and retention decisions. The impact on collection development behaviors will be critical, as libraries do indicate intentions to cancel print duplicates of MUSE titles and to monitor carefully the information provided on individual electronic title and article activity. Use information is beginning to flow to subscribing libraries, but there is no evidence yet of journal cancellations for Hopkins Press titles.

TABLE 15.1.   Project MUSE Subscribing
Libraries and Customer Print Subscriptions
as of June 1997

Subscribing Libraries	
ARL universities	65 libraries
Other universities	128 libraries
Liberal arts colleges	101 libraries
Community colleges	53 libraries
Public libraries	3 library systems

Customer Print Subscriptions	
No. of Print Subscriptions	Percentage of Libraries
0	27.8
1–4	7.6
5–9	6.8
10–14	15.8
15–19	13.0
20–24	11.8
25–29	9.0
30–34	6.2
35–40	2.0

An important area of analysis is user demography, that is, the characteristics of the individuals searching the Project MUSE database. An on-line user survey and focus group discussions are beginning to provide some insights:

- The status of the user, that is, undergraduate student, graduate student, faculty, staff, community member, or library employee. As Project MUSE is introduced, library staff are typically the heaviest users, followed by a growth in student use as campus awareness and understanding expands.

- Type of institution, that is, research university, comprehensive university, liberal arts college, community college, or public library setting. As Project MUSE subscriptions have increased and access has extended into new campus settings, heavier use has initially been in the research universities and liberal arts colleges where there is either traditional awareness of Project MUSE titles or organized and successful programs to promote availability.

- The computer experience of users, that is, familiarity with searching full-text electronic databases through a Web interface. Project MUSE users tend to be knowledgeable Internet searchers who have significant comfort with Web browsers, graphical presentations of information, and construction of searches in textual files.

- The location of use, that is, in-library, on-campus in faculty office and student residence hall, or off-campus. Preliminary data indicates that the searching of Project MUSE is taking place predominantly on library-based equipment. This finding can be explained by the inadequate network infrastructure that persists at many campuses or by the general lack of awareness of Project MUSE until a user is informed by library staff about its availability during a reference exchange.

- The browsers used to search the Project MUSE database. An analysis of searches over an 18-month period confirms that Netscape browsers are used now in over 98% of the database activity, with a declining percentage of Lynx and other nongraphical options.

Project MUSE enables searching by author, title, or keyword, in the table of contents or the full text of the journals, and across all the journals or just selected titles. All articles are indexed with Library of Congress subject headings. Hypertext links in tables of contents, articles, citations, endnotes, author bibliographies, and illustrations allow efficient navigation of the database. User searching behavior is an important area for investigation, and some preliminary trends can be identified:

- The predominant search strategy is by keyword, with author and title inquiries occurring much less frequently. This strategy can be partially explained by the heavy undergraduate student use of the database and the rich results enabled by keyword strategies.

- Use of the database is equally distributed across the primary content elements: tables of contents, article abstracts, images linked to text, and the articles. An issue for future analysis is the movement of users among these files.

- Given the substantial investment in the creation of LC subject headings and the maintenance of a structured thesaurus to enhance access to articles, their value to search results and user success is being monitored carefully.

- With the expansion of both internal and external hypertext links, the power of the Web searching environment is being observed, the user productivity gains are being monitored, and the willingness to navigate in an electronic journal database is being tested.

- Users are directed to the Project MUSE database through several channels. Libraries are providing links from the bibliographic record for titles in the on-line catalog. Library Web sites highlight Project MUSE or collections of electronic journals. Subject pages list the Project MUSE titles that cluster in a particular discipline.

- Users are made aware of Project MUSE through a variety of promotional and educational strategies. Brochures and point-of-use information are being prepared. In some cases, campus media have included descriptive articles. Library instructional efforts have focused on Project MUSE and its structure and searching capabilities.

- Printing and downloading to disk are important services linked to the effective use of Project MUSE, given the general unwillingness of users to read articles on-line. Libraries have an interest in maximizing turnover on limited computer equipment and are focused on implementing cost-recovery printing programs.

- Project MUSE is increasingly enabling users to communicate with publishers, journal editors, and the authors of articles through e-mail links embedded in the database. Correspondence has been at a very low level but is projected to expand as graduate student and faculty use increases and as familiarity and comfort with this feature grows.

With over 400 subscribing libraries and over three million potential users of Project MUSE in the communities served, it is possible to document global use trends and the changing intensity of searching activity (see Table 15.2). The progression of use over time as a library introduces access to Project MUSE is being monitored. Early analysis suggests that the first two quarters of availability produce low levels of use, while third quarter use expands significantly.

Data is also being collected on the number of requests for individual journal titles. During the 12-month period ending August 1, 1997, the total number of requests to the MUSE database was just over nine million, for an average of just under 25,000 hits per day. For data on the average number of requests per month for individual journal titles, see Table 15.3.

In addition, data is now being collected on the number of requests for individual journal articles. During the 12-month period ending August 1, 1997, 100 articles represented 16.5% of the total articles requested. The article receiving the largest number of requests was hit 3,944 times. Two journals, *Postmodern Culture* (33 articles) and *Configurations* (22 articles), included 55% of the most frequently requested articles.

User satisfaction with the quality and effectiveness of Project MUSE will be the central factor in its long-term success. Interactions with users seek to understand expectations, response to system design and performance, and satisfaction with results. The degree to which individuals and libraries are taking advantage of expansive fair use capabilities should also be gauged.

Project MUSE has focused on various technical considerations to maximize the dependability and efficiency of user searching. Detailed information on platforms and browsers is collected, for example, and access denials and other server responses that might indicate errors are automatically logged and routed for staff investigation.

Expectations for technology are generally consistent: more content, expanded access, greater convenience, new capabilities, cost reduction, and enhanced pro-

TABLE 15.2.   Project MUSE Global Use Trends

	4th Quarter 1996	1st Quarter 1997
Total requests	1,833,692	2,618,069 (+42.8%)
Requests per day	19,922	29,090 (+46.0%)
Total subscribers	199	322 (+61.8%)
Requests per subscriber	9,214	8,131 (−12.0%)

ductivity. It will be important to monitor the impact of Project MUSE in the subscribing communities and to assess whether it is delivering a positive and effective experience for users.

It is also important to maximize the core advantages of using information in digital formats:

- accessibility, that is, delivery to locations wherever users can obtain network connections
- searchability, that is, the range of strategies that can be used to draw relevant information out of the database
- currency, that is, the ability to make publications available much earlier than is possible for print versions
- researchability, that is, the posing of questions in the digital environment that could not even be conceived with print materials
- interdisciplinarity, that is, the ability to conduct inquiries across publications in a range of diverse disciplines and discover new-but-related information
- multimedia, that is, access to text, sound, images, video in an integrated presentation
- linkability, that is, the hypertext connections that can be established among diverse and remote information sources
- interactivity, that is, the enhancement of user control and influence over the flow of information and the communication that can be integrated into the searching activity

Project MUSE will be evaluated against these quantitative and qualitative models. Its success will ultimately be determined by its support for the electronic scholarly publishing objectives outlined in the work of the American Association of Universities and the Association of Research Libraries:

- foster a competitive market for scholarly publishing by providing realistic alternatives to prevailing commercial publishing options
- develop policies for intellectual property management emphasizing broad and easy distribution and reuse of material

TABLE 15.3.   Average Requests for Individual Journal Titles
per Month as of August 1997

Journal Title	No. of Issues On-line	Average No. of Requests per Month
American Imago	10	12,328
American Jewish History	5	3,718
American Journal of Mathematics	6	4,596
American Journal of Philology	6	4,126
American Quarterly	6	8,162
Arethusa	5	6,195
Bulletin of the History of Medicine	6	10,392
Callaloo	8	23,649
Configurations	13	36,917
Diacritics	5	7,083
ELH	15	25,796
Eighteenth-Century Life	4	2,113
Eighteenth-Century Studies	8	7,605
Human Rights Quarterly	11	10,718
Imagine	2	1,656
Journal of Democracy	7	22,032
Journal of Early Christian Studies	6	6,454
Journal of Modern Greek Studies	3	5,316
Journal of the History of Ideas	8	7,550
Kennedy Institute of Ethics Journal	6	3,803
Late Imperial China	2	1,742
Literature and Medicine	5	6,667
MLN	14	13,139
Milton Quarterly	1	253
Modern Fiction Studies	11	20,381
Modern Judaism	5	3,155
Modernism/Modernity	8	14,488
New Literary History	7	7,253
Performing Arts Journal	5	3,363
Philosophy and Literature	3	12,037
Philosophy, Psychiatry, and Psychology	6	6,601
Postmodern Culture	21	74,564
Review of Higher Education	4	5,621
Reviews of American History	10	18,509
SAIS Review	5	6,390
The Henry James Review	8	10,610
The Lion and the Unicorn	6	10,764
The Yale Journal of Criticism	3	6,108
Theatre Journal	6	9,322
Theatre Topics	3	3,199
Theory and Event	3	39
Wide Angle	6	4,324
World Politics	6	6,454

- encourage innovative applications of information technology to enrich and expand the means for distributing research and scholarship
- ensure that new channels of scholarly communication sustain quality requirements and contribute to promotion and tenure processes
- enable the permanent archiving of research publications and scholarly communication in digital formats

CHAPTER 16

A New Consortial Model
for Building Digital Libraries

Raymond K. Neff

Libraries in America's research universities are being systematically depopulated of current subscriptions to scholarly journals. Annual increases in subscription costs are consistently outpacing the growth in library budgets. This problem has become chronic for academic libraries that collect in the fields of science, engineering, and medicine, and by now the problem is well recognized (Cummings et al. 1992). At Case Western Reserve University, we have built a novel digital library distribution system and focused on our collections in the chemical sciences to investigate a new approach to solving a significant portion of this problem. By collaborating with another research library that has a strong chemical sciences collection, we have developed a methodology to control costs of scholarly journals and have planted the seeds of a new consortial model for building digital libraries. This paper summaries our progress to date and indicates areas in which we are continuing our research and development.

For research libraries in academia, providing sufficient scholarly information resources in the chemical sciences represents a large budgetary item. For our purposes, the task of providing high-quality library services to scholars in the chemical sciences is similar to providing library services in other sciences, engineering, and medicine; if we solve the problem in the limited domain of the chemical sciences, we can reasonably extrapolate our results to these other fields. Thus, research libraries whose mission it is to provide a high level of coverage for scholarly publications in the chemical sciences are the focus of this project, although we believe that the principles and practices employed in this project are extensible to the serial collections of other disciplines.

A consortium depends on having its members operating with common missions, visions, strategies, and implementations. We adopted the tactics of developing a consortial model by having two neighboring libraries collaborate in the initial project. The University of Akron (UA) and Case Western Reserve University

(CWRU) both have academic programs in the chemical sciences that are nationally ranked, and the two universities are fewer than 30 miles apart. It was no surprise to find that both universities have library collections in the chemical sciences that are of high quality and nearly exhaustive in their coverage of scholarly journals. To quantify the correlation between these two collections, we counted the number of journals that both collected and found the common set to be 76% in number and 92% in cost. The implications of the overlap in collecting patterns is plain; if both libraries collected only one copy of each journal, with the exception of the most used journals, approximately half of the cost of these subscriptions could be saved. For these two libraries, the cost savings is potentially $400,000 per year. This cost savings seemed like a goal worth pursuing, but to do so would require building a new type of information distribution system.

The reason scholarly libraries collect duplicative journals is that students and faculty want to be able to use these materials by going to the library and looking up a particular volume or by browsing the current issues of journals in their field. Eliminating a complete set of the journals at all but one of our consortial libraries would deprive local users of this walk-up-and-read service. We asked ourselves if it would be possible to construct a virtual version of the paper-based journal collection that would be simultaneously present at each consortium member institution, allowing any scholar to consult the collection at will even though only one copy of the paper journal was on the shelf. The approach we adopted was to build a digital delivery system that would provide to a scholar on the campus of a consortial member institution, on a demand basis, either a soft or hard copy of any article for which a subscription to the journal was held by a consortial member library. Thus, according to this vision, the use of information technology would make it possible to collect one set of journals among the consortium members and to have them simultaneously available at all institutions. Although the cost of building the new digital distribution system is substantial, it was considered as an experiment worth undertaking. The generous support of The Andrew W. Mellon Foundation is being used to cover approximately one-half of the costs for the construction and operation of the digital distribution system, with Case Western Reserve University covering the remainder. The University of Akron Library has contributed its expertise and use of its chemical sciences collections to the project.

It also seemed necessary to us to want to invite the cooperation of journal publishers in a project of this kind. To make a digital delivery system practical would require having the rights to store the intellectual property in a computer system, and when we started this project, no consortium member had such rights. Further, we needed both the ongoing publications and the backfiles so that complete runs of each serial could be constructed in digital form. The publishers could work out agreements with the consortium to provide their scholarly publications for inclusion in a digital storage system that would be connected to our network-based transmission system, and thus, their cooperation would become essential. The chemical sciences are disciplines in which previous work with electronic libraries had been started. The TULIP Project of Elsevier Science (Borghuis et al. 1996) and the CORE Project undertaken by a consortium of Cornell University, the American Chemical Society, Bellcore, Chemical Abstracts, and OCLC were known to us, and we certainly wanted to benefit from their experiences. Publications of the American Chemical Society, Elsevier Science, Springer-Verlag, Academic Press, John Wiley & Sons, and many other publishers were central to our proposed project because of the importance of their journal titles to the chemical sciences disciplines.

We understood from the beginning of this effort that we would want to monitor the performance of the digital delivery system under realistic usage scenarios. The implementation of our delivery system has built into it extensive data collection facilities for monitoring what users actually do. The system is also sensitive to concerns of privacy in that it collects no items of performance information that may be used to identify unambiguously any particular user.

Given the existence of extensive campus networks at both CWRU and UA and substantial internetworking among the academic institutions in northeastern Ohio, there was sufficient infrastructure already in place to allow the construction and operation of an intra- and intercampus digital delivery system. Such a digital delivery system has now been built and made operational. The essential aspects of the digital delivery system will now be described.

A DIGITAL DELIVERY SYSTEM

The roots of the electronic library are found in landmark papers by Bush (1945) and Kemeny (1962). Most interestingly, Kemeny foreshadowed what prospective scholarly users of our digital library told us was their essential requirement, which was that they be able to see each page of a scholarly article preserved in its graphical integrity. That is, the electronic image of each page layout needed to look like it did when originally published on paper. The system we have developed uses the ACROBATR page description language to accomplish this objective.

Because finding aids and indices for specialized publications are too limiting, users also have the requirement that the article's text be searchable with limited or unlimited discipline-specific thesauri. Our system complements the page images with an optical character recognition (OCR) scanning of the complete text of each article. In this way, the user may enter words and phrases the presence of which in an article constitutes a "hit" for the scholar.

One of the most critical design goals for our project was the development of a scanning subsystem that would be easily reproducible and cost efficient to set up and operate in each consortium member library. Not only did the equipment need to be readily available, but it had to be adaptable to a variety of work flow and staff work patterns in many different libraries. Our initial design has been successfully tailored to the needs of both the CWRU libraries and the Library at the University of Akron. Our approach to the sharing of paper-based collections is to use a scanning device to copy the pages of the original into a digital image format that may be readily transmitted across our existing telecommunications infrastructure. In addition, the digital version of the paper is stored for subsequent retrieval. Thus, repeated viewing of the same work would necessitate only a one-time transformation of format. This procedure is an advantage in achieving faster response times for scholars, and it promotes the development and use of quality control methods. The scanning equipment we have used in this project and its operation are described in Appendix E. The principal advantage of this scanner is that bound serials may be scanned without damaging the volume and without compromising the resulting page images; in fact, the original journal collection remains intact and accessible to scholars throughout the project. This device is also sufficiently fast that a trained operator, including students, may scan over 800 pages per average workday. For a student worker making $7.00 per hour, the person-cost of scanning is under $0.07 per page; the cost of conversion to searchable text adds $0.01 per page. Appendix E also gives more details regarding the scanning processes and work flow. Appendix F gives a technical justification for a digitization standard for the consortium. Thus, each consortium member is expected to make a reasonable investment in equipment, training, and personnel.

The target equipment for viewing an electronic journal was taken to be a common PC-compatible computer workstation, hereafter referred to as a client. This client is also the user platform for the on-line library catalog systems found on our campuses as well as for the growing collections of CD-ROM-based information products. Appendix B gives the specification of the workstation standards for the project. The implications for use of readily available equipment is that the client platform for our project would also work outside of the library—in fact, wherever a user wanted to work. Therefore, by selecting the platform we did, we extended the project to encompass a full campuswide delivery system. Because our consortium involves multiple campuses (two at the outset), the delivery system is general purpose in its availability as an access facility.

Just as we needed a place to store paper-based journals within the classical research library, we needed to specify a place to store the digital copies. In technical parlance, this storage facility is called a server. Appendixes B and C give some details regarding the server hardware and software configurations used in this project.

Appendix C also gives some information regarding the campuswide networks on both our campuses and the statewide network that connects them. It is important to note that any connected client workstation that follows our minimum standards will be able to use the digital delivery system being constructed.

Because the key to minimizing the operating costs within a consortium is interoperability and standardization, we have adopted a series of data and equipment standards for this project; they are given in Appendixes A and B.

RIGHTS MANAGEMENT SYSTEM

One of the most significant problems in placing intellectual property in a networked environment is that with a few clicks of a mouse thousands of copies of the original work can be distributed at virtually zero marginal cost, and as a result, the owner may be deprived of expected royalty revenue. Since we recognized this problem some years ago and realized that solutions outside of the network itself were unlikely to be either permanent or satisfactory to all parties (e.g., author, owner, publisher, distributor, user), we embarked on the creation of a software subsystem now known as Rights Manager™. With our Rights Manager system, we can now control the distribution of digitally formatted intellectual property in a networked environment subject to each stakeholder receiving proper due.

In this project, we use the Rights Manager system with our client server–based content delivery system to manage and control intellectual property distribution for digitally formatted content (e.g., text, images, audio, video, and animations).

Rights Manager is a working system that encodes license agreement information for intellectual property at a server and distributes the intellectual property to authorized users over the Internet or a campuswide intranet along with a Rights Manager–compliant browser. The Rights Manager handles a variety of license agreement types, including public domain, site licensing, controlled simultaneous accesses, and pay-per-use. Rights Manager also manages the functionality available to a client according to the terms of the license agreement; this is accomplished by use of a special browser that enforces the license's terms and that permits or denies client actions such as save, print, display, copy, excerpt, and so on. Access to a particular item of intellectual property, with or without additional functionality, may be made available to the client at no charge, with an overhead charge, or at a royalty plus overhead charge. Rights Manager has been designed to accommodate sufficient flexibility in capturing wide degrees of arbitrariness in charging rules and policies.

The Rights Manager is intended for use by individuals and organizations who function as purveyors of information (publishers, on-line service providers, campus libraries, etc.). The system is capable of managing a wide variety of agreements from an unlimited number of content providers. Rights Manager also permits customization of licensing terms so that individual users or user classes may be defined and given unique access privileges to restricted sets of materials. A relatively common example of this customization for CWRU would be an agreement to provide (1) view-only capabilities to an electronic journal accessed by an anonymous user located in the library, (2) display/print/copy access to all on-campus students enrolled in a course for which a digital textbook has been adopted, and (3) full access to faculty for both student and instructor versions of digital editions of supplementary textbook materials.

Fundamental to the implementation of Rights Manager are the creation and maintenance of distribution rights, permissions, and license agreement databases.

These databases express the terms and conditions under which the content purveyor distributes materials to its end users. Relevant features of Rights Manager include:

- a high degree of granularity, which may be below the level of a paragraph, for publisher-defined content
- central or distributed management of rights, permissions, and licensing databases
- multiple agreement types (e.g., site licensing, limited site licensing, and pay-per-use)
- content packaging where rights and permission data are combined with digital format content elements for managed presentation by Web browser plug-in modules or helper applications

Rights Manager maintains a comprehensive set of distribution rights, permissions, and charging information. The premise of Rights Manager is that each publication may be viewed as a compound document. A publication under this definition consists of one or more content elements and media types; each element may be individually managed, as may be required, for instance, in an anthology.

Individual content elements may be defined as broadly or narrowly as required (i.e., the granularity of the elements is defined by the publisher and may go below the level of a paragraph of content for text); however, for overall efficiency, each content element should represent a significant and measurable unit of material. Figures, tables, illustrations, and text sections may reasonably be defined as individual content elements and be treated uniquely according to each license agreement.

To manage the distribution of complete publications or individual content elements, two additional licensing metaphors are implemented. The first of these, a Collection Agreement, is used to specify an agreement between a purveyor and its supplier (e.g., a primary or secondary publisher); this agreement takes the form of a list of publications distributed by the purveyor and the terms and conditions under which these publications may be issued to end users (one or more Collection Agreements may be defined and simultaneously managed between the purveyor and a customer).

The second abstraction, a Master Agreement, is used to broadly define the rules and conditions that apply to all Collection Agreements between the purveyor and its content supplier. Only one Master Agreement may be defined between the supplier and the institutional customer. In practice, Rights Manager assumes that the purveyor will enter into licensing agreements with its suppliers for the delivery of digitally formatted content. At the time the first license agreement is executed between a supplier and a purveyor, one or more entries are made into the purveyor's Rights Manager databases to define the Master and Collection Agreements. Optionally, Publication and/or Content-Element usage rules may also be defined. Licensed materials may be distributed from the purveyor's site (or perhaps by an authorized service provider); both the content and associated licensing rules are transferred by the supplier to the purveyor for distributed license and content management.

Depending on the selected delivery option, individual end users (e.g., faculty members, students, or library patrons) may access either a remote server or a local institutional repository to search and request delivery of licensed publications. Depending on the agreement(s) between the owner and the purveyor, individual users are assigned access rights and permissions that may be based on individual user IDs, network addresses, or both.

Network or Internet Protocol addresses are used to limit distribution by physical location (e.g., to users accessing the materials from a library, a computer lab, or a local workstation). User identification may be exploited to create limited site-licensing models or individual user agreements (e.g., distributing publications only to students enrolled in Chemistry 432 or, perhaps, to a specific faculty member).

At each of the four levels (Master Agreement, Collection Agreement, Publication, and Content-Element), access rules and usage privileges may be defined. In general, the access and usage permissions rules are broadly defined at the Master and Collection Agreement level and are refined or restricted at the Publication and Content-Element levels. For example, a Master or Collection Agreement rule could be defined to specify that by default all licensed text elements may be printed at a some fixed cost, say 10¢ per page; however, high value or core text sections may be individually identified using Publication or Content-Element override rules and assessed higher charges, say 20¢ per page.

When a request for delivery of materials is received, the content rules are evaluated in a bottom-up manner (e.g., content element rules are evaluated before publication rules, which are, in turn, evaluated before license agreement rules, etc.). Access and usage privileges are resolved when the system first recognizes a match between the requester's user ID (or user category) and/or the network address and the permission rules governing the content. Access to the content is only granted when an applicable set of rules specifically granting access permission to the end user is found; in the case where two or more rules permit access, the rules most favorable to the end user are selected. Under this approach, site licenses, limited site licenses, individual licensing, and pay-per-use may be simultaneously specified and managed.

The following use of the Rights Manager rules databases is recommended as an initial guideline for Rights Manager implementation:

1. Use Master Agreement rules to define the publishing holding company or imprint, the agreement's term (beginning and ending dates), and the general "fair use" guidelines negotiated between a supplier and the purveyor. Because of the current controversy over the definition of "fair use," Rights

Manager does not rely on preprogrammed definitions; rather, the supplier and purveyor may negotiate this definition and create rules as needed. This approach permits fair use definitions to be redefined in response to new standards or regulatory definitions without requiring modifications to Rights Manager itself.

2. Use Collection Agreement rules to define the term (beginning and ending dates) for specific licensing agreements between the supplier and the purveyor. General access and permission rules by user ID, user category, network address, and media type would be assigned at this level.

3. Use Publication rules to impose any user ID or user category–specific rules (e.g., permissions for students enrolled in a course for which this publication has been selected as the adopted textbook) or to impose exceptions based on the publication's value.

4. Use Content-Element rules to grant specific end users or user categories access to materials (e.g., define content elements that are supplementary teaching aids for the instructor) or to impose exceptions based on media type or the value of content elements.

The Rights Manager system does not mandate that licensing agreements exploit user IDs; however, maximum content protection and flexibility in license agreement specification is achieved when this feature is used. Given that many institutions or consortium members may not have implemented a robust user authentication system, alternative approaches to uniquely identifying individual users must be considered. While there are a variety of ways to address this issue, it is suggested that personal identification numbers (PINs), assigned by the supplier and distributed by trusted institutional agents at the purveyor's site (e.g., instructors, librarians, bookstore employees, or departmental assistants) or embedded within the content, be used as the basis for establishing user IDs and passwords. Using this approach, valid users may enter into registration dialogues to automatically assign user IDs and passwords in response to a valid PIN "challenge."

While Rights Manager is designed to address all types of multimedia rights, permissions, and licensing issues, the current implementation has focused on distribution of traditional print publication media (text and images). Extensions to Rights Manager to address the distribution of full multimedia, including streaming audio and video, are being developed at CWRU.

The key to understanding our approach to intellectual property management is that we expect that each scholarly work will be disseminated according to a comprehensive contractual agreement. Publishers may use master agreements to cover a set of titles. Further, we do not expect that there will be only one interpretation of concepts such as fair use, and our Rights Manager system makes provision for arbitrarily different operational definitions of fair use, so that specific contractual agreements can be "enforced" within the delivery system.

A NEW CONSORTIAL MODEL

The library world has productively used various consortial models for over 30 years, but until now, there has not been a successful model for building a digital library. One of the missing pieces in the consortial jigsaw puzzle has been a technical model that is both comprehensive and reproducible in a variety of library contexts. To begin our approach to a new consortial model, we developed a complete technical system for building and operating a digital library. Building such a system is no small achievement. Similar efforts have been undertaken with the Elsevier Science TULIP Project and the JSTOR project.

The primary desiderata for a new consortial model are as follows:

- Any research library can participate using agreed upon and accepted standards.

- Many research libraries each contribute relatively small amounts of labor by scanning a small, controlled number of journal issues. Scanning is both systematic and based on a request for an individual article.

- Readily available off-the-shelf equipment is used.

- Intellectual property is made available through licensing and controlled by the Rights Manager software system.

- Publishers grant rights to libraries to scan and store intellectual property retrospectively (i.e., already purchased materials) in exchange for the right to license use of the digital formats to other users. Libraries provide publishers with digital copies of scholarly journals for their own use, thus enabling publishers to enrich their own electronic libraries.

A PAYMENTS SYSTEM FOR THE CONSORTIUM

It is unrealistic to assume that all use of a future digital library will be without any charging mechanisms even though the research library of today charges for little except for photocopying and user fines. This is not to assume that the library user is charged for each use, although that would be possible. A more likely scenario would be that the library pay on behalf of the members of the scholarly community (i.e., student, professor, researcher) that it supports. According to our proposed consortial model, libraries would be charged for use of the digital library according to the total pages "read" in any given user session. It could be easily worked out that users who consult the digital library on the premises of the campus library would not be charged themselves, but if they used the digital library from another campus location or from off-campus through a network, that they would pay a per-page charge analogous to the cost of photocopying. A system of charging could include categorization by type of user, and the Rights Manager system provides for a wide variety of charging models, including the making of distinctions of usage in soft-copy format, hard-copy format, and downloading of a work in whole or in part. Protecting the rights of the owner is an especially interesting problem when the entire work is downloaded in a digital format. Both visible and invisible watermarking are techniques with which we have experience for protecting rights in the case of downloading an entire work.

We also have in mind that libraries that provide input via scanning to the decentralized, digital library would receive a credit for each page scanned. It is clear that the value of the digital library to the end user will increase as higher degrees of completeness in digitized holdings is achieved. Therefore, the credit system to originating libraries should recognize this value and reward these libraries according to a formula that charges and credits with a relative credit-to-charging ratio of perhaps ten to one; that is, an originating library might receive a credit for scanning one page equal to a charge for reading ten soft-copy pages.

The charge-and-credit system for our new consortial model is analogous to that used for the highly successful Online Computer Library Center's cataloging system. Member libraries within OCLC contribute original cataloging entries in the form of MARC records for the OCLC database as well as draw down a copy of a holding's data to fill in entries for their own catalog systems. The system of charging for "downloads" and crediting for "uploads" is repeated in our consortial model for retrospective scanning and processing of full-text journal articles. Just as original cataloging is at the heart of OCLC, original scanning is at the heart of our new consortial model for building the library of the future.

DATA COLLECTION

One of the most important aspects of this project is that the underlying software system has been instrumented with many data collection points. In this way we can find out through actual usage by faculty, students, and research staff what aspects of the system are good and which need more work and thought. Over the past decade many people have speculated about how the digital library might be made to work for the betterment of scholarly communications. Our system as described in this paper is one of the most comprehensive attempts yet to build up a base of usage experience data.

To appreciate the detailed data being collected by the project, we will describe the various types of data that the Rights Manager system captures. Many types of transactions occur between the Rights Manager client and the Rights Manager server software throughout a user session. The server software records these transactions, which will permit detailed analysis of usage patterns. Appendix D gives some details regarding the data collected during a user session.

PUBLISHERS AND DIGITAL LIBRARIES

The effects of the new consortial model for building digital libraries are not confined to the domain of technology. During the period when the new digital distribution system was being constructed, Ohio LINK, an agency of the Ohio

Board of Regents, commenced an overlapping relationship with Academic Press to offer its collection of approximately 175 electronic journals, many of which were in our chemical sciences collections. Significantly, the Ohio LINK contract with Academic Press facilitated the development of our digital library because it included a provision covering the scanning and storage of retrospective collections (i.e., backfiles) of their journals that we had originally acquired by subscription. In 1997, Ohio LINK extended the model of the Academic Press contract to an offering from Elsevier Science. According to this later agreement, subscriptions to current volumes of Elsevier Science's 1,153 electronic journals would be available for access and use on all of the 57 campuses of Ohio LINK member institutions, including CWRU and the University of Akron. The cost of the entire collection of electronic journals for each university for 1998 was set by the Ohio LINK–Elsevier contract to be approximately 5.5% greater than the institution's Elsevier Science expenditure level for 1997 subscriptions regardless of the particular subset these subscriptions represented; there is a further 5.5% price increase set to take effect in 1999. Further, the agreement between Ohio LINK and Elsevier constrains the member institutions to pay for this comprehensive access even if they cancel a journal subscription. Notably, there is an optional payment discount of 10% when an existing journal subscription (in a paper format) is limited to electronic delivery only (eliminating the delivery of a paper version). Thus, electronic versions of the Elsevier journals that are part of our chemical sciences digital library will be available at both institutions regardless of the existence of our consortium; pooling collections according to our consortial model would be a useless exercise from a financial point of view.

Other publishers are also working with our consortium of institutions to offer digital products. During spring 1997, CWRU and the University of Akron entered into an agreement with Springer-Verlag to evaluate their offering of 50 or so electronic journals, some of which overlapped with our chemical sciences collection. A similar agreement covering backfiles of Elsevier journals was considered and rejected for budgetary reasons. During the development of this project, we had numerous contacts with the American Chemical Society with the objective of including their publications in our digital library. Indeed, the outline of an agreement with them was discussed. As the time came to render the agreement in writing, they withdrew and later disavowed any interest in a contract with the consortium. At the present time, discussions are being held with other significant chemical science publishers about being included in our consortial library. This is clearly a dynamic period in journal publishing, and each of the societal and commercial publishers sees much at stake. While we in universities try to make sense of both technology and information service to our scholarly communities, the publishers are each trying to chart their own course both competitively and strategically while improvements in information technology continually raise the ante for continuing to stay in the game.

The underlying goal of this project has been to see if information technology could control the costs of chemical sciences serial publications. In the most extreme case, it could lower costs by half in our two libraries and even more if departmental copies were eliminated. As an aside, we estimated that departmentally paid chemical sciences journal subscriptions represented an institutional expenditure of about 40% of the libraries' own costs, so each institution paid in total 1.4 times each library's costs. For both institutions, the total was about 2.8 times the cost of one copy of each holding. Thus, if duplication were eliminated completely, the resulting expenditures for the consortium for subscriptions alone would be reduced by almost two-thirds from that which we have been spending. Clearly, the journal publishers understood the implications of our project. But the implications of the status quo were also clear: libraries and individuals were cutting subscriptions each year because budgets could not keep up with price increases. We believed that to let nature take its course was irresponsible when a well-designed experiment using state-of-the-art information technology could show a way to make progress. Thus, the spirit of our initial conversations with chemical sciences publishers was oriented to a positive scenario: libraries and the scholars they represented would be able to maintain or gain access to the full range of chemical sciences literature, and journals would be distributed in digital formats. We made a crucial assumption that information technology would permit the publishers to lower their internal production costs. This assumption is not unreasonable in that information technology has accomplished cost reductions in many other businesses.

In our preliminary discussions with the publishers, we expressed the long-term objective that we were seeking—controlling and even lowering our costs through the elimination of duplication as our approach to solving the "cancellation conundrum"—as well as our short-term objective—to receive the rights to scan, store, and display electronic versions of both current and back files of their publications, which we would create from materials we had already paid for (several times over, in fact). Current and future subscriptions would be purchased in only one copy, however, to create the desired financial savings. In exchange, we offered the publishers a complete copy of our PDF-formatted current issue and backfiles for their use, from which they could derive new revenue through licensing to others. Since these once-sold backfiles were being considered on the publishers' corporate balance sheets as a depleted resource, we thought that the prospect of deriving additional revenue from selling them again as a digital resource would seem to be an attractive idea. In the end, however, not one publisher was willing to take us up on this exchange. To them, the backfiles that we would create were not worth what we were asking. One chemical sciences journal publisher was willing to grant the rights to backfiles for additional revenue from our consortium. But this offer made no sense unless the exchange could be justified on the basis of savings in costs of library storage space and the additional convenience of electronic access (the digital library is never closed, network access from remote locations would likely increase marginal usage, etc.). When we saw the proposed charge, we rejected this offer as being too expensive. Another publisher did grant us the rights we sought as part of the overall statewide Ohio LINK electronic and print subscription contract, but this arrangement locked in the current costs (and annual increments) for several years, so the libraries could not benefit directly in terms of cost savings. With that particular limited agreement, however, there still is the definite possibility for savings on departmentally paid, personal subscriptions.

When we began to plan this project, it was not obvious what stance the publishing community would take to it. Our contacts in some of the leading publishing houses and in the Association of American Publishers (AAP) led us to believe that we were on the right track. Clearly, our goal was to reduce our libraries' costs, and that goal meant that publishers would receive less revenue. However, we also believed that the publishers would value receipt of the scanned backfiles that we would accumulate. Thus, the question was whether the backfiles have significant economic value. Clearly, libraries paid for the original publications in paper formats and have been extremely reluctant to pay a second time for the convenience of having access to digital versions of the backfiles. In our discussions, the publishers and AAP also seemed interested in doing experiments in learning whether a screen-based digital format could be made useful to our chemical sciences scholars. Thus, there was a variety of positive incentives favoring experimentation, and a benign attitude toward the project was evinced by these initial contacts with publishers. Their substantial interest in the CWRU Rights Management system seemed genuine and sincere, and their willingness to help us with an experiment of this type was repeatedly averred. After many months of discussion with one publisher, it became clear that they were unwilling to participate at all. In the end, they revealed that they were developing their own commercial digital journal service and that they did not want to have another venue that might compete with this. A second publisher expressed repeated interest in the project and, in the end, proposed that our consortium purchase a license to use the backfiles at a cost of 15% more than the price of the paper-based subscription; this meant that we would have to pay more for the rights to store backfiles of these journals in our system. A third publisher provided the rights to scan, store, display, and use the backfiles as part of the overall statewide Ohio LINK contract; thus this publisher provided all the rights we needed without extra cost to the consortium. We are continuing to have discussions with other chemical sciences journal publishers regarding our consortium and Ohio LINK, and these conversations are not uncomplicated by the overlap in our dual memberships.

It is interesting to see that the idea that digital distribution could control publisher costs is being challenged with statements such as "the costs of preparing journals for World Wide Web access through the Internet are substantially greater than the costs of distributing print." Questions regarding such statements abound: For example, are the one-time developmental costs front-loaded in these calculations, or are they amortized over the product's life cycle? If these claims are true, then they reflect on the way chemical sciences publishers are using information technology, because other societies and several commercial publishers are able to reflect cost savings in changing from print to nonprint distribution. Although we do not have the detailed data at this time (this study is presently under way in our libraries), we expect to show that there are significant cost savings in terms of library staff productivity improvement when we distribute journals in nonprint versions instead of print.

As a result of these experiences, some of these publishers are giving us the impression that their narrowly circumscribed economic interests are dominating the evolution of digital libraries, that they are not fundamentally interested in controlling their internal costs through digital distribution, and that they are still pursuing tactical advantages over our libraries at the expense of a different set of strategic relationships with our scholarly communities. As is true about many generalizations, these are not universally held within the publishing community, but the overwhelming message seems clear nonetheless.

CONCLUSIONS

A digital distribution system for storing and accessing scholarly communications has been constructed and installed on the campuses of Case Western Reserve University and the University of Akron. This low-cost system can be extended to other institutions with similar requirements because the system components, together with the way they have been integrated, were chosen to facilitate the diffusion of these technologies. This distribution system successfully separates ownership of library materials from access to them.

The most interesting aspect of the new digital distribution system is that libraries can form consortia that can share specialized materials rather than duplicate them in parallel, redundant collections. When a consortium can share a single subscription to a highly specialized journal, then we have the basis for controlling and possibly reducing the total cost of library materials, because we can eliminate duplicative subscriptions. We believe that the future of academic libraries points to the maintenance of a basic core collection, the selective acquisition of specialty materials, and the sharing across telecommunications networks of standard scholarly works. The consortial model that we have built and tested is one way to accomplish this goal. Our approach is contrasted with the common behavior of building up ever larger collections of standard works so that over time, academic libraries begin to look alike in their collecting habits, offer almost duplicative services, and require larger budgets. This project is attempting to find another path.

Over the past decade, several interesting experiments have been conducted to test different ideas for developing digital libraries, and more are under way. With many differing ideas and visions, an empirical approach is a sound way to make progress from this point forward. Our consortium model with its many explicit standards and integrated technologies seems to us to be an experiment worth continuing. During the next few years it will surely develop a base of performance data that should provide insights for the future. In this way, experience will benefit visioning.

REFERENCES

Borghuis, M., Brinckman, H., Fischer, A., Hunter, K., van der Loo, E., Mors, R., Mostert, P., and Zilstra, J.: TULIP Final Report: *The University LIcensing Program*. New York: Elsevier Science, 1996.

Bush, V.: "As We May Think," *The Atlantic Monthly*, 176, 101–108, 1945.

Cummings, A. M., Witte, M. L., Bowen, W. G., Lazarus, L. O., Ekman, R. H.: *University Libraries and Scholarly Communication: A Study Prepared for The Andrew W. Mellon Foundation*. The Association of Research Libraries, 1992.

Fleischhauer, C., and Erway, R. L.: *Reproduction-Quality Issues in a Digital-Library System: Observations on the Reproduction of Various Library and Archival Material Formats for Access and Preservation*. An American Memory White Paper, Washington, D.C.: Library of Congress, 1992.

Kemeny, J. G.: "A Library for 2000 A.D." in Greenberger, M. (Ed.), *Computers and the World of the Future*. Cambridge, Mass.: The M.I.T. Press, 1962.

APPENDIX A

Consortial Standards

MARC

- Enumeration and chronology standards from the serials holding standards of the 853 and 863 fields of MARC
  - Specifies up to 6 levels of enumeration and 4 levels of chronology, for example

    853 |aVolume|bIssue|i(year)|j(month)

    853 |aVolume|bIssue|cPart|i(year)|j(month)
- Linking from bibliographic records in library catalog via an 856 field
  - URL information appears in subfield u, anchor text appears in subfield z, for example

    856 7 |uhttp://beavis.cwru.edu/chemvl|zRetrieve articles from the Chemical Sciences Digital Library

    Would appear as

    Retrieve articles from the Chemical Sciences Digital Library

TIFF

- The most widely used multipage graphic format
- Support for tagged information ("Copyright", etc.)
- Format is extensible by creating new tags (such as RM rule information, authentication hints, encryption parameters)
- Standard supports multiple kinds of compression

Adobe PDF

- Container for article images
- Page description language (PDF)
- PDF files are searchable by the Adobe Acrobat browser
- Encryption and security are defined in the standard

SICI (Serial Item and Contribution Identifier)

- SICI definition (standards progress, overview, etc.)
- Originally a key part of the indexing structure
- All the components of the SICI code are stored, so it could be used as a linking mechanism between an article database and the Chemical Sciences Digital Library
- Ohio LINK is also very interested in this standard and is urging database creators and search engine providers to add SICI number retrieval to citation database and journal article repository systems
- Future retrieval interfaces into the database: SICI number search form, SICI number search API, for example
  0022–2364(199607)121:1<83:TROTCI>2.0.TX;2-I

APPENDIX B

Equipment Standards for End Users

Minimum Equipment Required

Hardware: An IBM PC or compatible computer with the following components:

- 80386 processor
- 16 MB RAM
- 20 MB free disk space
- A video card and monitor with a resolution of 640 × 480 and the capability of displaying 16 colors or shades of gray

Software:

- Windows 3.1
- Win32s 1.25
- TCP/IP software suite including a version of Winsock
- Netscape Navigator 2.02
- Adobe Acrobat Exchange 2.1

Win32s is a software package for Windows 3.1 that is distributed without charge and is available from Microsoft.

The requirement for Adobe Acrobat Exchange, a commercial product that is not distributed without charge, is expected to be relaxed in favor of a requirement for Adobe Acrobat Reader, a commercial product that is distributed without charge.

The software will also run on newer versions of compatible hardware and/or software.

Recommended Configuration of Equipment

This configuration is recommended for users who will be using the system extensively. Hardware: A computer with the following components:

- Intel Pentium processor
- 32 MB RAM
- 50 MB free disk space
- A video card and monitor with a resolution of 1280 × 1024 and the capability of displaying 256 colors or shades of gray

Software:

- Windows NT 4.0 Workstation
- TCP/IP suite that has been configured for a network connection (included in Windows NT)
- Netscape Navigator 2.02
- Adobe Acrobat Exchange 2.1

The requirement for Adobe Acrobat Exchange, a commercial product that is not distributed without charge, is expected to be relaxed in favor of a requirement for Adobe Acrobat Reader, a commercial product that is distributed without charge.

Other software options that the system has been tested on include:

- IBM OS/2 3.0 Warp Connect with Win-OS/2
- IBM TCP/IP for Windows 3.1, version 2.1.1
- Windows NT 3.51

APPENDIX C

Additional Hardware Specifications

Storage for Digital Copies

To give us the greatest possible flexibility in developing the project, we decided to form the server out of two interlinked computer systems, a standard IBM System 390 with the OS/390 Open Edition version as the operating system and a standard IBM RS/6000 System with the AIX version of the UNIX operating system. Both these components may be incrementally grown as the project's server requirements increase. Both systems are relatively commonplace at academic sites. Although only one system pair is needed in this project, it is likely that eventually two pairs of systems would be needed for an effort on the national scale. Such redundancy is useful for providing both reliability and load leveling.

Campuswide Networks

Both campus's networks and the statewide network that connects them uses the standards-based TCP/IP protocols. Any networked client workstation that follows our minimum standards will be able to use the digital delivery system being constructed. The minimum transmission speed on the CWRU campus is ten million bits per second (M bps) to each client workstation and a minimum of 155 M bps on each backbone link. The principal document repository is on the IBM System 390, which uses a 155 M bps ATM (asynchronous transfer mode) connection to the campus backbone. The linkage to the University of Akron is by way of the statewide network in which the principal backbone connection from CWRU is also operating at 155 M bps, and the linkage from the UA to the statewide network is at 3 M bps. The on-campus linkage for UA is also a minimum of 10 M bps to each client workstation within the chemical sciences scholarly community and to client workstations in the UA university library.

APPENDIX D

System Transactions as Initiated by an End User

A typical user session generates the following transactions between client and server.

1. User requests an article (usually from a Web browser). If the user is starting a new session, the RM system downloads and launches the appropriate viewer, which will process only encrypted transactions. In the case of Adobe Acrobat, the system downloads a plug-in. The following transactions take place with the server:
   a. Authenticate the viewer (i.e., ensure we are using a secure viewer).
   b. Get permissions (i.e., obtain a set of user permissions, if any. If it is a new session, the user is set by default to be the general purpose category of PUBLIC).
   c. Get Article (download the requested article. If step b returns no permissions, this transaction does not occur. The user must sign on and request the article again).
2. User signs on. If the general user has no permissions, he or she must log on. Following a successful logon, transactions 1b and 1c must be repeated. Transactions during sign-on include:
   a. Sign On
3. Article is displayed on-screen. Before an article is displayed on the screen, the viewer enters the RM protocol, a step-by-step process wherein a single Report command is sent to the server several times with different state flags and use types. RM events are processed similarly for all supported functions, including display, print, excerpt, and download. The transactions include:
   a. Report Use BEGIN (just before the article is displayed).
   b. Report Use ABORT (sent in the event that a technical problem, such as "out of memory," prevents display of the article).
   c. Report Use DECLINE (sent if the user declines display of the article after seeing the cost).
   d. Report Use COMMIT (just after the article is displayed).
   e. Report Use END (sent when the user dismisses the article from the screen by closing the article window).
4. User closes viewer. When a user closes a viewer, an end-of-session process occurs, which sends transaction 3e for all open articles. Also sent is a close viewer transaction, which immediately expires the viewer so it may not be used again.
   a. Close Viewer

The basic data being collected for every command (with the exception of 1a) and being sent to the server for later analysis includes the following:

- Date/time
- Viewer ID
- User ID (even if it is PUBLIC)
- IP address of request

These primary data may be used to derive additional data: Transaction 1b is effectively used to log unsuccessful access attempts, including failure reasons. The time interval between transactions 3a and 3e is used to measure the duration that an article is on the screen. The basic data collection module in the RM system is quite general and may be used to collect other information and derive other measures of system usage.

APPENDIX E

Scanning and Work Flow

Article Scanning, PDF Conversion, and Image Quality Control

The goal of the scan-and-store portion of the project is to develop a complete and tested system of hardware, software, and procedures that can be adopted by other members of the consortium with a reasonable investment in equipment, training, and personnel. If a system is beyond a consortium member's financial means, it will not be adopted. If a system cannot perform as required, it is a waste of resources.

Our original proposal stressed that all existing scholarly resources, particularly research tools, would remain available to scholars throughout this project. To that end, the scan-and-store process is designed to leave the consortium's existing journal collection intact and accessible.

Scan-and-Store Process Resources

- Scanning workstation, including a computer with sufficient processing and storage capacity, a scanner, and a network connection. Optionally, a second workstation can be used by the scanning supervisor to process the scanned images. The workstation used in this phase of the project includes:
  — Minolta PS-3000 Digital Planetary Scanner
  — Two computers with Pentium 200 MHz CPU, 64 MB RAM, 4 GB HD, 21″ monitor
  — Windows 3.11 OS (required by other software)
  — Minolta Epic 3000 scanner software
  — Adobe Acrobat Capture, Exchange, and Distiller software
  — Image Alchemy software
  — Network interface cards and TCP/IP software for campus network access
- Scanner operator(s), typically student assistants, with training roughly equivalent to that required for interlibrary loan photocopying. Approximately 8 hours of operator labor will be required to process the average 800 pages per day capacity of a single scanning workstation.

- Scanning supervisor, typically a librarian or full-time staff, with training in image quality control, indexing, and cataloging, and in operation of image processing software. Approximately 3 hours of supervisor labor will be required to process 800 scanned pages per day.

Scan-and-Store Process: Scanner Operator

- Retrieve scan request from system
- Retrieve materials from shelves (enough for two hours of scanning)
- Scan materials and enter basic data into system
  — Evaluate size of pages
  — Evaluate grayscale/black and white scan mode
  — Align material
  — Test scan and adjust settings and alignment as necessary
  — Scan article
  — Log changes and additions to author, title, journal, issue, and item data on request form
  — Repeat for remaining requested articles
- Transfer scanned image files to Acrobat conversion workstation
- Retrieve next batch of scan requests from system
- Reshelve scanned materials and retrieve next batch of materials

Scan-and-Store Process: Acrobat Conversion Workstation

- Run Adobe Acrobat Capture to automatically convert sequential scanned image files from single-page TIFF to multi-page Acrobat PDF documents, as they are received from scanner operator
- Retain original TIFF files

Scan-and-Store Process: Scanning Supervisor

- Retrieve request forms for scanned materials
- Open converted PDF files
- Evaluate image quality of converted PDF files
  — Scanned article matches request form citation
  — Completeness, no clipped margins
  — Legibility, especially footnotes and references
  — Minimal skewing
  — Clarity of grayscale or halftone images
  — Appropriate margins, no excessive white space
- Crop fingertips, margin lines, and so on, missed by Epic 3000 scanner software
  — Retrieve TIFF image file
  — Mask unwanted areas
  — Resave TIFF image file

    — Repeat PDF conversion
    — Evaluate image quality of revised PDF file
- Return unacceptable scans to scanner operator for rescan or correction
- Evaluate, correct, and expand entries in request forms
- Forward corrected PDF files to the database
- Delete TIFF image files from conversion workstation

Notification to and Viewing by User of Availability of Scanned Article

Insertion of the article into the database

- The scanning technician types the scan request number into a Web form.
- The system returns a Web form with most of the fields filled in. The technician has an opportunity to correct information from the paging slip before inserting the article into the database.
- The Web form contains a "file upload" button that when selected allows the technician to browse the local hard drive for the article PDF file. This file is automatically uploaded to the server when the form is submitted.
- The system inserts the table of contents information into the database and the PDF file to the Rights Manager system.

Notification/delivery of article to requester

- E-mail to requester with URL of requested article (in first release)
- No notification (in first release)
- Fax to requester an announcement page with the article URL (proposed future enhancement)
- Fax to requester a copy of the article (proposed future enhancement)

APPENDIX F
———————

Technical Justification
for a Digitization Standard for the Consortium

A major premise in the technical underpinnings of the new consortial model is that a relatively inexpensive scanner can be located in the academic libraries of consortium members. After evaluating virtually every scanning device on the market, including some in laboratories under development, we concluded that the 400 dot-per-inch (dpi) scanner from Minolta was fully adequate for the purpose of scanning all the hundreds of chemical sciences journals in which we were interested. Thus, for our consortium, the Minolta 400 dpi scanner was taken to be the digitization standard. The standard that was adopted preserves 100% of the informational content required by our end users.

More formally, the standard for digitization in the consortium is defined as follows:

> The scanner captures 256 levels of gray in a single pass with a density of 400 dots per inch and converts the grayscale image to black and white using threshold and edge-detection algorithms.

We arrived at this standard by considering our fundamental requirements:

- Handle the smallest significant information presented in the source documents of the chemical sciences literature, which is the lowercase *e* in superscript or subscript as occurs in footnotes
- Satisfy both legibility and fidelity to the source document
- Minimize scanning artifacts or "noise" from background
- Operate in the range of preservation scanning
- Be affordable by academic and research libraries

The scanning standard adopted by this project was subjected to tests of footnoted information, and 100% of the occurrences of these characters were captured in both image and character modes and recognized for displaying and searching.

At 400 dpi, the Minolta scanner works in the range of preservation quality scanning as defined by researchers at the Library of Congress (Fleischhauer and Erway 1992).

We were also cautioned about the problems unique to very high resolution scanning in which the scanner produces artifacts or "noise" from imperfections in the paper used. We happily note that we did not encounter this problem in this project because the paper used by publishers of chemical sciences journals is coated.

When more is less: images scanned at 600 dpi require larger file sizes than those scanned at 400 dpi. Thus, 600 dpi is less efficient than 400 dpi. Further, in a series of tests that we conducted, a 600 dpi scanner actually produced an image of effectively lower resolution than 400 dpi. It appears that this loss of information occurs when the scanned image is viewed on a computer screen where there is relatively heavy use of anti-aliasing in the display. When viewed with software that permitted zooming in for looking at details of the scanned image (which is supported by both PDF and TIFF viewers), the 600 dpi anti-aliased image actually had lower resolution than did an image produced from the same source document by the 400 dpi Minolta scanner according to our consortium's digitization standard. With the 600 dpi scanner, the only way for the end user to see the full resolution was to download the image and then print it out. When a side-by-side comparison was made of the soft-copy displayed images, the presentation image quality of 600 dpi was deemed unacceptable by our end users; the 400 dpi image was just right. Thus, our delivery approach is more useful to the scholar who needs to examine fine details on-screen. We conducted some tests on reconstructing the journal page from the scanned image by printing it out on a Xerox DocuTech 6135 (600 dpi). We found that the smallest fonts and fine details of the articles were uniformly excellent. Interestingly, in many of the tests we performed, our faculty colleagues judged the end result by their own "acid test": how the scanned image, when printed out, compared with the image produced by a photocopier. For the consortium standard, they were satisfied with the result and pleased with the improvement in quality that the 400 dpi scanner provided in comparison with conventional photocopying of the journal page.

CHAPTER 17

On-line Books at Columbia
Early Findings on Use, Satisfaction, and Effect

Mary Summerfield and Carol A. Mandel

with Paul Kantor, Consultant

INTRODUCTION

The Online Books Evaluation Project at Columbia University explores the potential for on-line books to become significant resources in academic libraries by analyzing (1) the Columbia community's adoption of and reaction to various on-line books and delivery system features provided by the libraries over the period of the project; (2) the relative life-cycle costs of producing, owning, and using on-line books and their print counterparts; and (3) the implications of intellectual property regulations and traditions of scholarly communications and publishing for the on-line format.

On-line books might enhance the scholarly processes of research, dissemination of findings, teaching, and learning. Alternatively, or in addition, they might enable publishers, libraries, and scholars to reduce the costs of disseminating and using scholarship. For example:

- If the scholarly community were prepared to use some or all categories of books for some or all purposes in an on-line format instead of a print format, publishers, libraries, and bookstores might be able to trim costs as well as enhance access to these books.[1]

- If on-line books made scholars more efficient or effective in their work of research, teaching, and learning so as to enhance revenues or reduce operating costs for their institutions, on-line books might be worth adopting even if they were no less costly than print books.

- If an on-line format became standard, publishers could offer low-cost on-line access to institutions that would not normally have purchased print copies, thus expanding both convenient access to scholarship to faculty and students at those institutions and publishers' revenues from these books.[2]

This paper focuses on user response to on-line books and reports on:[3]

1. the conceptual framework for the project
2. background information on the status of the collection and other relevant project elements, particularly design considerations
3. the methodology for measuring adoption of on-line books by the Columbia community
4. early findings on use of on-line books and other on-line resources
5. early findings on attitudes toward on-line books

CONCEPTUAL FRAMEWORK

The variables representing usage of a system of scholarly communication and research are both effects and causes. Since scholars, the users of the system, are highly intelligent and adaptive, the effect of the system will influence their behavior, establishing a kind of feedback loop. As the diagram in Figure 17.1 shows, there are two key loops. The upper one, shown by the dark arrows, reflects an idealized picture of university administration. In this picture, the features of any system are adjusted so that, when used by faculty and students, they improve institutional effectiveness. This adjustment occurs in the context of continual adaptation on the part of the users of the system, as shown by the lighter colored arrows in the lower feedback loop.

These feedback loops are constrained by the continual change of the environment, which affects the expectations and activities of the users, affects the kind of features that can be built into the system, and affects the very management that is bringing the system into existence. The dotted arrows show this interaction.

Our primary research goal, in relation to users, uses, and impacts, is to understand these relationships, using data gathered by library circulation systems, Internet servers, and surveys and interviews of users themselves.

THE ON-LINE BOOKS COLLECTION

The project began formal activity in January 1995. However, discussions with publishers began in 1993, if not earlier. As noted in the project's Analytical Principles and Design document, "The Online Books Evaluation Project is a component of the developing digital library at Columbia University. As part of its digital library effort, the Columbia University Libraries is acquiring a variety of reference and monographic books in electronic format to be included on the campus network; in most cases, those books will be available only to members of the Columbia community. Some of the books are being purchased; others are being provided on a pilot project basis by publishers who are seeking to understand how the academic community will use online books if they become more widely available in the future."

Interrelationship of Key
Variables or Factors

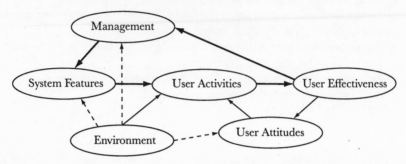

Figure 17.1. Interrelation of Factors Involved in the Use and Impact of On-line Books

Design of the On-line Books Collection

When this project was proposed, the World Wide Web was just emerging, and we expected to develop custom SGML browsers, just as other on-line projects were doing at the time. However, by the time the project was ready to mount books on-line,[4] the Web seemed the best delivery system for maximizing availability of the books to scholars.

Many other on-line projects are providing users with materials in PDF, scanned, or bitmapped format. These formats are effective for journal articles, which are finely indexed through existing sources and which are short and easily printed. However, the greatest potential for added value from on-line books comes with truly digital books. Only this on-line format allows the development of interactive books that take advantage of the current and anticipated capabilities of Web technology, such as the inclusion of sound and video, data files and software for manipulating data, and links to other on-line resources. Perhaps only such enhanced on-line books will offer sufficient advantages over traditional print format that scholars will be willing to substitute them for the print format for some or all of their modes of use and for some or all classes of books.

As of June 1997, the project included 96 on-line texts. The libraries have each book in print form—circulating from the regular collection or from reserves or noncirculating in reference—as well as in one or more on-line formats. Appendix A summarizes the print access modes for all the modern books in the collection.

METHODOLOGY FOR STUDYING USE OF
AND REACTIONS TO VARIOUS BOOK FORMATS

The project's Analytical Principles and Design document lays out the evaluation methodology.[5] Formulated in the first year of the project, this methodology remains the working plan. Here are some of the key measures for documenting use of the on-line books:

- The records of the Columbia computing system provide, for the most part, the use data for the on-line books. For books accessed via the World Wide Web, information on date, time, and duration of session involving an on-line book, user's cohort, location of computer, number of requests, amount of the book requested, and means of accessing the book will be available. These data became available in summer 1997 with the full implementation of the authentication system and related databases.

- Circulation data for each print book in the regular collection provides information on number of times a book circulates, circulation by cohort, duration of circulation, number of holds, and recalls. For most libraries, the data available for reserve books is the same as that for books in the regular collection as the CLIO circulation system is used for both.

- The records of the Columbia computing system provide, for the most part, the use data for the books accessed via CNet, Columbia's original, gopher-based Campus Wide Information System, including the number of sessions and their date and time. These records do not include the duration of the session, the activity during the session, e.g., printing or saving, or anything about the user. Thus, all we can analyze are the patterns of use by time of day, day of week, and over time.

- Until March 15, 1997, for books accessed via CWeb, we knew the use immediately preceding the hit on the book and the day and time of the hit. For data collected through that point, our analysis is constrained to patterns of use by time of day, day of the week, and over time. By manual examination of server data, we counted how many hits a user made on our collection during one session and the nature of those hits.

- Since March 15, 1997, we are able to link user and usage information and conduct a series of analyses involving titles used, number of hits, number of books used, and so on by individual and to group those individuals by department, position, and age. These data do not yet include sessions of use, just the magnitude of overall use during the period. Session-specific data are available starting in fall 1997.

We are using a wide range of tools in trying to understand the factors that influence use of on-line books. Table 17.1 summarizes our complex array of surveys and interviews.

USE OF BOOKS IN ON-LINE COLLECTION

At this point we will report on (1) trends in use of the on-line books; (2) user location and cohort; and (3) use of the on-line books by individuals. Summarized

TABLE 17.1.   Types of Surveys

Population	Method	Contact	Response Rate	Remarks
Users of on-line books	On-line instrument	Passive	Low	
Users of on-line books	On-line post-use survey	Passive	Very low	
Users of paper alternatives	Response slips in books	Passive	Unknown	Levels of use not known
Users of course materials in either form	Interviews distributed in class	Active	High	
Users and nonusers	Library & campus-wide surveys	Active	Moderate	No full active survey of the campus has been done
Discipline-specific potential users	Surveys & interviews	Active	High	Thus far only conducted before books were on-line

NOTE: Passive instruments are ones which the user must elect to encounter. Active instruments are distributed in some way, to the attention of the user. High response rates are in the range of 80–90% completion, with better than 60% usable.

below separately are findings for reference works and nonreference books, e.g., monographs and collections.

Reference Books

Three reference works have been available on-line long enough to have generated substantial usage data.[6] These are *The Concise Columbia Electronic Encyclopedia*, *Columbia Granger's World of Poetry*, and *The Oxford English Dictionary*. Three other titles (*Chaucer Name Dictionary*, *African American Women*, *Native American Women*) have been on-line only since early 1997, so usage data are very short-term for these titles. All three are accessible both through CNet and CWeb.

Most available reference books are used more heavily on-line than in print.
Of the six reference works in the collection, only *The Oxford English Dictionary* receives sizable use in its print form in the Columbia libraries. At most a handful of scholars use the library copies of the others each month. As the accompanying tables and figure show, each of these books receives much more use on-line. On-line availability seems to increase awareness of these resources as well as make access more convenient.

Early on-line reference books have experienced falling usage over time, substitution of use of a new delivery system for an old one, or a smaller rate of growth of use than might be expected given the explosion in access to and use of on-line resources in general.

In the early to mid-1990s, novelty may have brought curious scholars to the on-line format somewhat without concern for design, the utility of the delivery system, or the qualities of the books. With enhancement in delivery systems and expansion in the number of on-line books, being on-line is no longer a guarantee that a book will attract users. As access to the Web spreads, new graphical Web delivery systems are offering superior performance that is increasingly likely to draw scholars away from these early, text-based systems. In addition, as more competing resources come on-line and provide information that serves the immediate needs of a user better or offer a more attractive, user-friendly format, scholars are less likely to find or to choose to use any single resource.

The Oxford English Dictionary is the most heavily used reference work in the collection. Its CNet format offers good analytic functionality but it is difficult to use. The CWeb format is attractive and easy to use, but its functionality is limited to looking up a definition or browsing the contents.[7]

OED CNet usage dropped 59% from fourth quarter 1994 (2,856 sessions) to first quarter 1997 (1,167 sessions). *OED* CWeb use increased by 27% from fall semester 1996 (1,825 hits) to spring semester 1997 (2,326 hits). *The OED* had 173 unique users in the period from March 15 to May 31, 1997, with an average of 2.8 hits per user.

The Concise Columbia Electronic Encyclopedia remains on the text-based platform CNet. As Figure 17.2 shows, usage declined 84% over the past three years, from 1,551 sessions in April 1994 to 250 sessions in April 1997. Usage declined most in the 1996–97 academic year; 7,861 sessions were registered from September 1995 to May 1996 and 2,941 sessions (63% fewer) from September 1996 to May 1997.

Columbia now provides CWeb access to the *Encyclopedia Britannica* (directly from the publisher's server); many scholars may be using this resource instead of the *Concise Encyclopedia*. Recently the Columbia community has registered about 5,000 textual hits a month on the *Encyclopedia Britannica*.

Columbia Granger's World of Poetry is available on both CNet and CWeb. The CNet version is a Lynx, nongraphical Web formulation of the CWeb version. This resource, which became available to the community in on-line form in October 1994, locates a poem in an anthology by author, subject, title, first line, or keywords in its title or first line. In addition, it provides easy access to the 10,000 most often anthologized poems. In first quarter 1995, CNet sessions totaled 718; in first quarter 1997, they totaled 90 (or about one a day). CWeb hits totaled about 700 in the first quarter of 1997. Thus, even though it has declined, total usage of *Granger's* is still considerable.

Garland's *Chaucer Name Dictionary* was added to the CWeb collection at the end of 1996. *Native American Women* was added in January 1997, and *African American Women* went on-line in February 1997. Their early usage on CWeb is shown in Table 17.2.

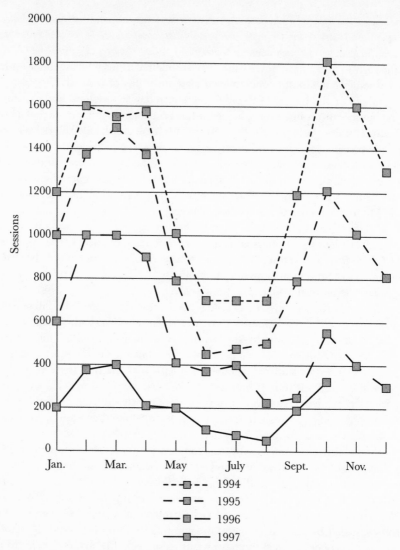

Figure 17.2. *Concise Columbia Electronic Encyclopedia* Sessions, 1994–1997: CNet

Nonreference Books

The Online Books Evaluation Project includes two types of nonreference books: *Past Masters*, 54 classical texts in social thought; and modern monographs and collections from Columbia University Press, Oxford University Press, and Simon and Schuster Higher Education. Most of these books came on-line during the 1996–97 academic year.

TABLE 17.2.   Use of Garland Reference Books on CWeb, January–May 1997

Title	*Jan.–May 1997*	*3/15–5/31/1997*	
	CWeb Hits	Unique Users	Mean Hits/ Unique User
Chaucer Name Dictionary	269	9	3.8
Native American Women	124	9	4.3
African American Women	230	6	5.5

On-line scholarly monographs are available to and used by more people than their print counterparts in the library collection.

Once a print book is in circulation, it can be unavailable to other scholars for hours (the reserve collection) or weeks or months (the regular collection). An on-line book is always available to any authorized user who has access to a computer with an Internet connection and a graphical Web browser.

Table 17.3 tracks usage of the contemporary nonreference books in the on-line collection for the last part of the spring semester 1997 and in the print circulation of these titles for the first six months of 1997. Fourteen of these books had no on-line use during this 2.5-month measurement period; 12 had no print circulations during their 6-month measurement period. In total, the on-line versions had 122 users while the print versions had 75 users. Looking at only the on-line books that circulated in print form, we find 122 on-line users and 45 print circulations, or that there were nearly three times as many on-line users as circulations. These data suggest that, compared for an equal period, these books will have many more users in on-line form than in print form.[8]

An on-line book may attract scholars who would not have seen it otherwise.

Once a group within the community becomes aware of the on-line books, they are likely to review books in the collection that seem related to their interests—at least while the collection is small. For example, half of the use of *Autonomous Agents: From Self Control to Autonomy* was from social work host computers. This title might seem related to social work issues even though it is not a social work book or part of the collection of the Social Work Library.

The fifth and sixth most used books—*Self Expressions: Mind, Morals, and the Meaning of Life* and *Bangs, Crunches, Whimpers, and Shrieks*—are both philosophy titles.

- *Self Expressions* is listed in the Current Social Science Web page along with the social work titles. Five of its seven users were from the School of Social Work, one from the Center for Neurobiology and Behavior, and one from Electrical Engineering.

TABLE 17.3. On-line and Print Circulation for Contemporary On-line Nonreference Books

Title	Online Activity: 3/15–5/31/97			Print Circulation Jan.–June/97	On-line Users/Circulation
	Users	Hits	Mean Hits/User		
Task Strategies: An Empirical Approach . . .	30	288	9.6	4	7.5
Mutual Aid Groups, Vulnerable Populations, & the Life Cycle	18	138	7.7	12	1.5
Supervision in Social Work	8	33	4.1	12	0.7
Philosophical Foundations of Social Work	8	21	2.6	0	NC
Self Expressions: Mind, Morals . . .	7	21	3.0	3	2.3
Bangs, Crunches, Whimpers, & Shrieks	7	21	3.0	0	NC
Handbook of Gerontological Services	6	31	5.2	1	6.0
Turning Promises into Performance	6	31	5.2	1	6.0
Qualitative Research in Social Work	6	10	1.7	1	6.0
Gender in International Relations	4	6	1.5	3	1.3
Other Minds	4	34	8.5	2	2.0
Seismosaurus	4	8	2.0	0	NC
Nietzsche's System	3	6	2.0	5	0.6
The Logic of Reliable Inquiry	3	7	2.3	0	NC
Sedimentographica	2	6	3.0	1	2.0
Free Public Reason	2	6	3.0	0	NC
Philosophy of Mathematics & Mathematical Practice in the 17th Century	2	3	1.5	0	NC
Real Rights	2	3	1.5	0	NC
Hemmed In	0	0	0	13	0

Jordan's Inter-Arab Relations					
Ozone Discourses	0	0	0	8	0
Children's Literature & Critical Theory	0	0	0	3	0
Freedom and Moral Sentiment	0	0	0	1	
Autonomous Agents	0	0	0	1	0
Novel & Globalization of Culture	0	0	0	1	0
Morality, Normativity & Society	0	0	0	1	0
Managing Indonesia	0	0	0	1	0
Littery Man	0	0	0	0	NC
Law & Truth	0	0	0	0	NC
Poetics of Fascism	0	0	0	0	NC
Majestic Indolence	0	0	0	0	NC
International Politics	0	0	0	0	NC
Total	122	673	5.5	75	1.6

NOTE: Titles in bold were on reserve for one or more courses in spring 1997. One book has been omitted from the list as it only went on-line in April 1997. NC: total or change is not calculable.

- *Bangs, Crunches, Whimpers, and Shrieks* is listed under Physics in the Current Science Web page. Two of its seven users were from the Physics department, another two from unidentified departments, and one each from Electrical Engineering, Engineering, and General Studies.

It is not clear whether scholars' productivity or work quality will be enhanced by such serendipity. The important concept of collation is transformed, in the networked environment, to a diversity of finding and navigational systems. As the on-line collection expands, browsing will require the focused use of on-line search tools rather than use of project-oriented Web pages. However, the Web's search systems may uncover a book's relevance to a scholar's work when the library catalog or browsing the library or bookstore shelves would not have done so. This new ability to identify relevant books should improve scholars' research and teaching.

Scholars use some on-line books relatively little.
As Table 17.3 shows, use of on-line books is not evenly balanced among titles. Instead it is driven by course demands or other interest in a book. The initial use of the 54 on-line *Past Masters* classic texts in social thought confirms this finding. In academic year 1996–97, these texts registered a total of about 2,460 hits from the Columbia scholarly community. However, 1,692 (69%) of these hits were on only eight (15%) of the titles, for an average total of 212 hits each, or 24 hits each per month. The other 46 texts averaged about 17 hits each over this period, or about two hits each per month.[9]

Patterns of usage may be expected to change over time as various texts are used in courses or by researchers and as the Columbia community becomes more aware of the on-line collections. In general, it is likely that nonreference books that are being used in courses, but which the students need not own, will be in greater demand on-line than will books that students must own or books that are of interest to only a small set of scholars.

The data to date suggest that to the extent that there are meaningful costs to creating on-line books and to maintaining them as part of a collection, publishing and library planners must select items for the on-line collection carefully. The decision rules will vary depending on what type of organization is taking on the risks of providing the access to the on-line books.

Some scholars, especially students with a reading assignment that is in the on-line collection, are looking at on-line books in some depth, suggesting that they find value in this means of access.
As Table 17.3 shows, the on-line books averaged 5.5 hits per unique user, suggesting that some users are looking at several elements of the book or at some elements repeatedly.[10] In fall 1996, three social work books were most intensively used because they were assigned reading for courses. We analyzed the server statistics through the end of 1996 for these books in an effort to learn how deeply the books

were used—to what extent use sessions included book chapters, the search engine, the pagination feature, and so on.

Table 17.4 shows that relatively few sessions (7%–24%) involved someone going only to the Title Page/Table of Contents file for a book. Many sessions (28%–59%) involved use of more than one chapter of the book; sessions averaged 1.4 to 3.5 hits on chapters, depending on the book used. Some users would seem to be repeat users who had set up a bookmark for a chapter in the book or had made a note of the URL because some sessions (9%–17%) did not include a hit on the Table of Contents/Title Page.

Table 17.5, illustrating the distribution of hits on the on-line books collection per unique user over the last part of the spring 1997 semester, indicates that while many users are making quite cursory use of the on-line books, more are looking at multiple files (e.g., reference entry, chapter) in the collection. As Table 17.6 shows, the distribution of unique titles viewed by these users over this period indicates that most users come to the collection to look at a single book. The greatest number of books used by a single person was seven (by two persons).

Not surprisingly, there is a certain correlation between number of hits and number of titles used. Those users with only one hit could only have looked at one title (42% of those using one book). The range of hits among those who used only one book is wide—20 (9%) had more than 10 hits. Six users had more than 25 hits; two of them looked at only one book, one each at two and three books, and two at seven books. These statistics indicate some significant use of the collection as measured by average number of hits per title used.

However, hits on several titles need not indicate heavy use of the on-line books collection. The individual who looked at five books had a total of only six to ten hits, as did four of the seven people who looked at four books (one to two hits each). The person who looked at six books had 11 to 15 hits in total (an average of about two hits per book).

Table 17.7 shows that graduate students tended to have more hits, and undergraduates and faculty, fewer hits.

The preceding discussion highlights the current data on usage by individuals. Using newer data on sessions, we will be able to derive valuable information on user behavior—not only number of books used and hits on those books but parts of the book used and repeat usership. We will begin to see revealed preference in user behavior and will be less reliant on responses to questionnaires. [11]

Data for the last half of the spring 1997 semester suggest that when a social work book available in both print and on-line formats was used in a course, the share of students using the on-line version was at most one-quarter.

Table 17.3 shows that the four most used nonreference books were all in the field of social work. Almost 91% of the users of these books were from the School of Social Work; they accounted for 98% of the hits on those books. The vast majority of these users (56 of 64) were graduate students. With the exception of the

TABLE 17.4. Session Analysis for Social Work Books, Fall 1996

	Handbook of Gerontological Services	Supervision in Social Work	Task Strategies
No. chapters in book	10	10	11
Sessions	41	46	58
Hits	128	128	284
Mean hits/session	3.1	2.8	4.9
Sessions w/TOC hit only	4 (10%)	11 (24%)	4 (7%)
Sessions w/no TOC hits	7 (17%)	7 (15%)	5 (9%)
Sessions w/ > 1 chapter hits	15 (37%)	13 (28%)	34 (59%)

Total Hits On	Number	Average/ Session	Number	Average/ Session	Number	Average/ Session
Table of contents	38	.9	47	1.0	60	1.0
Chapters	74	1.8	63	1.4	202	3.5
Page locator	5	.1	3	.1	7	.1
Search	5	.1	10	.2	4	.1
Bibliographic page	5	.1	4	.1	9	.2
Author biography	1	*	1	*	2	*

*Less than .05.

TABLE 17.5. Distribution of Hits per Unique User, March 15–May 31, 1997

Total Number of Hits	% of Total Users
1	34%
2	16%
3	8%
4	8%
5	4%
6–10	16%
11–15	5%
16–20	5%
21–25	2%
>25	2%

NOTE: Detail may not sum to 100% due to rounding.

TABLE 17.6.   Distribution of Unique Titles Viewed per User,
March 15–May 31, 1997

Number of Titles Viewed	Number of Users	% of Total Users
1	225	80%
2	32	11%
3	11	4%
4	8	3%
5	1	*
6	1	*
7	2	1%
Total	280	100%

NOTE: Detail may not sum to total due to rounding.
*Less than 0.5%.

TABLE 17.7.   Hits per Unique User by Academic Cohort,
March 15–May 31, 1997

Academic Cohort	N =	1 Hit	2–3 Hits	4–5 Hits	6–10 Hits	11–20 Hits	>20 Hits
Undergraduate	114	40%	28%	13%	14%	4%	1%
Graduate student	66	18%	14%	9%	20%	27%	12%
Professional student	9	33%	22%	22%	11%	0%	11%
Faculty	12	42%	25%	17%	8%	8%	0%

most used book, *Task Strategies,* these texts were on reserve for social work courses during the spring 1997 semester.

- Three sections, with a total of about 70 students, used *Supervision in Social Work* as a key text. Thus, potentially, if all seven graduate students who used this book were participants in these courses, about 10% of the most likely student user group actually used this book on-line during this period.[12]

- Three other course sections, again with about 70 students in total, used *Mutual Aid Groups.* This book was a major reading; in fact, one of its authors taught two of the sections in which it was used. Sixteen graduate students used this title for a potential penetration of about 23%.

- *Philosophical Foundations of Social Work* (as well as *Qualitative Research in Social Work*) was on reserve for a doctoral seminar that had an enrollment of 11 students. The instructor reported that this book was a major text in the course that students would have bought traditionally. She did not know how many of her students used the on-line version. If all eight users—seven graduate students and the one professional student—were class members, that suggests a substantial penetration for that small class. However, it is likely that some of these users were not enrolled in that course.

Location of Use of On-line Books

Scholars are not using on-line books from off-campus locations to the extent expected.
One of the key potential advantages to on-line books is their instant availability to scholars at any location at which they have access to a computer with a modem and a graphical Web browser. This benefit might well lead to substantial use of the on-line books from locations other than the Columbia campus. So far we are seeing only modest use of the books from off-campus.

From May 1996 to March 1997, 11% of the hits on the Columbia University Press nonreference books were dial-up connections from off-campus. Looking at the use of the social work titles, we find that computers in the School of Social Work were responsible for the following shares of hits on the social work titles:

Handbook of Gerontological Services	53%
Mutual Aid Groups, Vulnerable Populations	76%
Philosophical Foundations of Social Work	39%
Qualitative Research in Social Work	69%
Supervision in Social Work	48%
Task Strategies: An Empirical Approach	68%

Closer analysis of the usage data finds substantial use from the computer lab in the School of Social Work as well as from faculty computers. This finding suggests that many of the graduate students, most of whom do not live on or near campus, may not have Web access in their homes and, hence, are not equipped at this point in time to take full advantage of the on-line books.[13] Students who use the on-line books at the School of Social Work, however, avoid walking the several blocks to the social work library, worrying about the library's hours, or encountering non-availability of the book in its print form. In our interviews, scholars report that key constraining factors to using the on-line books and other Web resources from home are the expense of dialing in to campus or maintaining an Internet account, the lack of sufficiently powerful home computers and Web software, the frequency of busy signals on the dial-up lines, and the slowness of standard modems.

Students residing on campus may have Ethernet connections to the campus network— providing both speedy and virtually free access to the on-line collection.
At the end of the 1996–97 academic year, approximately 2,300 students were registered for residence hall network connections.[14] With the exception of the three Garland reference books, a very small share of reference collection use occurs on

computers in the libraries; the Columbia community is taking advantage of the out-of-library access to these resources. For example, 42% of the hits on *The Oxford English Dictionary* in the ten months following May 1996 were from residence hall network connections.

However, these undergraduates have shown little interest in the nonreference books on-line. Residence hall connections accounted for only 1% of the use of the Columbia University Press titles in social work, earth and environmental science, and international relations and 3% of the use of the Oxford University Press titles in literary criticism and philosophy from May 1996 to May 1997. These small shares are not surprising given that few of these books are aimed at the under-graduate audience. The undergraduates' use of the *Past Masters* classical texts in social thought from Ethernet connections in their rooms is somewhat higher—654 hits, or almost 13% of the total use of those texts from May 1996 to March 1997.

Scholars' Access to On-line Resources

We theorize that scholars with greater perceived access to networked computers and with greater familiarity with on-line resources are more likely first to sample on-line books and later to adopt them for regular use (assuming that books of interest are available on-line). All project questionnaires ask about both these factors. The access question is, "Is there a computer (in the library or elsewhere) attached to the campus network (directly or by modem) that you can use whenever you want?" The question about use of on-line resources asks, "On average this semester, how many hours per week do you spend in on-line activities (Email, Listservs & Newsgroups, CLIO Plus, Text, Image or Numeric Data Sources, Other WWWeb Uses)?" In some cases, the question asks for a single value; in others, it has five spaces in which respondents are asked to enter their hours for each of these activities.

Over 80% of Columbia library users report adequate access to a networked computer.
In the Columbia Libraries annual survey of on-site users in March 1997, 2,367 individuals responded to this question on access to networked computers. Almost 81% answered "Yes." Masters students were least likely to respond positively (67%) while the other scholarly cohorts—faculty, doctoral students, and undergraduate students—ranged from 85% to 87%. Users of science libraries were generally more likely to respond affirmatively.

Columbia library users report an average of about six hours a week in on-line activities with no significant difference across scholarly cohorts.
Even many of the survey respondents who did not claim easy access to a networked computer reported spending considerable time in on-line activities—22% spent four to six hours a week and 23% spent more than six hours a week.

Scholars' Choice among Book Formats

Scholars' patterns of using books in their various formats and their reactions to on-line books are being tracked through a variety of surveys, individual interviews, and focus groups (see Table 17.1).

One survey involves visiting a class session for which an assigned reading was in an on-line book. A question asks which format(s) of the book the student used for this assignment. Responses were distributed as shown in Table 17.8.

In 70% of the responses for fall 1996, as seen in Table 17.8, the student had used his or her own copy of the text. The next most common method was to use a friend's copy (14%). The shares for those two modes are insignificantly different in spring 1997. We are obtaining course syllabi from instructors so that, in the future, we can analyze these responses based on what portion of the book is being used in a course and whether students are expected to purchase their own copies.

Preferences for Studying Class Reading

We obtained far fewer responses (119 in fall 1996 and 88 in spring 1997) as to the preferred mode of studying. Table 17.9 shows that in both semesters, about two-thirds of respondents reported a preference for reading their own copy.

Scholars' Reactions to Book Formats and Characteristics

Scholars reporting easy access to a networked computer spend more time on-line and are more likely to prefer to use one of the forms of the on-line book.

In our in-class surveys in spring 1997, students claiming easy access to a networked computer (74% of the 209 respondents) were greater users of on-line resources overall. Only 27% of students claiming easy access reported as few as one to two hours on-line a week, while 53% of those lacking easy access had this low level of on-line activity. About 31% of the former group spent six or more hours a week on-line while 18% of the latter group did.

About 26% of the easy access group gave some form of on-line book (reading directly on-line, printout of text, or download of text and reading away from the Web) as their preferred method of reading an assignment for which an on-line version was available, while only 13% of the students lacking easy access did so.

This combination of responses suggests that, over time as members of the scholarly community obtain greater access to computers linked to the Web, on-line books will achieve greater acceptance.

Students report that they particularly value easy access to the texts that are assigned for class and an ability to underline and annotate those texts.

Students seek the ability to print out all or parts of the on-line texts that they use for their courses, again indicating their desire to have the paper copy to use in their

TABLE 17.8. Methods of Reading This Assignment

	Fall 1996		Spring 1997	
	Count	%	Count	%
Used own copy	269	70%	141	73%
Used friend's copy	54	14%	20	10%
Used library copy	33	8%	17	9%
Used photocopy	11	3%	17	9%
Read it directly from CWeb	0	0%	0	0%
Obtained JAKE printout of text[a]	10	3%	16	8%
Obtained printout using non-JAKE printer	4	1%	4	2%
Downloaded on-line text to disk & read away from CWeb	5	1%	1	*
Total	386	100%	216	111%

NOTE: % is share of responses, not cases, for individual methods of reading this assignment.
*Less than 0.5%.
[a]JAKE is the networked laser printer system maintained by AcIS. Undergraduates and social work students can print 100 pages a week at no charge.

TABLE 17.9. Preferred Method of Reading This Assignment

	Fall 1996		Spring 1997	
	Count	% of Cases	Count	% of Cases
Own copy	83	67%	56	64%
Friend's copy	9	8%	6	7%
Library copy	10	8%	6	7%
Photocopy	7	6%	8	9%
Directly from CWeb	2	2%	7	8%
JAKE printout of text	7	6%	6	7%
Printout using non-JAKE printer	3	2%	5	6%
Download of on-line text to disk to be read away from CWeb	3	2%	1	1%
Total responses	124	101%	95	109%
Total cases responding	119		88	

studying. Computer access to a needed text is not equivalent to having a paper copy (whole book or assigned portion) in one's backpack, available at any time and at any place (see Table 17.10).

The cross-tabulation of preferred method of use and reasons for that preference produces logically consistent results. For example, all the respondents who gave "Printout using non-JAKE printer" or "Download of on-line text to disk to be read away from CWeb" as their preferred method gave "Less costly" as one of their reasons, while few of those students who preferred their own copy gave that reason.

If the effective choice for completing a required reading is between borrowing a book from the library, probably on a very short-term basis from reserves, and accessing the book on-line, the student is facing a parallel situation of needing to photocopy or print out the reading to obtain portable, annotative media.[15] However, the on-line book's advantages are that it will never be checked out when the student wants to use it and that it will be accessible from a computer anywhere in the world at any time (as long as that computer has an Internet connection and a graphical Web browser).

In surveys and interviews, scholars indicate that they value the ability to do searches, to browse, and to quickly look up information in an on-line book.
They also like the ability to clip bits of the text and put them in an electronic research notes file. Willingness to browse and to read on-line for extended periods varies from person to person, but it does not seem to be widespread at this time.

Some scholars perceive gains in the productivity and quality of their work in using on-line books, particularly reference books.
Two key questions asked on all our questionnaires, other than those distributed in class, seek to determine the effect of on-line books on scholarly work:

1. In doing the type of work for which you used this book, do paper books or on-line books help you be *more productive*?
2. Do you find that you are able to do work of *higher quality* when you use paper books or on-line books?

The questionnaire offers a range of seven responses from "Much greater productivity (quality) with paper" through "No difference" to "Much greater productivity (quality) with on-line" plus "Cannot say."

As Table 17.11 shows, 52% of *OED* users felt that they were as productive or more productive using the on-line *OED*, while 39% of the users of the other on-line books felt that they are as productive or more productive using the on-line format. These responses are somewhat puzzling because the reference book most used on-line is *The OED*, suggesting that scholars do value it, and the CWeb version of the on-line *OED* provides as much if not more utility than does the print version (with the exception of being able to view neighboring entries at a

TABLE 17.10.   Reasons for Preferred Method

| | Fall 1996 | | Spring 1997 | |
Reasons for Preference	Count	%	Count	%
Always available	199	72%	108	74%
Easy to annotate	135	49%	57	39%
Easy to read	104	38%	70	48%
Less costly	60	22%	33	23%
Easy to search for words	30	11%	15	10%
Other reasons	25	9%	16	11%
Easy to copy	21	8%	20	14%
Easy to get to	0	0%	0	0%
Total responses	574	209%	319	219%
Total cases responding	276		146	

SOURCE: In-Class Survey.
NOTE: Respondents could give more than one reason for their preference.

TABLE 17.11.   CWeb On-line Survey: Productivity & Work Quality
by Book & Format, September 1996–June 1997

Response	OED (N = 64)	All Other Books (N = 21)
Productivity by Book Type		
Cannot say	12%	10%
Paper much greater	16%	24%
Paper greater	8%	14%
Paper somewhat greater	12%	14%
No difference	2%	19%
On-line somewhat greater	17%	5%
On-line greater	17%	5%
On-line much greater	16%	10%
Work Quality by Book Type		
Cannot say	16%	5%
Paper much greater	16%	24%
Paper greater	6%	14%
Paper somewhat greater	16%	14%
No difference	31%	29%
On-line somewhat greater	2%	0%
On-line greater	8%	0%
On-line much greater	6%	14%

glance). Thus, one might expect the productivity rating for the on-line *OED* to be higher.

The distribution of responses to the quality of work question supports the print format in general, although 47% of *OED* users and 43% of the users of all the other books felt that quality was as good or better with on-line books.

Table 17.12 shows considerable correlation in the responses to these two questions—those who supported the paper version for productivity tended to support it for quality as well.

In the last part of the spring 1997 semester, 52% of the on-line book users who went to the on-line survey responded to it, but only 15% of users chose to click on the button taking them to the survey.

Designing an on-line survey that is available to the reader without overt action might enhance the response rate significantly. We are working on doing that using HTML frames on the on-line books. We are also experimenting with other methods of reaching the users of the on-line books, e.g., registration of users that will bring e-mail messages about new books in their field while also enabling us to query them about their reactions to on-line books.

CONCLUSIONS

These preliminary results of the Online Book Evaluation Project suggest that, at this early point in its development, the on-line format is finding a place in the work patterns of scholars who have had an opportunity to try it.

Interviews and focus groups substantiate the findings from the server data and surveys. Together they suggest the following about scholars' reactions to the on-line format:

- It is a convenient way to access information in reference books and potentially to do textual analyses in individual books or whole databases like the *OED*.

- Using a search function, one can quickly determine if a book or set of books addresses a topic of interest and warrants further investigation.

- It is an easy way to browse through a book to determine whether it is worth deeper exploration or whether only a small section is pertinent to one's work. If the latter is the case, it is as easy to print out that small section of the on-line book as it is to take the typical next step of photocopying that section of the paper book.

- A scholar who wants to read and annotate only a modest section of a book, say a chapter or an essay for a course assignment, will find that accessing and printing out the section from the on-line book can be quicker than doing the equivalent with a library copy of the paper book.

TABLE 17.12.   CWeb On-line Survey: Quality & Productivity,
September 1996–June 1997

Productivity	Quality of Work			
	Cannot say	Better paper	No difference	Better on-line
Cannot say	8	0	2	0
Better paper	3	27	5	1
No difference	0	1	4	0
Better on-line	0	9	15	12

- Ready access from any location at any hour and not worrying about whether the book sought is on the library shelf are valued features of the on-line format.

On the other hand, if scholars want to read much or all of a book, they are likely to prefer the traditional format. If the book is core to their research or to a course, scholars are likely to prefer to own a copy. If they cannot afford such a copy, if the book is of more passing interest, or if they cannot obtain a print copy, scholars would typically prefer to retain a library copy for the duration of their interest in the book. If they cannot do so, say because the book is on reserve, scholars must decide among their options, e.g., buying their own copy or using an on-line copy, and decide which option is next preferred.

Over the duration of this project, we will continue to add books to the on-line collection and to pursue our explorations of scholars' reactions to this format. We will look for trends in the perceived accessibility of on-line books and in the desirability of this format for various uses. We will seek to measure the frequency with which scholars read such substantial portions of books borrowed from libraries that they will continue to seek library access to paper copies. In a related effort, we will assess the extent to which libraries now satisfy scholars' desires for access to such copies. If a library did not have a book in its collection in print format but did offer on-line access, a scholar would face a different trade-off between the two formats.

At the same time we will pursue our analyses of the cost and intellectual property issues involved in scholarly communication in an effort to determine whether the on-line book format can contribute to the perpetuation of research and learning and to the dissemination and preservation of knowledge.

NOTES

1. The book could be used entirely in an on-line format or scholars could choose to acquire a print version of all or part of the book once they had browsed the on-line version. Alternatively, at least at some point in time and for some forms of books such as textbooks, an electronic format such as a CD-ROM might be better—for technical, cost, or market

reasons—than either the on-line or the print format. Malcolm Getz addressed some of the format issues well in chapter 6.

2. In effect, funds that would have been spent on interlibrary loan activities, i.e., staff and mailing costs, would be redirected to the producers of the scholarly knowledge, thus supporting the production and dissemination of such scholarship.

3. Details on early project activities and findings are available in Summerfield, Mandel, and Kantor, *Online Books at Columbia—Measurement and Early Results on Use, Satisfaction, and Effect: Interim Report of The Andrew W. Mellon Foundation–Funded Columbia University Online Books Evaluation Project,* July 1997. This report is available at *http://www.arl.org/scomm/scat/summerfield.ind.html.* Background information on project design and collection issues is provided in the project's Analytical Principles and Design document of December 1995 and in its Annual Report of February 1997. Both are available at *http://www.columbia.edu/dlc/olb/.*

4. A few reference books were already on-line on a text-based campuswide information system.

5. As noted earlier, this document is included on the Web page for the project. Questionnaires and other research methodologies have been fine-tuned after pretests and early use, but the general concepts remain in place.

6. For Tables 17.2–17.7, Web data exclude hits by project staff. These hits were excluded because they can be substantial in number, as resources are in design phases, and do not reflect the scholarly use that we are studying.

7. Columbia's Academic Information Systems designed a Web version of the *OED* that has various analytical capabilities, but that version requires more server resources than we can devote to this single work.

8. Clearly, these measures are not absolutely equivalent. Scholars can access and use books from the regular collection without checking them out. (However, to use a book in the reserve collection, a scholar must check it out.)

9. This type of skewed distribution, or Bradford law, is typical of use of all types of library collections.

10. Each on-line book is comprised of several Web files—one for the table of contents, one for each chapter, one for the index, and so on.

11. For use data to show revealed preference, the collection must contain books that would repeatedly draw users to the collection—either books that users want to look at often or an assortment of books that pulls scholars to the collection for a variety of purposes.

12. Other students in these courses may have used the book earlier in the semester. Data for the fall 1997 semester will be complete.

13. The School of Social Work is strictly a graduate school. Many of its students have residences in New York before they begin studying at Columbia. Virtually all are involved in various internships that take them away from the campus. In fact, they are likely to be on campus for only two or three days a week. Another group of students take most of their courses at another campus about 20 miles away. All these factors led to an expectation that this cohort would particularly value on-line books and the ability to use them away from campus.

14. In January 1998, that count had grown to 2,700. By May 1998, it is likely to be at about 3,000. The residence hall network covers 15 buildings and has a total of 4,500 ports.

15. Software allowing annotation of an electronic document is available, but few people are aware of it. The project will seek to bring such software to the Columbia community as feasible.

Publisher/Title	Author	Subject	Print Status	Month Public
Columbia University Press				
Great Paleozoic Crisis	Erwin	Earth Science	Circulating	6/97
Seismosaurus: The Earth Shaker	Gillette	Earth Science	Circulating	10/96
Invasions of the Land	Gordon	Earth Science	Circulating	6/97
Folding of Viscous Layers[a]	Johnson	Earth Science	Circulating	
Dinosaur Tracks & Other Fossil Footprints[a]	Lockley	Earth Science	Circulating	
Sedimentographica: Photographic Atlas	Ricci-Lucchi	Earth Science	Circulating	1/97
Development of Biological Systematics[a]	Stevens	Earth Science	Circulating	
Consuming Subjects[a]	Kowaleski	Economic History	Circulating	
Jordan's Inter-Arab Relations	Brand	Internat'l Relations	Reserves	3/97
Managing Indonesia	Bresnan	Internat'l Relations	Reserves	3/97
Logic of Anarchy[a]	Buzan	Internat'l Relations	Reserves	
Hemmed In: Responses to Africa's . . .	Callaghy	Internat'l Relations	Reserves	3/97
China's Road to the Korean War[a]	Chen	Internat'l Relations	Circulating	
Culture of National Security[a]	Katzenstein	Internat'l Relations	Reserves	
International Relations Theory & the End of the Cold War[a]	Lebow	Internat'l Relations	Circulating	
The Cold War on the Periphery[a]	McMahon	Internat'l Relations	Circulating	
Losing Control: Sovereignty . . .[a]	Sassen	Internat'l Relations	Circulating	
Gender In International Relations	Tickner	Internat'l Relations	Reserves Circulating	11/96
The Inhuman Race[a]	Cassuto	Literary Criticism	Circulating	
Rethinking Class: Literary Studies . . .[a]	Dimock	Literary Criticism	Circulating	
The Blue-Eyed Tarokaja[a]	Keene	Literary Criticism	Circulating	
Ecological Literary Criticism[a]	Kroeber	Literary Criticism	Circulating	
Parables of Possibility[a]	Martin	Literary Criticism	Circulating	
The Text and the Voice[a]	Portelli	Literary Criticism	Circulating	
At Emerson's Tomb[a]	Rowe	Literary Criticism	Circulating	
Extraordinary Bodies: Figuring Physical . . . [a]	Thomson	Literary Criticism	Circulating	
What Else But Love? The Ordeal of Race . . .[a]	Weinstein	Literary Criticism	Circulating	
Columbia Granger's Index to Poetry	Granger	Poetry	Ref. Desk	10/94

Publisher/Title	Author	Subject	Print Status	Month Public
Ozone Discourses	Liftin	Political Science	Reserves	1/97
Concise Columbia Electronic Encyclopedia		Reference	Ref. Desk	3/91
Hierarchy Theory[a]	Ahl	Science	Circulating	
Refiguring Life: Metaphors of 20th Century . . .[a]	Keller	Science	Circulating	
The Molecular Biology of Gaia[a]	Williams	Science	Circulating	
Sampling the Green World[a]	Stuessy	Science	Circulating	
The Illusion of Love[a]	Celani	Social Work	Circulating	
Mutual Aid Groups, Vulnerable Populations, & the Life Cycle	Gitterman	Social Work	Reserves	11/96
Supervision in Social Work	Kadushin	Social Work	Reserves	9/96
Eating Disorders: New Directions[a]	Kinoy	Social Work	Circulating	
From Father's Property to Children's Rights[a]	Mason	Social Work	Circulating	
Handbook of Gerontological Services	Monk	Social Work	Reserves	9/96
Turning Promises Into Performance	Nathan	Social Work	Circulating	9/96
Philosophical Foundations of Social Work	Reamer	Social Work	Reserves Circulating	9/96
Task Strategies: An Empirical Approach	Reid	Social Work	Reserves	9/96
Experiencing HIV[a]	Sears	Social Work	Circulating	
Qualitative Research In Social Work	Sherman	Social Work	Reserves	1/97
The Empowerment Tradition in America[a]	Simon	Social Work	Circulating	

Garland Publishing

Native American Women	Bataille	Biography	Reference	1/97
African American Women	Salem	Biography	Reference	1/97
Chaucer Name Dictionary	de Weever	English Literature	Reference	12/96

Oxford University Press

Oxford English Dictionary		Language	Reference	9/96
Postcards from the Trenches: . . .[b]	Booth	Literary Criticism	Circulating	
The Erotics of Talk[b]	Kaplan	Literary Criticism	Circulating	

Publisher/Title	Author	Subject	Print Status	Month Public
"Littery Man": Mark Twain . . .	Lowrey	Literary Criticism	Circulating	11/96
Children's Literature & Critical Theory	May	Literary Criticism	Circulating	11/96
Poetics of Fascism	Morrison	Literary Criticism	Circulating	10/96
Novel & Globalization of Culture	Moses	Literary Criticism	Circulating	11/96
Modernism & the Theater of Censorship	Parkes	Literary Criticism	Circulating	6/97
Romances of the Republic[b]	Samuels	Literary Criticism	Circulating	
Majestic Indolence: English Romantic Poetry . . .	Spiegelman	Literary Criticism	Circulating	1/97
Making Mortal Choices: . . . Moral Casuistry[b]	Bedau	Philosophy	Circulating	
Morality, Normativity, & Society	Copp	Philosophy	Circulating	10/97
Free Public Reason: Making It Up . . .	D'Agostino	Philosophy	Circulating	10/96
Metaphilosophy and Free Will[b]	Double	Philosophy	Circulating	
Bangs, Crunches, Whimpers, & Shrieks	Earman	Philosophy	Circulating	10/96
Causation and Persistence: A Theory . . .[b]	Ehring	Philosophy	Circulating	
Self Expression: Mind, Morals, & Meaning . . .	Flanagan	Philosophy	Circulating	10/96
Logic of Reliable Inquiry	Kelly	Philosophy	Circulating	10/96
Philosophy of Mathematics & Mathematical Practice In the 17th Century	Mancosu	Philosophy	Circulating	10/96
Moral Dilemmas & Moral Theory[b]	Mason	Philosophy	Circulating	
Autonomous Agents: From Self Control . . .	Mele	Philosophy	Circulating	10/96
Other Minds: Critical Essays	Nagel	Philosophy	Circulating	10/96
The Last Word[b]	Nagel	Philosophy	Circulating	
Law & Truth	Patterson	Philosophy	Circulating	11/96
Nietzsche's System	Richardson	Philosophy	Circulating	10/96
Freedom & Moral Sentiment	Russel	Philosophy	Circulating	10/96
Living High and Letting Die[b]	Unger	Philosophy	Circulating	
The Human Animal[b]	Weston	Philosophy	not in yet	
Real Rights	Wellman	Philosophy	Circulating	10/96

Publisher/Title	Author	Subject	Print Status	Month Public
Simon & Schuster Higher Education				
Bond Markets[b][c]	Fabozzi	Business	Reserves	
Marketing Management[b][c]	Kotler	Business	Reserves	
Statistics for Business & Economics[b]	Newbold	Business	Reserves	
Investments[b]	Sharpe	Business	Reserves	
Financial Market Rates & Flows[b]	Van Horne	Business	Reserves	
Politics & the Media	Davis	Political Science	Reserves	4/97
Public Policy Analysis[b]	Dunn	Political Science	Reserves	
International Politics	Holsti	Political Science	Reserves	1/97

[a]Permission has been received, but the book is not yet on-line.
[b]Book is not yet on-line.
[c]A new edition has been issued for which we need the electronic file.

CHAPTER 18

The Library and the University Press

Two Views of Costs and Problems in Scholarly Publishing

Susan Rosenblatt and Sandra Whisler

INTRODUCTION

The conflicts becoming apparent in scholarly communication have been anticipated for almost two decades. In 1982 Patricia Battin wrote:

> During the decade of the 1970's, librarians faced declining budgets, increasing vol-
> ume of publication, relentless inflation, space constraints, soaring labor costs, a hor-
> rifying recognition of the enormous preservation problems in our stacks, increasing
> devastation of our collections by both casual and professional theft, and continuing
> pressure from scholars for rapid access to a growing body of literature. It is ironic
> that both librarians and publishers introduced computer applications into libraries
> and publishing houses to save the book, not to replace it. Both were looking for ways
> to reduce labor costs rather than for visionary attempts to redefine the process of
> scholarly communication. . . . The former coalition shattered and publishers, schol-
> ars and librarians became adversaries in a new and unprecedented struggle to sur-
> vive in the new environment, each trying in his or her own way to preserve the past
> and each seeing the other as adversary to that objective.[1]

LIBRARY COSTS

Library Materials: Print

The results of the economic crisis in scholarly publishing were documented statistically in 1992 in *University Libraries and Scholarly Communication*.[2] Some of the principal findings included the fact that although materials and binding expenditures remain a relatively constant percentage of total library expenses, there has been a
hidden, but significant, change in the ratio of books to serials expenses. Although
materials expenditures have steadily risen, the average numbers of volumes added
to library collections annually continue to decline. Not only are libraries spending
more and receiving fewer items in absolute terms, but also libraries are collecting

an ever smaller percentage of the world's annual output of scholarly publications. Since 1974, even increases in university press outputs have outstripped increases in library acquisition rates.

Moreover, the study documents that some of the fields experiencing the greatest increases in their share of the total output are precisely those with the highest average per-volume hardcover prices: business, law, medicine, science, and technology. According to the report, science had the highest average prices; social sciences and business experienced price increase rates closer to the GNP deflator (p. xix).

Another finding was that serials prices consistently increase faster than general inflation. Serials had an overall annual inflation rate of more than 11% from 1986 to 1990. Prices of scientific and technical journals rose at the highest rates (13.5% per year, on average, from 1970 to 1990), and the most expensive serials experienced the largest relative price increases. In contrast, book prices inflated at 7.2% per year, while the general inflation rate averaged approximately 6.1%. In some institutions, science journals could comprise only 29% of the total number of journal subscriptions but consumed 65% of the serials budget. According to the Mellon report, "three European commercial publishers (Elsevier, Pergamon, and Springer . . .) accounted for 43% of the increase in serials expenditures at one university between 1986 and 1987" (p. xxi). The report does not introduce the question of the extent to which these inflation rates in the prices of scientific journals reflect increasing costs of production, expansion in content, price gouging, or the market value of the information itself—a value that might extend well beyond the university.

Brian Hawkins's 1996 study of library acquisition budgets of 89 schools finds that although budgets nearly tripled from 1981 to 1995 and increased by an average of 82% when corrected for inflation using the Consumer Price Index, the average library in the study lost 38% of its buying power. In the 15 years covered by his study, the inflation rate for acquisitions was consistently in the midteens. Confirming the Mellon study, he finds that the costs of some science journals increase more than 20% per year. He also notes that the trend line for average increases in library acquisition budgets is downward, accelerating the rate of decline in volumes added to collections.[3]

Harrassowitz regularly alerts libraries to subscription pricing information so that its customers can plan in advance to adjust purchasing patterns to stay within budget. In November 1996, Harrassowitz provided firm 1997–98 subscription pricing for six publishers publishing the majority of the STM (science, technology, and medicine) journals.[4] The announced price increases ranged from 1.2% to 22%, averaging 11%. According to Harrassowitz's analysis, libraries categorized as "General Academic/including Sci-Tech" could expect average price increases from the six publishers of almost 14%.

Peter Brueggeman from the Scripps Institution of Oceanography (SIO) Library at UCSD has discussed the problem from the perspective of a science library.[5] During the five-year period from 1992 to 1996, journal subscription costs at SIO rose 57% but the recurring collections budget increased 2.3%. Brueggeman singles out Elsevier and Pergamon for particular analysis: "Elsevier titles had a 28% increase between 1995 and 1996 and a 32% increase between 1992 and 1993. Pergamon titles had a 29% price increase between 1995 and 1996 and a 17% price increase between 1992 and 1993."

Various authors have demonstrated that not only do the most expensive journals experience the highest rates of inflation, but they are also among the most used. Chrzastowski and Olesko found that over a period of eight years, the cost of acquiring the ten most used chemistry journals increased 159% compared to an increase of 137% for the 100 most used journals.[6] During the same period, usage of the top ten journals increased 60% compared to an increase of 41% for the top 100 journals.

Library budgets that inflate more slowly than the rate of inflation for scholarly journals will cause a steady decline in the number of titles held in each library. Because libraries generally cancel journals on the basis of use, high-use, high-inflating titles may be protected. This protection results in a gradual homogenization of collections among libraries. Lesser-used titles, many with low prices and low inflation rates, will be crowded out faster than the general rate of decline in library subscriptions.

Figure 18.1 illustrates a hypothetical scenario. This scenario assumes that the collections budget is inflated by 4% per year. However, the average rate of inflation in the cost of scholarly publications is greater. The graph shows that if science journals, because they demonstrate high usage patterns, are canceled more slowly than other titles, then science journals will eventually crowd out other journals. In the example, the budget for science journals is allowed to inflate at approximately 8% per year (slightly less than one-half the actual inflation rate, but twice the rate of inflation in the total serials budget). Other, lesser-used journals, with lower subscription prices and lower rates of inflation, therefore must be canceled more rapidly in order for the collections budget to be balanced. Within a few years, the crowding-out effect from protection of high-use/high-price/high-inflation journals is quite noticeable. While no particular library may implement a budget strategy exactly like that depicted, all libraries tend to retain subscriptions to the highest use journals and to cancel first the lesser-used journals. Although the curve may change as the time line lengthens or shortens, the eventual result will be similar to that shown.

Library Materials: Electronic

As yet, there is no evidence that the emergence of electronic journals will improve the fundamental economic problems in the cycle of scholarly communication. The basic premise of publishers is that they must protect their current revenue base and secure guarantees to cover future inflation and increases in content.

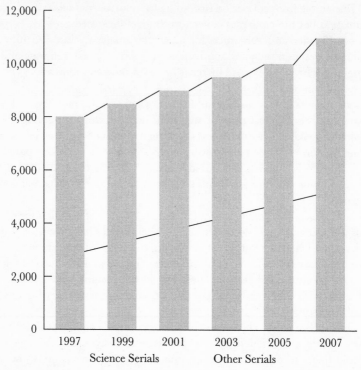

Figure 18.1. Crowding-out Effect

Thus, publishers frequently structure their initial subscription pricing for digital journals upon the actual cost of paper subscriptions acquired by the institution with which the publisher is negotiating. The proposed base subscription rate may include all subscriptions: library, departmental, personal, and other types identified with the campus, thereby greatly increasing the price that the library would have to pay to receive the digital journals. Clearly, publishers are concerned that network availability of electronic journals on the campus network will under-mine nonlibrary subscriptions to the print versions.

In early 1996, Ann Okerson reported that

> In general electronic licenses so far have cost on average $1/3$ more than print equiva-lents. . . . Publishers are setting surcharges of as much as 35% on electronic journals, and libraries simply do not have the capacity to pay such monies without canceling a corresponding number of the journals of that particular publisher or dipping into other publishers' journals.[7]

Moreover, during license negotiations for certain electronic journals, libraries may be asked to consent to such provisos as the following:

1. That there be multiyear price increase guarantees to compensate for inflation, often at somewhat lower rates than historical rates of price increase for print materials
2. That there be upward price adjustments for increases in content, often capped at lower rates than typical for print journals
3. That the publisher be protected against declines in revenue through cancellation
4. That fair use rights typical for print journals be abrogated for the digital journals

Maintaining a combination of print and electronic subscriptions for a multiyear period without incurring substantial new marginal costs for electronic versions and ensuring a cap on inflation are attractive to libraries. But neither "feature" of these new licenses will alter the basic economic difficulty facing libraries: inflation in the price of scholarly information outstrips libraries' ability to pay. In fact, by being locked into multiyear agreements that ensure price increases to particular publishers, libraries hasten the rate at which other journals and monographs are crowded out of the market.

Not all scientific publishers have negotiated as described above. For example, the American Physical Society and the American Mathematical Society offer electronic versions of their journals free to subscribers to the print editions. Clearly, publishers must find revenue streams that will enable them to survive, and the pricing structures for both print and digital journals are the key to those revenue streams. To base a pricing structure for electronic publishing on the costly print model will not be economically viable in the long run (it may, in fact, be unsustainable in the short term as well). Libraries' declining budgets will result inevitably in cancellations to avoid the structural problems associated with double-digit inflation, thereby undermining the publishers as well.

The current economic model for scholarly publication cannot be sustained. Continued escalation in the prices for scholarly journals, stagnation in library budgets, and isolation of the creators and consumers of scholarly information (the faculty) from the effects of the economy could lead to the collapse of the system of scholarly communication itself.

Operations Costs in Libraries

Library operations costs associated with printed scholarly journals include the costs to acquire, process, preserve, and circulate journals. Each library's costs differ based on the organizational structure, degree of centralization or decentralization of processes, differentials in salary and benefit scales, effectiveness of automated systems, success at reengineering internal operations, and other factors.

University Libraries and Scholarly Communication reports that "salaries as a percentage of total library expenditures have declined over the past two decades, while other operating expenditures (heavily reflecting computerization) have risen markedly" (p. xxii). The report infers that the increases in other operating expenditures reflect automation of technical service operations such as acquisition, cataloging, serials control, and circulation. It also notes that despite the decline in salaries as a percentage of total library expenses and the increase in other expenditures, "the number of volumes added per staff member has declined" (p. xxii), implying that there has not been a measurable staff efficiency gain from the investments in automation. In fact, on average, library staff increased by a total of 7% from 1970 to 1985 and by 6% from 1985 to 1991. Thus the rise in the nonsalary operations portion of the total operating expenses did not occur through staff reductions but rather as a result of budget augmentation for nonsalary items.

Presumably, greater efficiency in processing and circulation coupled with declining acquisitions should have resulted either in staff reductions or in substantial shifts of personnel away from the back room of technical processing to and into service to faculty and students, but it is not possible to discern from ARL statistics whether this is so. The ARL did not report service transactions until 1991, so one cannot discern changes in user demand for the earlier periods. Between 1991 and 1996, the ARL reports steady increases in interlibrary borrowing, library instruction, reference transactions, and total circulation. During the same period, total staff has declined by 2%.[8]

The inability to learn from the ARL reports or other reliable studies how libraries might be changing their staff allocation among operations and services reflects a serious flaw common to almost all analyses of library costs relating to both collections and operations. It is not obvious to what extent nonsalary investments, for example in automated systems, have actually improved processing productivity or the quality of services rendered by staff; nor is it clear whether or to what degree these investments have moderated the rate of rise of operations costs.

Library rankings typically reflect inputs such as budget, volumes acquired, number of serial subscriptions maintained, size of staff; or operational statistics such as the number of circulation transactions, titles cataloged, hours of opening, or items borrowed through interlibrary services. Ironically, the ARL Index ranks research libraries in part on the number of staff they employ; improving productivity and reducing staff accordingly would have the paradoxical effect of reducing a library's ranking vis-à-vis its peers. Developing measurements of service outcomes related to the mission of the institution would be more helpful as comparative data. For example, how do a library's collections and services contribute to research quality, faculty productivity, or student learning? The problem of defining productivity of knowledge workers was mentioned 30 years ago by Peter Drucker[9] and is further examined by Manuel Castells in his recent book *The Rise of the Network Society.*[10] Library operations represent a clear example of this productivity paradox.

William Massy and Robert Zemsky, discussing the use of information technology to enhance academic productivity in general, remark on its transformational potential, calling it a "modern industrial revolution for the university" that can create economies of scale, deliver broad information access at low marginal cost, and allow for mass customization.[11] The analysis they provide for the academy at large would appear to be even more pertinent to libraries, many of whose functions are of a processing nature similar to those in industry and whose services can also be generalized to a greater degree than is possible for teaching and research.

Massy and Zemsky suggest that although capital investments in technology to enhance productivity will increase the ratio of capital cost to labor cost, they may not actually reduce overall costs. But the writers argue that those investments will save money in the long term because over time labor costs rise with productivity gains and technology costs decline.

The primary purposes of automating processing operations in libraries have been to reduce the rate of rise of labor costs and to improve timeliness and accuracy of information. From the point of view of faculty and students, the service improvements are the most important result of automation. For example, on-line catalogs and automated circulation services provide users with more rapid access to information about the library's collections, reduce errors in borrowing records, and support more timely inventory control. Use of on-line indexing and abstracting services rather than the print versions preserves the scarce time of scholars and effectively extends the library's walls throughout the network.

Despite the efficiencies that automation has brought, labor costs to perform library processing operations such as ordering and receiving, cataloging, maintenance of the physical inventory, and certain user services including interlibrary lending and borrowing remain substantial. A transition to electronic publishing of journals (accompanied by the elimination of print subscriptions) could enable libraries to reduce or eliminate many of the costs of these labor-intensive operations. The freed-up resources might then be moved into higher priority services, necessary capital investments in technology, or provision of technology-based information resources. The benefits to end users could also be significant: less time spent in finding and retrieving physical issues of journals.

In the very long term, restructuring of library operations in response to electronic scholarly publishing could, in theory, result in major improvements to the quality of library services and also reduce operations costs. However, to maximize operations costs reductions, libraries will need to define better the desired outcomes of their operations investments, measure those outcomes effectively, and engage in rigorous reengineering of processes.

Several studies have attempted to quantify typical costs of acquiring journals. In a study funded by CLR (The Council on Library Resources), Bruce Kingma found the average fixed cost of purchasing a journal subscription to be $62.96.[12] In discussing the economics of JSTOR, Bowen estimates the costs of processing, check-in, and binding to be approximately $40.00.[13] In 1996, the library of the University of California, Berkeley estimated the physical processing costs, including check-in of individual issues, bindery preparation, and binding, for print serial subscriptions received and housed in the main library to be as low as $17.47 for a quarterly journal and up to $113.08 for a weekly journal. Berkeley's figures exclude the costs of ordering and order maintenance under the assumption that those costs will not differ significantly for electronic journals. The figures also exclude staff benefit costs and overhead and therefore understate the true cost to the university of receiving print subscriptions. Assuming an average annual processing cost of $50.00 per print serial subscription, a research library subscribing to 50,000 titles may incur an operations cost of $2.5 million per year simply to acquire journals.

Once the library acquires these journals, it begins to incur the costs of making them available to students, faculty, and other users. In the late 1980s, Michael Cooper reviewed the costs of alternative book storage strategies.[14] He found that circulation costs ranged from a low of $.53 per transaction in a medium-sized, open-stack research library to a high of $9.36 per transaction from a remote storage facility. Adjusted for inflation of 3% per year, these costs would range from approximately $.67 to $11.86 per transaction today. Berkeley calculates that an average circulation transaction costs approximately $1.07, and Bowen's estimate is $1.00. According to *ARL Statistics, 1995–96,* the mean number of initial circulations per library was 452,428. Using a circulation transaction cost of $1.00, the average ARL library spent almost $500,000 to circulate materials during the fiscal year 1995/96.

A review of the costs of acquiring and circulating print journals indicates that a transition from print to electronic journals would eventually reduce annual library operations costs related to providing the university community with the fruits of recent scholarship, but it is not clear how much of these savings might be offset by costs of technology infrastructure and equipment replacement. Large recurring expenses in support of historical print collections would continue but gradually diminish over time as the aging of the collection reduced the rate of usage. The long-term cost reductions could be substantial in the sciences where currency of information is of utmost importance. Costs associated with traditional operations and physical facilities might be more rapidly reduced were high-use print collections converted to digital form. Ultimately, the shift from labor-intensive processing operations to capital investments in electronic content (current journals and retrospective conversion of high-use print collections) might bring about the kinds of effects envisioned by Massy and Zemsky.

However, caution must be exercised in forecasting these types of savings. Despite the potential for long-range cost reductions, savings are unlikely to occur to any significant degree in the short term. The pace of transition from print to digital journals is moving slowly, and only those publishers with a strong financial base will be likely to succeed in quickly providing on-line access. As noted above and in the section of this paper relating to publishers' cost structures, there is no clearly viable economic path to move from print to digital publishing. Moreover, because user acceptance of digital journals may not occur rapidly and because of the many uncertainties about archiving digital information, libraries will need to maintain print collections—historical and prospective—into the foreseeable future, requiring that investments in operations and facilities be maintained.

Interlibrary borrowing and lending is a growing cost within research libraries,[15] and its rate of increase promises to escalate as the inflation-generated rate of serials cancellations escalates. According to the ARL, faculty and students borrowed more than twice as many items through interlibrary loan in 1996 as they did in 1986. The University of California Libraries recently reported an annual increase approaching 10% per year. Interlibrary services are labor-intensive operations; in 1993, the ARL conducted a cost study that determined the average cost of a borrowing transaction to be $18.62 and that of a lending transaction to be $10.93. The average ARL university library processed 17,804 interlibrary borrowing transactions and 33,397 interlibrary lending transactions during 1995–96, incurring an average annual cost of approximately $700,000. Given the rate of rise of interlibrary resource sharing transactions as well as the rate of rise of labor costs, research libraries are likely to experience increasing interlibrary borrowing and lending costs of about 10% per year. The rate of rise of interlibrary lending costs could be reduced through use of on-line journals rather than print journals; but if traditional print-based fair use practices are abrogated in the on-line environment, publishers might create pay-per-view contracts that would actually increase costs beyond the costs of manual interlibrary loans. Thus there are unknown cost implications in interlibrary resource sharing of digital information.

Capital Costs

Capital assets in libraries are of three basic types: buildings, collections, and equipment. Expenditures for the most costly of these assets, buildings, are typically not a part of library budgets and therefore are not generally considered by librarians in their discussions of library costs. This paper will not attempt to discuss capital costs for library buildings in any depth except to cite several relevant studies. In the late 1980s Cooper estimated the construction cost per volume housed in an on-campus open-stack library to range from $4.33 for compact shelving to $15.84 for traditional open stacks; he calculated the construction cost per volume of a remote regional storage facility to be $2.78.[16] Bowen uses Cooper's construction costs, adjusted for inflation, and Malcolm Getz's life cycle estimates to calculate an annual storage cost of $3.07 per volume.[17] Lemberg's research substantiates Bowen's premises regarding the capital cost that might be avoided through digitization of high-use materials.[18] He demonstrates that, even considering the capital costs of technology necessary to realize a digital document access system, research libraries as a system could accrue substantial savings over time if documents are stored and delivered electronically rather than in print form.

Extrapolating from Bowen's estimate of an annual storage cost of $3.07 per volume, a research library subscribing to 50,000 journal titles per year, each of which constitutes one volume, accrues $153,000 in new storage costs each year.

Over 10 years the cumulative cost to house the volumes received through the 50,000 subscriptions would exceed $8 million.

The growing dependence on information technologies to deliver scholarly information requires that universities make new investments in capital equipment and allocate recurring operations resources to the maintenance of that equipment and the network infrastructure. Although universities have invested heavily in network technologies, the true costs are still inadequately understood, and it is clear that increasing dependence on digital, rather than print, scholarly information will require that reliable funding for technology be developed. While capital costs for print libraries entail buildings, whose construction costs fall within known ranges and whose life cycle is long, and collections, the long-term costs of which can be rather reliably estimated, capital costs for the digital library are distributed across the campus and indeed the world. As yet, there is no clear formula to indicate how much initial capital investment in technology might be required to deliver a given number of digital documents to a given size academic community. Moreover, the life cycle for capital assets relating to delivery of digital library content is typically very short, perhaps shorter than five years. Thus funding allocations must be made frequently and regularly to ensure continued access to digital information. The Berkeley library, for example, estimates that annual equipment replacement costs for the existing installed base of equipment would be approximately $650,000, assuming a five-year life cycle. But the library has never had an explicit budget to support that expense, so investments in computer equipment, networking, and equipment replacement have been made through periodic redirection of the operating budget. Similar technology funding and renewal problems exist across the campus. Berkeley's situation is not unusual, and further work needs to be done to understand more fully the capital cost differentials between the physical plant investments required for print collections and the network investments required to make digital information available to the campus community.

It is possible that if libraries and their parent institutions, universities, could avoid some of the capital and operations costs associated with print-based dissemination of scholarly publications, these resources could be reallocated to capital investments in technology, provision of additional information resources available to the academic community, service improvements within libraries, and restoration of control of the system of scholarly publishing to universities and scholarly societies rather than the commercial sector.

THE ECONOMICS OF ELECTRONIC PUBLISHING:
A VIEW FROM THE UNIVERSITY OF CALIFORNIA PRESS

The market realities described in the first portion of this paper are sobering, but the basic outlines have been well known to libraries and scholarly publishers for more than a decade. This section discusses the realities for nonprofit journal publishers (university presses and scholarly societies) as a way of answering the question "So why don't publishers just reduce their prices—at least for electronic publications?" Although the focus is on nonprofit presses, the basic economics are equally true for commercial publishers, except that they require profits and have the considerable advantage of greater access to capital to fund innovation.

The largest constraint on all publishers' ability to radically change the price structure for electronic publications is the first-copy costs, which commonly range from 70% to 85% of the print price (see Table 18.1 for an example of first-copy costs for University of California Press journals).

These first-copy costs will remain whether the format is electronic, paper, or both. Any pricing model must provide sufficient income to cover these costs in addition to the unique costs associated with publishing in any particular medium. Publishers are not wedded to maintaining print revenues per se but to maintaining enough revenues to cover their first-copy and unique-format costs and to cover the costs of the technological shift. In the transition period, when both print and electronic editions must be produced, this objective will inevitably result in prices that are higher than print-only prices. Whether wholly electronic publications are, in the long run, more economical will depend on the costs of producing a uniquely electronic product and on the size of the market. If substantially fewer libraries subscribe to electronic publications than subscribed to their print predecessors, the cost per subscription will inevitably increase in order to cover a larger share of first-copy costs.[19]

Electronic Pricing Models

There are a number of models for pricing electronic resources. But all of them boil down to various ways of obtaining revenue to cover the same set of costs. They all ultimately depend on the same formula of first-copy costs plus print costs plus electronic costs. Table 18.2 shows humanities journal x.

Electronic Access Provided "Free"   Publishers that are providing electronic access "free" with print subscriptions are, in fact, subsidizing the costs of the electronic edition out of the surplus revenues generated by the print publication; the print publication already covers the first-copy costs allocated to each subscription. For relatively high-priced scientific journals with high first-copy costs, this subsidization can be done without inflating the price too substantially; the uniquely electronic costs are then subsidized by all institutional subscribers and hidden as a percentage of the total cost of publication. Because the basic subscription price is high enough, relatively modest additional increases will also cover the cost of lost individual subscriptions (since individual subscriptions typically cover the run-on costs of producing additional issues but make only a partial contribution to first-copy costs). This approach has the added advantage of sidestepping for now the problems of negotiating prices and guarantees with libraries (and the associated

TABLE 18.1. UC Press First-Copy Journal Costs, Average, 1994–95 (15 February 1997)

	Humanities	Social Sciences	STM	Press-Owned	Contract	Program-wide
Composition/ printing	$284,722	$253,005	$50,125	$362,488	$226,127	$588,615
Mailing	$12,696	$15,839	$3,266	$19,792	$12,009	$31,801
Postage	$30,138	$40,970	$5,574	$44,808	$31,874	$76,682
Royalties/edit. support	$133,602	$797,662	$27,697	$246,796	$712,164	$958,961
Press staff	$254,931	$412,675	$33,290	$401,613	$350,036	$751,649
Total costs	$716,089	$1,520,151	$119,952	$1,075,497	$1,332,210	$2,407,708
First-copy costs[a]	74.14%	87.94%	71.74%	77.14%	88.22%	83.27%

[a]First-copy costs include editorial support (including copyediting), composition, royalties to authors or societies, and press staff costs—all of the costs except for print, paper, bind, and mail costs.

TABLE 18.2.   Electronic Pricing Model

Print only		
First-copy costs	$48,000	80%
Print/paper/bind/mail	$12,000	
Print edition costs	$60,000	
Subscriptions to 1,000 libraries @ $60	$60,000	
Print and electronic		
First-copy costs	$48,000	
Print/paper/bind/mail	$12,000	
Electronic costs	$12,000	
Total costs	$72,000	
Subscriptions to 1,000 libraries @ $72	$72,000	
% increase in total costs		20%

overhead costs). However, it does not contribute to developing commonly under-stood and agreed upon cost recovery models that will cover the costs of electronic scholarly communication in the long run.

Extra Charge for Electronic Access, Bundled with Paper   An electronic edition that is provided with a print subscription for an extra charge is essentially the same as the previous cost recovery model, but the increase to cover electronic costs is made explicit. This approach may be especially necessary for journals whose base rate is low and whose markup for electronic costs cannot be covered by a typical inflationary increase. This model still has the advantage, for publishers, of spreading the cost over all institutional subscribers and of simplifying licensing negotiations.

Negotiated Price by Library Based on Paper Subscription Base   Some publishers take the basic institutional print subscription base and guarantee this revenue for a period of years (typically three). Publishers are willing to guarantee limits to inflationary increases for this period in exchange for the guaranteed income and protection from cancellations to help cover transition costs. Again, this approach works better with higher priced journals for which the added costs of electronic publishing are a smaller proportion of the total cost.

Separate Price and Availability for Electronic and Paper, with an Incentive for Bundling   Offering paper and electronic editions separately but with an incentive for bundling is the method deployed by SCAN and by Project MUSE. This model offers more flexibility to libraries, because libraries are allowed to cancel print and take only electronic or to select among the publications offered. Discount incentives encourage maintaining paper and electronic subscriptions (a strategy used by both projects) and ordering larger groups of journals (the entire list for MUSE; discipline clusters for SCAN). The advantage to this approach is that the costs of electronic publishing are made clear. (See the revenues section below for a discussion of the adequacy of this model for supporting humanities publishing in the long run and of the impact of consortia discounts.)

In all these models, the ultimate economic effect in the transition period is the same: costs for libraries go up. Publishers must cover their first-copy costs; continue to provide paper editions for individuals, many libraries, and international markets; and generate revenue to cover the infrastructure and overhead costs of electronic innovation. For nonprofit publishers, at least, these costs must all be supported by the revenues from current journal subscriptions.

Electronic Costs

It is likely, in the long run, that eliminating print editions entirely will reduce costs somewhat for some kinds of journals. However, for journals that are trying fully to exploit the new capabilities offered by electronic technologies, it seems likely that the additional costs of generating links, specialized formats, and so on will continue to cost as much, or nearly as much, as the cost of printing and binding.[20] But even for simpler humanities journals, the experience at the University of California Press raises questions about the assumption that ongoing electronic costs will be substantially lower.

Covering Costs of Development The University of California Press's original economic model assumed that the development costs were largely one-time expenses and that there was a single learning curve and set of skills to master, after which electronic publishing would be largely routinized; additional expenses would be easily absorbed by the margin generated by the savings in the paper edition. On the basis of the past three years, it seems apparent that this assumption was flawed. UC Press dedicated 3,500 staff hours on the SCAN project in 1994 (gopher site development); 4,100 hours in 1995 (WWW site development); and 3,700 hours in 1996 (largely on WWW development and on laying the groundwork for SGML implementation). It is apparent from ongoing trends in technological innovation that Internet technology and expectations for electronic publishing will continue to evolve very rapidly for at least the next 20 years. The Press's "bad luck" in initially developing for an outmoded platform (gopher) is an inevitable occurrence over the long term for electronic publishing projects. As a result, it seems foolhardy to assume that substantially less investment will be necessary for technical research, experimentation, and site redesign and revision in the future. Any viable economic model for the University of California Press must thus assume one or two technical FTE positions as part of ongoing overhead. (Please note that these positions will not include file server maintenance and enhancement, since the costs of file service for the SCAN project are presently borne by University of California/Berkeley Library.)

The SCAN project has experienced ongoing instability in technical staff at the library and at UC Press. Being located in a region with such a strong high-technology industry has actually proven to be a disadvantage, since current and potential employees can make so much more money at other jobs. This situation results in long staff vacancies and repeated training on the specifics of the project. In this way, the project again faces not one but rather a continual series of learning curves.

There is a third implication to this vision of a constantly evolving future. Functionality and continually changing platforms, combined with the Press's commitment to archiving and to long-term responsibility for viable electronic access, demand implementation of a coding system that is totally portable and highly functional. As a result, the commitment to SGML seems more and more wise as time goes on. This commitment leads the Press to reject image-based solutions like Acrobat, which would require less work and which would be faster to implement but which do not have long-term migration paths. Having experienced the painful process of completely recoding individual files, the Press does not want to face the same problem with a much larger set of files in the future. The necessity and the difficulty of repeated conversions of legacy text is sadly underestimated by many publishers and librarians. Scaleability, an important and underrated issue in any case, becomes even more vital in a scenario in which larger and larger amounts of material must be converted each time the technological environment evolves.

Electronic publishing is adding new duties (and requiring new resources) within the Press, without removing present duties. For example, the Press has added .5 FTE in the journals production staff (a 25% increase) to handle liaison with suppliers, scanning and archiving of all images being published, archiving of electronic files, and routine file conversion duties. This position will clearly grow into a full-time position as all the journals are mounted on-line; only the slowness of the on-line implementation permits the luxury of this low staffing level. The seven people working on Project MUSE or the seven people working on *The Astrophysical Journal Electronic Edition* confirm this assumption. In addition, clearing electronic rights for images in already published books and journals and maintaining an ongoing rights database creates a new staff responsibility, since many rights holders are requiring renewal of rights and payments every five to ten years. The need for technical customer support is still unknown but surely represents some portion of an FTE.

Marketing is another area requiring addition of new expertise and staff. Successfully selling electronic product requires a series of changes within the publishing organization. The marketing necessary to launch a new print journal successfully or to sell a book is expensive and time-consuming, but the approaches and tasks are familiar and can be performed by existing marketing staff as part of their existing marketing jobs. In contrast, successfully establishing a customer base of licensed libraries for electronic product requires new skills and abilities, a substantial staff commitment, a higher level of staff expertise and authority, and substantial involvement from the licensing libraries. Marketing electronic services requires all the brochures and ads that print publications do. In addition, it requires substantial publicity efforts, a travel schedule to perform demonstrations at a wide range of library and end user meetings, and participation in appropriate LIST-SERVs. There must be at least one staff member who has the requisite knowledge and authority and who can dedicate a large portion of time to outreach, negotiations, and liaison with potential and actual license customers and subscription agents. There are also demands for ongoing customer relations work, including the provision of quarterly or annual use reporting. The Press has found it very difficult to fit those new functions into its traditional marketing and distribution job descriptions and workloads. As the Press moves more seriously into electronic publication of current season books, it will surely need to hire a new person to market on-line books; these functions cannot possibly be integrated into the already busy jobs of books marketing professionals with their focus on current season bookstore sales.

In short, the Press anticipates a permanent addition of at least three or four full-time staff to the overhead of the publishing operation. For now, some of these positions are covered by the Mellon Foundation grant, and some of them have been deferred (to the detriment of the project), but in the long run the electronic publishing model must absorb this additional $200,000 in annual costs.

Finally, UC Press and the UC Library have just begun to step up to the costs of long-term archiving, including periodic refreshing of technology and the requisite reconversion of files—another argument for structured standardized coding of text.

Income for Electronic Product

Unfortunately, in a period when electronic publishing generates additional costs that must be funded, several trends apparent in the emerging purchase patterns of electronic products limit the income available to support publication costs and create further pressures on publishers to increase prices.

Slowness to Adopt   University presses attempting to sell electronic product directly (as opposed to bundling it automatically in the paper price and offering "free" access) are finding that sales to universities are progressing more slowly than projected. Project MUSE sales, for example, are at 378 after two years; sales to MIT's electronic-only journals hover at around 100; in no case are there more than 50 library subscriptions. There are under 25 subscriptions to the on-line edition of *The Cigarette Papers* at the University of California/San Francisco Library's Brown and Williamson Tobacco site after nine months (*http://www .library.ucsf.edu/tobacco/cigpapers/*). Sales to SCAN are a handful (although access has been restricted for less than one month at the time this paper is written). Even for publications for which no additional charge is being made, library adoptions are slow in coming. *The Astrophysical Journal Electronic Edition,* for example, has 130 libraries licensed to date. There are, of course, good reasons for this slowness: libraries face the same difficulties in building infrastructure, funding, and staff expertise that publishers do. But the low sales nevertheless make funding the transition more difficult, because publishers can't count on sales income from the electronic product to help to cover the costs of electronic publication. The growth curves to which publishers are accustomed from launching paper journals (even in this age of low library adoptions) are too optimistic when applied to electronic publications. This slowness has real consequences for funding electronic innovation.

New Discount Structures   Emerging business practices and discount expectations lessen the income per subscribing institution (at the same time that the efforts necessary to obtain that subscription are intensified). The expectations of consortia for deep discounting (both for number of consortia members and for adopting a bundle of publications) can go as high as 40% for academic institutions, with non-traditional markets receiving even deeper discounts. If 70–85% of the list price represents first-copy costs, a 40% discount means that these subscriptions are no longer carrying their full share of the first-copy costs. Deep discounting cannot be a long-term pricing strategy.

In addition, other consortial demands (for example, demands that inflationary increases not exceed a certain percentage for several years or that access be provided to high schools free of charge) further lessen the ability of publishers to fund electronic innovation out of electronic product sales. Again, it is easy to empathize with these library positions and to understand why they are evolving. But these efforts by libraries to control costs actually have an inflationary pressure on overall prices, since the base price must increase to make up the losses.

Loss of Subscriptions   Publishers are also worried about losing subscriptions. Some losses will surely happen. At a minimum, subscriptions will be reduced by another major wave (or waves) of cancellations as libraries try to cope with the ongoing costs of paper and electronic subscriptions from the major commercial science publishers and by the loss of any duplicate subscriptions still remaining on campuses. In addition, publishers are haunted by the potential for substantial shrinkage of individual subscriptions or society memberships as more and more scholars have "free" access from their campuses, though loss of individual subscriptions is less sure than library cancellations. (By December 1996, almost 60% of SCAN uses were coming from U.S. non-.edu addresses as more and more people obtain access from home workstations; it is possible that individuals will pay for the convenience of noncampus access, just as they now do for nonlibrary print access.) Nevertheless, because individual subscriptions play an increasingly important role in financing many journals (especially journals launched within the past ten years, when library support has been so eroded), widespread cancellation would have a substantial impact that would force journal prices higher.

Possible Increases in Sales   Two possible new revenue sources may somewhat balance the losses in income described above, although both are highly speculative at this point. First, publishers may obtain new institutional markets and wider distribution as consortia bring institutions like junior colleges and high schools to scholarly publications. Project MUSE has begun to see this trend. It is not clear, however, that these customers will be long-term subscribers. Given the present nature of scholarship, many of these new subscribers may conclude that any amount of money is too much to pay after two or three years of low use statistics, especially when on-demand access by article becomes widely available. There will be a substantial market for scholarship at junior college, high school, and public libraries only when the possibility of wider audiences through the Internet fundamentally changes the ways in which scholars write and present their work—a change that will surely take many years to materialize. Other publishers are more optimistic about this potential source of income.

Second, a substantial revenue stream may exist in sale of individual chapters and articles to scholars whose institutions do not have access, who do not have an institutional base, or who are willing to pay a few dollars for the convenience of immediate access at their workstations (people who are now presumably asking their research assistants to make photocopies in the stacks). And there may be substantial sales among the general public. This new product may represent enough income to relieve some of the pressure on journal finances, if the process can be entirely automated (at $6 or $7 per article, there is no room for the cost of an employee ever touching the transaction). This solution needs substantial traffic, because it takes seven or eight article sales to cover the first-copy costs of one typical humanities subscription.

Of course, the ability to purchase single chapters or articles will also diminish subscription revenues, as some libraries choose to fill user needs on demand and to cancel their present subscriptions. It is too soon to tell what the mix of new audiences and subscription cancellations will be, and whether the revenue stream from new sources will replace that from canceled subscriptions.

Aggregators   So far, the models we have examined have all assumed that the publisher is providing access to electronic resources. Publishers could, of course, avoid many of these costs by providing electronic files to aggregators and leaving marketing, file service, file conversion, and archiving to outside suppliers who would provide a single point of purchase for libraries and individuals. This scheme offers a number of advantages from a library point of view. The instant connection between search engine and ordering ability that the larger services like UnCover and OCLC offer may potentially bring more end users.

But from a publishing point of view, this model has two very large disadvantages. The first is strategic. In an electronic world, one of the major values that publishers have to offer is the branding value of our imprints as symbols of excellence resulting from peer review and gatekeeping functions, which will be ever more valuable in the time-starved world of the Internet. This brand identity is inevitably diluted in an aggregated world, especially if the aggregator is handling marketing and distribution.

Second, and more relevant to the discussion at hand, it is hard to see how the royalties most typically offered by aggregators (for institutional licenses or for on-demand use) can begin to replace the revenue lost from direct subscriptions. A 30–40% royalty does not cover first-copy costs of 80%. Only by retaining the entire fee can publishers hope to generate enough revenue for on-demand sales to make a sufficient contribution to the costs of publication. A wide-scale move to aggregation would have the effect of making the first-copy costs for the few remaining subscriptions very large indeed, in addition to reducing the perceived value of what we sell (yes, it is possible for a humanities quarterly to cost $1,200 annually!).

The University of California Press and most other nonprofit scholarly publishers would like nothing better than to price electronic products substantially lower than print. However, the low margins under which they operate, the demands of users that print continue to be provided, the high first-copy costs typical of scholarly publishing, the need to fund the development of electronic product, and the expenses of producing full-featured electronic publications all mitigate against low prices, at least during the transition period.

CONCLUSION

The university press and the library face economic pressures that neither can address alone. So long as journal prices escalate more rapidly than library collection budgets, libraries will continue to reduce serial subscriptions to balance the collections budget. These reductions will adversely affect the revenues to university presses. Pressure from science, technology, medicine, and business faculties to retain high-cost, high-use journals will crowd out less-used scholarly journals, many of which are published by university presses. Because libraries must continue to provide access to and preserve print inventories, housing them in large physical plants that must be maintained, they will be unable to implement large-scale, cost-reducing changes in operations to free up resources for investments in technology. The trends noted in *University Libraries and Scholarly Communication* and in Hawkins's paper will result in a catastrophic decline in the system of scholarly communication unless there is a fundamental shift in the way in which its processes, products, and costs are analyzed. Each of the two partners, the library and the press, serves as an inadequate unit of analysis for the system of scholarly communication as a whole.

Sandra Braman's description of the three stages in the conceptualization of the information society provides a useful context in which to view today's problems of press and library within the system of scholarly communication.[21] In her conceptualization, the first stage of the information economy is recognized by the increasing importance of information sector industries. In the second stage, certain forms of information never before recognized as commodities, become so recognized. In this stage, political controversy about information's value as a public good versus its market value as a commodity is highlighted. The rising commercialization of scholarly publishing and the declining ability of libraries to provide access to scholarly information may be interpreted as a second-stage information society phenomenon.

Braman postulates that the third stage of the information society produces a more sophisticated understanding of the flow of information: the flow may replace the market as the primary feature of the information economy. This stage represents a paradigm shift in which the information economy operates in a *qualitatively* different manner than in the two previous stages. According to Braman: "key insights of this perspective include identification of a new unit of analysis, the project, involving multiple interdependent organizations, as more useful than either the industry or the firm for analytical purposes"(p. 112). She further describes the third-stage conceptualization of the information economy as including a production chain, or "harmonized production flows," including information creation, processing, storage, transportation, distribution, destruction, seeking, and use, in short, all the stages of the system of scholarly communication from author to user, including the library. In the third stage, networked information economy, economic viability stems not from maximizing profit or economic stability within each component of the system, but rather through building long-term relationships and a stable system or flow of information.

Michael Hammer makes a similar point with respect to industrial or business reengineering but applicable to the operations of libraries and presses as well.[22] He notes that automation and other reengineering efforts frequently have not yielded the improvements that companies desire. He believes that heavy investments in information technology deliver disappointing results because the technology is used primarily to speed up traditional business processes, along with their inefficiencies, rather than to transform them. "Instead of embedding outdated processes in silicon and software, we should obliterate them and start over. We should . . . use the power of modern information technology to radically redesign our business processes in order to achieve dramatic improvements in their performance" (p. 104).

Both Braman and Hammer emphasize the disquieting qualities that characterize this kind of paradigm shift implied by the third stage of the information economy and by radical reengineering. According to Hammer,

> Reengineering cannot be planned meticulously and accomplished in small and cautious steps. It's an all-or-nothing proposition with an uncertain result. . . . At the heart of reengineering is the notion of discontinuous thinking—of recognizing and

breaking away from the outdated rules and fundamental assumptions that underlie operations. Unless we change these rules, we are merely rearranging the deck chairs on the Titanic. We cannot achieve breakthroughs in performance by cutting fat or automating existing processes. Rather, we must challenge old assumptions and shed the old rules that made the business under perform in the first place . . . Reengineering requires looking at the fundamental processes of the business from a cross-functional perspective.

Manuel Castells takes a different approach, suggesting that technology-driven productivity increases in the informational economy have not thus far been evident. His thesis is that technology-driven productivity increases were steady in the industrial sector between 1950 and 1973, but since 1973 productivity, particularly in the service sector, has stagnated despite the intensive investment in technology. He suggests three factors that appear to be relevant to the library and press sector as well as to the service sectors of the economy in general. These factors include the following.

1. *Diffusion:* before technological innovation can improve productivity markedly, it must have permeated the whole economy, including business, culture, and institutions.
2. *Measuring productivity:* Service industries traditionally find it difficult to calculate productivity statistically; thus the lack of observable productivity enhancements may in part be a symptom of the absence of relevant measures.
3. *The changing informational economy:* Productivity cannot easily be measured because of the broad scope of its transformation under the impact of information technology and related organizational change.

If Castells, Braman, and Hammer are correct, then libraries and presses, alone or together, cannot implement technological solutions that can transform the processes, productivity, and economics of scholarly publishing.

The Mellon projects have been useful in introducing two players in the information flow to the problems of the other, and in forging collaborative relationships to aid in sustaining the system of scholarly communication. These cooperative projects between university libraries and presses have helped participants begin to understand the system of scholarly publishing as an information flow rather than as separate operational processes. But their effectiveness is limited because, outside the parameters of the projects, the partners must still maintain their separate identities and economic bases.

A fuller exploration of the potential of transforming the flow of scholarly information would incorporate a more integrated approach, including the creators of the information, the university administration, and the information consumers as well as the publisher and the library. In this approach, costs and subsidies of the entire process of scholarly communication could be better understood and resources made more flexibly available to support it. For example, it might be possible to view operational and capital savings to libraries resulting from a transition to electronic publication as resources ultimately available to sustain the publication chain, or consumers could be asked to pay some or all of the costs of creating, storing, archiving, and delivering scholarly information. A critical flaw in the current system is the existence of a part of the gift economy, in the form of the library, within a monetary economy for commercial publishers. Because the consumers of the information within the university do not pay for it, they and the campus administration see the library as a "problem" when it cannot provide the information needed within the budget allotted.

A key problem in securing the future of scholarly communication is that both presses and libraries are undercapitalized. Although libraries incur huge capital costs over time in both inventory and facilities, they are not free individually nor as parts of the system of scholarly communication to reallocate present or future capital expenditures to investments in new modes of publication. However, such reallocation, if it occurs at all, will take place very slowly because the transition to digital publication will also be slow. It is possible that a more rapid transition to electronic publishing would reduce libraries' recurring operations costs, thereby enabling them to invest greater resources in information itself. But a more rapid transition is feasible for presses only if there is a rise in demand for digital publications from libraries and from end users or a substantial increase in subsidies from their parent universities. Presses can offer electronic publications, but they cannot change the demand patterns of their customers—libraries—nor the usage patterns of the end consumers in order to hasten a transition from print to electronic dissemination. As long as a substantial portion of their market demands print (or fails to purchase electronic product), presses will be forced to incur the resulting expenses, which, in being passed on to libraries as costs that inflate more rapidly than budgets, will reduce the purchases of scholarly publications.

Ironically, in the present environment, universities tend to take budgetary actions that worsen the economics of scholarly communication as experienced by both libraries and presses. University administrators increasingly interpret any subsidy of university presses as a failure of the press itself as a business; as university subsidies are withdrawn, presses must increase prices, which reduces demand and exacerbates the worsening fiscal situation for the presses. But in the networked economy where everyone can be an author and publisher, the value added by presses (for example, gatekeeping, editorial enhancement, distribution) may be more important than ever in helping consumers select relevant, high-quality information. At the same time, university administrators see the library as a black hole whose costs steadily rise faster than general inflation.[23] Since library materials budgets grow more slowly than inflation in the costs of scholarly publications, the inevitable result is reduced purchasing of scholarly publications of all types, but particularly of university press materials, which in general are of lesser commercial value in the commodity market. Unless the system as a whole changes, both university presses and university libraries will continue to decline, but at accelerated rates.

Although it is not possible to envision with certainty exactly how a successful transition from the present system to a more sustainable system might occur, one plausible scenario would be for universities themselves to invest capital resources more heavily in university-based information flows and new forms of scholarly publication as well as place increased market pressures on the commercial sector. If universities were to make strategic capital and staffing investments in university presses during the short term, the presses could be more likely to make a successful and rapid transition to electronic publication. At the same time, intensive university efforts (i.e., investments) to recover scientific, technical, medical, and business publishing from the private sector could be made to reduce the crowding out of university press publications by for-profit publishers. These efforts to recover scholarly publishing could be accompanied by libraries' placing strong market pressures on commercial publishers through cancellation of journals whose prices rise faster than the average rates for scholarly journals in general. The investments in these two areas: converting publication processes to electronic form and returning commercial scholarly publishing to the university could be recovered over time through reductions in capital investments in library buildings. Ultimately, the university itself would encompass most of the information flow in scholarly communication through its networked capability. That information having commodity value outside the academy could be sold in the marketplace and the revenues used as a subsidy to the system itself.

Another way of accomplishing a harmonization of the scholarly information economy was suggested by Hawkins:[24] the independent nonprofit corporation model in which universities and colleges would invest together in a new organization that would serve as a broker, negotiator, service provider, and focus for philanthropy. It would leverage individual resources by creating a common investment pool.

However the solution to the problem of the economic crisis in scholarly communication is approached, there must be a fundamental change in how the process as a whole is conceived and how intellectual property rights of both authors and universities are managed. Such a change cannot be made unilaterally by university libraries and presses but will require the strategic involvement and commitment of university administrators and faculty within the university and among universities. Patricia Battin, envisioning an integrated scholarly information flow, said almost ten years ago:

> Commitment to new cooperative interinstitutional mechanisms for sharing infrastructure costs—such as networks, print collections, and database development and access—in the recognition that continuing to view information technologies and services as a bargaining chip in the competition for students and faculty is, in the end, a counterproductive strategy for higher education. If the scholarly world is to maintain control of and access to its knowledge, both new and old, new cooperative ventures must be organized for the management of knowledge itself, rather than the ownership of formats.[25]

NOTES

1. Battin, Patricia. "Libraries, Computers and Scholarship." *Wilson Library Bulletin*, April 1982, 580–581.

2. *University Libraries and Scholarly Communication: A Study Prepared for The Andrew W. Mellon Foundation*. Published by the Association of Research Libraries for The Andrew W. Mellon Foundation, Washington, D.C., 1992.

3. Hawkins, Brian. "The Unsustainability of the traditional library and the threat to higher education." Paper presented at the Stanford Forum for Higher Education Futures, The Aspen Institute, Aspen Meadows, Colo., October 18, 1996.

4. "Price Comparison of STM Journals 1996/1997." Harrassowitz News: Press Release, November 1996; URL: *http://www.harrassowitz.de/news/9611pro1.html*.

5. Brueggeman, Peter. "Journal Subscription Price Increases." URL: *http://scilib.ucsd .edu/sio/guide/prices/*. For similar information from the University of Wisconsin– Madison, see University of Wisconsin–Madison. "University Library Committee Proposed Resolutions on Faculty Concerns on Copyright and the Role of Libraries (as adopted and amended May 6, 1996). Faculty Document 1214a, May 6, 1996. URL: *http://www .library.wisc.edu/libraries/issues/ulc-ipr.htm*. From Cornell, see Atkinson, Ross. "Summary of the 16 November 1995 Presentation to the Science Faculty." URL: *http://scilib.ucsd.edu/sio /guide/prices/prices4.html*.

6. Chrzastowski, Tina E., and Brian M. Olesko. "Chemistry Journal Use and Cost: Results of a Longitudinal Study." *Library Resources and Technical Services* 41, no. 2, 1997, 101–111.

7. Okerson, Ann. "A Librarian's View of Some Economic Issues in Electronic Scientific Publishing." Paper presented at the UNESCO Invitational Meeting on the Future of Scientific Information, Paris, February 1996. URL: *http://www.library.yale.edu/~okerson /unesco.html*.

8. *ARL Statistics, 1995–96*. Association of Research Libraries, Washington, D.C., 1997, 6.

9. See, for example, Drucker, Peter. *The Age of Discontinuity: Guidelines to Our Changing Society*. (New York: Harper and Row, 1969).

10. Castells, Manuel. *The Rise of the Network Society*. (Cambridge, Mass.: Blackwell, 1996). See especially chapter 2, "The informational economy and the process of globalization," which discusses "the productivity enigma."

11. Massy, William F., and Robert Zemsky. "Using information technology to enhance academic productivity." URL: *http://www.educom.edu/program.nlii/keydocs/massy.html*.

12. Kingma, Bruce R. "The Economics of Access versus Ownership: The Costs and Benefits of Access to Scholarly Articles via Interlibrary Loan and Journal Subscriptions." (New York: Haworth Press, 1996), p. 37.

13. Bowen, William G. "JSTOR and the Economics of Scholarly Communication." URL: *http://www.mellon.org/jsesc.html*.

14. Cooper, Michael. "A Cost Comparison of Alternative Book Storage Strategies." *Library Quarterly* 59, no.3, 1989, 239–260.

15. *ARL Statistics, 1995–96*. Association of Research Libraries, Washington, D.C., 1997, 11.

16. Cooper, "Cost Comparison."

17. Bowen, "JSTOR."

18. Lemberg, William Richard. *A Life-Cycle Cost Analysis for the Creation, Storage, and Dissemination of a Digitized Document Collection*. (Ph.D. dissertation, School of Library and Infor-

mation Studies, University of California, Berkeley, 1995). Also available on-line at URL: *http:// SIMS.berkeley.edu/research/publications/DigtlDoc.pdf.*

19. Costs for production of electronic journals in this paper are based on the experience of the University of California Press in its SCAN (Scholarship from California on the Net) project, funded by The Mellon Foundation. For details regarding these costs, seeAppendix A.

20. See *The Astrophysical Journal* at *http://www.journals.uchicago.edu/ApJ/*, *Earth Interactions* at *http://earth.agu.org/ei/*, or any humanities journal with lots of multimedia.

21. Braman, Sandra. "Alternative Conceptualization of the Information Economy." *Advances in Librarianship* 19, 1995, 99–116.

22. Hammer, Michael. "Reengineering Work: Don't Automate, Obliterate." *Harvard Business Review*, July–August 1990, 104–112.

23. *University Libraries and Scholarly Communication* reports, however, that the percentage of university budgets allocated to library budgets is gradually declining rather than consuming ever increasing proportions of institutional resources.

24. Hawkins, Brian. "Creating the Library of the Future: Incrementalism Won't Get Us There!" *Serials Librarian* 24, no.3/4, 1994, 17–47.

25. Battin, Patricia. "New Ways of Thinking About Financing Information Services." In *Organizing and Managing Resources on Campus*, ed. Brian L. Hawkins (McKinney, Texas: Academic Computing Publications, 1989), 382.

Hours	Total Calendar 1996	Total Calendar 1995
General plan & design		
Research	253	265
Design	258	270
Project management	570	1,182
Operations development	16	73
Monographs	30	167
Gopher site		
Research	0	2
Design	0	0
Modification	0	178
File preparation	0	108
Web site		
Research	300	99
Design	101	244
Modification	152	153
File preparation	428	323
Permissions	366	
Marketing	126	
SGML		
Research	309	336
Design	0	348.5
Modification	361	4
File preparation	319	0
Partnering	104	119.5
Fund-raising	0	36
Accounting	26	48
Reporting	20	134
Total hours	3,739	4,090

PART FOUR

Visions of the Future

CHAPTER 19

Licensing, Copyright, and Fair Use
The Thesauron Project
(Toward an ASCAP for Academics)

Jane Ginsburg

The Thesauron Project takes its name from the ancient Greek term meaning treasury or inventory.[1] This project envisions the creation of a digital depository and licensing and tracking service for unpublished "academic" works, including working papers, other works-in-progress, lectures, and other writings that are not normally published in formal academic journals. A centralized digital clearinghouse for this material confers a number of benefits on the academic authors and on users, particularly users of university libraries, including students, professors, and other researchers.

First, a centralized depository offers a more systematic and convenient means to discover the unpublished literature than does wandering around individual professors' or departments' Web pages. The depository's detailed and dynamic catalog of its works, identifying new and revised submissions, will significantly enhance the accessibility of this material.

Second, academic authors may not always have a significant financial stake in the electronic exploitation of their works (whether the works are unpublished or published; in the latter instance, many academics may have assigned all rights to publishers—sometimes inadvertently). But academics do have a very significant glory interest. A depository that undertakes what one might call "prestige accounting" for the authors adds an important feature and may serve as an incentive to participation.

What is "prestige accounting"? It is the tracking of use in a way that would permit authors to interrogate the depository to learn if and how their works are being used, for example, on reserve or in course packs at identified universities, for identified courses. Currently, academic authors generally do not know, apart from general sales figures (if they receive any), what has been the dissemination of their works. With some prodding of publishers, one might find out which bookstores placed orders for the book and thus infer which schools were using the work.

However, this kind of information is not generally available (or, at any rate, disseminated) for photocopied course packs, even when rights are cleared.

Third, and especially important to the digital environment, a service of this kind would add considerable value if it could ensure that the digital version made available is authentic. Many works may be traveling on the Web, but the user may not (or should not) be confident that the document downloaded is completely consistent with the work as created. This quality control is particularly significant when many different versions (e.g., prior drafts) are accessible at multiple Internet sites (not all of them with the author's permission).

DEFINING THE THESAURON UNIVERSE

What Kinds of Works Will the Thesauron Depository Include?

At least as an initial matter, the depository will be confined to unpublished works such as drafts, lectures, occasional pieces, conference proceedings, masters theses, and perhaps, doctoral dissertations. This definition should help avoid possible conflict with publishers (or those that are the copyright holders of works written by academics) who are or will be undertaking their own licensing programs. Moreover, the universe of "unpublished" works may grow as that of formal academic publications shrinks.

Whose Works Will Be Included in the Thesauron Depository?

Any academic (term to be defined; e.g., anyone with an institutional IP address) who wishes to deposit a work will be welcome to do so. There will be no screening or peer review.

Participating authors will register with the Thesauron depository and will receive a password (Thesauron registration information will also be relevant to terms and conditions and to authenticity; the password will tie into use reporting; see IIC, IVA, VB, infra).

DEPOSIT

Entry of Works

Deposits must be made by or under the authority of the author (if living) or successor in title (if dead); the depository will not accept submissions from unauthorized third parties.

Deposited works should be sent in HTML format.

Upon depositing, the author will supply information necessary to cataloging the work, including author name and the title of the work, and will categorize the work for the Thesauron catalog by selecting from LC classifications and subclassifications supplied on menu screens (see also IIIC, infra).

Every work deposited in Thesauron will automatically receive an identifying

ISBN-type number ("Thesauron number"). The number will be communicated to each author upon deposit as well as maintained in the catalog.

Exit of Works

The author, upon submitting the work, may demand that it self-delete from the depository by a date selected. Any document so designated should bear a legend that indicates at what date it will no longer be included in the depository.

The author may also demand deletion from the depository at any time. The catalog (see IIIC, infra) will indicate the date that a work has been deleted and whether it has been replaced by an updated version. A morgue catalog will be established to keep a record of these deletions.

Terms and Conditions

With each deposit, a participating author who wishes to impose terms and conditions on use of the work may select from a menu of choices. These choices will include:

What kind of access to permit (e.g., browsing only)
What purpose (e.g., personal research but not library reserve or course packs)
Whether to charge for access, storage, or further reproductions

ACCESS

What Users May Access the Thesauron Depository?

As a starting point, access will be limited to university-affiliated (or research institute–affiliated) users. These users will make their first contact with Thesauron from their institutional host in order to establish a user ID number from which they may subsequently gain access from both institutional and noninstitutional hosts (i.e., work or home).

When registering, the user will indicate a user category (e.g., professor, postdoctoral, graduate, undergraduate) and disciplines (research and teaching subject matter areas); this information will be relevant to the depository's catalog and tracking functions (see IIIC, VA, infra).

A second phase of the project would extend access to independent scholars who do not have institutional affiliations. At a later date, access to the depository might be expanded to the general public.

Conditions on Use

When registering, the user will encounter a series of screens setting forth the general conditions on using Thesauron. These conditions include agreement to abide by the terms and conditions (if any) that each author has imposed on the deposited works (e.g., the author permits browsing and personal copying, but not further copying or distribution). The user will also agree that in the event of a dispute between the user and Thesauron, or between the user and a Thesauron author, any judicial proceeding will be before the U.S. District Court for the Southern District of New York (or, if that court lacks subject matter jurisdiction, before the New York State Supreme Court) and will be governed by U.S. copyright law and New York law. (The choice of forum and of state law assumes that Thesauron will be established at Columbia University.)

How Will Users Know Thesauron's Holdings?

The depository will include an electronic catalog searchable by keyword or by Boolean logic. The catalog will also be organized in a scroll-through format employing LC subject headings. The catalog will be dynamic so as to reflect new submissions or revisions of material (and will also indicate when an author has deleted material from the depository).

The catalog will be dynamic in another way. Along the lines of SmartCILP (Current Index to Legal Periodicals) and similar products, it will regularly e-mail registered users with information about new submissions in the subject matter categories that the Thesauron user has requested.

How Will Users Access Material from the Thesauron Depository?

After finding the requested work's Thesauron number in the general on-line catalog or in the e-mailed updates, the registered user will click on the catalog listing or type in the Thesauron number to receive the work.

It is also possible to envision links to specific works in the depository from on-line course syllabi or other on-line reading lists.

In addition to the general conditions screens encountered on first registration with Thesauron, the terms and conditions (if any) pertinent to each work will appear on the initial screen prefacing each work. In order to access the rest of the document, the user will be obliged to click on a consent to those terms and conditions.

AUTHENTICITY
Delivery from the Thesauron Depository

Documents in the depository will be authentic when submitted by the author. The depository will add digital signatures or other marking material to identify the author, the work, and its date of submission.

Subsequent Generations of Documents Originally Obtained from the Depository

The Thesauron project does not now contemplate attempting to prevent users from making or circulating further copies of works obtained from the depository. But it is important to provide the means for anyone who obtains a document of uncertain provenance to compare it with the authentic version to ensure that no alterations have occurred. Thus, if a registered user has obtained a copy from a source other than Thesauron, the user should verify that copy against the version in the depository.

TRACKING

Identification of Uses

Registered users will respond to a menu screen indicating the purpose of their access, e.g., library reserve, course pack, personal research.

Reporting

Registered authors will have electronic "prestige" reports that they may interrogate at any time to learn:

   The number of hits each deposited work has received
   The source of the hit (institution, department, user category—names of users will not be divulged)
   The nature of the use (library reserve, course pack, research)

Billing

If the author has requested payment for access or copying, the registered user will need a debit account to access the work; the debit would be credited to the author's account. These operations may be implemented through links to a participating bank.

OTHER POTENTIAL APPLICATIONS OF THESAURON

As currently conceived, Thesauron's universe is unpublished academic works. But once all its features have been put into place, Thesauron could either expand its holdings or work in tandem with copyright owners of published works to supplement whatever rights clearance system the publisher has devised. Similarly, in situations in which authors have not assigned their copyrights or have at least retained electronic rights, Thesauron could work together with collective licensing agencies, such as the Authors' Registry, to supplement their rights clearance and reporting mechanisms.

COSTS OF IMPLEMENTATION AND MAINTENANCE

Initial Setup

The primary initial costs will be in acquiring hardware to accommodate the depository and in creating or adapting the software for the various components of the system: author registration; deposit; cataloging; user registration; use tracking and reporting; billing. It will also be important to publicize Thesauron to potential participating institutions, authors, and users; some portion of the initial budget should be allocated to this promotion.

Maintenance

Because most of the information in Thesauron is author- or user-generated, the maintenance costs should be largely limited to general system maintenance and gradual expansion of disk storage. It may be desirable to provide for part-time help line assistance.

Paying for Thesauron

It will be necessary to seek a grant to support the initial setup of and publicity for the system. The maintenance and help line costs should be covered by a modest subscription from participating institutions in exchange for the service of receiving and delivering works into and from the depository.

If the payment feature becomes a significant aspect of Thesauron, a portion of the access or copying charges could go to defray maintenance expenses.

NOTE

1. Plato refers to a storehouse of wisdom *(sophias . . . thesauron)*, at Philebus 15e. Similarly, Xenophon alludes to the "treasures, which they left behind written in books" *(thesaurous . . . , hous ekeinoi katelipon en bibliois grapsantes)*, at Memorabilia 1.6.14.

APPENDIX A

The Thesauron Project:
Annotated Bibliography of On-line Sources

Compiled by Deirdre von Dornum, J.D., Columbia, 1997.

Defining the Thesauron Universe

What Kinds of Works Will the Thesauron Depository Include?

1. See University of Texas Copyright Management Center *(www.utsystem .edu/OGC/intellectualproperty/)* for overview of "Faculty as Authors, Distributors and Users: The Roles of Libraries and Scholarly Presses in the Electronic Environment."

Whose Works Will Be Included in the Thesauron Depository?

1. General information on universities and copyright: Copyright Management Center at *copyinfo@indiana.edu.*
2. For definition of "educator," see Educational Fair Use Guidelines for Digital Images 1.4, available at *www.utsystem.edu/OGC/intellectualproperty/imagguid .htm.*
3. The WATCH file (Writers And Their Copyright Holders), a database of names and addresses of copyright holders of unpublished works primarily housed in libraries and archives in North America and the United Kingdom: *www.lib.utexas.edu/Libs/HRC/WATCH.*
4. Hypatia Electronic Library, a directory of research workers in computer science and pure mathematics, and a library of their papers: *http://hypatia.dcs .qmw.ac.uk.*

Deposit

Entry of Works

1. Existing depository: CORDS *(lcweb.loc.gov/copyright/):* U.S. Copyright Office's electronic system for receipt and processing of copyright applications; working with small number of representative copyright owners to establish digital depository.
2. How to assemble depository: ACM has guidelines for electronic submission of works to start a depository *(www.acm.com).*

Terms and Conditions

1. Copyright Clearance Center *(www.copyright.com):* has templates of rights and pricing schemes; individual publishers fill in specifics.
2. JSTOR *(www.jstor.org/about/license.html):* model licensing agreement.

Access

What Users May Access the Thesauron Depository?

1. European Copyright User Platform (accessible via *arl.cni.org/scomm/sum .html*) has a grid model for legitimate access considering the following dimensions:
   a. type of library: national, university, public, and so on.
   b. whether user groups are open (the general public), closed (a specific subset who have a formal relationship with the organization), or registered (individuals who have authorized passwords).

c. types of permissible activities, including digitization and storage, viewing, downloading, copying, exporting, and so on.

2. Project MUSE (Johns Hopkins University Press) *(128.220.50.88/proj_descrip /rights.html):* allows access through universities *only* to faculty, students, and staff (access expected to be enforced by subscribing universities).

3. University of Texas system *(www.utsystem.edu/OGC/intellectualproperty /l-resele.htm)* discusses restriction of electronic distribution of copyrighted materials to enrolled students.

4. Virginia Tech *(ei.cs.vt.edu/courses.html)* digital library in use for computer science courses.

Conditions on Use

1. Nontechnological means of control
   a. University of Texas system *(http://www.utsystem.edu/OGC/intellectualproperty /rsrvguid.htm)* suggests: retrieval of works in electronic reserve systems by course number or instructor name, but not by author or title of work.
   b. ASCAP *(www.ascap.com):* collective on-line licensing for all copyrighted musical works in ASCAP's repertory; does *not* allow reproduction, copy, or distribution by any means (enforced contractually, not technologically).

2. Technological devices
   a. CORDS *(lcweb.loc.gov/copyright/):* individual digital works will be assigned "handles" that code for access terms and conditions established by rights holders.
   b. Ivy League *(www.cultech.yorku.ca/projects/docs/ivymain.html):* Canadian consortium of companies, universities, and rights clearance organizations; employs encryption, fingerprinting, tagging, and copy prohibition to enforce limitations on user and use.
   c. IMPRIMATUR *(www.imprimatur.alcs.co.uk/):* U.K. consortium in development for copyright managed Internet server; interested in using numbering system and cryptography to limit access.
   d. Technology providers (information available through IMPRIMATUR site or *www.ncri.com/articles/rights_management/ifrro95.html)*

How Would Users Access Material from the Thesauron Depository?

1. Course syllabi/electronic reserve lists
   a. For summary of fair use and academic environment, see *arl.cni.org/aau /IP1.html#Background.* For a computer science–oriented digital library aleady in use with computer science courses at Virginia Tech, see *ei.cs.vt.edu/courses.html.*

b. model charters of electronic reserves: University of Kentucky (*www.uky
.edu/Libraries/elecrestf.html*);   Duke   (*http://www.lib.duke.edu/access/reserves
/intro.htm*)

c. links to further info: *www.columbia.edu/~rosedale.*

2. General search engine

a. The Computation and Language E-print Archive, an electronic archive
and distribution server for papers on computational linguistics, natural
language processing, speech processing, and related fields, is accessible
by a variety of means, such as: title/author search; abstract number;
most recent acquisitions; form interface searches. See *http://xxx.lanl.gov
/cmp-lg/.*

Authenticity

Delivery from the Thesauron Depository

1. CORDS *(lcweb.loc.gov/copyright/):* authenticity initially verified by Copyright
Office, and then guaranteed.

2. Clickshare *(www.clickshare.com)* operates across the Internet as an authentication and payment facilitator.

Subsequent Generations of Documents Originally Obtained from the Depository

1. ACM project *(www.acm.org):* very concerned about authenticity of documents.

Tracking

Reporting

1. Copyright Clearance Center *(www.copyright.com):* currently licenses on behalf
of over 9,200 publishers, representing hundreds of thousands of authors;
collects usage information from meters (appears to be volume and billing
rather than specific use) and reports to rights holders.

2. Technological devices: Clickshare *(www.clickshare.com)* operates across the Internet as an authentication and payment facilitator; can also provide user
profiling and user-access verification services. Publishers maintain their own
content on their own Internet server; the Clickshare software enables the
provider to track and receive royalties from users who click on content
pages; the publishers retain the copyrights.

Billing

1. Authors' Registry *(www.webcom.com/registry/):* accounting system for paying
royalties to registered authors for electronic media uses.

2. ASCAP *(www.ascap.com):* collective on-line licensing for all copyrighted muscial works in ASCAP's repertory; four different rate schedules (on-line service providers select one).

3. Publication Rights Clearinghouse (National Writers' Union) *(www.nwu.org /nwu/):* rights to previously published articles by freelance writers sold to fax-for-fee database. PRC sets royalties and forwards to authors when articles used, minus 20% fee.

4. Corbis *(www.corbis.com* or *www.corbisimages.com/):* licensing of digital images.

Notes

This project was developed by Jane C. Ginsburg, Morton L. Janklow Professor of Literary and Artistic Property Law, Columbia University School of Law, in consultation with James Hoover, Professor of Law and Associate Dean for Library and Computer Services, Columbia University School of Law; Carol Mandel, Deputy University Librarian, Columbia University; David Millman, Manager, Academic Information Systems, Columbia University; and with research assistance from Deirdre von Dornum, Columbia University School of Law, class of 1997.

CHAPTER 20

Technical Standards
and Medieval Manuscripts

Eric Hollas

Medieval manuscripts—that is, handwritten codices produced between the fifth century and the late fifteenth century—are counted among the greatest intellectual treasures of western civilization. Manuscripts are significant to scholars of medieval culture, art historians, calligraphers, musicologists, paleographers, and other researchers for a multiplicity of reasons. They contain what remains of the classical literary corpus; and they chronicle the development of religion, history, law, philosophy, language, and science from the Middle Ages into early modern times.

Even though manuscripts represent the most voluminous surviving artifact from the Middle Ages, the very nature of this resource presents challenges for usage. Each manuscript—as a handwritten document—is a unique creation. As such, copies of a particular work may contain variances that make all copies—wherever they might be—necessary for review by an interested scholar. Also, access to unique manuscripts that are spread across several countries or continents can be both costly and limited. A scholar wishing to consult manuscripts must often travel throughout Europe, the United States, and other countries to find and study manuscripts of interest. Such research is costly and time-consuming. The universities, museums, and libraries that own these manuscripts may lack the space and personnel to accommodate visiting scholars, and in some cases research appointments need to be arranged months in advance. Compounding these difficulties can be the challenge of inconvenient geography. While eminent collections reside in the great capitals of Europe, other collections of scholarly interest are housed in remote sites with no easy access at all. And finally, the uniqueness of each manuscript presents special issues of preservation. Because manuscripts represent finite and nonrenewable resources, librarians concerned with the general wear and tear on manuscripts have begun to restrict access to these codices.

In an effort to preserve medieval manuscripts and to create broader and more economical access to their contents, many libraries have in recent decades sought to provide filmed copies of their manuscripts to users. This practice has been a long-established one at such institutions as the British Library, the Bibliotheque National, and the Vatican Library. Additionally, some libraries have been established for the specific purpose of microfilming manuscript collections. The Institut de Recherche et d'Histoire des Textes in Paris, for example, for decades has been filming the manuscripts of the provincial libraries in France. Since its founding in 1965, the Hill Monastic Manuscript Library (HMML) at Saint John's University in Minnesota has filmed libraries in Austria, Germany, Switzerland, Spain, Portugal, Malta, and Ethiopia. And at the Vatican Film Library at Saint Louis University, one can find microfilms of 37,000 manuscript codices from the Biblioteca Apostolica Vaticana in Rome. Instead of traveling from country to country and from library to library, researchers may make a single trip to one of these microfilm libraries to consult texts, or in certain circumstances, they may order microfilm copy by mail. Microfilm was a great step forward in providing access to manuscripts, and it still offers tremendous advantages of economy and democratic access to scholars. Still, there are certain limitations because in some situations researchers must visit the microfilm institutions to consult directly, and the purchase of microfilm—even if ordered from a distance—can entail long waits for delivery. And compounding these difficulties can be the inconsistency or inadequacy of existing descriptions of medieval manuscripts.

Access to manuscripts in particular collections is guided by the finding aids that have been developed through the centuries. The medieval shelf list has given way to the modern catalog in most cases, but challenges in locating particular manuscripts and in acquiring consistent information abound. Traditionally, libraries in Europe, the United States, and elsewhere have published manuscript catalogs to describe their handwritten books. These catalogs are themselves scholarly works that combine identification of texts with a description of the codex as a physical object. Although these catalogs are tremendously valuable to scholars, they are not without their shortcomings. With respect to manuscript catalogs, there is presently no agreement within the medieval community on the amount and choice of detail reported, on the amount of scholarly discussion provided, and on the format of presentation. Moreover, to consult these published books in the aggregate requires access to a research library prepared to maintain an increasingly large collection of expensive and specialized books. And beyond that, the production of a modern catalog requires expertise of high caliber and the financial resources that facilitate the work. Because many libraries do not have such resources available, many collections have gone uncataloged or have been cataloged only in an incomplete fashion. The result for the scholar is a paucity of the kind of information that makes manuscript identification and location possible.

Existing and emerging electronic technologies present extraordinary opportunities for overcoming these challenges and underscore the need to create a long-term vision for the Electronic Access to Medieval Manuscripts project. Electronic access both to manuscript images and to bibliographic information presents remarkable opportunities. For one, the distance between the manuscript and the reader vanishes—providing the opportunity for a researcher anywhere to consult the image of a manuscript in even the remotest location. Second, electronic access obviates the security issues and the preservation concerns that accompany usage. Furthermore, electronic access will permit the scholar to unite the parts of a manuscript that may have been taken apart, scattered, and subsequently housed at different sites. It also allows for image enhancement and manipulation that conventional reproductions simply do not make available. Electronic access will also make possible comprehensive searches of catalog records, research information, texts, and tools—with profound implications in terms of cost to the researcher and a more democratic availability of materials to a wider public.

One may imagine a research scenario that contrasts sharply with the conventional methods that have been the mainstay of manuscript researchers. Using a personal computer in an office, home, educational institution, or library, scholars will be able to log on to a bibliographic utility (i.e., RLIN or OCLC) or to an SGML database on the World Wide Web and browse catalog records from the major manuscript collections around the world. To make this vision a reality requires adherence to standards, however—content standards to ensure that records include the information that scholars need and encoding standards to ensure that that information will be widely accessible both now and in the future.

This point may be demonstrated by considering several computer cataloging projects developed since the mid-1980s. These efforts include the Benjamin Catalogue for the History of Science, the International Computer Catalog of Medieval Scientific Manuscripts in Munich, the Zentralinventar Mittelalterlicher Handschriften (ZIH) at the Deutsche Staatsbibliothek in Berlin, MEDIUM at the Institut de Recherche et d'Histoire des Textes in Paris, and PhiloBiblon at the University of California, Berkeley. The Hill Monastic Manuscript Library has also embarked on several electronic projects to increase and enhance scholarly access to its manuscript resources. In 1985, Thomas Amos, then Cataloger of Western Manuscripts at HMML, began development of the Computer Assisted Cataloging Project, a relational database that he used to catalog manuscripts from Portuguese libraries filmed by HMML.

These electronic databases as well as others from manuscript institutions around the world represent an enormous advancement in scholarly communication in the field of manuscript studies. As in the case of printed catalogs and finding aids, however, these data management systems fall short of the ideal on several counts. First, each is a local system that must be consulted on-site or purchased independently. Second, the development and maintenance of these various databases involve duplication of time, money, and human resources. All rely on locally developed or proprietary software, which has posed problems for the long-term maintenance and accessibility of the information. Finally, and probably most important, each system contains its own unique set of data elements and rules and procedures for data entry and retrieval. When each of these projects was begun, its founders decided independently what information to record about a manuscript, how to encode it, and how to retrieve it. Each of the databases adopted a different solution to the basic problems of description and indexing, and the projects differed from each other with regard to completeness of the data entered and the modes in which it could be retrieved.

The lessons to be drawn from these experiences are clear and enunciate the hazards for the future if approaches distinctively different from the ones now being used are not pursued. First of all, local institutions could not maintain locally developed software and systems. In the instances of projects that chose to rely on proprietary software, it became apparent that the latter was dependent on support from the manufacturer, whose own longevity in business could not be guaranteed or who could easily abandon such software programs when advances provided new opportunities. Furthermore, experience has demonstrated that such material is not always easily translated into other formats, and if modified, it poses the same problems of maintenance as locally developed software. Beyond that, different projects made substantially different decisions about record content, and those decisions were sometimes influenced by the software that was available. This lack of consistency made it difficult to disseminate the information gathered by each project, and for their part funding agencies were reluctant to continue their support for such limited projects. All of which reiterates the fundamental need for content standards to ensure that records include the information that scholars need and encoding standards to ensure the wide accessibility of that information both now and into the future. It is the objective of Electronic Access to Medieval Manuscripts to address these issues.

Electronic Access to Medieval Manuscripts is sponsored by the Hill Monastic Manuscript Library, Saint John's University, Collegeville, Minnesota, in association with the Vatican Film Library, Saint Louis University, and has been funded by a grant from The Andrew W. Mellon Foundation. It is a three-year project to develop guidelines for cataloging medieval and renaissance manuscripts in electronic form. For this purpose it has assembled an international team of experts in manuscript studies and library and information science that will examine the best current manuscript cataloging practice in order to identify the information appropriate to describing and indexing manuscripts on two levels, core and detailed. Core-level descriptions, which will contain the basic or minimum elements required for the identification of a manuscript, will be useful for describing manuscripts that have not yet been fully cataloged, and may also be used to give access to detailed descriptions or to identify the sources of digital images or other information extracted from manuscripts. Guidelines for detailed or full descriptions will be designed to accommodate the kinds of information found in full scholarly manuscript cataloging.

In addition to suggesting guidelines for content, Electronic Access to Medieval Manuscripts will also develop standards for encoding both core-level and detailed manuscript descriptions in both MARC and SGML. The MARC (Machine-Readable Cataloging) format underlies most electronic library catalogs in North America and the United Kingdom, and it is used also as a vehicle for international exchange of bibliographic information. MARC bibliographic records are widely accessible through local and national databases, and libraries with MARC-based cataloging systems can be expected to maintain them for the foreseeable future. SGML (Standard Generalized Markup Language) is a platform-independent and extremely flexible way of encoding electronic texts for transmission and indexing. It supports the linking of texts and images, and SGML-encoded descriptions are easily converted to HTML for display on the World Wide Web. In developing standards for SGML encoding of manuscript descriptions, Electronic Access to Medieval Manuscripts will work closely with the Digital Scriptorium, a project sponsored jointly by the Bancroft Library at the University of California, Berkeley, and the Butler Library at Columbia University.

The project working group for Electronic Access to Medieval Manuscripts consists of representatives from a number of North American and European institutions. Drafts produced by the working group will be advertised and circulated to the international community of manuscript scholars for review and suggestions. The cataloging and encoding guidelines that result from the work of the project will be made freely available to any institution that wishes to use them.

For the purposes of Electronic Access to Medieval Manuscripts, the standards for cataloging medieval manuscripts are crucial, but so too is the application of content standards to the two encoding standards whose existence and ubiquitous usage address the issues noted earlier. At the risk of stating the obvious, Electronic Access to Medieval Manuscripts has chosen to work with two existing and widely used encoding standards because it is unwise for medievalists to reinvent the wheel and waste resources on solutions that are temporary and that will require added resources to take them into future applications.

With regard to encoding standards, the universal acceptance of MARC and the accessibility of MARC records on-line make it a particularly attractive option. But other compelling reasons make MARC an excellent choice. First, most libraries already have access to a bibliographic utility (such as OCLC and RLIN) that utilizes MARC-based records, and these institutions have invested considerable resources in creating catalog records for their printed books and other collections. Second, since most catalog records for printed books and reference materials are already in MARC-based systems, placing manuscript records in the same system makes good sense from the standpoint of proximity and one-stop searching. Third, by using MARC, local libraries need not develop or maintain their own database systems. Finally, although it may be unrealistic to expect that all manuscript catalog records will one day reside in a single database, therefore allowing for a universal search of manuscript records, it is likely that a majority of manuscript institutions in the United States will be willing to place their manuscript records in this bibliographic utility rather than in other existing environments.

Thus the value of selecting MARC as an encoding standard seems clear. MARC systems exist; they are widely accessible; they are supported by other, broader interests; and enough bibliographic data already exists in MARC to guarantee its maintenance or its automatic transfer to any future platform. A significant number of records for medieval manuscripts or microfilms of them, prepared and entered by the various institutions that hold these items, already exist in USMARC (RLIN and OCLC databases). Regrettably, there is generally little consistency in description, indexing, or retrieval for these records, which points back to the need for content standards as well as encoding standards. Furthermore, MARC as it currently exists has limits in its abilities to describe medieval manuscripts (e.g., it does not provide for the inclusion of incipits), but nonetheless it offers possibilities for short records that point to broader sets of data in other contexts. Still, MARC, with its records in existing bibliographic databases, is particularly advantageous for small institutions with few manuscript holdings, and it remains for them perhaps the most promising vehicle for disseminating information about their collections.

The second viable encoding option, particularly in light of the recent success of the Archival Finding Aid Project at the University of California, Berkeley, is the use of SGML. As a universal standard for encoding text, SGML can be used to encode and index catalog records and other data including text, graphics, images, and multimedia objects such as video and sound. A more flexible tool than MARC, SGML is more easily adapted to complex hierarchical structures such as traditional descriptions of medieval manuscripts, and it offers broad possibilities for encoding and indexing existing, as well as new, manuscript catalogs. As an encoding scheme, SGML demonstrates its value as a nonproprietary standard. In many respects it is much more flexible than MARC or any established database program, and it is possible to write a Document Type Definition (DTD) that takes into account the particular characteristics of any class of document. SGML offers the further advantage that encoded descriptions can be linked directly to digital images, sound clips (e.g., for musical performances), or other bodies of digital information relating to a manuscript. Numerous initiatives using SGML suggest great promise for the future. The experience of the American archival profession with the Encoded Archival Description (EAD) suggests that the latter can be a good approach to encoding manuscript descriptions, which have many structural analogies to archival finding aids. The Canterbury Tales project, based at Oxford, has demonstrated that SGML, based on a Text Encoding Initiative (TEI) format, can be used successfully to give sophisticated access to images of manuscripts, text transcriptions, and related materials. In addition, several English libraries have already experimented with SGML DTDs, mostly TEI-conformational, for manuscripts. And finally, MASTER, an Oxford-based group, is interested in developing a standard DTD for catalog descriptions of medieval manuscripts, and it and Electronic Access to Medieval Manuscripts have begun to coordinate their efforts toward achieving this common goal.

The emerging interconnectivity of MARC and SGML presents tremendous opportunities for Electronic Access to Medieval Manuscripts. Currently there is work on a DTD for the MARC format that will allow automatic conversion of MARC-encoded records into SGML. Recently, a new field (856) was added to the MARC record that will accommodate Web addresses. Implementation of this field will allow researchers seeking access to a cataloging record in a bibliographic utility to read the URL (Uniform Resource Locator) and then enter the address into a Web browser and link directly to a Web site containing a detailed manuscript record or other scholarly information. In the future, researchers who enter the bibliographic utility through a Web browser will find field 856 to be an active hypertext link. Electronic Access to Medieval Manuscripts envisions an environment in which institutions can enter their manuscript catalog records into MARC, display them in a bibliographic utility to maximize economy and access, and then embed a hypertext link to a more detailed catalog record, an image file, or scholarly information on an SGML server.

The cumulative experience of recent years has shaped the development and goals of Electronic Access to Medieval Manuscripts. Concerned with arriving at standards for cataloging manuscripts in an electronic environment, the project seeks to provide standards for both core-level and full, or detailed, manuscript records that will serve the expectations and needs of scholars who seek consistent information from one library to another; at the same time, these standards will afford flexibility to those catalogers and libraries wishing to provide various levels of information about their individual manuscripts. In structuring its program and goals, Electronic Access to Medieval Manuscripts also has sought to arrive at guidelines for encoding into MARC and SGML formats that will provide useful, economic, and practical long-term alternatives to the libraries that select one of these options in the future.

CHAPTER 21

Digital Libraries
A Unifying or Distributing Force?

Michael Lesk

INTRODUCTION

There are several future trends that everyone seems to agree upon. They include

- widespread availability of computers for all college and university students and faculty
- general substitution of electronic for paper information
- library purchase of access to scholarly publications rather than physical copies of them

Early steps in these directions have been followed by many libraries. Much of this movement has taken the form of digitization. Unfortunately some of the digitized material is not used as much as we would like. This lack of interest may reflect the choice of the material to convert; realistically, nineteenth-century books that have never been reprinted or microfilmed may have been obscure for good reasons and will not be used much in the future. But some more general problems with the style of much electronic library material suggest that the difficulties may be more pervasive.

THE WEB

The primary means today whereby people gain access to electronic material is over the World Wide Web. The growth of the Web is amply documented at *http://www.cyberatlas.com* and similar sites. Predictions for the number of Web users worldwide in the year 2000 run up to 1 billion (Negroponte 1996); students have the highest Web usage of any demographic group, with about 40% of them in 1996 showing medium or high Web usage; and people have been predicting the end of paper libraries since at least 1964 (Samuel 1964). Web surfing appears to be substituting for TV viewing and CD-ROM purchasing, taking its share of approximately 7 hours per day that the average American spends dealing with media of all forms. Advertisers are lining up to investigate Web users and find the best way to send product messages to them (Novak and Hoffman 1996). Figure 21.1 shows the growth of Web hosts just in the last few years.

ON-LINE JOURNALS AND THE WEB

Following the move of information to digital form, there have been many experiments with on-line journals. Among the best known projects of this sort are the TULIP project of Elsevier (Borghuis 1996) and the CORE project of Cornell, the American Chemical Society, Bellcore, Chemical Abstracts, and OCLC. These projects achieved more or less usage, but none of them approached the degree of epidemic success shown by the Web. The CORE project, for example, logged 87,000 sessions of 75 users, but when we ended access to primary chemical journals at Cornell, nobody stormed the library demanding the restoration of service. Imagine what would happen if the Cornell administration were to cut access to the Web.

In the CORE project (see Entlich 1996), the majority of the usage was from the Chemistry and Materials Science departments. They provided 70% of active users and 86% of all sessions with the journals. Various other departments at Cornell use chemical information (Food Sciences, Chemical Engineering, etc.) but make less use of the on-line journals. Apparently the overhead of starting to use the system and learning its use discouraged those who did not have a primary interest in it. Many of the users printed out articles rather than read them on-line. About one article was printed for every four viewed, and people tended to print an article rather than flip through the bitmap images. People accessed articles through both browsing and searching, but they read the same kinds of articles they would have read otherwise; they did not change their reading habits.

Some years ago the CORE project had compared the ability of people to read bitmaps versus reformatted text and found that people could read screen bitmaps just as fast as new text (Egan 1991). Yet in the actual use of the journals, the readers did not seem to like the page images. The Scepter interface provided a choice of page image or text format, and readers only looked at about one image page in every four articles. "This suggests that despite assertions by some chemists in early interviews that they particularly liked the layout of ACS journal pages, for viewing on-line they prefer reformatted text to images of those pages, even though they can read either at the same speed. The Web-like style is preferred for on-line viewing."

Perhaps it is not surprising that the Web is more popular than scientific journals. After all, *Analytical Chemistry* has never had the circulation among undergraduates of *Time* or *Playboy*. But the Web is not being used only to find out sports scores or other nonscholarly activities (30% of all AltaVista queries are about sex;

Jul 1992	992,000
Jan 1993	1,313,000
Jul 1993	1,776,000
Jan 1994	2,217,000
Jul 1994	3,212,000
Jan 1995	4,852,000
Jul 1995	6,642,000
Jan 1996	9,472,000
Jul 1996	12,881,000
Jan 1997	16,146,000
Jul 1997	19,540,000

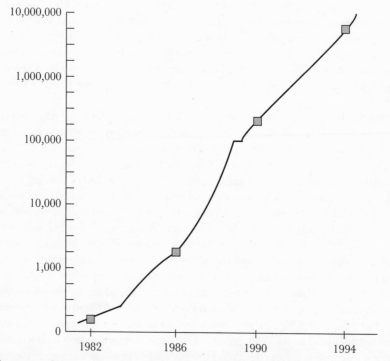

Figure 21.1. Internet Hosts (from Cyberatlas and Network Wizards)

Weiderhold 1997). The Web is routinely used by students to access all kinds of information needed in classroom work or for research. When I taught a course at Columbia, the students complained about reading that was assigned on paper, much preferring the reading that was available on the Web. The Web is preferred not just because it has recreational content but also because it is a way of getting scholarly material.

The convenience of the Web is obvious. If I need a chart or quote from a Mellon Foundation report, I can bring it up in a few tens of seconds at most on my workstation. If I need to find it on paper and it isn't in my office, I'm faced with a delay of a few minutes (to visit the Bellcore library) and probably a few weeks (because, like most libraries, they are cutting back on acquisitions and will have to borrow it from somewhere else). The Web is so convenient that I frequently use it even to read publications that I do have in my office.

Web use is greeted so enthusiastically that volunteers have been typing in (or scanning) out-of-copyright literature on a large scale, as for example for Project Gutenberg. Figure 21.2 shows the number of books *added* to the Project Gutenberg archive each year in the 1990s; by comparison, in the entire 1980s, only two books were entered.

By comparison, some of the electronic journal trials seem disappointing. Some of the reasons that digital library experiments have been less successful than they might have been involve the details of access. Whereas Web browsers are by now effectively universal on campuses, the specific software needed for the CORE project, as an example, was somewhat of a pain for users to install and use. Many of the electronic library projects involve scanned images, which are difficult to manipulate on small screens, and they have rarely involved material that was designed for the kind of use common on computer systems. By contrast, most HTML material is written with the knowledge of the format in which it will be read and is adapted to that style. I note anecdotal complaints even that Acrobat documents as not as easy to read as normal Web pages.

Web pages in particular may have illustrations in color, and even animations, beyond the practical ability of any conventional publisher. Only one in a thousand pages of a chemical journal, for example, is likely to have a color illustration. Yet most popular Web pages have color (although the blinking colored ad banners might be thought to detract rather than help Web users). Also, Web pages need not be written to the traditional standards of publishing; the transparencies that represent the talk associated with a scholarly paper may be easier to read than the paper itself.

Such arguments suggest that the issue with the popularity of the Web compared with digital library experiments is not just content or convenience but also style. In the same way that *Scientific American* is easier to read than traditional professional journals, Web pages can be designed to be easier for students to read than the textbooks they buy now. Reasons might include the way material is broken into fairly short units, each of which is easy to grasp; the informal style; the power of easy cross-referencing, so that details need not be repeated; the extreme personality shown by some Web pages; and the use of illustrations as mentioned before. Perhaps some of these techniques, well known to professional writers, could be encouraged by universities for research writing.

The attractiveness of the newer Web material also suggests that older material will become less and less read. In the same way that vinyl records have suddenly become very old or that TV stations refuse to show black-and-white movies, libraries may find that the nineteenth-century material in many libraries disappears

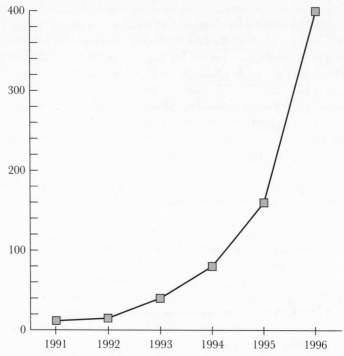

Figure 21.2. Project Gutenberg Texts

from the view of the students. Mere scanning to produce bitmaps results in material that cannot be searched and does not look like newly written text; scanning may produce material that, although more accessible than the old volumes, is still not as welcome to students as new material. How much conversion of the older bitmaps can be justified? Of course, many vinyl recordings are reissued on CD and some movies are colorized, but libraries are unlikely to have resources to do much updating. How can we present the past in a way that students will use? Perhaps the present will become a golden age for scholars because nearly the entire world supply of reference books will have to be rewritten for HTML.

RISKS OF THE WEB

Of course, access to Web pages typically does not involve the academic library or bookstore at all. What does this fact mean for the future of access to information at a university? There are threats to various traditional values of the academic system.

- *Shared experience.* Santayana wrote that it didn't matter what books students read as long as they all read the same thing. Will the great scattering of material on the Web mean that few undergraduates will be able to find some-body else who has been through the same courses reading the same books? When I was an undergraduate I had a friend who would look at people's bookshelves and recite the courses they had taken. This activity will become impossible.

- *Diversity.* Since we can always fear two contradictory dangers, perhaps the ease of getting a few well-promoted Web sites will mean that fewer sources are read. If nobody wants to waste time on a Web site that does not have cartoons, fancy color pictures, and animation, then only a few well-funded organizations will be able to put up Web sites that get an audience. Again, the United States publishes about 50,000 books each year, but produces less than 500 movies. Will the switch to the Web increase or decrease the variety of materials read at a campus?

- *Quality.* Much of the material on the Web is junk; Gene Spafford refers to Usenet as a herd of elephants with diarrhea. Are students going to come to rely on this junk as real? Would we stop believing that slavery or the Holo-caust really happened if enough followers of revisionist history put up a pre-dominance of Web pages claiming the reverse?

- *Loyalty.* It has already been a problem for universities that the typical faculty member in surface effect physics, for example, views as colleagues other ex-perts in surface effect physics around the world rather than the other mem-bers of the same physics department. Will the Web create this disloyalty in undergraduates as well? Will University of Michigan undergraduates read Web pages from Ohio State? Can the Midwest survive that?

- *Equality of access.* Will the need for computers to find information produce bar-riers for people who lack money, good eyesight, or some kinds of interface-using skills? Universities want to be sure that all students can use whatever information delivery techniques are offered; is the Web acceptable to at least as wide a span of students as the traditional library is?

- *Recognition.* Traditionally, faculty obtain recognition and status from publish-ing in prestigious journals. High-energy physicists used to get their latest in-formation from *Physical Review Letter;* today they rely on Ginsparg's preprint bulletin board at Los Alamos National Laboratory. Since this Web site is not refereed, how do people select what to read? Typically, they choose papers by authors they have heard of. So the effect of the switch to electronic pub-lishing is that it is now harder for a new physicist to attract attention.

A broader view of threats posed by electronics to the university, not just those threats arising from digital library technology, has been presented by Eli Noam (1995). Noam worries more about videotapes and remote teaching via television and about the possibility that commercial institutions might attempt to supplant universities by offering cheap education based entirely on electronic technologies.

Should these institutions succeed in attracting enough customers to force traditional universities to lower tuition costs, the financial structure of present-day higher education would be destroyed. Noam recommended that universities emphasize personal mentoring and one-to-one instruction to take the greatest advantage of physical presence.

Similarly, Van Alstyne and Brynjolfsson (1996) have warned of balkanization caused by the preference of individuals to select specialized contacts. They point to past triumphs involving cross-field work, such as the history of Watson and Crick, trained in physics and zoology respectively. In their view, search engines can be too effective, since letting people read only exactly what they were looking for may encourage overspecialization.

As an example of the tendency toward seeking collaborators away from one's base institution, Figure 21.3 shows the tendency of multiauthored papers to come from more than one institution. The figures were compiled by taking the first issue each year from the *SIAM Journal of Control and Optimization* (originally named *SIAM Journal of Control*) and counting the fraction of multiauthored papers in which all the authors came from one institution. The results were averaged over each decade. Note the drop in the 1990s. There has also, of course, been an increase in the total number of multiauthored papers (in 1965 the first issue had 14 papers and every paper had only one author; the first issue in 1996 had 17 papers and only two were single-authored). But few of the multiple-authored papers today came from only one research institution.

Of course, there are advantages to the new technology as well, not just threats. And it is clear that the presence of the Web is coming, whatever universities do— this is the first full paper I have written directly in HTML rather than prepared for a typesetting language. Much of the expansiveness of the Web is all to the good; for many purposes, access to random undergraduate opinions, and certainly to their fact gathering, may well be preferable to ignorance. It is hard to imagine students or faculty giving up the speed with which information can be accessed from their desktops any more than we would give up cars because it is healthier to walk or ecologically more desirable to ride trains. How, then, can we ameliorate or prevent the possible dangers elaborated before?

UNIVERSITY PUBLISHING

Bellcore, like many corporations, has a formal policy for papers published under its name. These papers must be reviewed by management and others, reducing the chance that something sufficiently erroneous to be embarrassing or something that poses a legal risk to the corporation will appear. Many organizations do not yet have any equally organized policy for managing their Web pages (Bellcore does have such a policy that deals with an overlapping set of concerns). Should universities have rules about what can appear on their Web pages? Should such rules distinguish between what goes out on personal versus organizational pages?

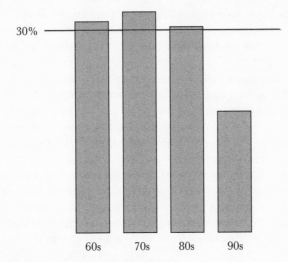

Figure 21.3. Percentage Coauthored from One Site

Should the presence of a page on a Harvard Web page connote any particular sign of quality, similar to the appearance of a book under the Harvard University Press imprint? Perhaps a university should have an approved set of pages, providing some assurance of basic correctness, decency of content, and freedom from viruses; then people wishing to search for serious content might restrict their searches to these areas.

The creation of a university Web site as the modern version of a university press or a journal offers a sudden switch from publishers back to the universities as the providers of information. Could a refereed, high-prestige section of a university Web site attract the publication that now goes to journals? Such a Web site would provide a way for students to find quality material and would build institutional loyalty and shared activities among the members of the university community. Perhaps the easiest way of accomplishing this change would be to make tenure depend on contributions to the university Web site instead of contributions to journals.

The community could even be extended beyond the faculty. Undergraduate papers could be placed on a university Web site; one can easily imagine different parts of the site for different genres ranging from the research monograph to the quip of the day. This innovation would let all students participate and get recognition; but some quality control would need to be imposed, and presence on the Web site would need to be recognized as an honor.

In addition to supporting better quality, a university Web site devoted to course reading could make sure that a diversity of views is supported. On-line reading lists, just like paper reading lists, can be compiled to avoid the problem of everyone relying on the same few sites. This diversity would be fostered if many of the search engines were to start making money by charging people to be listed higher in the list of matches (a recurrent rumor, but perhaps an urban legend). Such an action would also push students to look at sites that perhaps lack fancy graphics and animation.

Excessive reliance on a university Web site could produce too much inbreeding. If university Web sites replace the publications that now provide general prestige, will it be possible for a professor at a less prestigious university to put an article on, say, the Harvard or Stanford Web site? If not, how will anyone ever advance? I do not perceive that this problem will occur soon; the reverse (a total lack of organizational identification) is more likely.

Web sites of this sort would probably not include anonymous contributions. The Net is somewhat overrun right now with untraceable postings that often contain annoying or inflammatory material ranging from the merely boring commercial advertising to the deliberately outrageous political posting. Having Web sites that did not allow this kind of material might help to civilize the Net and make it more productive.

INFORMATION LOCATION

Some professors already provide Web reading lists that correspond to the traditional lists of paper material. The average Columbia course, for example, has 3,000 pages of paper reading (with an occasional additional audiotape in language courses). The lack of quality on the Web means that faculty must provide guidance to undergraduates about what to read there.

More important, it will be necessary for faculty to teach the skill of looking purely at the text of a document and making a judgment as to its credibility. Much of our ability to evaluate a paper document is based on the credibility of the publisher. On the Web, students will have to judge by principles like those of paleography. What do we know, if anything, about the source? Is there a motive for deception? How does the wording of the document read—credibly or excessively emotionally? Do facts that we can check elsewhere agree with those other sources?

The library will also gain a new role. Universities should provide a training service for how to search the Web, and the library is the logical place to provide that training. This logic is partly because librarians are trained in search systems, which are rarely studied formally by any other groups. In addition, librarians will need to keep the old information sources until most students are converted, which will take a while.

The art of learning to retrieve information may also bring students together. I once asked a Columbia librarian whether the advent of computers and networks in the dormitory rooms was creating a generation of introverted nerds lacking social skills. She replied that the reverse was true. In the days of card catalogs, students were rarely seen together; each person searched the cards alone. Now, she said, she frequently sees groups of two or three students at the OPAC terminals, one explaining to the others how to do something. Oh, I said, so you're improving the students' social skills by providing poor human interface software. Not intentionally, she replied. Even with good software, however, there is still a place for students helping each other find information, and universities can try to encourage this interaction.

Much has been written about the information rich versus the information poor and the fear that once information will need to be obtained via machines that cost several thousand dollars, poor people will be placed at a still greater disadvantage in society than they are today. In the university context, money may not be the key issue, since many university libraries provide computers for general use. However, some people face nonfinancial barriers to the use of electronic systems. These barriers may include limited eyesight or hearing (which of course also affect the use of conventional libraries). More important, perhaps, is the difficulty that some users may have with some kinds of interface design. These difficulties range from relatively straightforward issues such as color blindness to complex perceptual issues involving different kinds of interfaces and their demands on different individuals. So far, we do not know whether some users will have trouble with whatever becomes the standard information interface; in fact, we do not know whether some university students in the past had particular difficulties learning card catalogs.

The library may also be a good place to teach aspects of collaboration and sharing that will grow out of researching references, as hyperlinking replaces traditional citation. Students are going to use the Web to cooperate in writing papers as well as in finding information for them. The ease of including (or pointing to) the work of others is likely to greatly expand the extent to which student work becomes collaborative. Learning how to do collaborative work effectively and fairly is an important skill that students can acquire. In particular, the desire to make attractive multimedia works, which may need expertise in writing, drawing, and perhaps even composing music, will drive us to encourage cooperative work.

Students could also be encouraged to help organize all the information on the local Web site. Why should a student create a Web page that prefers local resources? Perhaps because the student receives some kind of academic credit for doing so. University Web sites, to remain useful, will require constant maintenance and updating. Who is going to do that? Realistically, students.

NEW CREATIVITY

Applets that implement animation, interactive games, and many other new kinds of presentation modes are proliferating on the Web. The flowering of creativity in these presentations should be encouraged. In the early days of movies and television, the amount of equipment involved was beyond the resources of amateurs, and universities did not play a major role in the development of these technologies. By contrast, universities are important in American theater and classical music. The Web is also an area in which equipment is not a limitation, and universities have a chance to play a role.

This innovation represents a chance for the university art and music departments to join forces with the library. Just as the traditional tasks of preparing reading lists and scholarly articles can move onto a university Web site, so can the new media. The advantage of collaborating with the library is that we can actually save the beginnings of a new form of creativity. We lack the first e-mail message; nobody understood that it was worth saving. Much of early film (perhaps half the movies made before 1950) no longer survives. The 1950s television entertainment is mostly gone for lack of recording devices. In an earlier age, the Elizabethans did not place a high value on saving their dramatic works; of the plays performed by the Admiral's Men (a competitor to Shakespeare's company), we have only 10% or 15% today. We have a chance not to make the same mistake with innovative Web page designs, providing that such pages are supported in some organized way rather than on computers in individual student dorm rooms.

Recognizing software as a type of scholarship is a change for the academic community. The National Science Foundation tends to say, "we don't pay for software, we pay for knowledge," drawing a sharp distinction between the two. Even computer science departments have said that they do not award a Ph.D. for writing a program. The new kinds of creativity will need a new kind of university recognition. Will we have honorary Web pages instead of honorary degrees? We need undergraduate course credit and tenure consideration for Web pages.

Software and data are new kinds of intellectual output that are not considered creative. Traditionally, for example, the design of a map was considered copyrightable; the data on the map, although representing more of the work, were not considered part of the design and were not protected. In the new university publishing model, data should be a first-class item whose accumulation and collection is valuable and leads to reward.

A switch toward honoring a Web page rather than a paper does have consequences for style, as discussed above. Web pages also have no size constraints; in principle, there is no reason why a gigabyte could not be published by an undergraduate. Universities will need to develop both tools and rules for summarizing and accessing very large items as needed.

CONCLUSION

Academic institutions, in order to preserve access to quality information while also preserving some sense of community in a university, should take a more active view of their Web sites. By using the Web as a reward and as a way of building links between people, universities could serve a social purpose as well as an information purpose. The ample space and low cost of Web publishing provide a way to extend the intellectual community of a university and to make it more inclusive. Web publishing may encourage students and faculty to work together, maintaining a local bonding of the students. The goal is to use university Web publishing, information searching mechanisms, and rewards for new kinds of creativity to build a new kind of university community.

REFERENCES

Borghuis, M., H. Brinckman, A. Fischer, K. Hunter, E. van der Loo, R. Mors, P. Mostert, and J. Zilstra. 1996. *TULIP Final Report*. (New York: Elsevier Science Publishers, 1996, ISBN 0-444-82540-1). See *http://www1.elsevier.nl/homepage/about/resproj/trmenu.htm* on the Web.

Egan, D., M. Lesk, R. D. Ketchum, C. C. Lochbaum, J. Remde, M. Littman, and T. K. Landauer. 1991. "Hypertext for the Electronic Library: CORE Sample Results." *Proc. Hypertext 91*, 229–312. San Antonio, Texas, 15–18 December.

Entlich, R., L. Garson, M. Lesk, L. Normore, J. Olsen and S. Weibel. 1996. "Testing a Digital Library: User Response to the CORE Project." *Library Hi Tech* 14, no. 4: 99–118.

Negroponte. 1996. "Caught Browsing Again." *Wired*, issue 4.05 (May). See *http://www.hotwired.com/wired/4.05/negroponte.html* on the Web.

Noam, Eli M. 1995. "Electronics and the Dim Future of the University." *Science* 270, no. 5234 (13 October): 247.

Novak, T. P., and D. L. Hoffman. 1996. "New Metrics for New Media: Toward the Development of Web Measurement Standards." Project 2000 White Paper, available on the Web at *http://www2000.ogsm.vanderbilt.edu*.

Samuel, A. L. 1964. "The Banishment of Paperwork." *New Scientist* 21, no. 380 (27 February): 529–530.

Van Alstyne, Marshall, and Erik Brynjolfsson. 1996. "Could the Internet Balkanize Science?" *Science* 274, no. 5292 (29 November): 1479–1480.

Wiederhold, Gio. 1997. Private communication.

CHAPTER 22

Digital Documents and the Future of the Academic Community

Peter Lyman

Today the academic community is the subject of an experiment in technological innovation. That experiment is the introduction of digital documents as a new currency for scholarly communication, an innovation that some think will replace the system of print publication that has evolved over the past century. What will be the long-term consequences of this innovation for the conduct of research and teaching, for the library and the campus as places, and ultimately for our sense of academic community?

This work on technology and scholarly communication has been focused upon one dimension of this process of innovation: the economics of scholarly publishing. The central focus has been to understand the formation and dynamics of new markets for digital information: will digital modes of publication be more cost-effective than print modes, both for publishers and for libraries? We must learn how readers use on-line journals and how the journal format itself will evolve in a digital medium: will digital publications change the form and content of scholarly ideas? Together these papers investigate the emerging outline of a new marketplace for ideas, one that will probably be reshaped by new kinds of intellectual property law, but that will certainly include new kinds of pricing, new products, and new ways of using information. These questions are important economically, yet if we knew the answers, would we know enough to understand the impact of technological innovation upon the academic community for which the system of scholarly publication serves as an infrastructure?

One reason this question must be asked is the debate about what economists call "the productivity paradox." This is the observation that the introduction of information technology into the office has not increased the productivity of knowledge workers thus far, unlike the productivity gains that technology has brought to the process of industrial production. Yet Peter Drucker has described the productivity of knowledge workers as the key management problem of the twenty-first century.[1] And more recently, Walter Wriston has described information as a new kind of capital that will be the key to wealth in the economy of the future, saying: "The pursuit of wealth is now largely the pursuit of information, and the application of information to the means of production."[2] Why, then, does it seem that information technology has not increased the productivity of knowledge workers?

Erik Brynjolfsson has defined three dimensions within which an explanation of the productivity paradox might be found: (1) perhaps this paradox is a measurement problem, since the outcomes of work mediated by information technology may not fit traditional categories and are perhaps difficult to measure with traditional methodologies; (2) the productivity paradox might be a consequence of the introduction of very different cultures of work based on new kinds of incentives and skills; hence productivity gains may require redesign and reorganization of work processes previously based on printed records; (3) perhaps information technology creates new kinds of economic value (such as variety, timeliness, and customized service), which change the very nature of the enterprise by introducing new dimensions and qualities of service.[3]

Although the analysis of the impact of information technology on scholarly communication has only indirectly been a discussion about productivity thus far, it should be understood that the question of productivity raises issues like changes in academic culture and the organization of academic work, not just about its efficiency.[4] For the purposes of this discussion, however, what is of immediate interest to me as a political theorist and university librarian is the way the productivity paradox frames the possible dimensions of the dynamics of technological innovation, thereby setting a research agenda for the future. How might our understanding of the *outcomes* or *impact* of research, teaching, and learning change? How might the *incentives* for academic work evolve, and would the *organization* of the process of research and teaching change? Will new kinds of *value* be introduced into academic work, changing its cultures, and will traditional kinds of value be lost? This broader research agenda provides a context for discussing the price, supply, and demand for digital publications.

In sum, how might the substance and organization of academic work change as information technology changes the infrastructure of scholarly communication? To borrow a term from a very different economic tradition, the question of the social impact of information technology concerns the *mode of production,* that is, the complex of social relationships and institutions within which academic work is organized, within which the products of academic work are created and consumed, and within which cultural valuation is given to academic work. In the course of this exploration of the changing modes of production that govern knowledge work, it will be necessary to think seriously about whether printed knowledge and digital information are used in the same way, if we are to understand the nature of demand; about the new economic roles of knowledge, if we are to understand issues of price and supply; and about how the management of knowledge might be a strategy for increasing the productivity of knowledge workers, if we are to understand the future of institutions like the research library and disciplinary guilds.

THE SYSTEM OF SCHOLARLY COMMUNICATION

The idea that there is a system of scholarly communication was popularized by the American Council of Learned Societies newsletter *Scholarly Communication*, which began by publishing a survey on the impact of personal computers on humanities research in 1985. "Scholarly communication" is a term invented to frame both print publication and digital communication within a single functional schema, tacitly asserting a continuity between them. It is this continuity that is in question, not least because the term "scholarly communication" encompasses the very research processes that are obviously being transformed by information technology, resulting in the creation of new kinds of information products and services that were not part of the scholarly publishing marketplace in the print era. These products and services include, for example, patents on methodological procedures and genetic information; software for gathering, visualizing and analyzing data; information services, such as document delivery and databases; network services; electronic mail, mailing lists, and Web pages; and electronic journals and CD-ROMs.

Today each of the institutional parts of the system of scholarly communication built over the past 50 years—research universities, publishing, and libraries—is changing, and it is unlikely that a new equilibrium will resemble the old. This system is unusual, perhaps, in that different participants perceive it from very different, perhaps contradictory, perspectives. From the perspective of the academic community, both the *production* and *consumption* of scholarly information are governed by a culture of gift exchange: production by the faculty as members of scholarly guilds, and consumption by free access to information in libraries. In gift exchange cultures, information is exchanged primarily (although not necessarily exclusively) in order to create and sustain a sense of community greater than the fragmenting force of specialization and markets. From the perspective of publishing, however, production for the academic marketplace is centered on the faculty as authors, a relationship governed by contract, and consumption is centered on academic research libraries, governed by copyright law in print publishing and by contract law in digital publishing. It is this variation in perspective, perhaps, that leads each side to hope that digital documents will replace printed journals without changing other aspects of the system of scholarly communication.

Gift and market exchange are symbiotic, not opposites. If scholarly publishing is governed by the rules of market exchange, it must manage the boundaries between two gift cultures, that within which knowledge is created and that within which knowledge is consumed. The crisis of scholarly communication has made these boundaries very difficult to manage, as ideas from the university are turned into intellectual property, then sold back to the university to be used as a common good in the library.

Why the crisis in boundary management? The immediate crisis that has desta-bilized the system is the problem of sharply increasing costs for scholarly journals in science, technology, and medicine. The causes of the crisis are varied, but they begin with the commercialization of scholarly publishing, a dramatic shift from nonprofit to for-profit publishing since the 1950s, that created the hybrid gift/mar-ket system. In turn, the historic growth in the amount of scientific, technical, and medical information, driven by federal funding, has increased costs, particularly as specialization has created journals with very small markets. And the waning of a sense of the legitimacy of library collection costs within the university has allowed the rate of growth of collection budgets to fall far below the rate of price in-creases.[5] Even with cost/price increases, the academic gift economy still subsidizes the market economy, for faculty give away their intellectual property to the pub-lishers, yet remarkably, those who subsidize research do not yet make a property claim on the research they support. Subsidies include, for example, the federal funding of research, institutional subsidies, and the voluntary labor of faculty in providing editorial services to publishers.

This system evolved at the turn of the twentieth century as a subsidy for non-profit university presses and disciplinary society publishers in order to circulate scholarly information and build a national intellectual infrastructure. Since 1950, however, federal research funding and commercial publishing have reshaped the system, creating the hybrid market-gift exchange system with many unrecognized cross subsidies.

Higher education is both the producer and consumer of scholarly publications. As creators of scholarship, faculty are motivated by nonmarket incentives, pri-marily promotion and tenure; yet at the same time, faculty see themselves as inde-pendent entrepreneurs, managing a professional career through self-governed dis-ciplinary guilds that cross all educational institutions. This guildlike structure is a deliberate anachronism, perhaps, but one that sustains a sense of professional identity through moral as well as material rewards.[6]

Scholarly publications are consumed within a gift culture institution called the library, a subsidized public good within which knowledge appears to the reader as a free good. Publishers would add that this gift culture is, in turn, subsidized by the owners of intellectual property through the fair use and first sale doctrines, which generally allow copyrighted information to be consumed for educational pur-poses.

The ambiguity at the boundary of gift and market extends to institutions of higher education as well, which are simultaneously corporation and community. But the dominant factor that has shaped the last 50 years of higher education is that universities have become a kind of public interest corporation that serves na-tional policy goals. Just as the Morrill Act created land grant colleges to promote research and education for the development of the agricultural economy, modern research universities have been shaped by federal research funding since World War II as "milieus of innovation," functioning as tacit national laboratories for a polity uncomfortable with the idea of a formal industrial policy.[7]

This system of scholarly communication is in crisis. Consider, for example, the possible consequences for this system if some of the ideas and questions being debated nationally were to come to pass:

- What is the future of university research? Does the research university still play a central role as a national milieu for innovation, or has the corporation become the focus of innovative research and national information policy?

- What is the future scope of higher education? Historically, colleges and universities have had a tacit monopoly of the education market based on accreditation and geographical proximity, but instructional technology and distance education have created new markets for education. With the Western Governors' University proposal, a national market for education would be created based on selling teaching services that will be evaluated by examination rather than the accreditation of traditional institutional settings for education. Moreover, corporate training and for-profit education is on the verge of competing directly with some sectors of education.

- What is the future of the library as a public good? In the polity, the idea of a national digital library has been modeled upon the universal access policies governing telephone and electric utilities. Here the public good is fulfilled by the provision of "access," but it will be the consumer's responsibility to pay for information used. The cultural legitimation crisis of public institutions within the polity extends to the funding of academic research libraries within the university as well.

- What is the future of the academic disciplines in a world of increasing specialization that makes it difficult for traditional disciplines to find common terms of discourse and at a time in which disciplinary metamorphosis is now creating new fields like molecular biology, neuroscience, cultural studies, and environmental science?

- What is the future of fair use? Rights that exist in print are not being automatically extended to the use of digital works. Federal policy discussions about intellectual property in the digital environment have not included fair use, giving priority to the creation of a robust market in digital publication and the creation of incentives for the publication of educational works.

These are questions, not predictions, but they are questions that are being discussed in the polity, so they are not mere speculation. They are intended only to point out that the system of scholarly communication is a historical creation, a response to certain conditions that may no longer exist.

Three new factors define the conditions within which a system of scholarly communication may evolve. First, the emergence of a global economy in which intellectual property is an important source of wealth creates a context in which the value of scholarly research may be a matter of national interest extending far beyond the traditional concerns of the academy. Second, the end of the cold war as a stimulus for national information policy that took the form of federal patronage of university research may fundamentally change the shape and content of federal funding for research. And third, information technology has created global communication, enabling new links between researchers around the world, creating the possibility that the intellectual disciplines of the future are likely to develop paradigms and concerns that transcend national boundaries.

DIGITAL DOCUMENTS AND ACADEMIC PRODUCTIVITY

What is the nature of digital documents as an innovation, that it is possible to ask whether they might affect the value of information and its use and the organization of academic research? Geoffrey Nunberg has identified two differences between digital and mechanical technologies that affect both the value of knowledge and the organization of its reproduction.

> Unlike mechanical antecedents like the printing press, the typewriter, or the telegraph, the computer isn't restricted to a single role in production and diffusion. In fact, the technology tends to erase distinctions between the separate processes of creation, reproduction and distribution that characterize the classical industrial model of print commodities, not just because the electronic technology employed is the same at each stage, but because control over the processes can be exercised at any point.
>   . . . The second important difference between the two technologies follows from the immateriality of electronic representations and the resulting reductions in the cost of reproduction.[8]

The fundamental consequence of these differences, Nunberg argues, is that the user[9] has much greater control of the process of digital reproduction of knowledge as well as its content, essentially transforming the meaning of publication by allowing the reader to replace the author in determining the context and form of knowledge.

However, these differences in the process of the reproduction of ideas do not apply to all digital information, only to information that is "born digital," sometimes also called "digital documents."[10] Today's marketplace consists largely of *digitized* documents, that is, works written for and reproduced in printed journals, then scanned and distributed on the network. Digitized documents conform to the modes of production of print journals: to the rhetorical rules of the genre of scientific and to the traditional relationships between author, publisher, and reader. If prior processes of technological innovation hold in this case, however, digitized documents represent only a transitional stage, one in which the attempt is made to use new technologies to increase the productivity of traditional modes of production and to reinforce traditional authority patterns. CD-ROM technology is a good example of the attempt to preserve the traditional modes of production yet take advantage of the capability of digital signals to include multimedia, by packaging them within a physical medium that can be managed just like a printed commodity. The immateriality of networked information is much more difficult to control, although encryption and digital watermarking are technologies that give to digital signals some of the characteristics that enable print copyright to be regulated.

The interesting points to watch will be whether the content of digital and print versions of the same works begin to diverge and whether readers will be allowed to appropriate published digital works and reuse them in new contexts. Markets are made by consumers, not just by publishers, and the fundamental question concerns the future of readers' behavior as the consumers of information. What, for example, is the unit of knowledge? Will readers want to consume digital journals by subscription? Or consume single articles and pay for them as stand-alone commodities through document delivery? Or treat a journal run as a database and pay for access to it as a searchable information service? As Nunberg points out, the intersection of technology and markets will be determined by the nature of the digital signal, which unifies the processes of production, reproduction, and use of information.

In thinking about the nature of digital documents and the kind of social relationships that they make possible, consider the credit card, which may well be the most successful digital document thus far. The credit card itself is only an interface to liquid cash and credit, taking advantage of mainframe computer technology and computer networks to manage market transactions wherever they occur around the world. It replaces printed currency and portable forms of wealth such as letters of credit and traveler's checks with a utility service. It creates new kinds of value: liquidity, through an interface to a worldwide financial system; timeliness and access, through 24-hour service anywhere in the world; and customized or personalized service, through credit. These new kinds of value are not easily measured by traditional measures of productivity; Brynjolfsson notes that by traditional measures, the ATM seems to reduce productivity by reducing the use of checks, the traditional output measure of banks. Yet to characterize the new kinds of value simply as improvements in the quality of service is not a sufficient description of the value of credit or debit cards, since they have created entirely new kinds of markets for financial services and a new interface for economic activity that supports entirely new styles of life, creating a mobile society.

One of these new markets is worthy of a second look, not only as an example of innovation, but to explore the *reflexive* quality of digital documents. When I use a debit card, a profile of my patterns of consumption is created, information that is of economic value for advertising and marketing; thus I often receive coupons for new or competing products on the back of my grocery receipt. Information about my use of information is a new kind of economic value and the basis of a new kind of market when used by advertisers and market analysts. In tracking the use of digital services, network technologies might also be described as keeping the consumer under surveillance. Issues of privacy aside, and they are not sufficiency recognized as yet, this tracking will make possible an entirely new, direct, and unmediated relationship between consumer and publisher.

Thus the discussion of protecting intellectual property on the Internet has focused not only on technologies that allow for the control of access to copyrighted material, but also on technologies that audit the use of information, including requirements for the authentication of the identity of the user and tracking patterns of use. The consequences of this reflexivity may well reflect a fundamental shift in how we conceive of the value of information. While markets for physical commodities were regulated by laws and inventory management techniques, markets for digital services will focus on both the content and use of information and will use the network as a medium for knowledge management techniques.[11]

To summarize this process of innovation, credit cards might be described in productivity terms as an efficient new way to manage money, but they might also be described as creating entirely new genres of wealth, literally a new kind of currency; as new ways of life that create new kinds of social and geographical mobility; and in terms of the new kinds of markets and organizations that they make possible. Digitized documents may lower the costs of reproduction and distribution of print journals and perhaps some first-copy costs, but they also create new kinds of value in faster modes of access to information, new techniques for searching, and more customized content. And in the longer run, true digital documents will produce new genres of scholarly discourse, new kinds of information markets, and perhaps new kinds of educational institutions to use them.

At the moment these new possibilities tend to be discussed in terms of the capacity of the new technology to disrupt the laws, cultures, and organizations that have managed research, reading, publishing, and intellectual property in the era of print. Most prominent among these disruptions has been the discussion of the protection of copyright on the Internet, but there is also active concern about the social impacts of digital documents. For example, we have just identified the problem of privacy and surveillance of networked communication, a capacity for surveillance that has already begun to change the nature of supervision in the workplace. Or, to take a second kind of social impact, pornography on the Web has been defined as a social problem involving the protection of children. But these problems are only two examples of a broader issue concerning the impact of a global communications medium on local norms, for the scope of the network transcends the jurisdiction even of national regulatory authorities. There is discussion about the quality of social relationships in Cyberia, negatively manifested by the problem of hostile electronic mail and positively manifested by emerging forms of virtual community.[12] And in national information policy, debate continues about the proper balance between the public interest in access to information and the commercialization of information in order to create robust information markets.

To summarize, digital technology is not so much about the introduction of intelligent machines, a process that Wriston described as "the application of information to the means of production," as it is about the productivity of knowledge workers. The process of technological innovation implies social and economic change and will be marked by changing knowledge cultures and new genres, which support new styles of life; by changing modes of production, which are likely to be manifested in new kinds of rhetoric, discourse, and new uses of information; and by new forms of communication and community, which will be the foundation of new markets and institutions.

DIGITAL DOCUMENTS AND ACADEMIC COMMUNITY

In an essay called "The Social Life of Documents," John Seeley Brown and Paul Duguid have argued that documents should not be interpreted primarily as containers for content, but as the creators of a sense of community. They say, "the circulation of documents first helps make and then helps maintain social communities and institutions in ways that looking at the content alone cannot explain. In offering an alternative to the notion that documents deliver meaning, [there is a] connection between the creation of communities and the creation of meaning."[13] That is, the central focus of analysis should not be on the artifact itself or even, perhaps, on the market as the primary social formation around documents, but instead the focus should be on the function of the artifact and market in creating and sustaining the social worlds, or communities, of the readers. Here, at last, we have identified the missing subject for discussions of the impact of technology and digital documents on social change: the academic community.

Recently the business management literature has begun to consider an interesting variant of this thesis, namely that the formation of a sense of community within electronic commerce on digital networks is the precondition for the creation and sustenance of markets for digital services. For example, John Hagel III and Arthur G. Armstrong argue that producers of digital services must adapt to the culture of the network.

> By giving customers the ability to interact with each other as well as with the company itself, businesses can build new and deeper relationships with customers. We believe that commercial success in the on-line arena will belong to those who organize virtual communities to meet multiple social and commercial needs.[14]

Whereas producers controlled traditional markets, they argue, the information revolution shifts the balance of power to the consumer by providing tools to select the best value, creating entirely new modes of competition. The markets of the future will take the form of virtual communities that will be a medium for "direct channels of communication between producers and customers" and that will "threaten the long-term viability of traditional intermediaries" (p. 204). In the context of scholarly communication, "traditional intermediaries" would mean libraries and perhaps educational institutions as well.

The questions concerning productivity and technological innovation might now be reconstituted as a kind of sociology of knowledge: What kind of academic community first created print genres and was in turn sustained by them? What kind of community is now creating digital genres and is in turn sustained by them? And what is the relationship between the two, now and in the future?

On a larger scale, the relationship between community and digital documents is a problem in national information policy. In the United States, national information policy has tended to focus on the creation of information markets, but the broader discussion of the social and political impact of digital communications has been concerned with issues of community. For example, the Communications Decency Act and subsequent judicial review has concentrated on Internet pornography and its impact on the culture and mores of local communities. Social and political movements ranging from Greenpeace to militia movements have used the Internet to organize dissent and political action; is this protected free speech and association? Universities are concerned about the impact of abusive electronic mail on academic culture.

The bridge between technology and community is suggested by the elements in the analysis of productivity: how new technologies add new value, create new incentives, and enable new kinds of organization. Brown and Duguid argue that our nation's sense of political community was created by newspapers, not so much in the content of the stories, but in their circulation:

> Reaching a significant portion of the population, newspapers helped develop an implicit sense of community among the diverse and scattered populace of the separate colonies and the emerging post-revolutionary nation. . . . That is, the emergence of a common sense of community contributed as much to the formation of nationhood as the rational arguments of Common Sense. Indeed the former helped create the audience for the latter.[15]

Similarly, and closer to the issue of scholarly communication, the scientific letters that circulated among the Fellows of the Royal Society were the prototype for scientific journals, which in turn sustained scholarly disciplines, which are the organizing infrastructure for academic literature and departments. New forms of value, which is to say new *uses* of information, create new genres of documents, which in turn create literature, which serves as the historical memory for new forms of community.[16]

In the case of print and digital documents, change is not evolutionary because these two kinds of information offer different kinds of value, but they are not opposites. Genre, for example, has been shaped by the physical characteristics of the print medium, including the *design* within which information is presented (e.g., page layout, font, binding) as well as the rhetorical norms governing the structure of information (e.g., essay, scientific article, novel). Rhetoric has been described as a structure to govern the allocation of attention, the scarcest resource of modern times. Our frequent complaints of information overload may well reflect the early stage in the development of rhetorical structures for digital media. Certainly we face more information and more kinds of information, but the real problem reflects the difficulty in determining the quality of digital information (e.g., the lack of reputation and branding); or the difficulty of knowing which kind of information is relevant for certain kinds of decisions (e.g., the problem of productivity); or the relatively primitive rhetorical practices that govern new media (e.g., the problem of flaming in electronic mail).

Consider, for example, the technology of scientific visualization and multimedia. Thus far, visual media tend to be consumed as entertainment, which require us to surrender our critical judgment in order to enjoy the show. Thus the problem of the quality of multimedia information is not simply technical, but requires the development of new genres and rhetorical norms within which visual media are used in a manner consistent with academic values such as critical judgment.

Or, consider some of the new genres for digital documents, which might well be described as adding new kinds of value to information: hypertext, the Boolean search, and the database. Most of us did not learn to read these new genres in childhood as part of the process of becoming literate, and we lack conceptual models for learning them other than those derived from our experience with print; there is, perhaps, a generational difference in this regard. The database raises new problems in defining the unit of knowledge: will consumers read the digital *journal* or the digital *articles,* or will the unit of knowledge be the *screen,* the digital analog of the paragraph, which is identified by a search engine or agent? HTML raises the question: who is responsible for the context of information, the author or the reader? As readers jump from text to text, linking things that had not previously been linked, they create context and therefore govern meaning, and reading becomes a kind of performing art. These questions might be described, perhaps, as a legitimation crisis, in that the traditional authorities that governed or mediated the structure and quality of print are no longer authoritative: the author, the editor, the publisher, and the library. Who are the new authorities?

Information technology was designed to solve the information problems of engineers and scientists, becoming instantiated into the hardware and software templates within which new genres and rhetorical forms have evolved, thence into computer literacy training for nontechnical users, and thence the user skills and modes of reading that the younger generation thinks of as intuitive relationships with the machine. Hypertext, for example, turns narrative into a database, which is a highly functional strategy for recovering specific bits of information in scientific research, as, for example, in searching for information with which to solve a problem. Electronic mail is a highly efficient means for exchanging messages but has little scope for lexical or rhetorical nuance. This limitation has little effect on groups sharing a common culture and background, but it becomes a problem given the diverse social groups that use electronic mail as a medium for communication today, hence, the frequency of flaming and misunderstanding.

In any case, as sociologists like Bruno Latour have noted, the original intent of the designers of a technology does not necessarily govern the process of technological innovation, for the meaning and purpose of a technology mutates as it crosses social contexts.[17] Thus the problem may not best be posed in terms of an emerging cultural hegemony of the sciences and technology over academic institutions, although many of us do not find it intuitive to be giving "commands" to a computer or pressing "control" and "escape" keys.

But the cultural and organizational consequences of information technology need to be thought about, as technologies designed for the military, business, and science are introduced across the academic community. Thus far the discussion of this topic has occurred primarily in the context of thinking about the uses of distance education, which is to say, the extension of the scope of a given institution's teaching services to a national, or perhaps global, market. But there is a broader question about the nature of the academic community itself in a research university: what is the substance of this sense of community, and what sustains it?

It is often claimed that digital communication can sustain a sense of *virtual* community, but what is meant by virtual, and what is meant by community in this context? The literature on *social capital*, for example, argues that civic virtue is a function of participation, and those who participate in one voluntary social activity are highly likely to participate in others, creating a social resource called civil society or community.[18] Robert Putnam argues that television, and perhaps other media, are a passive sort of participation that replace and diminish civic communities. The question is whether today's virtual communities represent a kind of social withdrawal or whether they might become resources for social participation and community. If this community is an important goal of digital networks, how might they be better designed to accomplish this purpose? Can networks be designed to facilitate the moral virtues of community, such as trust, reciprocity, and loyalty?

And finally, to return to the question of the productivity of knowledge workers in an information society, and mindful of the heuristic principle that documents can be understood in terms of the communities they sustain, is not the research library best conceptualized as the traditional knowledge management strategy of the academic community? If so, how well does the digital library perform this function, at least as we understand it thus far? The digital library is generally conceived of only as an information resource, as if the library were only a collection, rather than as a shared intellectual resource and site for a community.

The social functions of the library are not easily measured in terms of outcomes, but are an element in the productivity of faculty and students. To some extent, perhaps, libraries have brought this problem on themselves by measuring quality in terms of fiscal inputs and size of collections, and they must begin to define and measure their role in productivity. But in another sense, the focus on the content and format of information to the exclusion of consideration of the social contexts and functions of knowledge is a distortion of the nature and dynamics of scholarly communication and the academic community.

NOTES

1. Peter F. Drucker, *The Age of Discontinuity* (New York: Harper and Row, 1978).
2. Walter Wriston, *The Twilight of Sovereignty* (New York: Charles Scribner's Sons, 1992), xii.
3. Erik Brynjolfsson, "The Productivity Paradox of Information Technology: Review and Assessment," *Communications of the ACM* (December, 1993), 36(12)67–77.
4. See, for example, William F. Massy and Robert Zemsky, "Using Information Technology to Enhance Academic Productivity," a White Paper for the EDUCOM National Learning Infrastructure Initiative (NLII), 1995.
5. Anthony M. Cummings, Marcia L. Witte, William G. Bowen, Laura O. Lazarus, and Richard H. Ekman, *University Libraries and Scholarly Communication.* (Washington D.C.: The Association of Research Libraries, 1992).
6. See Stanley Chodorow and Peter Lyman, "The Responsibilities of Universities in the New Information Environment," in *The Mirage of Continuity,* ed. Brian L. Hawkins and Patricia Battin (Washington, D.C.: Council on Library and Information Resources, 1998), 61–78.
7. See Manuel Castells, *The Rise of the Network Society* (London: Blackwell Publishers, 1996), 56.
8. Geoffrey Nunberg, "The Places of Books in the Age of Electronic Reproduction," in *Future Libraries,* ed. R. Howard Bloch and Carla Hesse (Berkeley: University of California Press, 1993), 21–22.
9. The term "user" is applied to the consumption of digital documents the way the term "reader" has been applied to the consumption of printed works. "User" is a semantic strategy for pointing out that engagement with a technology mediates between the reader and the text, allowing for the direct control over content and format that Nunberg describes.
10. See, for example, the report on a workshop held at the Hawaii International Conference on System Sciences in January 1995: M. Stuart Lynn and Ralph H. Sprague Jr., eds., *Documents in the Digital Culture: Shaping the Future* (Honolulu, Hawaii: A HICSS Monograph, 1995).
11. On knowledge management, see, for example, Thomas H. Davenport, Sirkka L. Jarvenpaa, and Michael C. Beers, "Improving Knowledge Work Processes," *Sloan Management Review* (Summer 1996), 53–65.
12. The term "Cyberia" reflects the anthropologist's approach to analyzing the Internet as a site for culture and community and is best summarized by Arturo Escobar, "Welcome to Cyberia: Notes on the Anthropology of Cyberculture," *Current Anthropology* (June 1994), 35(4)211–231.
13. John Seeley Brown and Paul Duguid, "The Social Life of Documents," *Release 1.0: Esther Dyson's Monthly Report* (New York: Edventure Holdings Inc., October 11, 1995), 7.
14. John Hagel III and Arthur G. Armstrong, *net.gain: expanding markets through virtual communities* (Boston, Mass.: Harvard Business School Press, 1997), 5.

15. Brown and Duguid, 5. This argument is derived from Benedict Anderson's *Imagined Communities*.

16. The concept of virtual community was introduced by Howard Reingold, writing about the social relationships and sense of community that inter-relay chat, MOO, and MUD technology sustained. The term "community" is used provisionally, because the participants use it to describe their experience, not because virtual community has any necessary resemblance to more traditional meanings of the word.

17. Note that Latour chose the genre of the novel to discuss this phenomenon. Bruno Latour, *Aramis, or The Love of Technology*, trans. Catherine Porter (Cambridge, Mass.: Harvard University Press, 1996).

18. See, for example, Robert D. Putnam, "The Strange Disappearance of Civic America," *The American Prospect* (Winter 1996), 24(34–48). In the same issue, see also Sherry Turkle, "Virtuality and Its Discontents: Searching for Community in Cyberspace."

CHAPTER 23

The Economics of Electronic Journals

Andrew Odlyzko

INTRODUCTION

It is now practically universally accepted that scholarly journals will have to be available in digital formats. What is not settled is whether they can be much less expensive than print journals. Most traditional print publishers still claim, just as they have claimed for years, that switching to an electronic format can save at most 30% of the costs, namely the expenses of printing and mailing. Prices of electronic versions of established print journals are little, if any, lower than those of the basic paper versions. What publishers talk about most in connection with electronic publishing are the extra costs they bear, not their savings [BoyceD]. On the other hand, there is also rapid growth of electronic-only journals run by scholars themselves and available for free on the Internet.

Will the free electronic journals dominate? Most publishers claim that they will not survive (see, for example, [Babbitt]) and will be replaced by electronic subscription journals. Even some editors of the free journals agree with that assessment. My opinion is that it is too early to tell whether subscriptions will be required. It is likely that we will have a mix of free and subscription journals and that for an extended period neither will dominate. However, I am convinced that even the subscription journals will be much less expensive than the current print journals. The two main reasons are that modern technology makes it possible to provide the required services much more cheaply, and that in scholarly publishing, authors have no incentive to cooperate with the publishers in maintaining a high overhead system.

In section 2 I summarize the economics of the current print journal system. In section 3 I look at the electronic-only journals that have sprung up over the last few years and are available for free on the Net. I discuss the strange economic incentives that exist in scholarly publishing in section 4. Finally, in section 5 I present some tentative conclusions and projections.

This article draws heavily on my two previous papers on scholarly publishing, [Odlyzko1, Odlyzko2], and the references given there. For other references on electronic journals, see also [Bailey, PeekN]. It should be stressed that only scholarly journal publishing is addressed here. Trade publishing will also be revolutionized by new technology. However, institutional and economic incentives are different there, so the outcome will be different.

Scholarly publishing is a public good, paid for largely (although often indirectly) by taxpayers, students' parents, and donors. The basic assumption I am making in this article is that its costs should be minimized to the largest extent consistent with delivering the services required by scholars and by the society they serve.

COSTS OF PRINT JOURNALS

Just how expensive is the current print journal system? While careful studies of the entire scholarly journal system had been conducted in the 1970s [KingMR, Machlup], they were obsolete by the 1990s. Recent studies, such as those in [AMSS, Kirby], address primarily prices that libraries pay, and they show great disparities. For example, among the mathematics journals considered in [Kirby], the price per page ranged from $0.07 to $1.53, and the price per 10,000 characters, which compensates for different formats, from under $0.30 to over $3.00. Such statistics are of greatest value in selecting journals to purchase or (much more frequently) to drop, especially when combined with measures of the value of journals, such as the impact factors calculated by the *Science Citation Index*. However, those measures are not entirely adequate when studying the entire scholarly journal publishing system. For example, in the statistics of [Kirby], the *Duke Mathematics Journal* (*DMJ*), published by Duke University Press, is among the least expensive journals at $0.19 per page. On the other hand, using the same methodology as that in [Kirby], the *International Mathematics Research Notices* (*IMRN*), coming from the same publisher as *DMJ*, would have been among the most expensive ones several years ago and would be around the median now (its size has expanded while the price has stayed about constant). The difference appears to come from the much smaller circulation of *IMRN* than of *DMJ* and not from any inefficiencies or profits at Duke University Press. (This case is considered in more detail in Section 4.)

To estimate the systems cost of the scholarly journal publishing system, it seems advisable to consider total costs associated with an article. In writing the "Tragic Loss" essay [Odlyzko1], I made some estimates based on a sample of journals, all in mathematics and computer science. They were primary research journals, purchased mainly by libraries. The main identifiable costs associated with a typical article were the following:

1. revenue of publisher: $4,000
2. library costs other than purchase of journals and books: $8,000
3. editorial and refereeing costs: $4,000
4. authors' costs of preparing a paper: $20,000

Of these costs, the publishers' revenue of $4,000 per article (i.e., the total revenue from sales of a journal, divided by the number of articles published in that journal) attracts the most attention in discussions of the library or journal publishing "crises." It is also the easiest to measure and most reliable. However, it is also among the smallest, and this fact is a key factor in the economics of scholarly publishing. The direct costs of a journal article are dwarfed by various indirect costs and subsidies.

The cost estimates above are only rough approximations, especially those for the indirect costs of preparing a paper. There is no accounting mechanism in place to associate the costs in items (3) and (4) with budgets of academic departments. However, those costs are there, and they are large, whether they are half or twice the estimates presented here.

Even the revenue estimate (1) is a rough approximation. Most publishers treat their revenue and circulation data as confidential. There are some detailed accounts, such as that for the American Physical Society (APS) publications in [Lustig] and for the *Pacific Journal of Mathematics* in [Kirby], but they are few.

The estimate of $4,000 in publishers' revenue per article made in [Odlyzko1] has until recently been just about the only one available in the literature. It is supported by the recent study of Tenopir and King [TenopirK], which also estimates that the total costs of preparing the first copy of an article are around $4,000. The estimate in [Odlyzko1] was based primarily on data in [AMSS] and so is about five years out of date. If I were redoing my study, I would adjust for the rapid inflation in journal prices in the intervening period, which would inflate the costs. On the other hand, in discussing general scholarly publishing, I would probably deflate my estimate to account for the shorter articles that are prevalent in most areas. (The various figures for size of the literature and so on derived in [Odlyzko1] were based on samples almost exclusively from mathematics and theoretical computer science, which were estimated to have articles of about 20 pages each. This figure is consistent with the data for these areas in [TenopirK]. However, the average length of an article over all areas is about 12 pages.) Thus, on balance, the final estimate for the entire scholarly literature would probably still be $3,000 to 4,000 as the publisher revenue from each article.

The $4,000 revenue figure was the median of an extremely dispersed sample. Among the journals used in [Odlyzko1] to derive that estimate, the cost per article ranged from under $1,000 for some journals to over $8,000 for others. This disparity in costs brings out another of the most important features of scholarly publishing, namely lack of price competition. Could any airline survive with $8,000 fares if a competitor offered $1,000 fares?

Wide variations in prices for seemingly similar goods are common even in competitive markets, but they are usually associated with substantial differences in quality. For example, one can sometimes purchase round-trip trans-Atlantic tickets for under $400, provided one travels in the off-season in coach, purchases the tickets when the special sales are announced, travels on certain days, and so on. On the other hand, a first-class unrestricted ticket bought at the gate for the same plane can cost 10 times as much. However, it is easy to tell what the difference in price buys in this case. It is much harder to do so in scholarly publishing. There is some positive correlation between quality of presentation (proofreading, typography, and so on) and price, but it is not strong. In the area that matters the most to scholars, that of quality of material published, it is hard to discern any correlation. In mathematics, the three most prestigious journals are published by a commercial publisher, by a university, and by a professional society, respectively, at widely different costs. (Library subscription costs per page differ by more than a factor of 7 [Kirby], and it is unlikely that numbers of subscribers differ by that much.) In economics, the most prestigious journals are published by a professional society, the American Economic Association, and are among the least expensive ones in that field.

Many publishers argue that costs cannot be reduced much, even with electronic publishing, since most of the cost is the first-copy cost of preparing the manuscripts for publication. This argument is refuted by the widely differing costs among publishers. The great disparity in costs among journals is a sign of an industry that has not had to worry about efficiency. Another sign of lack of effective price competition is the existence of large profits. The economic function of high profits is to attract competition and innovation, which then reduce those profits to average levels. However, as an example, Elsevier's pretax margin exceeds 40% [Hayes], a level that is "phenomenally high, comparable as a fraction of revenues to the profits West Publishing derives from the Westlaw legal information service, and to those of Microsoft" [Odlyzko2]. Even professional societies earn substantial profits on their publishing operations.

> Not-for-profit scientific societies, particularly in the United States and in the UK, also often realize substantial surpluses from their publishing operations. . . . Net returns of 30% and more have not been uncommon. [Lustig]

Such surpluses are used to support other activities of the societies, but in economic terms they are profits. Another sign of an industry with little effective competition is that some publishers keep over 75% of the revenues from journals just for distributing those journals, with all the work of editing and printing being done by learned societies.

Although profits are often high in scholarly publishing, it is best to consider them just as an indicator of an inefficient market. While they are a substantial contributor to the journal crisis, they are not its primary cause. Recall that the publisher revenue of $4,000 per article is only half of the $8,000 library cost (i.e., costs of buildings, staff, and so on) associated with that article. Thus even if all publishers gave away their journals for free, there would still be a cost problem. The growth in the scholarly literature is the main culprit.

Even in the print medium, costs can be reduced. That they have not been is due to the strange economics of scholarly publishing, which will be discussed in Section 4. However, even the least expensive print publishers still operate at a cost of around $1,000 per article. Electronic publishing offers the possibilities of going far below even that figure and of dramatically lowering library costs.

COSTS OF "FREE" ELECTRONIC JOURNALS

How low can the costs of electronic publishing be? One extreme example is provided by Paul Ginsparg's preprint server [Ginsparg]. It currently processes about 20,000 papers per year. These 20,000 papers would cost $40 to $80 million to publish in conventional print journals (and most of them do get published in such journals, creating costs of $40 to $80 million to society). To operate the Ginsparg server in its present state would take perhaps half the time of a systems administrator, plus depreciation and maintenance on the hardware (an ordinary workstation with what is by today's standards a modest disk system). This expenses might come (with overheads) to a maximum of $100,000 per year, or about $5 per paper.

In presentations by publishers, one often hears allusions to big National Science Foundation (NSF) grants and various hidden costs in Ginsparg's operation. Ginsparg does have a grant from NSF for $1 million, spread over three years, but it is for software development, not for the operation of his server. However, let us take an extreme position, and let us suppose that he has an annual subsidy of $1 million. Let us suppose that he spends all his time on the server (which he manifestly does not, as anyone who checks his publications record will realize), and let us toss in a figure of $300,000 for his pay (including the largest overhead one can imagine that even a high-overhead place like Los Alamos might have). Let us also assume that a large new workstation had to be bought each year for the project, say at $20,000, and let us multiply that by 5 to cover the costs of mirror sites. Let us in addition toss in $100,000 per year for several T1 lines just for this project. Even with all these outrageous overestimates, we can barely come to the vicinity of $1.5 million per year, or $75 per paper. That is dramatically less than the $2,000 to $4,000 per paper that print journals require. (I am using a figure of $2,000 for each paper here as well as that of $4,000 from [Odlyzko1] since APS, the publisher of the lion's share of the papers in Ginsparg's server and among the most efficient publishers, collects revenues of about $2,000 per paper.) As Andy Grove of Intel points out [Grove], any time that anything important changes in a business by a factor of 10, it is necessary to rethink the whole enterprise. Ginsparg's server lowers costs by about two orders of magnitude, not just one.

A skeptic might point out that there are other "hidden subsidies" that have not been counted yet, such as those for the use of the Internet by the users of

Ginsparg's server. Those costs are there, although the bulk is not for the Internet, which is comparatively inexpensive, but for the workstations, local area networks, and users' time coping with buggy operating systems. However, those costs would be there no matter how scholarly papers are published. Publishers depend on the postal system to function, yet are not charged the entire cost of that system. Similarly, electronic publishing is a tiny part of the load on the computing and communications infrastructure and so should not be allocated much of the total cost.

Ginsparg's server is an extreme example of minimizing costs. It also minimizes service. There is no filtering of submissions nor any editing, the features that distinguish a journal from a preprint archive. Some scientists argue that no filtering is necessary and that preprints are sufficient to allow the community to function. However, such views are rare, and most scholars agree that journals do perform an important role. Even though some scholars argue that print plays an essential role in the functioning of the journal system (see the arguments in [Rowland] and [Harnad] for opposing views on this issue), it appears that electronic journals can function just as well as print ones. The question in this paper is whether financial costs can be reduced by switching to electronic publishing.

Hundreds of electronic journals are operated by their editors and available for free on the Net. They do provide all the filtering that their print counterparts do. However, although their ranks appear to double every year [ARL], they are all new and small. The question is whether a system of free journals is durable and whether it can be scaled to cover most of scholarly publishing.

Two factors make free electronic journals possible. One is advances in technology, which make it possible for scholars to handle tasks such as typesetting and distribution that used to require trained experts and a large infrastructure. The other factor is a peculiarity of the scholarly journal system that has already been pointed out above. The monetary cost of the time that scholars put into the journal business as editors and referees is about as large as the total revenue that publishers derive from sales of the journals. Scholarly journal publishing could not exist in its present form if scholars were compensated financially for their work. Technology is making their tasks progressively easier. They could take on new roles and still end up devoting less effort to running the journal system than they have done in the past.

Most scholars are already typesetting their own papers. Many were forced to do so by cutbacks in secretarial support. However, even among those, few would go back to the old system of depending on technical typists if they had a choice. Technology is making it easier to do many tasks oneself than to explain to others how to do them.

Editors and referees are increasingly processing electronic submissions, even for journals that appear exclusively in print. Moreover, the general consensus is that this procedure makes their life much easier. Therefore, if the additional load of publishing an electronic journal were small enough, one might expect scholars to do everything themselves. That is what many editors of the free electronic journals think is feasible. As the volume of papers increases, one can add more editors to spread the load, as the *Electronic Journal of Combinatorics* [*EJC*] has done recently (and as print journals have done in the past). The counterargument (cf. [Babbitt, BoyceD]) is that there will always be too many repetitive and tedious tasks to do and that even those scholars who enjoy doing them now, while they are a novelty, will get tired of them in the long run. If so, it will be necessary to charge for access to electronic journals to pay for the expert help needed to run them. Some editors of the currently free electronic journals share this view. However, none of the estimates of what would be required to produce acceptable quality come anywhere near the $4,000 per article that current print publishers collect. In [Odlyzko1] I estimated that $300 to $1,000 per article should suffice, and many others, such as Stevan Harnad, have come up with similar figures. In the years since [Odlyzko1] was written, much more experience in operations of free electronic-only journals has been acquired. I have corresponded and had discussions with editors of many journals, both traditional print-only and free electronic-only. The range of estimates of what it would cost to run a journal without requiring authors, editors, and referees to do noticeably more than they are doing now is illustrated by the following two examples (both from editors of print-only journals):

1. The editor-in-chief of a large journal, which publishes around 200 papers per year (and processes several times that many submissions) and brings in revenues of about $1 million per year to the publisher, thinks he could run an electronic journal of equivalent quality with a subsidy of about $50,000 per year to pay for an assistant to handle correspondence and minor technical issues. He feels that author-supplied copies are usually adequate and that the work of technical editors at the publisher does not contribute much to the scientific quality of the journal. If he is right, then $250 per paper is sufficient.

2. An editor of a much smaller journal thinks that extensive editing of manuscripts is required. In his journal, he does all the editing himself, and the resulting files are then sent directly to the printer, without involving any technical staff at the publisher. He estimates that he spends between 30 minutes and an hour per page and thinks that having somebody with his professional training and technical skills do the work leads to substantially better results. If we assume a loaded salary of $100,000 per year (since such work could often be done by graduate students and junior postdocs looking for some extra earnings in their spare time), we have an estimate of $25 to $50 per page, or $250 to $1,000 per article, for the cost of running an electronic journal of comparable quality.

All the estimates fit in the range of $300 to $1,000 per article that was projected in [Odlyzko1] and do not come close to the $4,000 per article charged by traditional publishers. Why is there such a disparity in views on costs? It is not caused by a simple ignorance of what it takes to run a viable journal on the part of advocates of free or low-priced publications, since many of them are running successful operations. The disparity arises out of different views of what is necessary.

It has always been much easier to enlarge a design or add new features than to slim down. This tendency has been noted in ship design [Pugh], cars, and airplanes as well as in computers, where the mainframe builders were brought to the brink of ruin (and often beyond) before they learned from the PC industry. Established publishers are increasingly providing electronic versions of their journals, but usually only in addition to the print version. It is no surprise therefore that their costs are not decreasing. The approach of the free electronic journal pioneers has been different, namely to provide only what can be done with the resources available. They are helped by what are variously called the 80/20 or 70/30 rules (the last 20% of what is provided costs 80% of the total, etc.). By throwing out a few features, publishers can lower costs dramatically. Even in the area of electronic publishing, the spectrum of choices is large. Eric Hellman, editor of *The MRS Internet Journal of Nitride Semiconductor Research [MRS]*, which provides free access to all readers but charges authors $275 for each published paper, commented [private communication] that with electronic publishing,

$250/paper gets you 90% of the quality that $1000/paper gets you.

Electronics offers many choices of quality and price in publishing.

An example of large differences in costs is provided by projects that make archival information available digitally. Astrophysicists are in the process of digitizing about a million pages of journal articles (without doing optical character recognition, OCR, on the output) and are making them available for free on the Web. The scanning project (paid for by a grant from NASA) is carried out in the United States, yet still costs only $0.18 per page in spite of the high wages. On the other hand, the costs of the JSTOR project, which was cited in [Odlyzko2] as paying about $0.20 per page for scanning, are more complicated. JSTOR pays a contractor around $0.40 per page for a combination of scanning, OCR, and human verification of the OCR output, and the work is done in a less-developed country that has low wage costs. However, JSTOR's total costs are much higher, about $1 to $2 per page, since they rely on trained professionals in the United States to ensure that they have complete runs of journals, that articles are properly classified, and so on. Since JSTOR aims to provide libraries with functionality similar to that of bound volumes, it is natural for it to strive for high quality. This goal raises costs, unfortunately.

It is important to realize how easy it is to raise costs. Even though lack of price competition in scholarly publishing has created unusually high profits [Hayes], most of the price that is paid for journals covers skilled labor. The difference in costs between the astrophysics and JSTOR projects is dramatic, but it does not come from any extravagance. Even at $2 per page, the average scholarly article would cost around $25 to process. At a loaded salary of $100,000 per year for a trained professional, that $25 corresponds to only half an hour of that person's time. Clearly one can boost the costs by doing more, and JSTOR must be frugal in the use of skilled labor.

Is the higher quality of the JSTOR project worth the extra cost? It is probably essential for JSTOR to succeed in its mission, which is to eliminate the huge print collections of back issues of journals. Personally I feel that JSTOR is a great project, the only one I am aware of in scholarly publishing that benefits all three parties: scholars, libraries, and publishers. Whether it will succeed is another question. It does cost more than just basic scanning, and it does require access restrictions. One can argue that the best course of action would be simply to scan the literature right away while there are still low-wage countries that will do the work inexpensively. The costs of the manual work of cutting open volumes and feeding sheets into scanners is not likely to become much smaller. At \$0.20 per page, the entire scholarly literature could probably be scanned for less than \$200 million. (By comparison, the world is paying several billion dollars per year just for one year of current journals, and the Harvard libraries alone cost around \$60 million per year to operate.) Once the material was scanned, it would be available in the future for OCR and addition of other enhancements.

The main conclusion to be drawn from the discussion in this section is that the monetary costs of scholarly publishing can indeed be lowered, even in print. Whether they will be is another question, one closely bound up with the strange economics of the publishing industry.

THE PERVERSE INCENTIVES IN SCHOLARLY PUBLISHING

Competition drives the economy, but it often works in strange ways. A study done a few years ago (before managed care became a serious factor) compared hospital costs in mid-sized U.S. cities that had either one or two hospitals. An obvious guess might be that competition between hospitals would lead to lower costs in cities that had two hospitals. However, the results were just the opposite, with the two-hospital cities having substantially higher prices. This result did not mean that basic economic laws did not apply. Competition was operating, but at a different level. Since it was doctors who in practice determined what hospital a patient went to, hospitals were competing for doctors by purchasing more equipment, putting in specialty wards, and the like, which was increasing their costs (but not making any noticeable difference in the health of the population they served). The patients (or, more precisely, their insurers and employers) were paying the extra price.

Scholarly publishing as a business has many similarities to the medical system, except that it is even more complicated. Journals do not compete on price, since that is not what determines their success. There are four principal groups of players. The first one consists of scholars as producers of the information that makes journals valuable. The second consists of scholars as users of that information. However, as users, they gain access to journals primarily through the third group, the libraries. Libraries purchase journals from the fourth group, the publishers, usually in response to requests from scholars. These requests are based overwhelmingly on the perceived quality of the journals, and price seldom plays a role (although that is changing under the pressure to control growth of library costs). The budgets for libraries almost always come from different sources than the budgets for academic departments, so that scholars as users do not have to make an explicit trade-off between graduate assistantships and libraries, for example.

Scholars as writers of papers determine what journals their work will appear in and thus how much it will cost society to publish their work. However, scholars have no incentive to care about those costs. What matters most to them is the prestige of the journals they publish in. Often the economic incentives are to publish in high-cost outlets. It has often been argued that page charges are a rational way to allocate costs of publishing, since they make the author (or the author's institution or research grant) cover some of the costs of the journal, which, after all, is motivated by a desire to further the author's career. However, page charges are less and less frequent. As an extreme example, in the late 1970s, *Nuclear Physics B,* published by Elsevier, took over as the "journal of choice" in particle physics and field theory from *Physical Review D,* even though the latter was much less expensive. This takeover happened because *Phys. Rev. D* had page charges, and physicists decided they would rather use their grant money for travel, postdocs, and the like. Note that the physicists in this story behaved in a perfectly rational way. They did not have to use their grants to pay for the increase in library costs associated with the shift from an inexpensive journal to a much pricier one. Furthermore, even if they had to pay for that cost, they would have come out ahead; the increase in the costs of just their own library associated with an individual decision to publish in *Nucl. Phys. B* instead of the less expensive *Phys. Rev. D* (could such a small change have been quantified) would have been much smaller than the savings on page charges. Most of the extra cost would have been absorbed by other institutions.

To make this argument more explicit, consider two journals: *H* (high priced) and *L* (low priced). Suppose that each one has 1,000 library subscriptions and no individual ones. *L* is a lean operation, and it costs them $3,000 to publish each article. They collect $1,000 from authors through page charges and the other $2,000 from subscribers, so that each library in effect pays $2 for each article that appears in *L*. On the other hand, *H* collects $7,000 in revenue per article, all from subscriptions, which comes to $7 per article for each library. (It does not matter much whether the extra cost of *H* is due to profits, higher quality, or inefficiency.)

From the standpoint of the research enterprise or of any individual library, it would be desirable to steer all authors toward publishing in *L,* as that would save a total of $4,000 for each article. However, look at this situation from the standpoint of the author. If she publishes in *L,* she loses $1,000 that could be spent on graduate students, conferences, and so on. If she publishes in *H,* she gets to keep that money. She does not get charged for the extra cost to any library, at least not right away. Eventually the overhead rates on her contract might go up to pay for the higher library spending at her institution. However, this effect is delayed and is weak. Even if we had accounting mechanisms that would provide instantaneous feedback (which we do not, with journal prices set more than a year in advance and totally insensitive to minor changes caused by individual authors deciding where to publish), our hypothetical author would surely only get charged for the extra $5 that she causes her library to spend ($7 for publication in *H* as opposed to $2 in *L*) and not for the costs to all the other 999 libraries. She would still save $995 ($1,000 − $5) of her grant money. Is it any wonder if she chooses to publish in *H*?

A secondary consideration for authors is to ensure that their papers are widely available. However, this factor has seldom played a major role, and with the availability of preprints through e-mail or home pages it is becoming even less significant. Authors are not told what the circulation of a journal is (although for established publications, they probably have a rough idea of how easy it is to access them). Further, it is doubtful this information would make much difference, at least in most areas. Authors can alert the audience they really care about (typically a few dozen experts) through preprints, and the journal publication is for the résumé more than to contact readers.

In 1993–94, there was a big flap about the pricing of *International Mathematics Research Notices* (*IMRN*), a new research announcement journal spun off from the *Duke Mathematical Journal*. The institutional subscriptions cost $600 per year, and there were not many papers in it. The director of publishing operations for Duke University Press then responded in the *Newsletter on Serials Pricing Issues* [*NSPI*] by saying that his press was doing the best it could to hold down prices. It's just that their costs for *IMRN* were going to be $60,000 per year, and they expected to have 100 [*sic*] subscriptions, so they felt they had to charge $600 per subscription. Now, one possibility is that the Duke University Press miscalculated and that it might have been easier for them to sell 400 subscriptions at $150 than 100 at $600, since *IMRN* did establish a good reputation as an insert to *Duke Math. J.* However, if their decision was right, then there seem to be two possibilities: (1) scholars will decide that it does not make sense to publish in a journal that is available in only 100 libraries around the world, or (2) scholars will continue submitting their papers to the most prestigious journals they can find (such as *IMRN*) no matter how small their circulation, since prestige is what counts in tenure and promotion decisions and since everybody that they want to read their papers will be able to get them electronically from preprint servers in any case. In neither case are journals such as *IMRN* likely to survive in their present form. (*IMRN* itself appears to have gained a longer lease on life, since it seems to have gained considerably more subscribers and, while it has not lowered its price, it is publishing many more papers, lowering its price per page, as mentioned in Section 2.)

The perverse incentives in scholarly publishing that are illustrated in the examples above have led to the current expensive system. They are also leading to its collapse. The central problem is that scholars have no incentive to maintain the current system. In book publishing, royalties align the authors' interests with those of publishers because both wish to maximize revenues. (This situation is most applicable in the trade press or in textbooks. In scholarly monograph publishing, the decreasing sales combined with the typical royalty rate of, at most, 15% are reducing the financial payoff to authors and appear to be leading to changes, with monographs becoming available electronically for free.) For the bulk of scholarly publishing, though, the market is too small to provide a significant financial payoff to the authors.

THE FUTURE

Although scholars have no incentive to maintain the current journal system, they currently also have no incentive to dismantle it. Even the physicists who rely on the Ginsparg preprint server continue to publish most of their papers in established print journals. The reason is that it costs them nothing to submit papers to such journals and also costs them nothing to have their library buy the journals. The data from the Association of Research Libraries [ARL] show that the average cost of the library system at leading research universities is about $12,000 per faculty member. (It is far higher at some, with Princeton spending about $30,000 per year per faculty member.) This figure, however, is not visible to the scholars, and they have no control over it. They are not given a choice between spending for the library and for other purposes.

Until the academic library system is modified, with the costs and trade-offs made clear to scholars and administrators, it is unlikely there will be any drastic changes. We are likely to see slow evolution (cf. [Odlyzko3]), with continuing spread of preprints (in spite of attempts of journals in certain areas, such as medicine, to play King Canute roles and attempt to stem this natural growth). Electronic journals will become almost universal but most of them will be versions of established print journals and will be equally expensive. Free or inexpensive electronic journals will grow, but probably not too rapidly. However, this situation is not likely to persist for long. I have been predicting [Odlyzko1, Odlyzko2] that change will come when administrators realize just how expensive the library system is and that scholars can obtain most of the information they need from other sources, primarily preprints. Over the decade from 1982 to 1992, library expenditures have grown by over a third even after adjusting for general inflation [ARL]. However, they have fallen by about 10% as a share of total university spending. Apparently the pressure from scholars to maintain library collection has not been great enough, and other priorities have been winning. At some point in the future more drastic cuts are likely.

Although library budgets are likely to be cut, total spending on information systems is unlikely to decrease. We are entering the Information Age, after all. What is likely to happen is that spending on information will increasingly flow through other channels. Traditional scholarly books and journals have always been only a part of the total communication system. Until recently they were the dominant part, but their relative value has been declining as the phone, the fax, and cheap airplane travel as well as the more widely noted computers and data networks have opened up other channels of communications among scholars. This decline, together with the feasibility of lower cost journal systems, is likely to lead to cutbacks in library budgets. How those cuts will be distributed is uncertain. In discussions of the library crisis, most attention is devoted to journal costs. However, for each $1 spent on journal acquisitions, other library costs come to $2. If publishers can provide electronic versions of not only their current issues, but also older ones (either themselves or through JSTOR), they can improve access to scholarly materials and lower the costs of the library system (buildings, staff, maintenance) without lowering their own revenues. It is doubtful whether those savings will be enough, though, and it is likely that spending on traditional scholarly journals as well as the rest of the library system will decrease. To maintain their position, publishers will have to move to activities in which they provide more value instead of relying on scholars to do most of the work for them.

NOTE

I thank Erik Brynjolfsson, Joe Buhler, Peter Denning, Mark Doyle, Paul Ginsparg, Stevan Harnad, Steve Heller, Eric Hellman, Carol Hutchins, Don King, Rob Kirby, Gene Klotz, Silvio Levy, Laszlo Lovasz, Harry Lustig, Robert Miner, Ann Okerson, Bernard Rous, Arthur Smith, Ron Stern, Edward Vielmetti, Lars Wahlbin, Bernd Wegner, and Ronald Wigington for their comments and the information they provided.

REFERENCES

[AMSS] Survey of American research journals, *Notices Amer. Math. Soc.* 40 (1993): 1339–1344.
[ARL] Association of Research Libraries, *http://arl.cni.org.*
[Babbitt] D. G. Babbitt, Mathematical journals: Past, present and future—a personal view, *Notices Amer. Math. Soc.* (Jan. 1997). Available at *http://www.ams.org.*
[Bailey] C. W. Bailey Jr., Scholarly electronic publishing bibliography, available at *http://info.lib.uh.edu/sepb/sepb.html.*
[BoyceD] P. B. Boyce and H. Dalterio, Electronic publishing of scientific journals, *Physics Today* (Jan. 1996): 42–47. Available at *http://www.aas.org/~pboyce/epubs/.*
[EJC] *The Electronic Journal of Combinatorics, http://www.combinatorics.org/.*
[Ginsparg] P. Ginsparg, Winners and losers in the global research village, available at *http://xxx.lanl.gov/blurb/pg96unesco.html.*
[Grove] A. Grove, *Only the Paranoid Survive,* Bantam Doubleday Dell, 1996.
[Harnad] S. Harnad, The paper house of cards (and why it's taking so long to collapse), *Ariadne,* issue # 8 (March 1997). Web version at *http://www.ariadne.ac.uk/.*
[Hayes] J. R. Hayes, The Internet's first victim? *Forbes* (Dec. 18, 1995): 200–201.
[KingMR] D. W. King, D. D. McDonald, and N. K. Roderer, *Scientific Journals in the United States. Their Production, Use, and Economics,* Hutchinson Ross, 1981.
[Kirby] R. Kirby, Comparative prices of math journals, available at *http://math.berkeley.edu/~kirby/journals.html.*
[Lustig] H. Lustig, Electronic publishing: economic issues in a time of transition, in *Electronic Publishing for Physics and Astronomy,* A. Heck, ed., Kluwer, 1997.

[Machlup] F. Machlup, K. Leeson, and associates, *Information Through the Printed Word: The Dissemination of Scholarly, Scientific, and Intellectual Knowledge*, vol. 2: Praeger, 1978.

[MRS] *The MRS Internet Journal of Nitride Semiconductor Research*, available at *http://nsr.mij.mrs.org/*.

[NSPI] *Newsletter on Serials Pricing Issues*, published electronically at Univ. of North Carolina, available at *http://www.lib.unc.edu/prices/*.

[Odlyzko1] A. M. Odlyzko, Tragic loss or good riddance? The impending demise of traditional scholarly journals, *Intern. J. Human-Computer Studies* (formerly *Intern. J. Man-Machine Studies*) 42 (1995): 71–122. Also in the electronic *J. Univ. Comp. Sci.*, pilot issue, 1994, *http://hyperg.iicm.tu-graz.ac.at*. Available at *http://www.research.att.com/~amo*.

[Odlyzko2] A. M. Odlyzko, On the road to electronic publishing, *Euromath Bulletin* 2, no. 1 (June 1996): 49–60. Available at author's home page, *http://www.research.att.com/ ~amo*.

[Odlyzko3] A. M. Odlyzko, The slow evolution of electronic publishing, in *Electronic Publishing—New Models and Opportunities*, A. J. Meadows and F. Rowland, eds., ICCC Press, 1998. Available at *http://www.research.att.com/~amo*.

[PeekN] R. P. Peek and G. B. Newby, eds., *Scholarly Publishing: The Electronic Frontier*, MIT Press, 1996.

[Pugh] P. Pugh, *The Cost of Seapower: The Influence of Money on Naval Affairs from 1815 to the Present Day*, Conway, 1986.

[Rowland] F. Rowland, Print journals: Fit for the future? *Ariadne*, issue # 7 (Jan. 1997). Web version at *http://www.ariadne.ac.uk/*.

[TenopirK] C. Tenopir and D. W. King, Trends in scientific scholarly journal publishing in the U. S., *J. Scholarly Publishing* 48, no. 3 (April 1997): 135–170.

CHAPTER 24

Cost and Value in Electronic Publishing

James J. O'Donnell

This chapter is perhaps best read through binocular lenses. On the one hand, it is an account of the value and function today and for the foreseeable future of electronic networked texts. But on the other hand, it questions our ability to account for such value and function. In search of the particular, it risks the anecdotal; in defense of value, it expresses skepticism about calculations of cost and price.

I am a student of the works of St. Augustine and shall begin accordingly with confession. For my own scholarship, the single most transforming feature of cyberspace as we inhabit it in 1997 can be found in a warehouse on the edges of downtown Seattle. I mean the nerve center of *www.amazon.com*. The speed with which a half-conceived interest in a book converts itself to a real book in my mailbox (48 to 72 hours later) has implications, retrospective and prospective, on the finances of my sector of higher education that could well be catastrophic.

If my approach seems whimsical, do not be misled. The real habits of working scholars often fall outside the scope of discussion when new and old forms of publication are considered. I will have some things to say shortly about the concrete results of surveys we have done for the *Bryn Mawr Reviews* project funded by Mellon, and more of our data appear in the paper by my colleague Richard Hamilton (see chapter 12), but first I want to emphasize a few points by personalizing them.

First, and most important, Amazon books is a perfect hybrid: a cyberspace service that delivers the old technology better and faster than ever before.

Second, my ritual allusion to the paradox of scholars wallowing in information that they do not actually read is not merely humorous: it is a fact of life. The file drawers full of photocopies, read and unread, that every working humanist seems now to possess are a very recent innovation. Photocopying is a service that has declined sharply in price—if measured in real terms—over the past 20 years, and it is certainly the case that graduate and undergraduate students can tell the same joke on themselves today. Perhaps only full professors today reach the point where they can joke similarly about books, but if so surely we are the leading edge of a wedge.

But abundance is not wealth, for wealth is related to scarcity. This, I think, is the point of our jokes. When each new book, pounced on with delight in a bookstore, was an adventure, and when each scholarly article was either a commitment of time or it was nothing, the mechanical systems of rationing that kept information scarce also kept it valuable. But if we now approach a moment when even quite serious books are abundantly available, then their individual value will surely decline.

I am fond of historical illustration. A student of mine at Penn is now working hard on a dissertation that involves late medieval indulgences—not just the theological practice of handing out remission of punishment but the material media through which that remission was attested. It turns out there were indeed some very carefully produced written indulgences before printing was introduced, but indulgences were among the first printed artifacts ever. The sixteenth century saw a boom in the indulgence business as mass production made the physical testimony easier to distribute and obtain. The "information economy" of indulgences showed a steady rise through several generations. (The *price* history of indulgences seems still obscure, for reasons my student has not yet been able to fathom; it would be interesting to see if supply and demand had more to do with the availability of the artifact or, rather, was measured by the number of years of purgatorial remission.) But there came a point at which, almost at a stroke, the superabundance of printed indulgences was countered by loud assertions of the worthlessness of the thing now overpriced and oversold. There followed the familiar cycle of business process reengineering in the indulgence business: collapse of market, restructuring, downsizing, and a focusing on core competencies. The indulgence business has never been the same.

A third and last confessional point: as founding coeditor of *Bryn Mawr Classical Review* (BMCR) since 1990, I may reasonably assert that I have been thinking about and anticipating the benefits of networked electronic communication for scholars for some time now. Yet as I observe my own practices, I must accept that my powers of prognostication have been at best imprecisely focused. Yes, a network connection at my desktop has transformed the way I work, but it has done so less through formal deployment of weighty scholarly resources and more through humbler tools. I will list a few:

1. On-line reference: Though I happened to have owned the compact OED for over 20 years and now, in fact, own a set of the Encyclopedia Britannica, I rarely used the former and rarely remember to look at the latter. But their electronic avatars I consult now daily: "information" sources on myriad topics far more detailed and scholarly than any previously in regular use.

2. On-line productivity information: Under this category I include far better information about weather and travel weather than ever before; access to current airline schedules and other travel information including hotel directories; nationwide telephone directories including yellow pages; on-line newspapers and news feeds.

3. E-mail as productivity tool: The positive impact of e-mail communication on scholarship for me cannot be underestimated. Relatively little of my e-mail has to do with my scholarship, but that proportion is important first of all: news of work in progress, often including copies of papers, and ongoing conversation with specialists elsewhere is a great boon, no question.

4. Formal on-line publishing endeavors: I confess that I use the kinds of resources that Mellon grants support far less than I might have expected. I did indeed point my students to a specific article in a MUSE journal a few months ago, and I browse and snoop, but it was only in writing this paper that I had the excellent idea to bookmark on my browser MUSE's *Journal of Early Christian Studies* and JSTOR's *Speculum*—they appear just below the exciting new URL for the *New York Times Book Review* on-line.

So we, or at least I, live in a world where electronic and print information are already intermarrying regularly, where the traditional content of print culture is declining in value, and where the value of electronic information is not so much in the content as in the interconnectedness and the greater usefulness it possesses. For a work as explicitly devoted as this one is to carrying traditional resources into electronic form, all three of those observations from experience should give pause. In fact, I am going to argue that the intermediacy and incompleteness of the mixed environment we inhabit *today* is an important and likely *durable* consideration. Later in this chapter I will return to the implications of this argument. To give them some weight, let me recount and discuss some of our experiences with BMCR. Some familiar tales will be told here, but with, I hope, fresh and renewed point.

When we began BMCR, we wrote around to publishers with classics lists and asked for free books. An engaging number responded affirmatively, considering we had no track record. Oxford Press sent many books, Cambridge Press did not respond: a 50% success rate with the most important British publishers seemed very satisfactory for a start-up. During our first year, we reviewed many OUP books but few if any Cambridge titles. There then appeared, sometime in 1991 or 1992, an OUP Classics catalog with no fewer than two dozen titles appending blurbs from *Bryn Mawr Classical Review*. (From this we should draw first the lesson that brand names continue to have value: OUP could have chosen to identify its blurbs, as it more commonly does, by author of the review than by title of the journal, but we had chosen our "brand" well.) Approximately two weeks after the OUP catalog appeared, we received unsolicited a first handsome box of books from Cambridge, and we now have a happy and productive relationship with both publishers. Our distinctive value to publishers is our timeliness: books reviewed in time to blurb them in a catalog while the books are still in their prime selling life, not years later. The practical value to scholars is that information about and discussion of current work moves more rapidly into circulation. (Can a dollar price be placed on such value? I doubt it. I will return later to my belief that one very great difficulty in managing technology transitions affecting research and teaching is that our economic understanding of traditional practices is often too poor and imprecise to furnish a basis for proper analysis. In this particular case, we must cope with the possibility that a short-term advantage will in the long term devalue the information by increasing its speed of movement and decreasing its lifetime of value.)

We began BMCR in part because we already had a circle of collaborators in place. Rick Hamilton had created *Bryn Mawr Commentaries* in 1980, offering cheap, serviceable, reliable texts of Greek and Latin authors with annotation designed to help real American students of our own time; in a market dominated by reprints of texts for students in the upper forms of British public schools in another century, the series was an immediate hit. It quickly became the most successful textbook series in American classics teaching. I had joined that project in 1984 and in slightly over a decade we had almost 100 titles in print. In the course of that project, Hamilton had assembled a team of younger scholars of proven ability to do good work on a short deadline without exclusive regard for how it would look on a curriculum vitae—textbook-writing is notoriously problematic for tenure committees. This group formed the core of both our editorial board and our reviewing team. If you had asked us in 1990 what we were doing, we would have said that we were getting our friends to review books for us. This statement was true insofar as it meant that we could do a better job more quickly of getting good reviews moving because we had already done the work of building the community on which to draw.

But what surprised us most was that a little more than a year after we began work, we looked at the list of people who had reviewed for us and found that it had grown rapidly beyond the circle of our friends and even the friends of our friends. A book review journal seems unusually well situated to build community in this way because it does not wait for contributions: it solicits them and even offers small compensation—free books—to win people over. If then it can offer timely publication, at least in this field, it is possible to persuade even eminent and computer-hostile contributors to participate. (To be sure, there are no truly computer-hostile contributors left. The most recent review we have published by someone not using at least a word processor is three years old.)

But the fact of networked communication meant that the reviewer base could grow in another way. A large part of our working practice, quite apart from our means of publication, has been facilitated by the Internet. Even if we only printed and bound our product, what we do would not be possible without the productivity enhancement of e-mail and word processing. We virtually never "typeset" or "keyboard" texts, a great savings at the outset. But we also do a very high proportion of our communication with reviewers by e-mail. Given the difficulties that persist even now of moving formatted files across platforms, we still receive many reviews on floppy disks with accompanying paper copies to ensure accuracy, but that step is only a last one in a process greatly improved by the speed of optical fiber.

Further, in July 1993 our imitation of an old practice led to a fresh transformation of our reviewing population. We began to publish a listing of books received—enough were arriving to make publishing this list seem like a reasonable practice, one we now follow every month. By stroke of simple intuition and good luck, Hamilton had the idea to prepend to that list a request for volunteers to review titles yet unplaced. (I may interpose here that Hamilton and I both felt acutely guilty in the early years every time one or two books were left unplaced for review after several months. Only when we read some time later the musings of a book review editor for a distinguished journal in another field well known for its reviews and found that he was publishing reviews of approximately 5% of the titles that came to his desk did we start to think that our own practice [reviewing, on a conservative estimate, 60 to 70% of titles] was satisfactory.) The request for volunteers drew an unexpected flood of responses. We have now institutionalized that practice to the point that each month's publication of the "books received" list needs to be coordinated for a time when both Hamilton and I are prepared to handle the incoming flood of requests: 30 to 40 a month for a dozen or so still-available titles.

But the result of this infusion of talent has been an extraordinary broadening of our talent pool. Though a few reviewers (no more than half a dozen) are household names to our readers as authors of more than a dozen reviews over the seven years of our life, we are delighted to discover that we have published, in the classical review journal alone, 430 different authors from a total of about 1,000 reviews. Our contributors come from several continents: North America, Europe, Africa, Asia, and Australia. By the luck of our having begun with a strategy based in praxis rather than ideology (beginning, that is, with people who had contributed to our textbook series), we have succeeded in creating a conversation that ranges widely across disciplinary and ideological boundaries. The difficulty of establishing working relations with European publishers remains an obstacle that perplexes us: but that difficulty chiefly resides in the old technology of postal delays and the fact that even e-mail does not eradicate the unfamiliarity that inheres when too few opportunities for face-to-face encounter exist.

Our experience with *Bryn Mawr Medieval Review* has been instructively different. There we began not with a cadre of people and an idea, but merely with an idea. Two senior editors, including myself, recruited a managing editor who tried to do in a vacuum what Hamilton and I had done with the considerably greater resources described above. It never got off the ground. We put together an editorial board consisting of smart people, but people who had no track record of doing good work in a timely way *with us:* they never really engaged. There was no cadre of prospective reviewers to begin with, and so we built painstakingly slowly. In the circumstances, there was little feedback in the form of good reviews and a buzz of conversation about them, and publication never exceeded a trickle.

We have speculated that some intrinsic differences between "classics" and "medieval studies" as organized fields in this country are relevant here. Classicists tend to self-identify with the profession as a whole and to know and care about materials well beyond their immediate ken. A professor of Greek history can typically tell you in a moment who the leading people in a subfield of Latin literature are and even who some of the rising talent would be. But a medievalist typically self-identifies with a disciplinary field (like "history") at least as strongly as with "medieval studies," and the historian of Merovingian Gaul neither knows nor cares what is going on in Provençal literature studies. I am disinclined to emphasize such disparities, but they need to be kept in mind for what follows.

After two and a half years of spinning our wheels, with, to be sure, a fair number of reviews, but only a fair number, and with productivity clearly flagging, we made the decision to transfer the review's offices to new management. We were fortunate in gaining agreement from Professor Paul Szarmach of the Medieval Institute of Western Michigan University to give the journal a home and some institutional support. Western Michigan has been the host for a quarter century of the largest "come-all-ye" in medieval studies in the world, the annual Kalamazoo meetings. Suddenly we had planted the journal at the center of a network of self-identified medievalists. The managing editorship has been taken up by two WMU faculty, Rand Johnson in Classics and Deborah Deliyannis in History, and since they took over the files in spring 1996, the difference has been dramatic. In the last months of 1996, they had the most productive months in the journal's life and on two occasions distributed more reviews in one month than BMCR did. BMCR looks as if it will continue to outproduce BMMR over the next twelve months by an appreciable pace, but the gap is narrowing.

Both BMCR and BMMR stand to gain from our Mellon grant. Features such as a new interface on the World Wide Web, a mechanism for displaying Greek text in Greek font, and enhanced search capabilities will be added to what is still the plain-ASCII text of our archives, which are still, I am either proud or embarrassed to claim, on a gopher server at the University of Virginia Library. Indeed, when we began our conversations with Richard Ekman and Richard Quandt in 1993, one chief feature of our imagined future for BMCR was that we would not only continue to invent the journal of the future, but we would put ourselves in the position of packaging what we had done for distribution to others who might wish to emulate the hardy innovation of an electronic journal. About the time we first spoke those words, Mosaic was born; about the time we received notice of funding from The Mellon Foundation, Netscape sprang to life. Today the "NewJour" archive based on a list comoderated by myself and Ann Okerson on which we distribute news of new electronic journals suggests that there have been at least 3,500 electronic journals born—some flourishing, some already vanished. Though BMCR is still one of the grandfathers of the genre (Okerson's 1991 pathbreaking directory of e-journals listed 29 titles including BMCR, and that list was near exhaustive), we are scarcely exemplary: it's getting crowded out here.

But meanwhile, a striking thing has happened. Our users have, with astonishing unanimity, not complained about our retro tech appearance. To be sure, we have always had regrets expressed to us about our Greekless appearance and our habit of reducing French to an accentless state otherwise seen in print chiefly in Molly Bloom's final soliloquy in the French translation of *Ulysses*. But those complaints have not increased. Format, at a moment when the Web is alive with animation, colors, Java scripts, and real audio, turns out to be far less importance than we might have guessed. Meanwhile, to be sure, our usage has to some extent plateaued. During the first heady years, I would send regular messages to my coeditors about the boom in our numbers. That boom has never ended, and I am very pleased to say that we have always seen fewer losses than gains to our subscription lists, but we are leveling out. Although Internet usage statistics continue to seek the stratosphere, we saw a "mere" 14% increase in subscriptions between this time 12 months ago and today. (Our paper subscriptions have always remained very consistent and very flat.) It is my impression that we are part of a larger Internet phenomenon that began in 1996, when the supply of sites began to catch up to demand and everyone's hits-per-site rate began to level off.

But we are still a success, in strikingly traditional ways. Is what we do worth it? How can we measure that? My difficulty in answering such questions is that in precisely the domain of academic life that feels most like home to me, we have always been astonishingly bad at answering such questions. Tony Grafton and Lisa Jardine, in their important book on Renaissance education, *From Humanism to the Humanities*, make it clear how deeply rooted the cognitive dissonance in our profession is between what we claim and what we do. Any discussion of the productivity of higher education is going to be inflammatory, and any attempt to measure what we do against the standards of contemporary service industries will evoke defenses of a more priestly vision of what we are and what we can be—in the face of economic pressures that defer little, if at all, to priesthoods.

But I will also suggest one additional reason why it is premature to begin measuring too closely what we do. Pioneers are entitled to be fools. Busting sod on the prairie was a disastrous mistake for many, a barely sustainable life for many more (read Wallace Stegner's luminous memoir *Wolfwillow* for chapter and verse), and an adventure rewarding to few. But it was also a necessary stage toward a productive and, I think we would all agree, valuable economy and culture. I suggest that if we do not know how to count and measure what we do now on the western frontier with any certainty, we do already know how to fret about it. We know what the issues are, and we know the range of debate.

By contrast, any attempt to measure the value of electronic texts and images or of the communities they facilitate is premature in a hundred ways. We have no common space or ground on which to measure them, for one thing: a thousand or a million experiments are not yet a system. We do not know what survives, what scales, what has value that proves itself to an audience willing to pay to sustain it. We can measure some of the costs, but academic enterprises are appallingly bad at giving fully loaded costs, inasmuch as faculty time, library resources, and the heat that keeps the fingers of the assistant typing HTML from freezing are either unaccounted for or accounted for far more arbitrarily than is the case for, for example, amazon.com. We can measure some of the benefits, but until there is an audience making intelligent choices about electronic texts and their uses, those measures will be equally arbitrary.

Let me put it this way. Was an automobile a cost-effective purchase in 1915? I know just enough of the early history of telegraphy to surmise, but not enough to prove, that the investment in the first generation of poles and wires—Ezra Cornell's great invention—could never possibly have recouped itself to investors. In fact, as with many other new technologies of the nineteenth century, one important stage in development was the great crash of bankruptcies, mergers, and reorganizations that came at the end of the first generation. Western Union, in which Cornell was a principal shareholder, was one economic giant to emerge in that way. A similar crash happened to railroads in the late nineteenth century. Such a reading of history suggests that what we really want to ask is not whether we can afford the benefits of electronic texts but whether and how far we can allow universities and other research institutions to afford the *risks* of such investment.

For we do not know how to predict successes: there are no "leading economic indicators" in cyberspace to help us hedge and lay our bets. Those of us who have responsibility for large institutional ventures at one level or another find this situation horribly disconcerting, and our temptation over the next months and years is always going to be to ask the tough, green-eyeshade questions, as indeed we must. But at the same time, what we must be working for is an environment in which not every question is pressed to an early answer and in which opportunity and openness are sustained long enough to shape a new space of discourse and community. We are not yet ready for systems thinking about electronic information, for all that we are tempted to it: the pace of change and the shifts of scale are too rapid. The risk is always that we will think we discern the system of the future and so seek to institutionalize it as rapidly as possible, to force a system into existing by closing it off by main force of software, hardware, or text-encoding choices. To do so now, I believe, is a mistake.

For one example: Yahoo and AltaVista are powerful tools to help organize cyberspace in 1997. But they are heavily dependent on the relative sizes of the spaces they index for the effectiveness of their results: they cannot in present form scale up. Accordingly, any and all attempts to measure their power and effectiveness are fruitless. For another example: there is as yet no systemic use of information technology in higher education beyond the very pedestrian and pragmatic tools I outlined above. Any attempt to measure one experiment thus falls short of its potential precisely because no such experiment is yet systemic. There is nothing to compare it with, no way to identify the distortions introduced by uniqueness or by the avenues in which the demands of present institutional structures distort an experiment so as to limit its effectiveness.

What we still lack is any kind of economic model for the most effective use of information technology in education and scholarship: that much must be freely granted. The interest and value of the Mellon grants, I would contend, lie in the curiosity with which various of our enterprises push our camel-like noses under one or another tent flap in search of rewarding treats. Until we find those treats, we must, however, be content to recognize that from a distance we all appear as so many back ends of camels showing an uncanny interest in a mysterious tent.

CHAPTER 25

The Future of Electronic Journals

Hal R. Varian

It is widely expected that a great deal of scholarly communication will move to an electronic format. The Internet offers much lower cost of reproduction and distribution than print, the scholarly community has excellent connectivity, and the current system of journal pricing seems to be too expensive. Each of these factors is helping push journals from paper to electronic media.

In this paper I want to speculate about the impact this movement will have on the form of scholarly communication. How will electronic journals evolve?

Each new medium has started by emulating the medium it replaced. Eventually the capabilities added by the new medium allow it to evolve in innovative and often surprising ways. Alexander Graham Bell thought that the telephone would be used to broadcast music into homes. Thomas Edison thought that recordings would be mostly of speech rather than music. Marconi thought that radio's most common use would be two-way communication rather than broadcast.

The first use of the Internet for academic communication has been as a replacement for the printed page. But there are obviously many more possibilities.

DEMAND AND SUPPLY

In order to understand how journals might evolve, it is helpful to start with an understanding of the demand and supply for scholarly communication today.

Supply of Scholarly Communication

The academic reward system is structured to encourage the production of ideas. It does this by rewarding the production and dissemination of "good" ideas—ideas that are widely read and acknowledged.

Scholarly publications are produced by researchers as part of their jobs. At most universities and research organizations, publication counts significantly toward salary and job security (e.g., tenure). All publications are not created equally: competition for space in top-ranked journals is intense.

The demand for space in those journals is intense because they are highly visible and widely read. Publication in a topflight journal is an important measure of visibility. In some fields, citation data have become an important observable proxy for "impact." Citations are a way of proving that the articles that you publish are, in fact, read.

Demand for Scholarly Communication

Scholarly communication also serves as an input to academic research. It is important to know what other researchers in your area are doing so as to improve your own work and to avoid duplicating their work. Hence, scholars generally want access to a broad range of academic journals.

The ability of universities to attract topflight researchers depends on the size of the library collection. Threats to cancel journal subscriptions are met with cries of outrage by faculty.

The Production of Academic Journals

Tenopir and King [1996] have provided a comprehensive overview of the economics of journal production. According to their estimates, the first-copy costs of an academic article are between $2,000 and $4,000. The bulk of these costs are labor costs, mostly clerical costs for managing the submission, review, editing, typesetting, and setup.

The marginal cost of printing and mailing an *issue* of a journal is on the order of $6. A special-purpose, nontechnical academic journal that publishes four issues per year with 10 articles each issue would have fixed costs of about $120,000. The variable costs of printing and mailing would be about $24 per year. Such a journal might have a subscriber list of about 600, which leads to a break-even price of $224.[1]

Of course, many journals of this size are sold by for-profit firms and the actual prices may be much higher: subscription prices of $600 per year or more are not uncommon for journals of this nature.

If the variable costs of printing and shipping were eliminated, the break-even price would fall to $200. This simple calculation illustrates the following point: fixed costs dominate the production of academic journals; reduction in printing and distribution costs because of electronic distribution will have negligible effect on break-even prices.

Of course, if many new journals are produced and distributed electronically, the resulting competition may chip away at the $600 monopoly prices. But if these new journals use the same manuscript-handling processes, the $200 cost per subscription will remain the effective floor to journal prices.

OTHER COSTS

Two other costs should be mentioned. First is the cost of archiving. Cooper [1989] estimates that the present value of the storage cost of a single issue of a journal to a typical library is between $25 and $40.

Another interesting figure is yearly cost per article read. This figure varies widely by field, but I can offer a few order-of-magnitude guesses. According to a chart in Lesk [1997, p. 218], 22% of scientific papers published in 1984 were not cited in the ensuing 10-year period. The figure rises to 48% for social science papers and a remarkable 93% for humanities papers!

Odlyzko [1997] estimates that the cost per reader of a mathematical article may be on the order of $200. By comparison, the director of a major medical library has told me that his policy is to cancel journals for which the cost per article read appears to be over $50.

It is not commonly appreciated that one of the major impacts of on-line publication is that use can be easily and precisely monitored. Will academic administrators really pay subscription rates implying costs per reading of several hundred dollars?

REENGINEERING JOURNAL PRODUCTION

It seems clear that reduction in the costs of academic communication can only be achieved by reengineering the manuscript handling process. Here I use "reengineering" in both its original sense—rethinking the process—and its popular sense—reducing labor costs.

The current process of manuscript handling is not particularly mysterious. The *American Economic Review* works something like this. The author sends three paper copies of an article to the main office in Princeton. The editor assigns each manuscript to a coeditor based on the topic of the manuscript and the expertise of the coeditor. (The editor also reviews manuscripts in his own area of expertise.) The editor is assisted in these tasks by a staff of two to three FTE clerical workers.

The manuscripts arrive in the office of the coeditor, who assigns them to two or more reviewers. The coeditor is assisted in this task by a half-time clerical worker. After some nudging, the referees usually report back and the coeditor makes a decision about whether the article merits publication. At the *AER*, about 12% of the submitted articles are accepted.

Typically the author revises accepted articles for both content and form, and the article is again sent to the referees for further review. In most cases, the article is then accepted and sent to the main office for further processing. At the main office, the article is copyedited and further prepared for publication. It is then sent to be typeset. The proof sheets are sent to the author for checking. After corrections are made, the article is sent to the production facilities where it is printed, bound, and mailed.

Much of the cost in this process is in coordinating the communication: the author sends the paper to the editor, the editor sends it to the coeditor, the coeditor sends it to referees, and so on. These costs require postage and time, but most important, they require coordination. This role is played by the clerical assistants.

Universal use of electronic mail could undoubtedly save significant costs in this component of the publication process. The major enabling technology are standards for document representation (e.g., Microsoft Word, PostScript, SGML, etc.) and multimedia e-mail.

Revelt [1996] sampled Internet working paper sites to determine what formats were being used. According to his survey, PostScript and PDF are the most popular formats for e-prints, with T$_{\text{E}}$X being common in technical areas and HTML for nontechnical areas. It is likely that standardization on two to three formats would be adequate for most authors and readers. My personal recommendation would be to standardize on Adobe PDF since it is readily available, flexible, and inexpensive.

With respect to e-mail, the market seems to be rapidly converging to MIME as a standard for e-mail inclusion; I expect this convergence to be complete within a year or two.

These developments mean that the standards are essentially in place to move to electronic document management during the editorial and refereeing process. Obviously, new practices would have to be developed to ensure security and document integrity. Systems for time-stamping documents, such as Electronic Postmarks, are readily available; the main barrier to their adoption is training necessary for their use.

IMPACT OF REENGINEERING

If all articles were submitted and distributed electronically, I would guess that the costs of the editorial process would drop by a factor of 50% due to the reduction in clerical labor costs, postage, photocopying, and so on. Such costs comprise about half the first-copy costs, so this savings would be noteworthy for small journals. (See Appendix A for the cost breakdown of a small mathematics journal.)

Once the manuscript was accepted for publication, it would still have to be copyedited and converted to a uniform style. In most academic publishing, copyediting is rather light, but there are exceptions. Conversion to a uniform style is still rather expensive because of the idiosyncrasies of authors' word processing systems and writing habits.

It is *possible* that journals could distribute electronic style sheets that would help authors achieve a uniform style, but experience thus far has not given great reason for optimism on this front. Journals that accept electronic submissions report significant costs in conversion to a uniform style.

One question that should be taken seriously is whether these conversion costs for uniform style are worth it. Typesetting costs are about $15 to $25 per page for moderately technical material. Markup costs probably require two to three hours of a copyeditor's time. These figures mean that preparation costs for a 20-page article are on the order of $500. If a hundred people read the article, is the uniform style worth $5 apiece to them? Or, more to the point, if 10 people read the article, is the uniform style worth $50 apiece?

The advent of desktop publishing dramatically reduced the cost of small-scale publication. But it is not obvious that the average quality of published documents went up. The earlier movement from hard type to digital typography had the same impact. As Knuth [1979] observes, digitally typeset documents cost less but had lower quality than did documents set manually.

My own guess about this benefit-cost trade-off is that the quality from professional formatted documents isn't worth the cost for material that is only read by small numbers of individuals. The larger the audience, the more beneficial and cost-effective formatting becomes. I suggest a two-tiered approach: articles that are formatted by authors are published very inexpensively. Of these, the "classics" can be "reprinted" in professionally designed formats.

A further issue arises in some subjects. Author-formatted documents may be adequate for reading, but they are not adequate for archiving. It is very useful to be able to search and manipulate subcomponents of an article, such as abstracts and references. This archiving capability means that the article must be formatted in such a way that these subcomponents can be identified. Standardized Generalized Markup Language (SGML) allows for such formatting, but it is rather unlikely that it could be implemented by most authors, at least using tools available today.

The benefits from structured markup are significant, but markup is also quite costly, so the benefit-cost trade-off is far from clear. I return to this point below.

In summary, reengineering the manuscript-handling process by moving to electronic submission and review may save close to half of the first-copy costs of journal production. If we take the $2,000 first-copy costs per article as representative, we can move the first-copy costs to about $1,000. Shifting the formatting responsibility to authors would reduce quality, but would also save even more on first-copy costs. For journals with small readership, this trade-off may be worth it. Indeed, many humanities journals have moved to on-line publication for reasons of reduced cost.[2]

Odlyzko [1997] estimates that the cost of Ginsparg's [1996] electronic preprint server is between $5 and $75 per paper. These papers are formatted entirely by the authors (mostly using $T_{E}X$) and are not refereed. Creation and electronic distribution of scholarly work can be very inexpensive; you have to wonder whether the value added by traditional publishing practices is really worth it.

ELECTRONIC DISTRIBUTION

Up until now we have only considered the costs of preparing the manuscript for publication. If the material were subsequently distributed electronically, there would be further savings. We can classify these as follows:

- Shelf space savings to libraries. As we've seen, these savings could be on the order of $35 per volume in present value. However, electronic archiving is not free. Running a Web server or creating a CD is costly. Even more costly is updating the media. Books that are hundreds of years old can easily be read today. Floppy disks that are 10 years old may be unreadable because of obsolete storage media or formatting. Electronic archives will need to be backed up, transported to new media, and translated. All these activities are costly. (Of course, traditional libraries are also costly; the ARL estimates this cost to be on the order of $12,000 per faculty member per year. Electronic document archives will undoubtedly reduce many of the traditional library costs once they are fully implemented.)

- Monitoring. As mentioned above, it is much easier to monitor the use of electronic media. Since the primary point of the editorial and refereeing process is to economize on readers' attention, it should be very useful to have some feedback on whether articles are actually read. This feedback would help university administrators make more rational decisions about journal acquisition, faculty retention, and other critical resource allocation issues.

- Search. It is much easier to search electronic media. References can be immediately displayed using hyperlinks. Both forward and reverse bibliographic searches can be done using on-line materials, which should greatly aid literature analysis.

- Supporting materials. The incremental costs to storing longer documents are very small, so it is easy to include data sets, images, detailed analyses, simulations, and so on that can improve scientific communication.

Chickens and Eggs

The big issue facing those who want to publish an electronic journal is how to get the ball rolling. People will publish in electronic journals that have lots of readers; people will read electronic journals that contain lots of high-quality material.

This kind of chicken-and-egg problem is known in economics as a "network externalities" problem. We say that a good (such as an electronic journal) exhibits network externalities if an individual's value for the product depends on how many other people use it. Telephones, faxes, and e-mail all exhibit network externalities. Electronic journals exhibit a kind of indirect form of network externalities since the readers' value depends on how many authors publish in the journal and the number of authors who publish depends on how many readers the journal has.

There are several ways around this problem, most of which involve discounts for initial purchasers. You can give the journal away for a while, and eventually charge for it, as the *Wall Street Journal* has done. You can pay authors to publish, as the *Bell Journal of Economics* did when it started. It is important to realize that the payment doesn't have to be a monetary one. A very attractive form of payment is to offer prizes for the best articles published each year in the journal. The prizes can offer a nominal amount of money, but the real value is being able to list such a prize on your curriculum vitae. In order to be credible, such prizes should be juried and promoted widely. This reward system may be an attractive way to overcome young authors' reluctance to publish in electronic journals.

WHEN EVERYTHING IS ELECTRONIC

Let us now speculate a bit about what will happen when all academic publication is electronic. I suggest that (1) publications will have more general form; (2) new filtering and refereeing mechanisms will be used; (3) archiving and standardization will remain a problem.

Document Structure

The fundamental problem with specialized academic communication is that it is specialized. Many academic publications have fewer than 100 readers. Despite these small numbers, the academic undertaking may still be worthwhile. Progress in academic research comes by dividing problems up into small pieces and investigating these pieces in depth. Painstaking examination of minute topics provides the building blocks for grand theories.

However, much can be said for the viewpoint that academic research may be excessively narrow. Rumor has it that a ghost named Pedro haunts the bell tower at Berkeley. The undergrads make offerings to Pedro at the Campanile on the evening before an exam. Pedro, it is said, was a graduate student in linguistics who wanted to write his thesis on Sanskrit. In fact, it was a thesis about one word in Sanskrit. And, it was not just one word, but in fact was on one of this word's forms in one of the particularly obscure declensions of Sanskrit. Alas, his thesis committee rejected Pedro's topic as "too broad."

The narrowness of academic publication, however, is not entirely due to the process of research, but is also due to the costs of publication. Editors encourage short articles, partly to save on publication costs but mostly to save on the attention costs of the readers. *Physics Letters* is widely read because the articles are required to be short. But one way that authors achieve the required brevity is to remove all "unnecessary" words—such as conjunctions, prepositions, and articles.

Electronic publication eliminates the *physical* costs of length, but not the attention costs. Brevity will still be a virtue for some readers; depth will be a virtue for others. Electronic publication allows for mass customization of articles, much like the famous inverted triangle in journalism: there can be a one-paragraph abstract, a one-page executive summary, a four-page overview, a 20-page article, and a 50-page appendix. User interfaces can be devised to read this "stretchtext."

Some of these textual components can be targeted toward generalists in a field, some toward specialists. It is even possible that some components could be directed toward readers who are *outside* the academic specialty represented. Reaching a large audience would, presumably, provide some incentive for the time and trouble necessary to create such stretchtext documents.

This possibility for variable-depth documents that can have multiple representations is very exciting. Well-written articles could appeal both to specialists and to those outside the specialty. The curse of the small audience could be overcome if the full flexibility of electronic publication were exploited.

FILTERING COSTS

As I noted earlier, one of the critical functions of the academic publishing system is to filter. Work cannot be cumulative unless authors have some faith that prior literature is accurate. Peer review helps ensure that work meets appropriate standards for publication. .

There is a recognized pecking order among journals, with high-quality journals in each discipline having a reputation for being more selective than others. This pecking order helps researchers focus their attention on areas that are thought by their profession to be particularly important.

In the last 25 years many new journals have been introduced, with the majority coming from the private sector. Nowadays almost anything can be published *somewhere*—the only issue is where. Publication itself conveys little information about quality.

Many new journals are published by for-profit publishers. They make money by selling journal subscriptions, which generally means publishing more articles. But the value of peer review comes in being selective, a value almost diametrically opposed to increasing the output of published articles.

I mentioned above that one of the significant implications of electronic publication was that monitoring costs are much lower. It will be possible to tell with some certainty what is being read. This monitoring will allow for more accurate benefit-cost comparisons with respect to purchase decisions. But perhaps even more significantly, it will allow for better evaluation of the significance of academic research.

Citation counts are often used as a measure of the impact of articles and journals. Studies in economics [Laband and Piette 1994] indicate that most of the citations are to articles published in a few journals. More articles are being published, a smaller fraction of which are read [de Sola Pool 1983]. It is not clear that the filtering function of peer review is working appropriately in the current environment.

Academic hiring and promotion policies contribute an additional complication. Researchers choose narrower specialties, making it more difficult to judge achievement locally. Outside letters of evaluation have become worthless because of the lack of guarantees of privacy. All that is left is the publication record and the quantity of publication, whose merits are easier to convey to nonexperts than quality of publication.

The result is that young academics are encouraged to publish as much as possible in their first five to six years. Accurate measures of the impact of young researchers' work, such as citation counts, cannot be accumulated in this short a time period. One reform that would probably help matters significantly would be to put an upper limit on the number of papers submitted as part of tenure review. Rather than submitting everything published in the last six years, assistant professors could submit only their five best articles. This reform would, I suggest, lead to higher quality work *and* higher quality decisions on the part of review boards.

Dimensions of Filtering

If we currently suffer from a glut of information, electronic publication will only make matters worse. Reduced cost of publication and dissemination is likely to make more and more material available. This proliferation isn't necessarily bad; it simply means that the filtering tools will have to be improved.

I would argue that journals filter papers on two dimensions: interest and correctness. The first thing a referee should ask is, "is this interesting?" If the paper is interesting, the next question should be, "is this correct?" Interest is relatively easy to judge; correctness is substantially more difficult. But there isn't much value in determining correctness if interest is lacking.

When publication was a costly activity, it was appropriate to evaluate papers prior to publication. Ideally, only interesting and correct work manuscripts would undergo the expensive transformation of publication. Furthermore, publication is a binary signal: either a manuscript is published or not.

Electronic publication is cheap. Essentially everything should be published, in the sense of being made available for downloading. The filtering process will take place *ex post*, so as to help users determine which articles are worth downloading and reading. As indicated above, the existing peer review system could simply be translated to this new medium. But the electronic media offer possibilities not easily accomplished in print media. Other models of filtering may be more effective and efficient.

A Model for Electronic Publication

Allow me to sketch one such model for electronic publishing that is based on some of the considerations above. Obviously it is only one model; many models should and will be tried. However, I think that the model I suggest has some interesting features.

First, the journal assembles a board of editors. The function of the board is not just to provide a list of luminaries to grace the front cover of the journal; they will actually have to do some work.

Authors submit (electronic) papers to the journal. These papers have three parts: a one-paragraph abstract, a five-page summary, and a 20- to 30-page conventional paper. The abstract is a standard part of academic papers and needs no further discussion. The summary is modeled after the *Papers and Proceedings* issue of the *American Economic Review*: it should describe what question the author addresses, what methods were used to answer the question, and what the author found. The summary should be aimed at as broad an audience as possible. This summary would then be linked to the supporting evidence: mathematical proofs, econometric analysis, data sets, simulations, and so on. The supporting evidence could be quite technical and would probably end up being similar in structure to current published papers.

Initially, I imagine that authors would write a traditional paper and pull out parts of the introduction and conclusion to construct the summary section. This method would be fine to get started, although I hope that the structure would evolve beyond this.

The submitted materials will be read by two to three members of the editorial board who will rate them with respect to how interesting they are. The editors will be required only to evaluate the five-page summary and will not necessarily be responsible for evaluating the correctness of the entire article. The editors will use a common curve; e.g., no more than 10% of the articles get the highest score. The editorial score will be attached to the paper and be made available on the server. Editors will be anonymous; only the score will be made public.

Note that all papers will be accepted; the current rating system of "publish or not" is replaced by a scale of (say) 1–5. Authors will be notified of the rating they received from the editors, and they can withdraw the paper at this point if they choose to do so. However, once they agree that their paper be posted, it cannot withdrawn (unless it is published elsewhere), although new versions of it can be posted and linked to the old one.

Subscribers to the journal can search all parts of the on-line papers. They can also ask to be notified by e-mail of all papers that receive scores higher than some threshold or that contain certain keywords. When subscribers read a paper, they also score it with respect to its interest, and summary statistics of these scores are also (anonymously) attached to the paper.

Since all evaluations are available on-line, it would be possible to use them in quite creative ways. For example, I might be interested in seeing the ratings of all readers with whom my own judgments are closely correlated (see Konstan et al. [1997] for an elaboration of this scheme). Or I might be interested in seeing all papers that were highly rated by Fellows of the Econometric Society or the Economic History Society.

This sort of "social recommender" system will help people focus their attention on research that their peers—whomever they may be—find interesting. Papers that are deemed interesting can then be evaluated with respect to their correctness.

Authors can submit papers that comment on or extend previous work. When they do so, they submit a paper in the ordinary way with links to the paper in question as well as to other papers in this general area. This discussion of a topic forms a thread that can be traversed using standard software tools. See Harnad [1995] for more on this topic.

Papers that are widely read and commented on will certainly be evaluated carefully for their correctness. Papers that aren't read may not be correct, but that presumably has low social cost. The length of the thread attached to a paper indicates how many people have (carefully) read it. If many people have read the paper and found it correct, a researcher may have some faith that the results satisfy conventional standards for scientific accuracy.

This model is unlike the conventional publishing model, but it addresses many of the same design considerations. The primary components are as follows:

- Articles have varying depths, which allows them to appeal to a broad audience as well as satisfy specialists.

- Articles are rated first with respect to interest by a board of editors. Articles that are deemed highly interesting are then evaluated with respect to correctness.

- Readers can contribute to the evaluation process.

- The unit of academic discourse becomes a thread of discussion. Interesting articles that are closely read and evaluated can be assumed to be correct and therefore serve as bases for future work.

APPENDIX A

Cost of a Small Math Journal

The production costs of the *Pacific Journal of Mathematics*[3] have been examined by Kirby [1997]. This journal publishes 10 issues of about 200 pages each per year. A summary of its yearly costs is given in Table 25.1.

The *PJM* charges $275 per subscription and has about 1,000 subscribers. The journal also prints about 500 additional copies per year, which go to the sponsoring institutions in lieu of rent, secretarial support, office equipment, and so on.

The first-copy costs per page are about $64, while the variable cost per page printed and distributed is about 3.5 cents. The average article in this journal is about 20 pages long, which makes the first-copy cost per article about $1,280, somewhat smaller than the $2,000 figure in Tenopir and King [1996]. However, the *PJM* does not pay for space and for part of its secretarial support; adding in

TABLE 25.1.   Pacific Journal of Mathematics Yearly Costs

First-copy costs	typesetting and art	$64,200
	salary and overhead	64,000
	total FC	128,200
Variable costs	distribution	44,300
	printing and binding	60,500
	total VC	104,800
Miscellaneous	reprints	6,000
	electronic edition	10,000
	total misc.	16,000
Total costs		$249,000

these costs would reduce the difference. The cost of printing and distributing a 200-page issue is about $7 per issue, consistent with the figure used in this paper.

NOTES

Research support from NSF grant SBR-9320481 is gratefully acknowledged.

1. This figure neglects fixed costs such as marketing, overhead, and so on, which would typically be included in a publisher's costs calculation.
2. Odlyzko [1997] and Harnad [1997] have similar cost estimates.
3. *http://www.math.uci.edu/pjm.html.*

REFERENCES

Michael Cooper. A cost comparison of alternative book storage strategies. *Library Quarterly*, 59(3), 1989.

Ithiel de Sola Pool. Tracking the flow of information. *Science*, 221(4611):609–613, 1983.

Paul Ginsparg. Winners and losers in the global research village. Technical report, Los Alamos, 1996. *http://xxx.lanl.gov/blurb/pg96unesco.html.*

Stevan Harnad. The paper house of cards (and why it's taking so long to collapse). *Ariadne*, 8, 1997. *http://www.ariadne.ac.uk/issue8/harnad/.*

Stevan Harnad. The post-Gutenberg galaxy: How to get there from here. *Times Higher Education Supplement*, 1995. *http://cogsci.ecs.soton.ac.uk:80/harnad/THES/thes.html.*

Rob Kirby. Comparative prices of math journals. Technical report, UC Berkeley, 1997. *http://math.berkeley.edu/kirby/journals.html.*

Donald Knuth. T_EX and Metafont: New Directions in Typesetting. American Mathematical Society, Providence, R.I., 1979.

Joseph A. Konstan, Bradley N. Miller, David Maltz, Jonathan L. Herlocker, Lee R. Gordon, and John Riedl. Grouplens: Applying collaborative filtering to usenet news. *Communications of the ACM*, 40(3):77–87, 1997.

David N. Laband and Michael J. Piette. The relative impact of economics journals: 1970–1990. *Journal of Economic Literature*, 32(2):640–66, 1994.

Michael Lesk. *Books, Bytes, and Bucks: Practical Digital Libraries*. Morgan Kaufmann, San Francisco, 1997.

Andrew Odlyzko. The economics of electronic journals. Technical report, AT&T Labs, 1997.

David Revelt. Electronic working paper standards. Technical report, UC Berkeley, 1996. *http://alfred.sims.berkeley.edu/working-paper-standards.html.*

Carol Tenopir and Donald W. King. Trends in scientific scholarly journal publishing. Technical report, School of Information Sciences, University of Tennessee, Knoxville, 1996.

SUMMARY COMMENTS

Deanna B. Marcum

I have been asked to bring my individual perspective to summarizing this collective work. I offer my comments from the perspective of a librarian.

I believe that all the contributors to this work share at least one major assumption: that the purposes of the library will remain unchanged, though the means through which it achieves those purposes may be quite new and different. The library still exists to provide whatever resources are necessary to meet the research and inquiry needs of students and faculty members. At the same time, the library as a physical place still serves as a community symbol of knowledge and its importance to society.

Against the backdrop of this shared assumption, contributors possess at least three different perspectives: (1) technology enthusiasts, who see how technology can change the essential nature of our work and who urge all of us to accelerate the pace of transformation; (2) librarians, who are concerned about managing "hybrid" organizations that will support massive paper-based collections while also taking full advantage of electronic resources; and (3) publishers, who want to understand how electronic scholarly communication will affect the publishing business.

In all these chapters, writers eloquently portray the promise of technology for increasing access to information. Far less clear are answers to the following questions:

1. Can technology reduce the cost of scholarly communication?
2. Do students learn better when using technology?
3. Are libraries organized to take full advantage of the possibilities for enhanced access?

I find these questions raised by the writers more compelling than their reports of progress, perhaps because so many of the projects they discuss are not far enough advanced to offer solid conclusions. I would summarize these questions, which have come up in many different guises, as follows:

1. Where should we concentrate our efforts—on converting print documents to digital form to increase access, or on adding digital files *that were born digi-tally* to existing library resources? Can we do both?

2. How do we shift the focus from individual institutional holdings to the provision of more extensive access to materials for our students and scholars? How do we budget for this shift?

3. How can digital libraries be discussed without taking into account the networks for delivering information resources and the equipment necessary for reading digital files? Libraries have never been islands unto themselves, but we are becoming increasingly aware of their interdependency.

4. What, exactly, do we want to count? How do we count? Our tradition is to collect quantitative data about the size of collections, budgets, staffs, transactions. If we keep in mind that the library's primary purpose is to provide resources for scholarship and teaching, what should we be counting in the digital environment? Thus far, only one conclusion is clear: counting hits on a Web site is useless.

5. Will we be able to read anything we are now producing in electronic form a few years from now? Digital preservation has been alluded to many times, but it remains an area of great uncertainty.

These chapters have described in detail several pilot projects and their outcomes and users' reactions. As these projects continue to develop, I hope that we can learn more about the following areas:

1. *Desirable future states.* We read a great deal about changes we can expect, but we need to have more intense discussions about those changes we are prepared to pursue and effect. Descriptions of the various projects have given us much to ponder. We must now spend more time specifying the desirable future outcomes and conditions against which we can measure project results.

2. *The nature of collections.* Electronic information resources alter both our notions about the significance of very large collections and our methods of allocating resources for the provision of information. How are these changed perceptions to be accommodated within higher education?

3. *Variations in disciplines.* There appear to be genuinely different requirements for research resources from discipline to discipline. In describing projects, we should look carefully at the types of resources involved and the audience, or audiences, for them. It is not possible to generalize about what scholars need and want.

4. *Users' views.* To date, the projects have provided considerable data about how information resources have been scanned and indexed and how they can be

retrieved. In the future, we must learn more about users' reactions to the new format and about the utility of digital information to them.

5. *Digital archiving*. Kevin Guthrie (see chapter 7) rightly pointed out that there are not technological barriers to archiving and to meeting our societal obligation to preserve the intellectual record. But now we must find the most suitable—and the most cost-effective—methods for fulfilling that obligation.

Though most of the contributors to this work advocate continued support for pilot projects, many have also asked that more specific requirements for reporting results be established. The future of scholarly communication may not be clear, but the need for all of us to understand better the implications of electronic publishing is entirely evident.

SELECTED BIBLIOGRAPHY

Allen, T. J., "Managing the Flow of Scientific and Technical Information," unpublished doctoral dissertation, (1966), Massachusetts Institute of Technology, Cambridge, MA.

Allen, T. J., "Distinguishing Engineers from Scientists," (1988), in R. Katz (ed.), *Managing Professionals in Innovative Organizations: A Collection of Readings*, Cambridge, MA: Ballenger Publishing Company, pp. 3–18.

Altbach, P. G., "Examining the Conflicts," *Journal of Academic Librarianship* 15(2) (1989), pp. 71–72.

Association of Research Libraries, *Report of the ARL Serials Prices Project* (1989), Washington, DC: ARL.

Association of American Universities in collaboration with the Association of Research Libraries, *Reports of the AAU Task Forces on Acquisition and Distribution of Foreign Language and Area Studies Materials, A National Strategy for Managing Scientific and Technological Information and Intellectual Property Rights in an Electronic Environment* (1994), Washington, DC.

Astle, Deana, and Charles Hamaker, "Journal Publishing: Pricing and Structural Issues in the 1930s and the 1980s," *Advances in Serials Management* 2 (1988), pp. 1–36.

Astle, Deana, and Charles Hamaker, "Pricing by Geography: British Journal Pricing 1986 Including Developments in Other Countries," *Library Acquisitions: Practice and Theory* 10 (1986), pp. 165–181.

Bakos, Y., and E. Brynjolfsson, "Bundling Information Goods: Pricing, Profits, and Efficiency" (January 23–25, 1997), paper presented at Economics of Digital Information and Intellectual Property Conference, John F. Kennedy School of Government.

Banerjee, Dwarika N., "The Story of Libraries in India," *Daedalus* (Fall 1996), pp. 353–361.

Barshall, Henry H., "The Cost Effectiveness of Physics Journals," *Physics Today* 41 (July 1988), pp. 56–59.

Baumol, W. J., and W. G. Bowen, *Performing Arts: The Economic Dilemma* (1966), New York: Twentieth Century Fund.

Bennett, S., "The Copyright Challenge: Strengthening the Public Interest in the Digital Age," *Library Journal* (November 15, 1994), pp. 34–37.

Bensman, Stephen J., "The Structure of the Library Market for Scientific Journals: The Case of Chemistry," *Library Resources & Technical Services* 40(2) (April 1996), pp. 145–170.

Berg, S. V., "An Economic Analysis of the Demand for Scientific Journals," *Journal of the American Society for Information Science* 21(1) (1970), pp. 23–29.

Besser, H., and R. Yamashita, "Museum Site Licensing Project: Studying the Economics of Network Access to Information" (August 1997), Interim Draft Report.

Billington, James H., "Libraries, the Library of Congress, and the Information Age," *Daedalus* (Fall 1996), pp. 35–54.

Blinder, A. S., "Fact and Fancy in the Growth Debate," (1997), working paper no. 45, Center for Economic Policy Studies, Princeton University.

Blinder, A. S., and R. E. Quandt, "Waiting for Godot: Information Technology and the Productivity Miracle?" *Atlantic Monthly* (October 1997).

Boissonnas, Christian M., "ALA/ACRL Journal Prices in Academic Libraries Discussion Group, Copyright: The TRLN Document, 'University Policy Regarding Faculty Publications in Scientific and Technical Scholarly Journals'," *Library Acquisitions: Practice and Theory* 18 (Spring 1994), pp. 99–101.

Boyce, Bert R., "Meeting the Serials Cost Problem: A Supply Side Proposal," *American Libraries* 24/3 (March 1993), pp. 272–273.

Braunstein, Y. M., "An Economic Rationale for Page and Submission Charges by Academic Journals," *Journal of the American Society for Information Science* 28(6) (1977), pp. 355–358.

Bryant, E., "Reinventing the University Press," *Library Journal* 119(14) (1994), pp. 147–149.

Carpenter, Kenneth E., "A Library Historian Looks at Librarianship," *Daedalus* (Fall 1996), pp. 77–102.

Chamberlin, Edward, *The Theory of Monopolistic Competition* (1935), Cambridge: Harvard University Press.

Charles River Associates, Inc., *Development of a Model of the Demand for Scientific and Technical Information Services* (1979), Cambridge, MA: CRA (NTIS No. PB 297826).

Chen, C. C., "The Use Patterns of Physics Journals in a Large Academic Research Library," *Journal of the American Society for Information Science*, 23(4) (1972), pp. 254–270.

Chressanthis, George A., and June D. Chressanthis, "Publisher Monopoly Power and Third-Degree Price Discrimination of Scholarly Journals," *Technical Services Quarterly*, 11/2 (1993a), pp. 13–36.

Chressanthis, George A., and June D. Chressanthis, "The Relationship between Manuscript Submission Fees and Journal Quality," *Serials Librarian* 24/1 (1993b), pp. 71–85.

Chressanthis, George A., and June D. Chressanthis, "The Determinants of Library Subscription Prices of the Top-Ranked Economics Journals: An Econometric Analysis," *Journal of Economic Education*, 25/4 (Fall 1994a), pp. 367–382.

Chressanthis, George A., and June D. Chressanthis, "A General Econometric Model of the Determinants of Library Subscription Prices of Scholarly Journals: The Role of Exchange Rate Risk and Other Factors," *The Library Quarterly*, 64/3 (1994b), pp. 270–293.

Christensen, John O., "Cost of Chemistry Journals to One Academic Library," *Serials Review* 18 (Fall 1992), pp. 19–36.

Christensen, John O., "Do We Know What We are Paying For? A Comparison of Journal Subscription Costs," *Serials Review* 19/2 (Summer 1993), pp. 39–61.

Cummings, A. M., M. L. Witte, W. G. Bowen, L. O. Lazarus, and R. H. Ekman, *University Libraries and Scholarly Communication* (1992), Washington, DC: Association of Research Libraries.

Daniel, H. D., *Guardians of Science: Fairness and Reliability of Peer Review* (1993), W. E. Russey, Trans., Weinheim: VCH.

De Gennaro, Richard, "Escalating Journal Prices: Time to Fight Back," *American Libraries* 8 (February 1977), pp. 69–74.

de Sant'Anna, Affonso Romano, "Libraries, Social Inequality, and the Challenge of the Twenty-First Century," *Daedalus* (Fall 1996), pp. 267–281.

Dickson, S. P. and V. Boucher, "A Methodology for Determining Costs of Interlibrary Lending" (1989), in *Research Access Through New Technology*, ed. Mary E. Jackson, New York: AMS Press.

Directory of Electronic Journals, Newsletters, and Academic Discussion List (1991–1995), Washington, DC: Association of Research Libraries.

Dougherty, Richard M., "A 'Factory' for Scholarly Journals," *Chronicle of Higher Education* 38/41 (June 17, 1992), pp. b1–b2.

Dougherty, Richard, and Brenda Johnson, "Periodical Price Escalation: A Library Response," *Library Journal* 113 (May 15, 1988), pp. 27–29.

Dowlin, Kenneth E., and Eleanor Shapiro, "The Centrality of Communities to the Future of Major Public Libraries," *Daedalus* (Fall 1996), pp. 173–190.

Dyl, Edward A., "A Note on Price Discrimination by Academic Journals," *Library Quarterly* 53/2 (April 1983), pp. 161–169.

Economic Consulting Services, Inc., "A Study of Trends in Average Prices and Costs of Certain Serials over Time" (1989), in *Report of the ARL Serials Prices Project*, Washington, DC: ARL.

Ekman, R., and R. Quandt, "Scholarly Communication, Academic Libraries, and Technology" (February 1994), The Andrew W. Mellon Foundation discussion paper.

Ekman, R., and R. Quandt, "Scholarly Communication, Academic Libraries, and Technology," *Change* (January/February 1995), pp. 34–44.

Elder, N., "Am I Ready for Electronic Journals? Are Electronic Journals Ready for Me?" (1994), in S. B. Ardis (ed.), *Library without Walls: Plug In and Go*, Washington, DC: Special Libraries Association, pp. 119–121.

Favier, Jean, "The History of the French National Library," *Daedalus* (Fall 1996), pp. 283–291.

Fisher, Janet H., John Tagler, Beth J. Shapiro, and Mary Beth Vanderpoorten, "The Balance Point: Perspectives on Firm Serials Prices," *Serials Review* 19 (Winter 1993), pp. 63–72.

Franks, J., "The Impact of Electronic Publication on Scholarly Journals," *Notices of the American Mathematical Society* 40(9) (1993), pp. 1200–1202.

Garvey, W. D., *Communication, The Essence of Science: Facilitating Information Exchange Among Librarians, Scientists, Engineers, and Students* (1979), New York: Pergamon Press.

Getz, Malcolm, "Document Delivery," *The Bottom Line* (1991), pp. 40–44.

Getz, Malcolm, "Electronic Publishing: An Economic View," *Serials Review* 18(1–2) (Spring and Summer 1992), pp. 25–31.

Griffith, B. C., and N. Mullins, "Coherent Social Groups in Scientific Change," *Science* 177 (1972), pp. 959–964.

Griffiths, J. M., B. C. Carroll, D. W. King, M. E. Williams, and C. M. Sheetz, "Description of Scientific and Technical Information in the United States: Current Status and Trends" (1991), unpublished technical report to the National Science Foundation— Knoxville, TN, University of Tennessee, Center for Information Studies, School of Information Sciences.

Griffiths, J. M., and D. W. King, "Special Libraries: Increasing the Information Edge" (1993), Washington, DC: Special Libraries Association.

Grycz, Czeslaw Jan, "Economic Models for Networked Information," *Serials Review* 18(1–2) (Spring and Summer 1992), pp. 11–18.

Haley, Jean Walstrom, and James Talaga, "Academic Library Responses to Journal Price Discrimination," *College & Research Libraries* 53 (January 1992), pp. 61–70.

Hamaker, Charles, and Deana Astle, "Recent Price Patterns in British Journal Pricing," *Library Acquisitions: Practice and Theory* 8 (1984), pp. 225–232.

Harnad, Stevan, "Electronic Scholarly Publication: Quo Vadis?" *Serials Review* (Spring 1995), pp. 78–80.

Harnad, Stevan, "Post-Gutenberg Galaxy: The Fourth Revolution in the Means of Production of Knowledge," *Public-Access Computer Systems Review* 2 (1) (1991), pp. 39–53.

Harter, Stephen P., "The Impact of Electronic Journals on Scholarly Communication: A Citation Analysis," *Public-Access Computer Systems Review* 7(5) (1996), pp. 5–34.

Hayes, John R., "The Internet's First Victim?" *Forbes* 156/14 (December 18, 1995), pp. 200–201.

Joyce, Patrick, and Thomas E. Merz, "Price Discrimination in Academic Journals," *Library Quarterly* 55/3 (July 1985), pp. 273–283.

Joyce, Patrick, "Price Discrimination in 'Top' Scientific Journals," *Applied Economics* 22/8 (1990), pp. 1127–1135.

Kent, A., K. I. Montgomery, J. Cohen, J. G. Williams, S. Bulick, R. Flynn, W. N. Sabar, and J. R. Kern, "A Cost-Benefit Model of Some Critical Library Operations in Terms of Use of Materials" (1978), Pittsburgh, PA: University of Pittsburgh (NTIS No. PB 282059).

Kent, Susan Goldberg, "American Public Libraries: A Long Transformative Moment," *Daedalus* (Fall 1996), pp. 207–220.

Kepper, Jan, *Monopolistic Competition Theory: Origins, Results, and Implications* (1994), Baltimore: Johns Hopkins University Press.

Ketcham, Lee, and Kathleen Born, "Projecting Serials Costs: Banking on the Past to Buy for the Future, Periodical Price Survey, 1994," *Library Journal* 119 (April 14, 1994), pp. 44–50.

King, D. W., *Communication by Engineers: A Literature Review of Engineers' Information Needs, Seeking Processes, and Use* (1994), Washington, DC: Council on Library Resources, Inc.

King, D. W., and J. M. Griffiths, *Study of Interlibrary Loan and Reference Referral Services in the State of Arizona* (1990), unpublished report prepared for Arizona Department of Library, Archives, and Public Records, Knoxville, TN: King Research, Inc.

King, Donald W., and José-Marie Griffiths, "Economic Issues Concerning Electronic Publishing and Distribution of Scholarly Articles," *Library Trends* 43(4) (Spring 1995), pp. 713–740.

King, D. W., F. W. Lancaster, D. D. McDonald, N. K. Roderer, and B. I. Wood, *Statistical Indicators of Scientific and Technical Communication (1960–1980)*, (1976), Rockville, MD: King Research, Inc. (Vol. 1: GPO No. 083-000-00295-3; Vol. 2: NTIS No. PB 254060).

King, D. W., D. D. McDonald, and C. H. Olsen, "A Survey of Readers, Subscribers, and Authors of the *Journal of the National Cancer Institute*" (1978), Knoxville, TN: King Research, Inc.

King, D. W., D. D. McDonald, and N. K. Roderer, *Scientific Journals in the United States: Their Production, Use, and Economics* (1981), New York: Academic Press.

King, D. W., and N. K. Roderer, *Systems Analysis of Scientific and Technical Communication in the United States: The Electronic Alternative to Communication through Paper-Based Journals* (1978), Knoxville, TN: King Research, Inc. (NTIS No. PB 281847).

Kingma, Bruce R., and Philip B. Eppard, "Journal Price Escalation and the Market for Information: The Librarians' Solution," *College & Research Libraries,* 53/6 (1992), pp. 523–535.

Lamm, Donald S., "Libraries and Publishers: A Partnership at Risk," *Daedalus* (Fall 1996), pp. 127–146.

Lang, Brian, "Bricks and Bytes: Libraries in Flux," *Daedalus* (Fall 1996), pp. 221–234.

Lehmann, Klaus-Dieter, "Making the Transitory Permanent: The Intellectual Heritage in a Digitized World of Knowledge," *Daedalus* (Fall 1996), pp. 307–329.

Lerner, Abba, "The Concept of Monopoly and the Measurement of Monopoly Power," *Review of Economic Studies* (June 1934), pp. 157–175.

Lesk, Michael, "Pricing Electronic Information," *Serials Review* 18(1–2) (Spring and Summer 1992), pp. 38–40.

Leskien, Hermann, "Allocated Parts: The Story of Libraries in Germany," *Daedalus* (Fall 1996), pp. 331–352.

Leslie, J., "Goodbye, Gutenberg," (1994), *Wired* 2(10).

Lewis, David, "Economics of the Scholarly Journal," *College and Research Libraries* 50/6 (November 1989), pp. 674–688.

Leibowitz, S. J., "Copying and Indirect Appropriability: Photocopying of Journals," *Journal of Political Economy*, 93/5 (1985), pp. 945–957.

Lor, Peter Johan, "A Distant Mirror: The Story of Libraries in South Africa," *Daedalus* (Fall 1996), pp. 235–265.

Lufkin, J. M., and E. H. Miller, "The Reading Habits of Engineers—A Preliminary Survey," *IEEE Transactions on Education* E-9(4) (1966), pp. 179–182.

Lyman, Peter, "What Is a Digital Library? Technology, Intellectual Property, and the Public Interest," *Daedalus* (Fall 1996), pp. 1–33.

Lynch, Clifford A., "Scholarly Communication in the Networked Environment: Reconsidering Economics and Organizational Missions," *Serials Review* (Fall 1994), pp. 23–30.

Lynch, Clifford A., "Reaction, Response, and Realization: From the Crisis in Scholarly Communication to the Age of Networked Information," *Serials Review* 18(1–2) (1992), pp. 107–112.

MacEwan, Bonnie, and Mira Geffner, "The Committee on Institutional Cooperation Electronic Journals Collection (CIC-EJC): A New Model for Library Management of Scholarly Journals Published on the Internet," *The Public-Access Computer Systems Review* 7(4) (1996).

Machlup, Fritz, "Publishing Scholarly Books and Journals: Is It Economically Viable?" *Journal of Political Economy* 85 (February 1977), pp. 217–225.

Marcum, Deanna B., "Redefining Community through the Public Library," *Daedalus* (Fall 1996), pp. 191–205.

Marks, Kenneth E., and Steven P. Nielsen, "A Longitudinal Study of Journal Prices in a Research Library," *Serials Librarian* 19 (1991), pp. 105–135.

Mason, Marilyn Gell, "The Yin and Yang of Knowing," *Daedalus* (Fall 1996), pp. 161–171.

McCarthy, Paul, "Serial Killers: Academic Libraries Respond to Soaring Costs," *Library Journal* 119 (June 15, 1994), pp. 41–44.

Meadows, Jack, David Pullinger, and Peter Such, "The Cost of Implementing an Electronic Journal," *Journal of Scholarly Publishing* (July 1995), pp. 84–90.

Metz, Paul, and Paul M. Gherman, "Serials Pricing and the Role of the Electronic Journal," *College and Research Libraries* (July 1991), pp. 315–327.

Metzl, Jamie Frederic, "Searching for the Catalog of Catalogs," *Daedalus* (Fall 1996), pp. 147–160.

Meyer, Richard W., "Management, Cost, and Behavioral Issues with Locally Mounted Databases," *Information Technology and Libraries* 9/3 (September 1990), pp. 226–241.

Miller, C., and P. Tegler, "An Analysis of Interlibrary Loan and Commercial Document Supply Performance," *Library Quarterly* 58 (1988), pp. 352–366.

Miller, William, "Troubling Myths about On-Line Information," *The Chronicle of Higher Education* (August 1, 1997).

Newsletters on Serials Pricing Issues (1989–), Marcia Tuttle (ed.), Chapel Hill: University of North Carolina.

Noll, Roger, and W. Edward Steinmueller, "An Economic Analysis of Scientific Journal Prices: Preliminary Results," *Serials Review* 18(1–2) (Spring and Summer 1992), pp. 32–37.

Odlyzko, Andrew M., "Tragic Loss or Good Riddance? The Impending Demise of Traditional Scholarly Journals," *International Journal of Man-Machine Studies* 42/1 (January 1995), pp. 71–122. (Available from *amo@research.att.com*)

Okerson, Ann Shumelda, "Buy or Lease? Two Models for Scholarly Information at the End (or the Beginning) of an Era," *Daedalus* (Fall 1996), pp. 55–76.

Okerson, Ann, "The Missing Model: A 'Circle of Gifts'," *Serials Review* 18(1–2) (1992), pp. 92–96.

Petersen, H. Craig, "The Economics of Economics Journals: Statistical Analysis of Pricing Practices by Publishers," *College & Research Libraries,* 53 (March 1992), pp. 176–181.

Petersen, H. Craig, "Variations in Journal Prices: A Statistical Analysis," *Serials Librarian* 17/1&2 (1989), pp. 1–9.

Petersen, H. Craig, "University Libraries and Pricing Practices by Publishers of Scholarly Journals," *Research in Higher Education* 31 (1990), pp. 307–314.

Pinelli, T. E., M. Glassman, W. E. Oliu, and R. O. Barclay, "Technical Communications in Aeronautics: Results of an Exploratory Study" (1989), Report 1 (Part 1), NASA TM-101534, Part 1. (NTIS No. 89N6772)

Quandt, Richard E., "Simulation Model for Journal Subscription by Libraries," *Journal of the American Society for Information Sciences,* 47(8) (1996), pp. 610–617.

Quandt, Richard E., "Electronic Publishing and Virtual Libraries: Issues and an Agenda for The Andrew W. Mellon Foundation," *Serials Review* (Summer 1996), pp. 9–23.

Quinn, Frank, "A Role for Libraries in Electronic Publication," *Serials Review* 21/1 (1995), pp. 27–30.

Rosenbloom, R. S., and F. W. Wolek, *Technology, Information, and Organization: Information Transfer in Industrial R&D* (1967), Boston, MA: Harvard University.

Schaffner, A. C., "The Future of Scientific Journals; Lessons from the Past," *Information Technology and Libraries* 13(4) (1994), pp. 239–247.

Schauder, D., "Electronic Publishing of Professional Articles: Attitudes of Academics and Implications for the Scholarly Communication Industry," *Journal of the American Society for Information Sciences* 45(2) (1994), pp. 73–100.

Schuchman, H. L., *Information Transfer in Engineering* (1981), Unpublished technical report to the National Science Foundation, Glastonbury, CT: The Futures Group.

Schwartz, Charles A., "Scholarly Communication as a Loosely Structured System: Reassessing Prospects for Structural Reform," *College and Research Libraries* 55/2 (March 1994), pp. 101–117.

Sichel, Daniel E., *The Computer Revolution: An Economic Perspective* (1997), Washington, DC: Brookings Institution.

Simpson, D. B., "Library Consortia and Access to Information: Costs and Cost Justification," *Journal of Library Administration*, 12(3) (1990), pp. 83–97.

Sirbu, Marvin A., "Creating an Open Market for Information," *The Journal of Academic Librarianship* (November 1995), pp. 467–471.

Spence, M., and B. Owen, "Television Programming, Monopolistic Competition, and Welfare," *Quarterly Journal of Economics* 91 (1977), pp. 103–126.

Stix, G., "The Speed of Write," *Scientific American* 276(6) (1994), pp. 106–111.

Stoller, Michael A., Robert Christopherson, and Michael Miranda, "The Economics of Professional Journal Pricing," *College and Research Libraries* 57/1 (January 1996), pp. 9–21.

Tagler, John, "Counterpoint: A Publisher's Perspective," *American Libraries* 19 (October 1988), p. 767.

Talaga, James, and Jean Walstrom Haley, "Marketing Theory Applied to Price Discrimination in Journals," *Journal of Academic Librarianship* 16 (January 1991), pp. 348–351.

Thompson, James C., "Journal Costs: Perception and Reality in the Dialogue," *College & Research Libraries* 49 (November 1988), pp. 481–482.

Thatcher, S. G., "Latin American Studies and the Crisis in Scholarly Communication" (September 22, 1992), paper presented at the Latin American Studies Association meetings, Los Angeles, CA

Tushman, M. L., "Special Boundary Roles in the Innovation Process," *Administrative Science Quarterly* 22(4) (1977), pp. 587–605.

Williams, G. R., "Library Subscription Decisions," *IEEE Transactions on Professional Communication* 18(3) (1975), pp. 207–209.

Young, Peter R., "Librarianship: A Changing Profession," *Daedalus* (Fall 1996), pp. 103–125.

Zaitsev, Vladimir, "Problems of Russian Libraries in an Age of Social Change," *Daedalus* (Fall 1996), pp. 293–306.

CONTRIBUTORS

SCOTT BENNETT is the University Librarian at Yale University.

JOANN BROOKS is a PhD candidate in the Information and Organization Program in the School of Public Policy at the University of Michigan.

RICHARD EKMAN is Secretary of The Andrew W. Mellon Foundation.

THOMAS A. FINHOLT is Assistant Research Scientist and Director of the Collaboratory for Research on Electronic Work in the School of Information at the University of Michigan.

JANET H. FISHER is Associate Director of Journals Publishing at MIT Press.

MALCOLM GETZ is Associate Professor of Economics at Vanderbilt University.

JANE GINSBURG is the Morton L. Janklow Professor of Literary and Artistic Property Law at Columbia University School of Law.

KEVIN M. GUTHRIE is President of JSTOR.

RICHARD HAMILTON is the Paul Shorey Professor of Greek at Bryn Mawr College.

SUSAN HOCKEY is Professor and Director of the Canadian Institute for Research Computing in Arts at the University of Alberta.

ERIC HOLLAS is Director of the Hill Monastic Manuscript Library at St. John's University, Collegeville, Minn.

KAREN HUNTER is Senior Vice President of Elsevier Science.

ANNE R. KENNEY is Associate Director of the Department of Preservation at the Cornell University Library.

ANDREW LASS is Professor of Anthropology at Mount Holyoke College and the project manager for the Czech and Slovak Library Information Network.

MICHAEL LESK is Director of Information and Intelligent Systems at the National Science Foundation.

PETER LYMAN is Professor and Associate Dean in the School of Information Management and Systems at the University of California, Berkeley.

CAROL A. MANDEL is Deputy University Librarian at Columbia University.

DEANNA B. MARCUM is the President of the Council on Library and Information Resources in Washington, DC.

RICHARD W. MEYER is the Director of the Library at Trinity University.

JAMES G. NEAL is the Dean of University Libraries and Sheridan Director of the Milton S. Eisenhower Library at Johns Hopkins University.

RAYMOND K. NEFF is Vice President for Information Services at Case Western Reserve University.

ANDREW ODLYZKO is head of the Mathematics and Cryptography Research Department at AT&T Labs.

JAMES J. O'DONNELL is Professor of Classical Studies and the Vice Provost for Information Systems and Computing at the University of Pennsylvania.

ANN S. OKERSON is the Associate University Librarian at Yale University.

RICHARD E. QUANDT is Senior Advisor at The Andrew W. Mellon Foundation and Senior Research Scholar at Princeton University.

WILLIS G. REGIER was Director of the University of Nebraska Press from 1987 to 1995 and Director of the Johns Hopkins University Press from 1995 to 1998. He is currently the Director of the University of Illinois Press. In 1998–99 he was a Visiting Scholar in the Department of Comparative Literature at Harvard University.

SUSAN ROSENBLATT is the former Deputy University Librarian at the University of California, Berkeley. She is now an independent consultant.

ROBERT SHIRRELL is Journals Manager at University of Chicago Press.

MARY SUMMERFIELD is the coordinator of the Online Books Project for the Columbia University Libraries.

HAL R. VARIAN is Dean of the School of Information Management and Systems at the University of California, Berkeley.

SANDRA WHISLER was Assistant Director of the University of California Press and now has her own consulting firm.

INDEX

ABI/Inform, 230, 232, 233, 235
academic community, and digital documents, 374–78. *See also* scholarly communication
academic journals. *See* electronic journals; print journals
Academic Press, 115, 268
academic productivity. *See* productivity
Acrobat, 26
administrative control, and Scully Project's productivity, 79–84
Adobe
  Acrobat Exchange, 274
  Portable Document Format, 96, 98, 123, 273, 278–79
Adonis, 227
Adorno, Theodor, 160
advertising
  and network tracking, 373
  revenues, from American Economic Association journals, 108
  See also marketing
African American Women, 286, 287
aggregators, 62–63, 65, 326–27
aliasing, 43
Alfa Informatica Group, 23
Allen, Brian, 75
Amazon Books, 202
American Association of Universities, scholarly publishing objectives, 255, 257

American Chemical Society
  CORE project, 355, 357
  and Ohio LINK, 268
American Economic Association (AEA), 169–70
  publishing costs, 105–8
  publishing revenue, 108–9
    campus license, 109–10
    economies of scope, 115
    enhanced member services, 112–13
    pay-per-look, 110–11
    rents, 116
American Economic Review (AER), in JSTOR study, 178, 185, 191
American Historical Review, in JSTOR study, 178, 187, 191
American Institute of Physics, CD-ROM subscription options, 155
America Online (AOL), 122
Amos, Thomas, 349
Andrew W. Mellon Foundation. *See* Mellon Foundation
Archival Finding Aid Project, 352
Armstrong, Arthur G., 374
ARTFL, 161
ArticleFirst, 232
Associated Colleges of the South (ACS), 230
  libraries, 242
  Palladian Alliance, 231, 235
Association for Computational Linguistics, 23
Association for Computers and the Humanities, 23

Compositor: Impressions Book and Journal Services, Inc.
Text: 10/12 Baskerville
Display: Baskerville
Printer: Edwards Brothers, Inc.
Binder: Edwards Brothers, Inc.